OTHER BOOKS BY WILLIAM SAFIRE

LANGUAGE

On Language
In Love with Norma Loquendi
Quoth the Maven
Coming to Terms
Fumblerules
Language Maven Strikes Again
You Could Look It Up
Take My Word for It
I Stand Corrected
What's the Good Word?
Watching My Language
Spread the Word
Let a Simile Be Your Umbrella
Safire's New Political Dictionary

POLITICS

The First Dissident
Safire's Washington
Before the Fall
Plunging into Politics
The Relations Explosion

FICTION

Full Disclosure
Sleeper Spy
Freedom
Scandalmonger

ANTHOLOGIES

Lend Me Your Ears: Great Speeches in History

(WITH LEONARD SAFIR)

Good Advice
Good Advice on Writing
Leadership
Words of Wisdom

NO UNCERTAIN TERMS

MORE WRITING FROM THE POPULAR
"ON LANGUAGE" COLUMN IN
THE NEW YORK TIMES MAGAZINE

WILLIAM SAFIRE

SIMON & SCHUSTER

NEW YORK   LONDON   TORONTO   SYDNEY   SINGAPORE

SIMON & SCHUSTER
Rockefeller Center
1230 Avenue of the Americas
New York, NY 10020

SIMON & SCHUSTER and colophon are registered trademarks
of Simon & Schuster, Inc.
For information about special discounts for bulk purchases (the purchase, not the book, is bulky),
please contact Simon & Schuster Special Sales:
1-800-456-6798 or business@simonandschuster.com

Manufactured in the United States of America

2 4 6 8 10 9 7 5 3

Library of Congress Cataloging-in-Publication Data
Safire, William, date.
No uncertain terms : more writing from the popular On language column
in the New York times magazine / William Safire.
p.   cm.
On language columns from July 1997 to Feb. 2000 and selected letters from readers.
1. English language—Usage. 2. English language—Style. I. New York times magazine.
II. Title.
PE1421.S229 2003
428—dc21   2003042393
ISBN 0-7432-4243-2

To Lisbeth and Daniel Schorr

A definition, like the barke with the tree, is to be neither straiter nor larger than the thing defined; and so it comprehend all, the shorter it is, the better.

—JOHN BARLOW, 1632

NO
UNCERTAIN
TERMS

TRACKING THE FAST TRACK

To BE REVEALED before your very eyes is the anatomy of an "On Language" column. You will discover its impetus, its motive, its little research tricks, its blinding flashes of lexicographic insight and the way the writer, straining to show how language illuminates The Meaning of Life, settles for the meaning of a word.

1. Glom onto a vogue word just as it passes its peak.
"White House Finds '*Fast Track*' Too Slippery" was the *Washington Post* headline over a story by Peter Baker. His lead: "Attention White House speechwriters: The term *fast track* is no longer in vogue." As the drive for free-trade legislation began, the phrase of choice was "Renewal of Traditional Trading Authority."

Just as many of you were getting your engines steamed up to take the *fast track*, your track gets renamed. Why?

"*Fast-track* legislation" made its burst for fame in the mid-70s as Congress gave the President a right that stretched to twenty years to negotiate trade treaties with other nations without having to face amendments back home; as a result, subsequent treaties would be ratified or turned down, all-er-nuthin'. Robert Cassidy, a lawyer who helped draft the Trade Act of 1974, recalls the adjective surfacing toward the end of the Tokyo Round in the late 70s; it did not appear in legislation until 1988.

When presidential authority to zip a treaty through expired, a Republican Congress was not so eager to hand that power back to Democrat Clinton. That's the reason White House wordmeisters derailed the use of *fast track* (too hasty-sounding) in favor of the solid, stodgy, nothing-new-here "Renewal of Traditional Trading Authority," as if George Washington had been born with the old *fast track* in his crib.

2. Involve the reader.
Here is a postcard from a slum dweller in Grosse Pointe, Michigan,

with an incomprehensible scrawl for a name asking: "What's with *fast track?* Whatever happened to 'life in the fast lane'?"

Now our linguistic train begins to leave the station, and we

3. *Follow the usage trail.*

The *fast lane* comes from auto racing. The trusty *Oxford English Dictionary,* supplemented and on CD-ROM, has a 1966 citation from Thomas Henry Wisdom's *High Performance Driving:* "One is frustrated on a motorway by the driver ahead in the *fast lane* (if only he understood it is the overtaking lane)."

How did the term get popularized in its metaphorically broadened form? A 1972 novel by Douglas Rutherford was titled *Clear the Fast Lane,* but that was still about auto racing. Then, in 1976, a rock group named the Eagles put out an album, *Hotel California,* that included the single "Life in the Fast Lane" by Joe Walsh, Don Henley and Glenn Frey.

"They knew all the right people/They took all the right pills/They threw outrageous parties/They paid heavenly bills/There were lines on the mirror, lines on her face/She pretended not to notice she was caught up in the race. . . ." The chorus: "Life in the *fast lane/*Surely make you lose your mind. . . ."

Since that song, the *fast lane* has had overtones of the drug culture and impending disaster, a speeded-up, sinister, modern version of Shakespeare's "primrose path of dalliance."

At this point, the language columnist thinks he has come to the fundament of it all, fulfilling his obligation to

4. *Satisfy the slavering etymological urge in roots-deprived readers.*

We have seen the *OED* make clear that the derivation is from highway driving. In Britain, the *fast lane* is the overtaking lane; in the United States, it is usually officially called the "passing lane." And as *fast lane* was being adopted, it spawned, or influenced, *fast track.*

Not so fast. The phrase *fast track* has a long history in horse racing, to mean "dry, conducive to speed." On the other hand, if it has been raining, the wet track is described as "slow," and the touts race about urging you to put your money on a "mudder," a horse that digs slogging. Count on some reader to find a metaphoric extension of *fast track* in a Jane Austen or Henry James novel.

Nor is that the only untapped root. Soon the vast legion of railroad buffs will check in with yards of lore about fast railroad tracks, where expresses roar past with whistles in the night.

I remember Richard Nixon using *fast track* in 1964, after he moved to New York City following his defeat for California governor. He told *The New York Times* a year later: "New York is a place where you can't slow down—a *fast track*. Any person tends to vegetate unless he is moving on a *fast track*."

And so the column falls together, requiring the writer only to

5. *Leave with a snapper, or sometimes a peroration.*

When next you hear of Congress disputing the president's bid for *fast-track* authority, think of the well-mentored business executives and political loners on the rise, following the racing drivers careening around the speedways, following the jockeys booting their mounts home on a sunny day, following John Luther (Casey) Jones, the hero engineer, slamming on the brakes and giving up his life to save his passengers from death on the *fast track*.

ACHILLES' HEELS

THE LEGAL COLUMNIST Bruce Fein of *The Washington Times*, attacking the attacker-attackers who have been blasting his friend Ken Starr, expressed astonishment at "mass-media gullibility in peddling bogus portraits of the Whitewater independent counsel sold by *myrmidons* of President Clinton."

What's a *myrmidon?* The poet Homer, often caught nodding but now probably shaking his head at the Clintonian odyssey, would point us to the *Myrmidones*, an Achaean race in Thessaly, Greece, who fought under Achilles in the Trojan War. They assumed their ancestor to be the issue of the mating of Zeus with Eurymedusa, a woman wooed by the god when he took the shape of an ant. (Some wags suggest that this may have been the origin of "ants in the pants.")

An alternative mythic source is the changing of ants into men by Zeus in answer to the prayers of King Aeacus, who had lost his army to the plague. But the metaphoric intent is the same, describing a race of antlike men, and the meaning of *myrmidon*, which should not be capitalized in its extended meaning, is "slavish follower; subordinate who obeys the orders of his leader without mercy."

The Greek word was introduced into American politics by Alexander Hamilton in his efforts to block Aaron Burr from becoming president in 1800. Hamilton wrote to Gouverneur Morris that Burr, to accomplish his end, "must lean upon unprincipled men, and will continue to adhere to the *myrmidons* who have hitherto surrounded him."

One man's *myrmidon*, however, is another man's *die-hard*.

ACRONYMANIA

In South Africa, an organization that hands out free condoms to prostitutes calls itself the Sex Worker Education and Advocacy Taskforce (Sweat).

In Chicago, an antidrug outfit calls itself Children Requiring a Caring Kommunity (Crack).

Serious business should eschew jazzy acronyms. Time for Citizens Militant on Nomenclature (C'MON).

ADVENTURER

The word *adventurer* has been through a half-millennium of exciting times.

Disrepute was its cradle. The Latin *advenir* meant "come to," as in "come to pass; arrive, happen," and a vestige lingers in gambling lingo as "betting on the come" in the hope that what will come next will enable the gambling *adventurer* to win. *Adventure* meant "coming by chance; the luck of the draw."

Applied to a person, *adventurer* meant "gamester," what we would now call "gambler." Accordingly, an English ordinance in 1474 decreed that the royal household would bar the "swearer, brawler, backbyter" and "*adventorer.*" Five centuries ago the *adventorer* was a fit companion for the secretive *backbyter*, the calumniator who whispered his slanders, stabbing reputations in the back.

Gambling and war combined as soldiers of fortune bet their lives on their livelihood; a 1555 usage derided "our *adventurers*, that serve withoute wages," supported only by their plunder. Just seven years before that, Edward Hall in his *Chronicle* provided the etymology: "He gave them a Pennon of St. George and bade them, *Adventure* (of whiche they were called *Adventurers*)." Most soldiers of fortune were self-glorified brigands; to be called an *adventurer* was to be insulted.

Then the pejorative word had a run of good luck. John Milton, in his 1667 *Paradise Lost*, wrote of "the Heav'n-banished host" of fallen angels awaiting the return of their satanic leader "now expecting/Each hour their great *adventurer* from the search/Of foreign worlds." (Though devilish, Lucifer was "great.") Meanwhile, a commercial company was founded in Antwerp and chartered in England called the Merchant *Adventurers*, in the sense of "enterprise," and led in the exploration and colonization of North America. The hazard to be undertaken was no longer a time-wasting game but a dangerous journey, an exploration for riches or a moral crusade. Jonathan Swift wrote in his *Tale of a Tub* (1704) "to encourage all aspiring adventurers."

But then it was applied to Prince Charles Edward Stuart in the pretender's desperate insurrection of 1745; his sobriquet was "the Young

Adventurer." Then *adventuring* became an -ism and lost even more respect. An English review in 1843 lumped together "Concubinage, Socialism and *Adventurism*," scorning all three as evidence of social decline. The *Oxford English Dictionary* defined it as "the principles and practice of an *adventurer* or *adventuress;* defiance of the ordinary canons of social decorum." An adventuress, especially, was not just a kept woman but was stigmatized as "loose."

Worse, *adventurism* was taken up by politics to define the most dangerous form of policy. Russian Communists in the 1920s called it *avantyruizm,* and Lenin considered it so deviationist as to border on revisionism. Britain's Harold Nicolson, in his 1932 *Public Faces,* deplored the way the public "had ousted the Churchill government on a charge of *adventurism.*" In 1957, the *Observer* wrote, "Of the three official accusations against Marshal Zhukov, that of '*adventurism*' appears to be based on no evidence whatsoever." Under the Communists, it was not merely the practice of a rash, reckless, precipitate or impetuous policy; it was a crime.

Today, an *adventurer* is no longer a person to be feared. The word has reasserted the romantic, courageous quality that the poet Keats, in "Endymion," gave it: "*Adventuresome,* I send/My herald thought into a wilderness." Today, to be *adventuresome* is to be "bold, daring," taking risks without a connotation of impetuosity or imprudence. Foolhardy—having the hardiness of a fool—is no longer automatically attached to today's *adventurers.* The battered old word that gambled on the come to make its comeback has at last arrived.

ALL PHAT! AND A BAG OF CHIPS

"They used to wear that stuff, y'know, *back in the day,*" says one teenager.

"It's not just *phat,*" observes another. "It's da *bomb.*"

"*Jiggy,*" the first agrees. "But the way she wears it is *all that.* Musta cost a *scrillion.*"

Welcome to the evanescent village of teenage slang, land of fleeting meanings and laid-back superlatives. In the interest of transgenerational interaction, here is a translation of some recent usages, which by the time they get to me are probably on the way out.

All that means "conceited." It is a shortening of *all that and a bag of chips*, with the emphasis on the *and*. The rhythm is similar to the ancient *pretty please with a cherry on top*, but the reference is to fast-food excess, as if to complain "too much." Although the *Los Angeles Times Magazine* wrote of Leonardo DiCaprio that "Hollywood's newest heartthrob is *all that and a bag of chips*," the primary meaning is not "overpowering" but "stuck up."

Back in the day is an updating of "in olden times." To teenagers this can reach back six months to a year. "My students use *back in the day* to impart a nostalgic feel," reports Marcia Tanner, a teacher in Michigan. "It seems to apply to anything that happened prior to their own involvement, as far back as last season." Reporting from Woodstock, New York, James Cobb wrote in *The New York Times* that "Eric Halpern, 21, a student at Rockland Community College, shouted, 'That is *phat!*' when he spotted the new Beetle, a reintroduced Volkswagen, at a filling station." Though some have postulated the origin of *phat* as an acronym for "pretty hips and thighs" or even more lascivious constructions, the word is more likely a deliberate misspelling of *fat*, which has for centuries had a slang meaning of "rich," as in "fat and happy."

"Veejay Day for 4,000 *Jiggy* Souls" headlined *The Washington Post* over a story about MTV tryouts for video jockeys, many of whom were transfixed by Will Smith's rendition of "Gettin' *Jiggy* wit It." The writer Michael Colton noted that *jiggy*, like *mangy*, means "cool, funky, kind of fly." It also has a sense of "nervous, crazed." The etymology is uncertain: In *From Juba to Jive: A Dictionary of African-American Slang*, Clarence Major defines *jig* as "a dance" and *jigaboo*, from the Bantu for "slavish," as a racist slur aimed at dark-skinned African Americans. *Jiggy* could also be related to the verb "to jiggle."

Da bomb blows your mind and the world up. And *scrillion* is easy. It means "a gazillion gazillion."

In the teenage world your definition of all that *is wrong. At least in my little corner of the world,* all that *means ALL THAT! I understand teenage slang is hard to decipher, so I'll try my best to explain expressions. All that, used in the context of: that guy is* all that *and* a bag of chips*, means he is hot, cute, fine and a bag of chips (meaning he is* Extra fine, hot 1/2, in other words, this guy is really cute!)*
Phat *means cool. Wow that's* phat*, whoa that's cool. My friends and I*

never use the word jiggy *except when we're listening to Will Smith. Da* bomb *is another expression for, hey, that is the coolest; hey, that is* da bomb!!! *Means it blows all other things compared to it away, too cool to be true. I have never heard the word* scrillion, *but I will be sure to because if that is what grown-ups think we say, well then I better fill out their expectations.*

Words some of us really do say: teenyboppers—*girls who have pictures of teenage heartthrobs like Leo [Leonardo DiCaprio—Ed.] in their room, go to Hanson concerts, sing Spice Girls songs during class, sit on each other's laps, and constantly wear flares and tank tops;* granola—*people who are not in touch with the 90s (hippies, thespians to the extreme);* corn flakes—*people who are "flaky."*

Liz Manashil
San Rafael, California

Phat *started in the world of graffiti.* Phat *was actually a style of writing where the letters look like they've been inflated close to the point of bursting. Creative spelling has emerged as an integral part of the hip-hop culture, aided by the early 80s abbreviations (or whatever U call them) used in song titles by the artist formerly known as Prince.*

Steve Spencer
Little Rock, Arkansas

ALONE WITH "ALONE," OR WHAT "IS" IS

"It depends on how you define *alone*," President Clinton told the grand jury. At another point he said, "It depends on what the meaning of the word *is* is."

Some readers and viewers, including Democratic congressional leaders, found this "legalistic parsing" off-putting. To construe words and tenses so narrowly, they felt, was trickily misleading, deliberately deceptive or even perjurious. Those of us in the language dodge, on the other hand, were delighted to see someone demonstrating the glories of terminological exactitude.

To millions of schoolchildren, the word *tense* meant only how you felt before a pop quiz. Now its grammatical sense comes into its newsworthy own with what *is* is.

Asked if he had (past tense) a sexual relationship with Monica Lewinsky, the President replied under oath and later to interviewers, "There's no sexual relationship," with that elided *"s"* capable of being construed as *is* or *was*. Unless asked afterward, "Was there ever" (past tense) or "Has there been" (past perfect), he could say that he was telling the literal truth—that no relationship was taking place at that moment.

The present third-person singular of the verb *to be* comes from the Latin *esse*, as in Bishop George Berkeley's *esse est percipi*, "to be is to be perceived." It's a short jump from *esse* to *is*. Mr. Clinton's formulation of "what *is* is" lends itself to metaphysical discussions about being and essence, and will surely be the title of tracts about virtual reality in the age of image.

Since so much depends on how we define *alone*, let's take a crack at it. The word is an odd combination of *all* and *one;* to say "all *alone*" is to be redundant. The original meaning is "wholly one"—that is, "unaccompanied; absolutely by oneself"—as in Shakespeare's *Julius Caesar* when Brutus says, "Good countrymen, let me depart *alone*." A seeming oxymoron is *alone* together, which is what was asked of Mr. Clinton. In the Paula Jones deposition, he said he did not remember being *alone* with Ms. Lewinsky; in his grand-jury testimony, he admitted nine occasions when they were together unobserved by others. His secretary, Betty Currie, gave the meaning a stretch when she said, "The President, for all intents and purposes, is never *alone*. . . . There's always somebody around him." In current usage, *alone with* means "unobserved by a third party."

Euphemism entered the testimony at least twice, once deceptively, once in a kindly way. In answering a question about what a prosecutor called "phone sex," Mr. Clinton admitted to "inappropriate sexual banter."

The etymology of *banter* is a mystery. Jonathan Swift, in the introduction to his *Tale of a Tub*, wrote in 1710 that this bit of slang "was first borrowed from the bullies in White Friars, then fell among the footmen, and at last retired to the pedants." Originally used to mean "raillery, ridicule," it softened in time to a sense of "good-humored teasing" or "joking dialogue, merry jesting." It never had, and does not now have, a connotation of sex talk.

The gentling quality of euphemism came in reference to Ms. Lewinsky's report of Mr. Clinton's denial of an affair with another White House aide. The President was quoted as referring to the other woman as *small-breasted*. A generation ago, the lack of an impressive bosom was often derided as *flat-chested;* the current use, as indicated in the testimony, is both more anatomically accurate and less cruel and pejorative.

Mr. Clinton's sensitivity to the nuance of language was exhibited in his answer to questions about an episode at a White House gate in which a Secret Service officer revealed to Ms. Lewinsky that another woman was in the Oval Office with the President. A prosecutor asked, "Weren't you *irate?*" The President responded, "What I remember was being *upset.*"

Irate is rooted in the Latin *irasci,* "to be angry," which also spawned *ire* and *irascible.* At the low end of *irate's* meaning is "wrathful" and at the high end is "incensed," one stop short of "enraged."

But Mr. Clinton, who knew his reaction had already been the subject of testimony by his aides, did not want to admit to anger that could be interpreted as leading to a threat to fire an agent. Hence his admission only to being *upset,* from the Middle English *upsetten,* originally meaning "toppled, overturned," but which in this modern extension of the metaphor means "disturbed," more worried or annoyed than angered or *irate.* A person who is *irate* strikes fear into others; one who is *upset* evokes sympathy from them.

The President used a similar term to accuse his accusers of "trying to *set me up* and trick me." A prosecutor countered by asking if he thought he had the right to commit perjury "because you think the case was a political case or a *setup.*"

The slang term had its origin in 1880 regarding free drinks, and later as the ice-and-soda fixings that needed only a shot of booze to turn into a highball. The entrapment sense (made famous by the Washington mayor Marion Barry's cry, "The bitch set me up!" which soon appeared on T-shirts in the nation's capital) appears closely associated with boxing. In 1926, setups were defined in *Hearst's International* as "has-beens or never-wases who get paid to stand up just long enough to be knocked out." A further development of the idea—to make an opponent vulnerable to a knockout blow—was expressed by the former heavyweight champion Jack Dempsey in 1950: "If you can land solidly with a straight left or with a left hook, you'll generally knock your opponent off balance, at least, and 'set him up' for a potshot with your right."

The extended metaphor of this fighting image, now meaning "to entrap or ensnare," was the sense used by both witness and prosecutor in the historic Clinton testimony.

"The singular verb to be *comes from the Latin* esse. . . ." *This is simply not true. Related to* esse—*true; sort of a first cousin once removed. Latin* est, *Germanic* ist, *Slavonic* yest, *and Sanskrit* asti, *all originated in the same (to us unknown) Indo-European root.*

Our is *came to England with the Angles and Saxons from North Germany. The low German and Dutch* is *is identical to ours, and was perfectly good English long before William the Conqueror imported the Latin and French version:* est.

John Foster Leich
Cornwall Bridge, Connecticut

Bill—First, you say that the present perfect form *has there been* is a past perfect. You will of course recognize a real past perfect in sentences such as "Had it already started snowing when you left the house?" Then you say that the English word *is* "comes from Latin esse." None of the forms of English *be* come from anything Latin. Is *is* not a descendant of esse; rather the s of is *is a distant cousin of the first* s *of the Latin infinitive* esse, *the second* s *is a verb root that occurred in the prehistoric Indo-European antecedents of English* am, is, are, *and of the infinitive and non–perfect tense forms of the Latin counterpart of* be; *the remainder of the paradigms of both* be *and* esse *developed out of forms of other verbs: one of them giving rise to* be, been, *and the perfect tenses (*fui, *etc.) of Latin* esse, *and one of them giving rise to* was, were.

Professor James D. McCawley*
Department of Linguistics
University of Chicago
Chicago, Illinois

NOBODY'S PERFECT

In a smirking swipe at the use of *what* is *is* by President Clinton, a language maven noted that *has there been* was in the past perfect tense.

As Lise Nazarenko, a lecturer in English at the University of Vienna, noted: *"Has there been* is not in the *past* perfect tense, but rather in the *present* perfect tense. Past perfect would be *had there been."*

*Professor McCawley died on April 10, 1999. See page 168 and page 180.

Perfect, in its most familiar sense, means "flawless"; in an earlier sense, it meant "complete." That sense of "finished" is what we use in grammar: a verb form expressing an action that is complete at the time of speaking or at the time spoken of. And since *has* is present and *had* is past, "*has* there been" is, as the entire Gotcha! Gang has gleefully pointed out, in the *present perfect* tense.

AND THE HORSE YOU RODE IN ON

James Carville, the best-selling author and keen debater who is President Clinton's most unwavering loyalist, is writing a book for Simon & Schuster about a group he calls "the President's enemies," foremost among them prosecutor Ken Starr. The Louisianan whose sobriquet is "the Ragin' Cajun" has chosen a tentative title: . . . *And the Horse You Rode In On*. That title is intended to strike a note of defiance. As Thomas Bowdler might expurgate it, "Be off with you and, for emphasis, take with you whatever brought you to this point." As the ellipsis indicates, the obscene beginning of the line is cut: The missing words can be any of a variety of contemptuous imprecations, none of which is suitable for book titles or family newspapers. But because the concluding trope is so widely known—and its origin such a mystery to students of English as a foreign language—the burden of explication falls to the linguistic mavenim.

The country-music songwriters D. Rock, C. Blake and B. Fischer titled their 1989 ditty "You and the Horse (You Rode In On)." A year later the group called Soul Asylum used the phrase as an album title, and a variant was the title of a 1993 mystery novel by Martha Grimes. A 1992 self-help paperback by Bill Wear used it in a subtitle: *Recovering from Divorce: And the Horse You Rode In On*, presumably expressing the confrontational attitude of an offended former spouse.

The first use in fictional dialogue that I can find is in George V. Higgins's 1972 classic hard-boiled novel, *The Friends of Eddie Coyle*.

"I first heard it when I was driving a truck for Coca-Cola," recalls Mr. Higgins, whose most recent novel is *A Change of Gravity*. "It must have been about the summer of 1960." The late 50s appears to be the time of the phrase's genesis; Michael Seidman, editor of Charles Durden's 1976 *No Bugles, No Drums*, another novel using the entire line, remembers the insult he heard growing up in the Bronx in that post–Korean War era: ". . . and the white horse you rode in on and all your relatives in Brooklyn."

The key word is *in*. "The horse he rode on," without the necessary *in* to conjure the image of a scene, is an ordinary phrase that can be found in use as far back as Shakespeare. ("Some hilding fellow, that had stolen the horse he rode on," with *hilding* meaning "bent downward, twisted waywardly aside.") But *rode in on* suggests a startling entrance.

A clue to the term's origin is immortalized in the halls of the Treasury Department in Washington. In the background of the oil painting that hangs as the official portrait of Donald Regan, who served as Secretary of the Treasury in the Reagan Administration, can be found a book titled *And the Horse You Rode In On*. No other book title is visible. In their 1987 book, *Showdown at Gucci Gulch*, Jeffrey H. Birnbaum and Alan S. Murray, then reporters for *The Wall Street Journal,* note that it was not a real book title but rather a favorite saying of Mr. Regan's. He attributed it to his friend John (Buck) Chapoton, who claimed he heard the phrase appended to its obscene imperative during a poker game in Texas.

This is an example of a vestigial metaphor. It occurs in such phrases as "my turn in the barrel" or "where were you when, etc." The jokes or anecdotes are deservedly forgotten, but the punch lines, or portions of them, live on. In this case, though the sentiment is not as elegantly expressed as in Churchill's alliterative "in defeat, defiance," the intensifying message stands tall in the linguistic saddle.

As the artist who painted the portrait of Donald Regan, I can tell you how it came about.

Secretary Regan posed for me in his White House office when he was President Reagan's chief of staff. During the first sitting I noticed a framed inscription in Japanese on his wall and asked what it was. He felt obliged to tell me the joke and that the Marines he commanded in Japan gave it to him as a parting gift. Obviously he enjoyed it.

When composing the portrait I decided to include some books, but I don't normally make the titles legible. After his enthusiastic approval of the painting at the last sitting, I pointed out that title, which was intended to be so nearly illegible that no one would notice unless directed to. It was to be his secret, to share with others only if he chose. He clapped his hands in delight and said, "I love it!"

Herbert E. Abrams
Warren, Connecticut

So lissen arready Wolfie (from Velvl, from the German Wölfl, diminutive of Wolf, pronounced Vulf, meaning Wolf)—again with the mistakes in Yiddish, when you wrote and they printed mavenim! I'll give you the singular, maven, as the Anglicization of the correct mavin. But the plural was, has been, and always will be or should be mavinim. And what would it hurt if you maybe transliterated it as mayvin so it shouldn't come out like mahvin, which is no longer the preferred English equivalent for Moisheh? And for the same 20¢ I can point out that on the occasion of birth, circumcision, bar mitzvah, marriage and burial Ze'eyev is appended; that's the Hebrew for Wolf. Hey, lokka this; a whole lecture on a pussel kart (also putzel kart) and enough room left over to correct your next mistake.

Arnold Lapiner, Major, U.S. Army retired
Trumansburg, New York

APPLE-PIE ORDER

"Chancellor Helmut Kohl," wrote *Business Week*'s Thane Peterson in a February 1998 article, "has turned European unity and the euro common currency into *motherhood-and-apple-pie* issues."

Meaning: "redolent with values that cannot easily be opposed." Origin? Here is one political lexicographer's speculation about its derivation.

One half of that portmanteau phrase began as *against motherhood*, meaning "a position that no politician in his right mind would take."

The other half of the suitcase is *as American as apple pie*. The United States produces more apples than any other country in the world, and the pie made from the fruit has come to signify traditional values.

When the expressions were combined in *motherhood and apple pie* (hyphenated when used as a modifier), the result became a worthy competitor to the flag and the Fourth of July. So how come there's no Apple Pie Day?

AS FAR AS THE EYE CAN SEE

Practitioners of what Thomas Carlyle called the dismal science—economics—are in a cheery mood these days. Nowhere is the mood swing from gloom and doom to sweetness and light more vivid than in the use of the phrase *as far as the eye can see.*

Walter Heller, an economic adviser to Presidents Kennedy and Johnson, was prescient in concerns he expressed in August 1981: "Even with the Reagan tax cut and the investment stimuli, businessmen are worried about the huge budget deficits *as far as the eye can see.*"

Two years later, Reagan's director of the Office of Management and Budget, David Stockman, made the figure of speech more famous in the economics dodge when he warned more specifically that without more budget discipline, there would be $200 billion deficits *as far as the eye can see.*

As recently as 1996, the Republican presidential candidate Bob Dole was thundering, "We have a president who's vetoed a balanced budget and submitted budgets with debt *as far as the eye can see.*"

But then President Clinton embraced the GOP goal as his own, and after long-sustained prosperity produced an unexpected tide of tax revenues, his economic aide Gene Sperling found it possible to use the magic phrase in a different direction early in 1998: "You'll see surpluses *as far as the eye can see.*"

Sure enough, in Mr. Clinton's State of the Union address, the phrase came shining through: "And if we maintain our resolve, we will produce balanced budgets *as far as the eye can see.*"

Walter Heller would be proud. He was the one who underscored the efficacy of jawboning—price control by public presidential hectoring—and popularized an apocryphal quotation attributed to the gangster Al Capone: "You can get a lot more done with a kind word and a gun than with a kind word alone."

How far can the human eye really see? Much depends on the brightness of the object in view. For astronomers, even the naked eye can see stars thousands of light-years out in space; for economists, however, a couple of fiscal years is considered pretty good.

AS THE WIND BLOWS

Headline writers are sometimes blessed with the names of people that lend themselves to wordplay. The independent counsel Ken Starr, for example, has run the gamut from "Starr Turn" to "Starr Chamber."

When Louis Freeh, director of the FBI, stepped forward to disagree semipublicly with his nominal boss, Attorney General Janet Reno, one writer recalled the famous Martin Luther King Jr. line and wrote, "Freeh at Last."

Senator Arlen Specter of Pennsylvania recalled a Lincoln speech and felt the punning urge to tell a right-wing columnist that "the Department of Justice cannot survive half slave and half Freeh."

As the years roll by, if Freeh tries something new, the headline will be "Freeh Enterprise"; his closest aides will be known inside the Bureau as "Freeh Agents"; the narcotics chasers will be "Freeh Based"; the person who forces him to leave will be the "Freeh Booter," leading to the "Freeh Fall"; any objection he raises to this will be known as the "Freeh Kick."

In the same way, we can envision his cotton security blanket being called the "Freeh Throw"; the question "Freeh Better?" being answered negatively in "Freeh Verse"; restrictions placed on his agency called "Freeh Rein," and the sack of pretzels sold at the Ninth Street Luncheonette labeled "Freeh Lunch."

Lance, load, love; way, wheel, will: The possibilities seem endless. But *U.S. News & World Report* is trying to spoil the fun with its recent headline: "Time to End the Freeh-for-All?"

I, for one, pledge not to base any puns on anybody's family name. The appellation "Freeh" was originally the German *Früh*, with an umlaut, evolving into its present state at least a generation ago, and was not a result of any shortening or changing on the Director's part. He was born Freeh.

ASK MR. MAVEN

"Charles Dickens assigned names to his characters that reflected their personality traits," writes Jerome Schwartz of Bloomfield, New Jersey. "Such names as *Fezziwig, Scrooge* and *Bumble* come to mind. Can you recall the name of this technique?"

Anthony Trollope did it, too: He named a doctor character Abel *Fillgrave*, M.D. The practice of novelists—or the occasion in real life—is the reverse of an eponym, which applies the name of a real person to a noun or verb. ("The nominee was *borked*.") And you notice these perfect appellations all the time: There used to be a helpful fellow in the *Times*'s payroll department named Harry *Cash*, and now there's a clerk here in the

Washington bureau named John *Files*. The head of the Passenger Vessel Association, which warned passengers not to climb on bow railings after viewing *Titanic*, is John *Groundwater*.

Assuming it all began in Shakespeare, I turned to the Bardophile Jeffrey McQuain, who immediately remembered the superficial Justice *Shallow* in *The Merry Wives of Windsor* and the fast-and-loose Mistress *Quickly* in *Henry IV*, Part 1.

Deeper research found the marriage of name and quality of character in allegories written two centuries earlier: Larry Scanlon, professor of English at Rutgers and editor of *Studies in the Age of Chaucer*, notes that *Constance*, the protagonist of "The Man of Law's Tale," is a model of constancy, and *Prudence* in another Canterbury tale offers wise advice. At that time, William Langland's *Piers Plowman* was a farmer whose first name is a play on an earlier Peter, the apostle whose name comes from the Greek *petra*, "rock." In Matthew 16:18, Jesus is quoted as saying, "Thou art Peter, and upon this rock I will build my church." (Plowman's daughter is named *Do-Just-So-or-Thy-Dame-Shall-Beat-Thee*, a name that seems to have atrophied over the centuries along with severe parental discipline.)

"The apt word you seek," McQuain says, "is *aptronym*, said to be coined by the American newspaper columnist Franklin P. Adams, who in 1938 joined the panel of radio's 'Information Please.' " FPA, as he was called, rearranged the first two letters of *patronym*, the naming for one's father, to spell *apt*, with its Latin root for "fasten, attach," which now means "fitted."

McQuain, who happened to know about FPA's coinage because his Internet word column is at www.infoplease.com, steered me to Merriam-Webster's *What's in a Name?* by Paul Dickson. That word maven applies this word to real people with euonymous (a mouth-filling word for "apt") names: Matt *Batts*, former major-league catcher; I. *Bidwell*, contractor; Dick *Curd*, Carnation Milk spokesman; Mike *Bassett*, veterinarian.

"Collecting aptronyms is generally good fun," Dickson writes, "but gets a bit unnerving when you run into the horrifyingly apt *Will Drop*, a Montreal window cleaner who died in a fall; and *Wilburn* and *Frizzel*, who on the grim morning of October 6, 1941, went to the electric chair at the Florida State prison."

Years ago I had a friend, a physician, who was dean of the University of Massachusetts School of Medicine. His name was Bill Butcher. In a gath-

ering I once asked him whether he had been called to the operating room to perform emergency surgery on an accident victim. When his name was announced over the intercom, one of the attending nurses became hysterical and had to be replaced.

Another doctor present at the same time, hearing this, informed the group that there was, several decades ago, in Boston a noted physician named Dr. Killum.

*The problem is that you never suggest what name we should call perfectly competent people who are wrongly named—malonyms?**

Alan Shaler
East Hampton, Massachusetts

My favorites include Lord Brain, the leading British neurologist; Coach Cramp, longtime swimming coach at Horace Mann Prep School; Dr. Donald Kuntz, gynecologist; Postmaster General Anthony M. Frank; Billboard *movie critic Michele Magazine; scholar and professor A. J. Cave, who wrote at length on the anatomy and society of the Neanderthals; and Blaise Wick, president of Zippo Lighter Corporation.*

Seth M. Siegal
New York, New York

A dentist named Dr. Payne. *A dermatologist named* Dr. Skinner. *A bank teller named* Mr. Outlaw. *A minister named* Paradise. *A rabbi named* Rabbi Angel. *A policeman named* Officer Secret. *A hairdresser named* Mrs. Brunetti. *A paint-store proprietor named* Mr. I. Schmier. *A baker named* Mr. Flakowitz.

David L. Garner
Dix Hills, New York

Their history extends well before Chaucer. The Hebrew Bible/Old Testament includes dozens. For example, the Book of Ruth presents Illness (Mahlon) *and* Failing (Chilion), *both of whom die by the fifth verse. Their mother* Naomi's *name means* Pleasant; *when she returns to her home of Bethlehem after the death of her husband and sons, she finds this name no longer apt, and asks, "Do not call me* Naomi (Pleasant), *call me*

*Dysonyms.—W.S.

Marah (Bitter), *for the Almighty has made my life forever bitter." By the happy ending of the story, though, she is again unambiguously* Naomi.

Aaron L. Mackler, Ph.D.
Department of Theology
Duquesne University
Pittsburgh, Pennsylvania

Perhaps you could explore inaptronyms, if I may coin a word: persons whose names are patently inappropriate to their callings. For example, when I was a student at the University of Notre Dame, the head of the sociology department was a Mr. Loveless *and the dean of the Law School was a* Mr. Lawless.

James P. Finnegan
Chappaqua, New York

BACK TO MY ROOTS

"DEAR SIRS," begins a letter to *The New York Times* from Stephen Sondheim, the noted Broadway songwriter whose "Send in the Clowns" won the 1975 Grammy Award for Song of the Year and whose *Sunday in the Park with George* won the 1985 Pulitzer Prize for drama.

Because his excoriation is written with his usual flair, I reprint it here in full:

In his weekly contribution to your Sunday magazine section, William Safire writes, "Let others fight their way through the maelstrom of charge and countercharge about low sex in high places; the duty of this column is to get to the bottom of the origins and development of the hot phrases." Yes, indeed. Would that he practiced what he preached.

His column used to be about language. For a long time now it has been nothing but a sly forum for his virulent, bilious and, in my opinion, psychopathic hatred of Bill Clinton. His pretended interest in the linguistic fallout from such notable phrasemakers as Paula Jones, Susan Carpenter-McMillan, Ken Starr, Dick Armey, Trent Lott and their like, often filtered through the remarks of their friends, colleagues and commentators, is a transparent excuse to remind the reader of his [Mr. Safire's] political obsessions. Like his fellow reactionaries, he's an unregenerate pork-barreler: He attaches his views, no matter how irrelevant, to anything that moves.

Safire already has two shots a week on the Op-Ed page. Isn't that enough? To call his Sunday salvo On Language is only one of his hypocrisies. The column used to be a vehicle for his often-entertaining observations about words and phrases as linguistic outcroppings of national culture, not an excuse to slather us with his shrill opinions.

Tell him to go back to his roots.

Yours,
Stephen Sondheim

That is what is called in the trade "a good pop." Although a self-imposed discipline prohibits my taking issue in this space with the political substance of his charges, it may be instructive to deal in temperate and scholarly fashion with some of Mr. Sondheim's semantic and rhetorical usages.

Virulent, bilious and, in my opinion, psychopathic. The earliest meaning of the adjective *virulent* (from the Latin *virus*, "poison") was the nature of an infection "marked by a rapid, malignant course." This precursor of *poisonous*, like the synonym "venomous," has since been extended to mean "malicious, mean-spirited, excessively harsh." *Virulent*, especially to the many now attuned to the dangers of viruses, is a more apt word than the overused *vicious* or the unfamiliar *vituperative* ("berating abusively").

Bilious is how you feel when your liver secretes too much bile, or how you look when so afflicted (sickly yellowish, almost green, leading to the characterization of the latest Paris fashion color as "a *bilious* green"). A sense derived from that, accurately used by Mr. Sondheim here, is "peevish" or "ill-tempered."

Because *psychopathic* is rhetorically excessive—any charge of "having a mental disorder often leading to criminal behavior" tends to turn reasonable readers off—it would ordinarily lessen the impact of the two previous adjectives. But note the writer's skillful interjection of *in my opinion* before the third word. The phrase not only introduces a dramatic pause before a point, but also seems to say that *virulent* and *bilious* were self-evident fact and that only *psychopathic* was a matter of opinion. The writer's admittedly debatable medical evocation is reinforced in the next sentence with a specific form of psychopathy, *obsessions.* Such progression of images is what goes into a good pop.

He's an unregenerate pork-barreler: He attaches his views, no matter how irrelevant, to anything that moves. The meaning of *unregenerate* is "stubborn, obstinate," which are run-of-the-mill words. Better, in a pop, to use a less familiar, longer term with a good rhythm that most readers sort of understand in the context. The writer's choice here is among *unreformed* (the original meaning, but too closely associated with political reform), *unreconstructed* (colored by Civil War Reconstruction and connoting resistance to the Union) and *unregenerate* (which can be nicely confused with degenerate).

I would have gone with *unreconstructed* with its historically reactionary

Confederate connotation, because it would set up *pork barrel,* a political Americanism derived from the barrel in which salt pork was distributed to slaves in pre–Civil War days. "Oftentimes the eagerness of the slaves," wrote C. C. Maxey in *The National Municipal Review* in 1919, "would result in a rush upon the pork barrel. . . . Members of Congress in the stampede to get their local appropriation items into the omnibus river and harbor bills behaved so much like Negro slaves rushing *the pork barrel* that these bills were facetiously styled '*pork barrel*' bills."

Sondheim's use of the noun *pork-barreler* takes the word-picture of a politician larding "pork," or governmental largess, into unrelated legislation, and extends that image to a writer attaching irrelevant views to a faster-moving subject. That's an effective extension of a metaphor.

Many would take exception to the stilted salutation *Dear Sirs;* like *Gentlemen,* it is an archaism as hoary as "carbon copy." *Dear Editors* is more pointed and less sexist.

The closing line, *Tell him to go back to his roots,* is not a derogation of the Bronx, where I went to high school. The great lyricist's double meaning is to the Nixon White House, from which the lifelong biliousness of the object of his ire was presumably derived, as well as to this column's primary concern with etymology, the roots of words.

Deconstruction of a well-built pop opens a vein of inquiry that is always worthwhile. Isn't it rich?

Now that's what I call an entertaining column. Thank you.
                                    Stephen Sondheim
                                    New York, New York

I would like to take issue with your analysis of bilious. *I believe the word is rooted in the medieval doctrine of humors—the four bodily fluids which we supposed to determine mental equilibrium. (This meaning of the word* humor *as a bodily fluid is now preserved in the aqueous and vitreous humors of the eyeball.) The medieval humors were blood, phlegm, yellow bile and black bile. The confusion obviously comes with the two types of bile. Yellow bile was associated with the liver, and an excess was thought to produce* melancholy. *My Oxford American dictionary still lists* liverish *as irritable, glum. While this usage has mostly disappeared from English, it is apparently still common for the French to refer to having a touch of* liver *when we would say that we have the* blues *or the* blahs. *Since you chose the liver's yellow bile as the departure for your analysis, the most derogatory synonym you could find was* peevish.

I think this is somewhat wide of Mr. Sondheim's meaning and that something stronger was intended. Webster's bile– ill-nature, bitterness of feeling, spleen *reveals that the basis for Mr. Sondheim's invective probably resides not in the melancholy yellow bile but rather in black bile which, with a fine disregard for medical facts, became associated with* spleen. *Hence "splenetic" and "to vent one's spleen" as expressions of* unreasoning anger *or* vindictiveness. *Merited or not, this is, I believe, Mr. Sondheim's meaning in his perception of your pursuit of the Clintons.*

Gregg Lauterbach
New York, New York

Your last paragraph begins: "Deconstruction of a well-built pop opens a vein of inquiry that is always worthwhile." Are you certain that deconstruction *is the proper word here? It seems to me that your column was not at all a deconstruction of Sondheim's letter. Rather, it was a* close reading *or, better, an exercise in* practical criticism.

As you likely know, deconstruction is associated mainly with postmodern literary theory. A deconstructionist will supposedly analyze a text and, seizing on inner contradictions and tensions, demonstrate that in fact the text does not mean what we think it means, or that it has multiple, irreconcilable meanings. Nowhere did you suggest that this was the case with Mr. Sondheim's letter. Instead, you set out to answer the question: What makes Mr. Sondheim's missive an effective piece of rhetoric? If anything, you placed yourself in the anti-deconstructionist camp because your theoretical premise seemed to be that, ultimately, a literary text—Mr. Sondheim's letter—is knowable.

When people use the verb deconstruct, *99 percent of the time they mean nothing more than* analyze *or* critique—*though evidently they feel* deconstruct *lends an air of sophistication to the activity.*

Leonard Stern
The Ottawa Citizen
Ottawa, Ontario, Canada

I wish to formally disagree with your characterization of bilious *as "how you feel when your liver secretes too much bile."* Bilious *and* jaundiced *are not synonyms. The former word does not refer to oversecretion but rather to* regurgitation *of bile and acids from the proximal intestine and stomach into the oral cavity. The taste of digestive fluids is both bitter and sour, providing the desired flavor in Mr. Sondheim's remarks.*

Robert S. Goldsmith, M.D.
Stamford, Connecticut

BARRY'S GHOST

"WILLIAM F. BUCKLEY JR. tells us," writes Jackson Williams of Austin, Texas, "that Brent Bozell was the ghostwriter of Barry Goldwater's 1960 book, *The Conscience of a Conservative.* The very next day, William Safire flatly credits Stephen Shadegg. . . . One of them might actually be right. I wonder which one."

Nobody's righter than Buckley. Shadegg (whose son John now serves in the House) wrote many of Goldwater's speeches in the late 50s, but Bill Buckley, who was inside that conservative circle, informs me that "Brent wrote the entire thing *ex nihilo,* from nothing. He had been writing speeches for Barry for a couple of years, but the book we're talking about, which I saw *prepartum, in partu* and *postpartum* [before, during and after birth] was Brent's." (The bracketed translations of Buckley's Latin are mine; I presume *antepartum* would have spoiled the alliteration.)

But what of the most memorable line Goldwater spoke? At the Republican Convention of 1964, as Rockefeller-Scranton forces were calling themselves "moderates" and calling the Goldwater supporters "extremists," the victorious candidate intoned the words that split and sank the party: "I would remind you that extremism in the defense of liberty is no vice, and let me remind you also that moderation in the pursuit of justice is no virtue."

I credited that to Karl Hess. This is disputed by Seth Leibsohn of Washington, who holds that "the author of that speech was a then-professor of political science at the University of Ohio and now at Claremont, Henry Jaffa."

As best I can reconstruct it, the inflammatory speech was largely written by Hess, with a quotation—of Marcus Tullius Cicero defying the conspiratorial Catiline—contributed by Professor Jaffa; Goldwater (or one of his acknowledged ghosts) wrote later that "I had heard it earlier from the writer Taylor Caldwell."

Cicero, criticized for his hasty execution of five of Catiline's supporters, said, "I must remind you, Lords, Senators, that extreme patriotism in the defense of freedom is no crime, and let me respectfully remind you that pusillanimity in the pursuit of justice is no virtue in a Roman."

It may have worked oratorically for Cicero but backfired when used by Goldwater.*

"BE THOU AS PURE . . ."

When independent counsel Ken Starr went before the House Judiciary Committee, he complained that "a number of my prosecutors are being *calumnied* and criticized." He repeated the unfamiliar verb: "To criticize and to *calumny* the men and women with whom I'm privileged to serve . . . is unfair, and I think it's unfortunate."

The use of *calumny* as a verb is infrequent. Although the verb form has a history in the language—in 1895, the *Pall Mall Gazette* wrote, "The President has not been in office 12 hours . . . and is already *calumnied*"— the preferred form is *calumniate*. "The highest personages have been *calumniated*," wrote Miles Smith in the "Letter from the Translators to the Reader," the preface to the 1611 King James version of the Bible.

It is as a noun that *calumny* is best known. The word is rooted in the Latin *calvi*, "to trick, deceive, intrigue against" (also the root of *challenge*), which progressed to *calumnia*, "false accusation." The old *Century Dictionary* defined it well as "untruth maliciously spoken, to the detraction of another; a defamatory report; slander."

Calumniate is to be preferred as the verb, because the perpetrator can then be called a *calumniator*, which has a zestier flavor than *calumnizer* and avoids the *calumnist/columnist* confusion. For an adjective, *calumnious* has the usage edge over *calumniatory*; Shakespeare, in *Hamlet*, had Laertes observe, "Virtue itself 'scapes not *calumnious* strokes." The Bard liked the word; later in the play, after one of his bawdiest puns, Hamlet says to the innocent Ophelia, "Be thou as chaste as ice, as pure as snow, thou shalt not escape *calumny*."

In mock modesty, an unidentified columnist is sometimes referred to in this space as "a vituperative right-wing *calumniator*," but it was not until Starr's use that the word was widely heard in political discourse. Its

*Barry Goldwater died on May 29, 1998.

origin in that sense was the ancient Latin advice to solons, *Fortiter calum-niari, aliquid adhærebit;* its English translation, "Throw plenty of mud and some of it will be sure to stick."

BELLYBUTTON

A full-page color advertisement in respectable newspapers for the movie *American Beauty* zeroed in on a female abdomen. Staring out at the reader, like the inescapable single eye of a Cyclops, was the model's *umbilicus.*

Showing that portion of the anatomy was not in bad taste because *umbilici* are omnipresent these days. Fashion models sashay down the runway with the smooth flesh of their flat stomachs proudly exposed, and nubile shoppers parade through malls with breezes causing goose bumps on their midsections. And at the center of attention is the rounded depression or the sometimes slight protuberance, the dialectical synonymy of which we examine today. We're talking *bellybuttons,* the focus of fashion at the *fin de millénaire.* A post-monokini shock was needed. If the display of nipples no longer titillated, designers asked one another, could the showing of bottoms be far behind? But when even the thong lost its shock value, fashion's eye landed on the center of it all.

"Between the emotion and the response," wrote the poet, "falls the Shadow." Between the *halter* and the *hip-hugger,* or between the *cropped top* and the *low-slung pants,* falls the *Navel.*

The Romans called the point at which the cord connecting the fetus with the placenta was cut and tied off the *umbilicus,* from *umbo,* "knob, projection." Speakers of Old High German and Old English preferred a Greek root, *omphalos,* which led to *nabalo* and *nafela,* and then popped up in Shakespeare as "he unseamed him from the *naue* to the chops," and developed into Sir Thomas Browne's 1646 observation, "The use of the *Navell* is to continue the infant into the mother." From there to James Russell Lowell's 1873 poetry: "He lifted not his eyes from off his *navel's* mystic knot."

That notion of self-absorption was picked up by the playwright Eugene O'Neill: "I had a mental view of him regarding his *navel* frenziedly by the hour," and by the BBC's publication, the *Listener,* in 1966: "One sits in a New York traffic jam, contemplating, as it were, the city's *navel.*" Those who do this religiously are called *omphalopsychic,* from a sect of quietists who induced hypnotic trances by gazing at their navels.

Today, many continue the introspective study. *"Bellybuttons*—there are two kinds," said a character in the 1973 *Odd Couple*, "the kind that go in and the kind that go out. I want an *outie!* No, no! I want an *innie!"* But today many more of us are contemplating the navels of other people, forcing synonymists to consider the varied nomenclature.

Bellybutton was first noted by John Bartlett in the 1877 edition of his *Dictionary of Americanisms.* Rudyard Kipling liked that noun in 1934, scorning fights with those "who do not come up to your *bellybutton.*" Although Aldous Huxley preferred *tummy-button,* J. B. Priestley in 1946 minted a nice trope with this sign of stomach-tightened nervousness: "with your *bellybutton* knockin' against your backbone." (It's two words in Merriam-Webster, one word in *Webster's New World.* I go with the analogy of *bellyache,* not *belly dancer.*)

Dialect-delighting Americans, however, have worked out a variety of names for the same anatomical place. Thanks to the editors of the *Dictionary of American Regional English* (now hard at work at the University of Wisconsin at Madison on their fourth volume, covering the letters P to S), we can examine a few answers to their Question X34/1: "What are some other names and nicknames for the navel?"

One-eyed Mabel was one response, probably derived from the popular *nabel,* a variant of *navel* recalling the Old High German *nabalo. Button* and *buttonhole* were frequent choices, and a fair sampling called it a *belly-hole. Chicken butt* and *chicken peck* were noted. Those interested in content preferred *lint-catcher, lint-getter* and *lint-strainer.* Perhaps a Greek influence can be found in one respondent's *oompalikis* and several *piko* answers. The midriff midrash includes the Yiddish *pupik.*

Many responses to *DARE*'s survey began with the word *where.* In the South, it was *where the Yankee shot you;* in the West, *where the Indians shot you,* and across the country, *where I got shot in the war.* Two interviewees eschewed the violent gunfire–bullet hole metaphor and replied with the less bellicose *where you got hit with a pick.*

Shucks! Any pre-television senior citizen could tell you that an umbilicus is where you keep the salt while eating celery in bed.

Joe McHale
Houston, Texas

BILL O' RIGHTS

Sir William Blackstone, working away at his *Commentaries on the Laws of England* in 1765, had to deal with a list of stated rights passed by Parliament in 1689 in "An Act Declaring the Rights and Liberties of the Subject and Settling the Succession of the Crown." Just as Parliament settled on William and Mary of Orange as king and queen, Blackstone settled on the list of powers to which their subjects were entitled as "the *bill of rights*."

Like most members of America's Continental Congress in 1774, Edward Rutledge, a delegate from South Carolina, read Blackstone. According to notes taken by John Adams, Rutledge rose in Carpenters' Hall in Philadelphia on September 28 to say, "I came with an Idea of getting a *Bill of Rights*." He didn't get one. However, fourteen years and one revolution later, Alexander Hamilton wrote in Federalist Paper No. 84, "The most considerable remaining objection to the Constitution is that the plan of the Convention contains no *bill of rights*." Hamilton thought it was unnecessary, but James Madison disagreed, and Thomas Jefferson wrote that he favored "the annexation of a *bill of rights* to the Constitution." Madison offered a dozen amendments; the states brushed aside two dealing with apportionment and congressional pay and ratified ten; though the list never had a formal title, the United States had what became known as "the *Bill of Rights*," capitalized.

Cut to two centuries later. I invited Judge Samuel I. Rosenman, one of FDR's great speechwriters, to visit the Nixon speechwriters at the White House. He told us how Roosevelt's writers had enlivened his 1944 State of the Union message by inserting an *Economic Bill of Rights* (to a job, to a decent home, to a good education, "to adequate protection from the economic fears of old age"). Some time later, when I noticed one of the newer speechwriters, Lee Huebner, slaving over the world's dullest economic message, I passed along the Rosenman tip: Do a preamble called an *economic bill of rights*. He did, and our turbid message with a ringing label got pretty good coverage.

The day before FDR's 1944 use of the *Economic Bill of Rights*, Senator Joel Bennett Clark of Missouri introduced legislation drafted by Harry Colmery of the American Legion, who called it a *Bill of Rights for G.I. Joe and G.I. Jane*. "The House sent the *G.I. Bill of Rights* to the White House," reported the *Times* on June 14, 1944, as millions became entitled to guarantees on home mortgages and support for college education. Crime came next. In 1983, according to the National Center for Victims of Crime, in Virginia, the International Association of Chiefs of Police adopted a *Crime Victims' Bill of Rights*. Voters were victims, too, in the eyes of Max Macauley of Sacramento in 1988, and he proposed a *Voters' Bill of Rights*. Six years later, this label was picked up by a group of Chicago professors who plumped for "truthful, understandable messages" and no last-minute tricks. The millionaire Ron Unz now has that phrase going in California, where it means spending limits, partial public financing, a ban on corporate gifts and fast Web site disclosure of fundraising.

Which brings us to the *Patients' Bill of Rights*, now the subject of lively debate and very likely to be a battleground in the campaign of 2000.

As 1973 began, the American Hospital Association, in Chicago, packaged a policy statement in the catchy phrase. Lawrence K. Altman, the doctor reporting on medicine for *The New York Times*, put it in his lead, which earned it a front-page headline: "*Hospital Patients' 'Bill of Rights' Backed.*" Dr. Altman explained, "What the hospital association has done is to collect the most commonly questioned situations and put them in one document." Included were the right to respectful care, confidentiality of records, a primary physician, and notification of experimentation.

Twenty-six years later, Senators Tom Daschle and Ted Kennedy went to the White House to announce that "by passing a *Patients' Bill of Rights*—national standards—we can make sure that all Americans have the same right to health care."

The other day I hopped in a cab, read the *Taxi Passengers' Bill of Rights* (to a clean cab and a respectful driver) and went to the supermarket, where I was reassured by a *Consumers' Bill of Rights* (to fresh produce and no hassling over returns). I am now at work on a *Bill-of-Rights Writers' Bill of Rights*. These include "the right to full coverage" and "entitlement to public attention."

You are misleading when you suggest that Madison, unlike Hamilton, favored the addition of a bill of rights to the Constitution.

In fact, Madison's initial position was closer to Hamilton's than that of Jefferson's. Madison believed that the document as drafted in Philadelphia in the summer of 1787, and then ratified by the states, was itself a bill of rights. It protected the people from many governmental infringements on their liberties (like the prohibition denying habeas corpus to those under arrest, the prohibition of bills of attainder, and so on).

Writing from Paris to Madison, Jefferson strenuously argued that a separate bill of rights would strengthen the Constitution's guarantees of the citizen's liberties, and only later did Madison come around to agreeing with him. Of course, it was clear that many of the states' ratifying conventions only ratified the document with the proviso that the first Federal Congress would pass a bill of rights.

And don't forget: Madison's amendment dealing with congressional pay was eventually ratified on May 7, 1792, as the 27th amendment (so the states did not, as you put it, "brush it" aside).

Jack Fruchtman Jr.
Towson University
Towson, Maryland

BLOOPIES 1997!

The moment dreaded on Madison Avenue is at hand. It's time for the highest honor that can be bestowed on the flubs of those copywriters who practice the poetry of persuasion: the ever-less-coveted Bloopie Awards.

The airline industry dominates. "British Airways," snarls its competitor, Virgin Atlantic, "is encouraging any passenger who can say that their business class isn't the most comfortable in the air to write and tell them why." Virgin is encouraging the reader to think of British Airways in the singular: "British Airways *is*." Fine; that's American usage. But it (Virgin, construed as singular) cannot with consistency use pronouns about B.A., one single unit, such as *their* and *them*.

The only correct forms are *its* and *it*. (The way to get around that is to make the subject "the folks at British Airways" or "those Establishment stiffs trying to drive us upstarts out of business," which would then take a more personal personal pronoun.)

Over at Continental Airlines they boast that customers at Newark Airport know "shops and restaurants are abundant and customs are speedy." While studies of Aborigines in Australia may deal with their *customs*, which is the plural of *custom*, the United States Customs Service considers itself singular, and you'd better believe it or the customs officer will make you lay out all your Paris-purchased underwear in front of all those other passengers. *Customs*, when used to mean the organization that collects duties, is singularly tough.

A company—even one that makes airplanes—may be a neutral entity, a beloved institution or a despised conglomerate, but it is not a living thing. Gulfstream Shares asserts, "Companies who own business jets outperform companies who don't." The antecedent of *who* should be a person; I am willing to extend this to a dog with a personality, but an inanimate object or organization takes a *which*. The flexible *that* can apply to either people or things.

And speaking of life: L'Oréal, the French cosmetics firm that has come out with a line of shampoos and conditioners called Vive, contributes to global linguistic confusion with its slogan *"Vive* means life!" Not quite. The French word *vive* is the imperative form of the verb *vivre*, "to live," and means "live!" or "long live," as in "Long live frizzy hair!" But the noun for *life* in French is *vie*, which can sometimes be *en rose*. As they never say in Paris, *C'est la vive*.

In a similar error reflecting a cultural gap, Isuzu has a line in its television advertisement for its Trooper utility vehicle that goes, "You don't have to buy the farm to get one." Unfortunately, *to buy the farm* is an old aviation expression meaning "to crash and burn."

Worse than the French not knowing French or Japanese not being hip to macabre Americanisms is the communications company who (whoops!) that communicates clumsily. "Never has a dangling modifier fetched such a handsome price," writes Peter Maiken at Beloit College in Wisconsin, enclosing a full-page ad from *The Wall Street Journal* by Lucent Technologies that reads, "Since inventing cellular and after introducing digital wireless, wireless office systems and cordless phones, it seems that anyone can get ahold of you no matter where you are."

As it stands, that sentence makes no sense at all. It could be improved, though not undangled, by changing *inventing* and *introducing* to *the invention of* and *the introduction of.* (Nothing wrong with *ahold*, in use since 1872; it needs no hyphen.)

Lucent's Digi-Bloopie outshone this Canon ad from last year: "What better way to show you Total Document Processing, then to put on a show." *Than* would have worked, with no comma preceding, but in its bungled form the sentence appears to be a line from an Andy Hardy movie.

Hyphenphobia is afflicting the drug advertisers. Efidac/24 promises "24 Hour Relief of Nasal Congestion," while Tavist-D advertises "12 Hour Relief," and Tagamet blocks acid with a "One Tablet Dose." Should be *24-hour, 12-hour,* one-tablet as befit compound adjectives. "Try Our New Italian *Four Cheese* Sticks!" shouts copy for Farm Rich products, illustrating the problem: It looks as if the company is selling four sticks made of cheese, but it is actually trying to sell sticks made of four cheeses, which would be clear with the hyphenated *four-cheese* sticks.

A heart-stopping headline reads, "Do You Have Chest Pain?" A special Bloopie for unintended vividness in ad copy goes to the Columbia-Presbyterian Medical Center, which describes itself as "a leader in cutting-edge research and heart surgery." The hyphen helps a little.

Proof that ideas are better than automobiles can be found in a Mercedes-Benz accessories ad that rates this year's Disaster Bloopie. "Her trademark has always been making art out of the everyday," the copy begins. "First, she was taken with fruits and vegetables. Next, she was inspired by popcorn, footballs and sharks. Then one day, Nicole Miller was struck by a Mercedes-Benz."

Some copywriters have lively grandparents and others—unfamiliar with apostrophes—complain of wooden expressions. Perhaps that explains this observation by Bruce Hardwood Floors: "Solid oak, just like your grandmothers."

Time for a coffee break. Says Maxwell House, "Always has and always will be good to the last drop." Unfortunately, there is something wrong with that last drop. Each parallel verb phrase must be complete in itself. *Always will be good* expresses a complete idea, but *always has good* lacks the past participle *been.* Change the slogan to "Always has been and always will be good to the last drop."

You think these awards don't get results? Last year a Bloopie went to Bayer aspirin for "Only Genuine Bayer can help save your life when taken regularly." That taking of life suggested copy written by Kevorkian Advertising. This year, the Bloopie Awards Committee is pleased to report that our heads are no longer pounding, because the new TV ads say, "And taken regularly, only Bayer can help save your life."

Never expressed in the infinitive, "bought the farm" was quite common usage by the Army careerist Georgia Boys and other southerners I served with, many of whom were, in those pre-build-up days, rotating in and out of Viet-

nam and Laos between CONUS tours [CONUS, Continental United States—Ed.]. Simply put, "bought the farm" was taken, by me, to mean that an individual was killed while on military service and that his G.I. insurance was used by the family to pay off the mortgage on the family farm.

James D. Storozuk
Fair Lawn, New Jersey

You gave only one meaning of vive, *the present subjunctive of the verb* vivre, *which in the case of L'Oréal's product doesn't make much sense.*

However, if you had used the other meaning of vive, *the company's slogan, "Vive means life!" isn't quite so incomprehensible. Vive is the feminine singular form of the adjective vif, meaning "alive." (Jeanne d'Arc fut brûlée vive—ugh!). So their slogan completely rendered into English, "Alive means life," ain't quite so crazy as you would have it. There is a certain bizarre logic to it.*

Mary Kimbrough
Rockport, Texas

You are definitely right that no self-respecting officer of the U.S. Customs Service would ever drop the s in our first name, even though some dictionaries do not seem very sure about our singularity. On the other hand, where many of my Customs colleagues have trouble is in the name of the buildings where our port offices are located around the country. Many insist, incorrectly, on adding an s to the inexplicably s-less Customhouse *or* Custom House. *(Both forms seem to be acceptable.) Nor are we very clear on whether the total revenue we collect is duty or duties. We will gladly review anything you have to declare on this, but with our customary skepticism.*

You might also want to consider the plight of our colleagues in France. They never seem to know if they work for La Douane Française, *or* Les Douanes Françaises.

Eric J. Francke
New York, New York

BLOOPIES 1998!

We begin the award of this year's coveted Bloopie Awards—for outstandingly sloppy solecisms in advertising copy—by holding our noses. "Don't let snoring come between you and a good night's sleep," says an ad for Breathe Right Nasal Strips in Smart Source. (That Sunday supplement styles itself SmartSource, but I like to put a space between whole words, especially when the second word is capitalized. The name of this column will never be OnLanguage.) "Try them for a week," urges the snoring copywriter, "so your bed partner can learn to breathe through their nose, instead of their mouth."

The personal pronoun *their*, like *them*, is plural, referring to more than one person. In this case, the writer wanted to refer to either one or the other of the bed partners, not both. That meant choosing the singular *his* or *her*. But the writer was in a bind: He or she could not choose either *his* or *her* because he or she could not specify whether the male or the female was doing the snoring; the product is designed for either one. Solution: Drop the *your* and make it all plural—"so bed partners can learn to breathe through their noses, instead of their mouths." This is an improvement but not a perfect way out because the sales pitch is aimed at only one of the bedmates: the bleary-eyed partner kept awake by the other's nasal vibrations. (I will now leave this award because I can hear the reader falling asleep, noisily.)

Runner-up in the "There's No Their There" category is IBM, among whose solutions for a small planet is this headline: "You can't begin to help a client until you've walked a mile in their shoes." The writer did not want to say his shoes, which would infuriate female customers, or to stretch his copy to his or her shoes. The fix: Make client plural. The ad continues: "Improving the quality of education in our schools is the most important challenge IBM has ever tackled." Yeah, right.

Not content with that entry, IBM took a full page to ask, "Can You Really Buy a Computer That Makes Someone Feel Differently About Their Job?" Howard Pelzner of Miami notes IBM's *their* problem (a virus loose, perhaps) and adds, "It should be different, the adjective, not differently, the adverb." This suggests the bad/badly differentiation: "to feel bad" is to be depressed, while "to feel badly" means to have a numbness in the fingers. A purist would extend that feeling to different/differently: To feel different is to be a stranger in a strange land, while to feel differently is to receive sensation from antennae rather than fingers. But you won't find that fine distinction made by most, and certainly not on a computer's grammar checker.

The Spelling Bloopie goes to the Orvis catalogue for inadvertently restraining newly married women who tend to take the bits in their mouths. "Beautifully made bridal leathers" are advertised as going into its brown "Bridal trim belt" for waist sizes 30 to 44. Sorry, but Flirtation Walk is no bridle path. *Bridal*, an adjective, refers to a woman being married, who gets a bridal shower and gets to throw the bridal bouquet and spend a night in the bridal suite. *Bridle*, a noun derived from the Old English *bregden*, "to move quickly," has to do with the leather headgear used to control a horse. When the bridle is yanked, it causes the animal to bridle—the verb's meaning has been extended to "to show hostility at an affront." When a newly married woman takes offense and rips off her veil to holler at the groom, we can witness a scene of bridal bridling.

"World MasterCard—more living, less limits" is the slogan of the bankers' credit combine, and it is more or less bankrupt grammar. "Shouldn't this read fewer limits?" writes Andrew Goldberg, a shoofly copywriter in New York. "The less/fewer problem is getting worse by the hour!" *Less* describes quantity; *fewer* deals with number. Years ago, Safeway was given a Bloopie for its sign at a checkout counter that read "Ten Items or Less," and lo! Ever since, I've gone zinging through with my nine items past a sign that correctly says "Ten Items or Fewer." The elitist media strike again.

Here comes a picture of the actress Susan Sarandon in an ad for the American Museum of Natural History, asking, "What part do each of us play?" Writes the Bloopie nominator Maxine Skopov of Orangeburg, New York: "Shouldn't that read 'What part does each of us play?' Could so many proofreaders, editors, printers have missed what virtually leaped out at me?" The part played by each of that phalanx of editors does not guarantee correct usage. Remember the famous 1940s radio line "the Shadow knows"? A black comedian liked to use Black English in spoofing it: "Who knows what evil lurks in the hearts of men? The Shadow do."

And what of the literary set? The Ivy League Bloopie goes to Princeton University Press for advertising *Disarming Strangers* by Leon V. Sigal as "an inside look at how the Korean nuclear crisis originated, escalated and was ultimately diffused." Mark Thompson of *Time* magazine notes, "If they can't tell the difference between diffuse and defuse at Princeton, what's the hope for the rest of us?"

Charles Krauthammer, the only pundit trained as a psychiatrist, wrote an article in the *Weekly Standard* about President Clinton's self-absorption, aptly headlined "The Solipsist-in-Chief." That reminded me that in a recent polemical harangue, I had knocked some politicians who made merely grammatical mistakes as solipsistic solons. Richard Wardlow of Cornelius, North Carolina, led the charge of the Gotcha! Gang: "Solipsism is the theory that the self is the only thing really existent while solecism is a violation of grammatical rules. It seems to me that your mistaken solons are solecistic rather than solipsistic."

O Solecism Mio. I earned a Bloopie of my own.

The definition of solipsism *that you cite brings the red herring of a notion of "the self"; more in harmony with the traditional use of that word in the* Oxford Dictionary of Philosophy's *definition. "The belief that only oneself and one's own experience exists." The* ODP's *entry goes on to note that "Russell reports meeting someone who claimed that she was a solipsist and was surprised that more people were not so as well"; I find the idea of democratic solipsism appealing: Only I really exist, but I recognize your right to believe that only you exist.*

*James D. McCawley**
Department of Linguistics
University of Chicago
Chicago, Illinois

The Ivy League Bloopie Award? The difference between diffuse *and* defuse *is a subtle and literary one, and one not lost on Princetonians.*

The editors of the Oxford English Dictionary *know the difference, too. In my proletarian two-volume* OED *under "diffuse" you'll find, first, the meaning as used in physical chemistry: "to pour out as a fluid with wide dispersion of its molecules." The second meaning is a more literary one: "to pour or send forth as from a center of dispersion." The* OED *cites as meaning 2(c) the figurative sense of the word: "the reverse of collect or concentrate, to dissipate."*

When editors at the Princeton University Press wrote that the "Korean nuclear crisis . . . was diffused," they had deftly found a more literary way to say "defused" or "disarmed" without the excessively obvious and trite allusion to the defusing of a bomb. (A détente expert such as yourself should appreciate this usage.)

*See page 180.

Contrary to the views of the gentleman from Time *magazine, I thought Princeton's usage was elegant and subtle—an interesting trope echoing faintly the principles of quantum physics and chemistry that made the cold war possible in the first place.*

Michael C. Alcamo
New York, New York

" . . . Newly married women who tend to take the bits in their mouths." A bit in the mouth is a bit that will do its job—unless it's then taken in the teeth. Then you can yank all you want to, but Dobbin won't give a damn.

Milton Werner
Brooklyn, New York

THAT FLEXIBLE THAT

I GAVE A BLOOPIE AWARD to a copywriter for writing "Companies who own business jets outperform," explaining that *who* is for living things, not inanimate objects. Instead, I urged the use of *which* or "the flexible *that*" for companies.

Lotsa flak from the Gotcha! Gang for permitting *which* to lead a restrictive clause; go for *that*. But then Robert Hodierne, an editor at Newhouse News Service (who is right about eschewing *which* in this case), pointed to my statement, "The flexible *that* can apply to either people or things," and asked, "Can you offer an example of *that* referring to people?"

Let's sing a few songs: "The Man That Got Away," "Someone That I Used to Love" and then my favorite, "The Girl That I Marry."

The list of examples of that *referring to people would not be complete without Shakespeare's use in Romeo's line, "He jests at scars that never felt a wound." How I remember my confusion when first encountering this usage, in a high school literature class, and puzzling over the paradox of how a scar could exist having "never felt a wound." It's been a favorite ever since.*

John Yavroyan
New York, New York

BLOOPIES 1999!

The moment has arrived for the 1999 coveted Bloopie Awards. Note how the adjective *coveted* (from *cupidus*, "desirable," its heart penetrated by Cupid's arrow) is wedded to the proper noun *Bloopie* (from *blooper*, an oops sound influenced by *blunder*, originally a baseball term for a ball looped by the batter just beyond the infield, and if not caught synonymous with *Texas leaguer*).

Jamming words together, with the second word capitalized in lieu of a space separation (you hear this, TimeWarner, DaimlerChrysler and PriceWaterhouseCoopers?), is the ultimate symbol of merger used by giant corporations eager to get really close. And because *coveted* is most often married to any award, why not the covetedBloopie Awards for solecisms in advertising copy?

The envelopes, please.

A triple Bloopie to Motorola for its "Digital DNA" ad in *Newsweek* and *The New Yorker*, showing an unhelpful repairman with the name tag "Earl" sitting next to an unused phone. (No, not the Maytag man; Motorola stole the idea.) The caption reads, "Who'd of thought that an electronic chip inside your car could help you avoid curbs, other cars, and best of all, Earl in repair."

Steve Allen,* the literate comedian, sent me a copy of a note he shot off to Christopher Galvin, boss of Motorola. "Question: At the advertising agency that placed this ad for you, was there literally no one in a position of authority aware of the fact that the phrase 'would of' is grammatically unjustified and that the correct version is 'would have' or 'would've'?"

The pronunciation of contractions is called verbal reduction. (Why? I dunno, but ommina find out.) If spoken in jest, a dialectical *who'd a thunk* would have worked, and so woulda *who woulda thought* (as in woulda-coulda-shoulda). But to write *of* to express the contraction *'ve* is a solecism.

But that's not the half of it. As Harvey Phillips of New York points out, Motorola's sentence has three errors; its digital DNA is all thumbs. The second is a misplaced comma: In "avoid curbs, other cars, and best of all, Earl in repair" we have a series. As the *Times* stylebook says, "In general, do not use a comma before *and* in a series." (Strunk and White disagree, citing red, white, and blue, but theirs is a little book.) Even if you accept as correct a serial comma after the next-to-last item in a series, I think it is a mistake to write curbs, other cars, and best of all, Earl in repair. The interjected *best of all* should stand alone, separated from the rest of the sentence by commas, dashes or parentheses. Thus, the punctuation should be "curbs, other cars and, best of all, Earl in repair."

Finally, in this triple-helixed DNA of error, let's look at the Motorola "Who'd of thought" sentence in its totality, as Grace Thaler of Boston

---

*Steve Allen died on October 30, 2000.

suggests. It's a question. How do you punctuate a question? With a question mark, not with a period.

The chagrined but good-humored CEO, Galvin (let's face it, what happened to Coke in Belgium was worse), wrote back to Steve Allen, who caught only one of the errors: "Couldn't agree more! It was stupid. We pulled the ad series."

And now to the "There's No Their There" Bloopie, named after the Oakland Mayor Jerry Brown's campaign against Gertrude Stein's municipal slur. (Brown is a brown is a brown.)

In an ad by Crystal Cruises in *The New Yorker*, we read, "A different writer, editor, or cartoonist from *The New Yorker* will join us for each segment, offering their thoughts and observations through on-board discussions." "Alas," writes Sharon King Hoge of New York, "where are the fact checkers?" (She means copy editors; fact checkers are in a lower pay grade.)

A horror of seeming sexist forces some writers into the improperly disagreeing use of the nonspecific plural pronoun. "A different writer, editor, or cartoonist [they go for the Strunk advice on serial commas, not mine] . . . offering their thoughts" is a mistake. The subject is singular (a different writer, not different writers), and the agreeing pronoun should be *his, her* or the tedious *his or her*. One solution is to make the subject plural: "Different writers . . . offering their thoughts," but that would commit the cruise line to dragging more than one writer out of the ship's bar to each segment. The best formulation: get rid of the *their* there. Thus: "A different writer . . . will join us . . . offering thoughts and observations."

Runner-up in this category is Chivas Regal Scotch whisky (Chivas comes from the old Gaelic *seimh* as, "a narrow place," and is the name of the distillery's founders), for "Some are born with a silver spoon in their mouth." As Michael Stronger of Brooklyn notes, *Some*, construed as plural ("Some are"), agrees with *their*, but leaves one spoon in one mouth. To the sound of "oom-pah-pah," say, "Some are born with silver spoons in their mouths."

The Veddy Veddy Wrong Use of Latin covetedBloopie to Bloomingdale's for advertising "Veni-Vedi-Vici" ("I Came, I Saw, I Conquered") cuff links.

If you believe the historian Suetonius, Julius Caesar succinctly summed up his Pontic triumph with the alliterative "Veni, vidi, vici," with the *V* pronounced as *W.* That middle V-word is the Latin *vidi,* from the root *videre,* "to see," and is not *vedi,* from the Bloomingdale's copy department, rooted in error. (I never took Latin but am told that *vidi* is in the first-person singular perfect active indicative, and sounds like one flake of the Breakfast of Champions.)

Finally, a covetedBloopie to Columbia House, the Squad Squad's favorite home video mail-order company: "Each video contains two 1-hour episodes on each video."

Just noticed the line about fact checkers being in a lower pay grade than copy editors. Ain't necessarily so. Here at The New York Times Maga-zine, *copy editors and fact checkers make the same big bucks. Gotcha!*

Linda Magyar
Chief of Research
The New York Times Magazine
New York, New York

May I offer a correction to your correction of the use of vidi—*which is pro-nounced not like one flake of the Breakfast of Champions but like the con-dition of a lawn or garden overgrown with unwanted vegetation. Or should I have ended the previous sentence with a question mark?*

Carl Bowman
New York, New York

Go stand in the corner with Bloomingdale's. Videre *is not the* root, *but the* infinitive. Vid *is the root.*

Digging a bit, you will unearth a root system in Greek and Sanskrit (cf. infra). The Greek word sports a digamma, which probably supports your W pronunciation of the V.

Edward Fischer
Jersey City, New Jersey

In your scathing critique of Motorola and its "Digital DNA" as in Newsweek, *you missed yet another confusing element of the statement, "Who'd of thought that an electronic chip inside your car could help you avoid curbs, other cars, and best of all, Earl in repair."*

"Yoking" together three objects of the verb, avoid, *as in "avoid curbs, cars, and Earl," is a* zeugma, *which, while not really ungrammatical, is a bit confusing for an advertisement.*

The Webster's Third International Dictionary *defines* zeugma *as the "use of a word [e.g.,* avoid] *to modify or govern two or more words [*curbs, cars, Earl] *in a manner that applies to each in a different sense." Certainly, chips helping to miss cars and curbs and Earl is zeugmatic, just as is the example in the dictionary: "The woman opened the door and her heart [and pocketbook] to the orphan."*

                                        Bruce S. Cooper, Ph.D.
                                        Fordham University
                                        New York, New York

BLUENOSES

"Both were single," wrote the *Times* columnist Anthony Lewis about some snooping into a relationship, "so the most prurient bluenose could not have objected." And in David Shaw's book, *The Pleasure Police*, the media reporter provided the subtitle *How Bluenose Busybodies and Lily-Livered Alarmists Are Taking All the Fun out of Life.*

The color blue has long been associated with sex and profanity. In 1864, John Hotten's slang dictionary had this entry: "Blue, said of talk that is smutty or indecent," and the slanguist John Farmer noted in 1890 that to make the air blue meant "to curse; to swear; to use profane language." A century before, laws enforcing public morality were christened blue laws.

But whence *bluenose?* That word was used by Washington Irving in 1809 about a New England cheese, and in 1836 by Thomas Haliburton, Canadian creator of *Sam Slick, the Clockmaker,* to describe natives of Nova Scotia. (One theory: It's cold up there, and noses can turn blue. Another: Fishermen would rub their noses on their wet blue sweaters, picking up the dye.) The word was also applied to a purplish potato and a shellfish known to that area. In 1858, Oliver Wendell Holmes spoofed the term with "ceruleo-nasal" (from the Latin *caerule*, "deep blue"), in reference to a Canadian provincial character working on the transatlantic submarine cable.

Blue-nose was later used to derogate Scottish Presbyterians, but gained a happier connotation as the name of a speedy fishing schooner that

Canadian yachtsmen still revere, and appeared in 1937 on that nation's ten-cent piece.

Then came Demon Rum. The word was used by friends of John Barleycorn to sneer at temperance forces inveighing against the users of alcohol. The *Oxford English Dictionary* cites a 1927 usage during the rise of Prohibition: "a lot of blue noses on the Board." In that year, hard-drinking newspapermen who frequented Lipton's saloon in New York City, near the *New York Times* building, then on Nassau Street, referred to the prohibitionists' "Blue-Nozzle Curse."

Etymology now has a great tool in cybersearching. I don't personally indulge, but my research assistant, Kathleen Miller, with the help of JSTOR, a zingy database that includes obscure academic publications, found a reference to *bluenose* in a 1990 article by David Jaffee in *The William and Mary Quarterly*. That led to an early-nineteenth-century *Farmer's Almanack* in which Robert B. Thomas made up a character, "Tom Bluenose," along with a saloonkeeper, "Toddy Stick," to deliver the message of temperance. (This makes me feel like the madman who contributed citations to the *OED*'s Sir James Murray.)

The sense of *bluenose* we seek goes beyond the temperance movement to mean "one who is excessively puritanical; a moralizing snoop." Merriam-Webster has the earliest dictionary citation, from the 1903 Frank Norris novel, *The Pit:* "I was vegetating there at Barrington, among those wretched old blue-noses." Today it has become an attack on all moralists, whether sincere defenders of moral principles or the hypocritical hounds: Its meaning is now "disapproving busybodies."

BREAD 'N' BUTTER

I am not in the least superstitious, but I know enough not to open an umbrella indoors, leave shoes on a table or a hat on a bed, touch somebody with a broom or rock an empty rocking chair. When any of these surefire invitations to misfortune occur, I—like anyone who hears a sneeze—say, "Bless you!" The latest medieval research tells us that this phrase—in German, *Gesundheit*, "a state of good health"—keeps the Devil from possessing your soul.

But folklorists know there are more specific expressions that are used to ward off evil in special situations. At a gathering of media biggies, I posed this query to Corinne Boggs Roberts: When you are walking along hand in hand with a friend, and an obstacle like a tree or a lamp-post forces you to break your handclasp momentarily, what expression do you use to ward off a quarrel or, worse, permanent separation? Without hesitation, Cokie, as she is known to intimates, replied, "Bread and butter."

Peter Bartis, at the American Folklife Center of the Library of Congress, explains, "*Bread and butter* go together, a sign of unity." He finds a citation in the seven-volume Frank C. Brown *Collection of North Carolina Folklore:* "If two persons are walking and they come to an object (high object) in their path, and one goes on one side and one on the opposite side, they will have a fuss."

A California source shows the expression to be national: "When something goes between two people while walking, and nothing is said afterward, the two will quarrel."

Thousands of bytes of e-mailed expostulations will be onloaded to my head from folklorists certain that the only expression to be used in that case is *needles and pins.* Hold your ire. According to a 1920s usage cited in the *Dictionary of American Regional English* (*DARE*), when two people accidentally said the same thing in unison, "one would then say 'needles' and the other 'pins,' then hook little fingers and make a silent wish." (I used to say "Snap!" before hooking pinkies. Today I say, "Great minds think alike," and eschew the digital signals.) "When walkers were separated and did not use this phrase or *bread and butter,*" *DARE* adds, "it was believed they would have a quarrel."

Here's another version of what to do when two people happen to say the same thing in unison, from my childhood, c. 1950, in Wisconsin. One of the two would initiate this exchange:
    "Pins."
    "Needles."
    "Cups."
    "Saucers."
    "What goes up the chimney?"
    "Smoke."
    "What comes down?"
    "Santa Claus."
    "I hope this wish may never be broken."

Then the two would hook little fingers and pull like a tug of war. The wish made by the one whose finger didn't unhook would be granted.

John Hetland
New York, New York

BROACHING THE TELLTALE BROOCH

Pinning down a pronunciation leads to a split decision.

Let us now broach the sensitive subject of Monica's brooch.

A front-page *New York Times* article by Jeff Gerth and Steve Labaton introduced President Clinton's secretary to the world and included this sentence: "The secretary, Betty Currie, has also retrieved and turned over to investigators several gifts—a dress, a brooch and a hat pin—that the President had given to Ms. Lewinsky, the lawyers said."

My phone immediately began ringing off the hook. (When did they stop making phones that hung on hooks? There's another preserved anachronism.) Investigative reporters, White House sources and other conspirators from the vasty deep demanded in unison: Forget about the dress and the hat pin—how do you pronounce *brooch?* Does it rhyme with *pooch* or with *coach?*

Not so fast; pronunciation is not a matter for a rush to judgment.

The story begins with the Middle English word *broche*, from the Latin *brocca*, spike, with the *o* pronounced as in *Oh, yeah?* As a noun, *broche* meant a tapering pointed instrument, "like a spear, a bodkin or a spit on which to roast meat," and centuries later, a chisel used by masons or a pick used by dentists. That meaning exists today in the French *en brochette*, with the skewer sticking through chunks of meat and onion and tomato. (Don't try to get it off with your fork or you'll splatter the bed of rice all over the table; let the waiter do it.)

As a verb, *to broach* carried forward that meaning of turning. Ships *broach to* when they turn broadside to wind or waves and thereby risk capsizing. Vintners tap a cask by *broaching* it, or enlarging a hole with a boring-bit also called a *broach*. That digging into "sense" led to the current major meaning, "to introduce, to give vent to, to utter," which is why we have been able to *broach* this subject today.

While this was happening to the verb, the noun rooted in *broche* was developing in the jewelry business. "Send hire letters, tokens, *brooches*, rynges," advised Chaucer's narrator in 1385, in *The Legend of Good*

Women, possibly against his amanuensis's better judgment, with the *brooch* denoting a pin (the original spike) attached to an ornament or jewel to form a clasp. Today, it is often synonymous with "pin" but retains a special meaning of an ornamental device intended to clasp two garments, or sections of a garment, together—or at least seeming to.

Note the way the word broke into two spellings: the verb *broach*, meaning to "open up, introduce, address," and the noun *brooch*, meaning "an ornamental pin sticking through a garment."

To me, that spelling split is a signal to pronounce the verb *broach* to rhyme with *coach*, and to pronounce the noun *brooch* to rhyme with *pooch*. (Nice dog, Buddy.)

Many respected dictionaries do not agree with me on this. They hold fast to the "oach" pronunciation for both verb and noun. Be patient; they'll catch up.

A broach *is not a* boring-bit. *It does not bore a round hole as does a bit. It drives a hole, any shape but round, through a piece of material, usually metal. First a pilot hole is bored, and then the broach of the required shape is driven through the pilot hole by great force to enlarge the hole to the desired shape. Admittedly, a small point.*

> Brooke Nihart
> McLean, Virginia

BROUGHT TO HEAL

A DELICIOUS TYPOGRAPHICAL ERROR appeared in *The Wall Street Journal* the other day: "Instead of a visionary revolutionary, Newt Gingrich is now more the old-fashioned ward healer. . . ."

The phrase is *ward heeler,* meaning "party hack." The *ward* is a political subdivision in some big cities, and *heeler*—derived from a dog that a master brings to heel—was first cited in 1876 about a minor politician who slavishly followed his ward leader.

The Boston Democratic boss Martin Lomasney, known as the Mahatma in the era of Mayor James M. Curley, was famous for an aphorism of advice that is tightly embraced by pols today who live in fear of eavesdroppers or subpoena-bearers: "Never write if you can speak; never speak if you can nod; never nod if you can wink." (I am indebted to Paul Allen of Ogilvy Adams & Rinehart for finding this apt axiom.)

Some political junkies also remember Lomasney for coming to the defense of ward heelers: "There's got to be in every ward," said the boss, "somebody that any bloke can come to—no matter what he's done—and get help. Help, none of your law and justice, but help." Such a caring person, binding up the wounded egos of voters sought by heartless cops, might justify the spelling of "ward healer."

In explaining the term ward heeler, *you described a* heeler *as "derived from a dog that a master brings to heel," used to describe "a minor politician who slavishly followed his ward leader." Let me proffer another explanation. Out here in the West, we may be more familiar with sheep- and cattle-herding dogs, who are categorized as either* heelers *or* headers. *The* heelers *herd by nipping at the animals' heels, while* headers *bite at the nose.*

Somehow, I prefer the image of the old ward politician, nipping at the heels of his voters to bring them into line and herd them to the polls (to cast a ballot for the right candidate, of course!).

Evelyn Cruz Stroufe
Seattle, Washington

Burn Before Reading

ASIAN-MONEY HEARINGS provide a quick look into the language of the intelligence world. Across the top of classified material shown to Department of Commerce official John Huang was this initialese: WNINTEL, NOFORN, ORCON. Senator Arlen Specter, who as former chairman of the Senate Intelligence Committee was familiar with the acronyms, elicited definitions from John Dickerson, a CIA official, to inform the uncleared public:

WNINTEL: "Warning notice: intelligence sources and methods."

NOFORN: "No foreign dissemination."

ORCON: "Originator controlled," meaning "no dissemination without going back to the originating agency."

Ah, spookspeak. I remember writing a draft of a presidential speech back in the Vietnam era that had some figures in it given me by Henry Kissinger. Feeling it should not be shown around, I typed at the top, "Top Secret/Sensitive/Eyes Only," phrases I'd picked up from spy novels.

When the speech did not come back to me from the Oval Office, I queried H. R. Haldeman: What cooks with my draft? Deadline time was approaching, and I would have to incorporate President Nixon's changes into the final draft to be typed up for reading on television.

"He'll have to fix it himself" was Bob Haldeman's reply. "You're not cleared for 'Top Secret/Sensitive/Eyes Only.'"

CANNOT CAN

"CAROLEE WESTCOTT says she was canned from the Olive Garden restaurant" for calling a congressman a "turncoat," according to an Associated Press dispatch from Lakeland, Florida.

Ruth Rados of Atlanta sent me that clip with an objection: *Canned?*

The slang term means "discharged" or its synonym from the shooting of a cannon, "fired." Asked about this rather informal usage, Norm Goldstein, editor of the *A. P. Stylebook,* writes: "No, it is surely not A. P. style to use *canned* for *fired.* It's a slang word we don't recommend in serious stories. (It was not used in followup stories on the same incident.)"

It's good to see the news agency upholding standards—and to note that it is blazing the trail to drop the hyphen in *follow-up.*

CHICOMS

Authors of historical fiction worry about anachronism. "And now the clock strikes one," says Dromio of Syracuse, but it was a Shakespearean comedy of error: mechanical clocks, not invented until the fourteenth century, were not available in ancient Ephesus. I had the same problem writing a novel set in our Federal period, and wondered what phrase a man of that era would have used for what we now call *hush money.* (Turns out Thomas Jefferson used the words *hush money* in a letter nearly a century after Steele and Swift.)

Thus it was when I came to the word *Chicom* in Seymour Topping's *Peking Letter,* a riveting novel of the Chinese civil war, I wondered: Was that word—a portmanteau of "Chinese Communist"—in use in the late 40s?

The earliest citation in the *Oxford English Dictionary* is 1966; the *Random House Historical Dictionary of American Slang* found a 1964 use by Robin Moore in his novel *The Green Berets.* So I called Top, a longtime *New York Times* colleague and now administrator of the Pulitzer Prizes, and put it to him. He was the Associated Press correspondent in Peking (now spelled Beijing) reporting on that war; was the word in use at the time?

"You bet it was, and it was no derogation," he recalled. "The truce teams of our Military Advisory Group referred to the Nationalist Chinese as the *Nats* and the Communist Chinese as the *Chicoms*. I can hear it now: 'The *Chicoms* took Mukden, and the *Nats* didn't put up much of a fight.'"

Such is the value to political etymology of the historical novel. Years from now our descendants will be reading dramas about the struggle between today's *Chicoms* and their rivals on politically free Taiwan, the *Chidems*.

CHILLING EFFECT

"A CHILLING SWEAT o'er-runs my trembling joints," says the frightened Quintus in Shakespeare's *Titus Andronicus*. Such a flush of fear stimulates the sweat glands, which then cool the skin with perspiration, metaphorically dampening ardor and freezing action. In underworld lingo, the verb *to chill* is to change a warm body into a cool corpse.

When it was discovered last month that City College of New York had installed a surveillance camera inside a smoke detector outside a student meeting room, three graduate students sued the school on privacy grounds. Brad Sigal, a graduate student, said, "It definitely has a *chilling effect*."

This phrase has now become the great cliché in First Amendment and libel law. Chief Justice Warren Burger used it fifteen times in a 1972 opinion. A *chilling effect* is one that intimidates, makes timorous and turns timid (all from *timere*, "to fear") the ordinarily gutsy journalist, causing the sin of self-censorship.

Who coined it? Forget early cases about coolants. According to Bryan A. Garner, editor of the *Dictionary of Modern Legal Usage*, the earliest metaphoric use found so far was in 1899, by Vice-Chancellor Henry Cooper Pitney of New Jersey: "This letter the wife swears she interpreted as one of intentional discouragement to her return, and that it had a *chilling effect* on her."

Thus are we coming up to the centennial of *chilling effect*. Break out the very cold champagne and toast the phrase good-bye.

CHUM FOR NONCHUMS

A BROOCH is a gift; *chum* so happily received is only in the category of trinkets treasured by people who think they can hear presidential seals bark.

"Officials also recall she was always eager for '*chum*,'" wrote Deborah Zabarenko of Reuters, helpfully defining the word as White House slang for inexpensive trinkets such as cuff links and scarf pins with the presidential seal.

This is not related to the *chum*, or buddy, of Cambridge University slang, thought to be derived from "chamber fellow," or roommate. In the sense used in the White House, *chum* borrows from fishing, a peaceful activity in which chopped-up fish is tossed overboard as bait to attract bigger and better fish.

The object of passing out the *chum*, in fishing as in politics, is to attract them with something glittery and then to hook 'em and reel 'em in.

CLARA BOW LIVES

In the Roaring Twenties, after her smash performance on the silent screen in the movie *It*, she was called "the 'It' Girl." Clara Bow had it, and every flapper wanted it.

In Bob Woodward's book about presidential hubris, *Shadow*, the reporter writes about the thoughts of Sydney Hoffmann, a lawyer for Monica Lewinsky: "She concluded it was highly possible that Lewinsky had a form of Clara Bow syndrome, named after the famous silent-film actress who couldn't say no."

This is a classic example of a *mondegreen*—a mishearing, or passed-along garble, of another's spoken communication. An example is a child's rendition of the opening of the Pledge of Allegiance as "I led the pigeons to the flag."

In 1922 (the year Clara was starring in *Down to the Sea in Ships*), an eminent French psychiatrist observed and reported a syndrome in which a woman has a delusional belief that an older, powerful, often celebrated man is in love with her. He called it *psychose passionelle*, which translates roughly as "erotomanic passion psychosis."

It is listed in *Longman's Dictionary of Psychology and Psychiatry*, however, under the name of the French doctor who identified the syndrome. His name was Clérambault.

COCKTAIL ATTIRE

An invitation came in from Metro-Goldwyn-Mayer to a showing of *Red Corner* with this strange notation: "Cocktail Attire."

What is that supposed to signify—dress like some kind of drunk? I called MGM to check out the meaning and was told, "Just nice dress—not too casual, not too fancy."

That seems to be "business attire," which means a suit or dark blazer and tie for men, anything this side of dressy evening wear for women. But it carries the connotation of "after business hours," which could mean either more or less dressy.

I went in a blazer without a tie and nobody gave me a dirty look. Richard Gere, the star, wore a suit and tie and looked better. That, I presume, is the range of *cocktail attire* at the movies. (If I had gone up to Gere and asked, "What do we do now?" I bet he would have known to reply, "We wait.")

COMPULSIVE COMPELLING

"We've made a compulsive, a compelling case," opined Henry Hyde, chairman of the House Judiciary Committee. Which did he mean?

Both words are rooted in the Latin *pellere*, "to drive." *Compel* is "to drive forcefully," *impel* is "to drive with moral pressure" and *propel* is "to drive forward." Although *compelling* and *compulsive* are usually taken to be synonyms, the meanings of the two adjectives are differentiating usefully.

Compulsive, which still means "having the power to compel," is being overtaken by its secondary meaning, "under the psychological coercion of obsession." One of these days, psychiatrists will adopt the verb *compulse*.

Meanwhile, *compelling* (though its root of *compel* still means "to force" or "to urge irresistibly") is more often being used to mean "driving toward a conclusion or action by cogent argument."

Chairman Hyde meant *compelling*, I hope.

COULD THE BODY
TAKE DOWN THE HAMMER?

For most of the twentieth century, it seemed the sobriquet was in decline. These nicknames of affection or derision, from the French slang *soubriquet*, "a chuck under the chin," enlivened the political language of a previous era. From *the American Fabius* (Washington) to *the Machiavelli of Massachusetts* (John Adams) to *the Sage of Monticello* (Jefferson), American presidents sported these monikers. Jackson was *Old Hickory*, and Grover Cleveland was *the Man of Destiny* to some, *the Stuffed Prophet* to others. Teddy Roosevelt was *the Rough Rider*.

Then the long night of innocuous desuetude set in. Only in sports and crime were heroes and villains immortalized with sobriquets. Honus Wagner, the great Pittsburgh Pirate shortstop in the first two decades of the century, was called *the Flying Dutchman* for his speed and Germanic background (based on the 1841 Richard Wagner opera *Der Fliegende Holländer*). According to Brenda Wilson and James Skipper Jr., making a case for socio-onomastics in the December 1990 *Names*, the journal of the American Name Society, Honus Wagner was responsible for the nickname of his Pirate teammate John Barney (Dots) Miller. When a sportswriter asked Wagner the name of the rookie trying out in the infield, the heavily accented Dutchman replied, "Dot's Milla." Miller proudly carried the nickname Dots through a twelve-year career in the major leagues.

"There has been a change in cultural orientation during the past century," note the onomastic linguists, "from one where there was a sense of solidarity and common identity rooted in tradition and personal relationships." Military leaders tried to keep it going: from the Civil War's Gen. Winfield Scott—*Old Fuss and Feathers*—to World War I's *Black Jack* Pershing, to World War II's *Old Blood and Guts*, applied to Gen. George Patton.

Baseball in mid-century preserved the tradition: After Babe Ruth's *the Sultan of Swat* came *Joltin'* Joe DiMaggio, also known as *the Yankee Clipper*, and Stan (*the Man*) Musial. And today we have Mark (*Big Mac*) McGwire and Frank (*the Big Hurt*) Thomas. In football, Elroy (*Crazylegs*) Hirsch was succeeded by Jerome (*the Bus*) Bettis. You can find more sobriquets in popular music: Frank Sinatra was *Ol' Blue Eyes*, Billie Holiday was *Lady Day*, and Benny Goodman *the King of Swing*.

But it was in organized crime that the dwindling practice of awarding a title based on a quality best held on. A previous century's Billy (*the Kid*) Bonney and Jack *the Ripper* led to *Scarface* Al Capone and Frank (*the Enforcer*) Nitti. Thomas B. Kirkpatrick, president of the Chicago Crime Commission, sent me his latest report on leader profiles in the "Chicago outfit" once headed by Tony Accardo. It includes the new boss, John (*No Nose*) DiFronzo; his adviser, Joe (*the Clown*) Lombardo; and area boss John (*Johnny Apes*) Monteleone. Crime figures in other ethnic groups cannot boast such colorful nomenclature.

In recent years, sobriquets have been making their way back into politics, often based on modifications of first names: *Landslide Lyndon* Johnson, *Tricky Dick* Nixon, *Slick Willie* Clinton (that last stolen from the bank robber *Slick Willie* Sutton, from his habit of slicking down his hair as well as his smooth way with safes). Ronald Reagan had a good run as *the Great Communicator*, but it was President Clinton who successfully styled himself *the Comeback Kid*.

That reversal of trend, with all its socio-onomastic resonance in a return to personalization of leadership, picked up speed with the election of James G. Janos to the governorship of Minnesota. The former professional wrestler ran under, and serves under, the service mark he registered in the United States Patent and Trademark Office, "Jesse (*the Body*) Ventura," which he established as the exclusive "nickname and not the name of any other particular living individual."

On top of that came the emergence, during the House of Representatives' impeachment debate, of Majority Whip Tom (*the Hammer*) DeLay. He's not happy with it: "Sometimes I'm a little blunt and forthright in what I believe, and that's created an image I don't think I am, quite frankly."

Don't knock it, Tom. Beats *the Screwdriver* or *the Monkey Wrench*, or as President James Buchanan described himself, *the Old Public Functionary*.

The anti-Italian segment of the liberal media (of which I know you are not a member) lists only nicknames of Italo-Americans, leaving out such classics as Benjamin (Bugsy) Siegel, Meyer (Little Man) Lansky, Edward (Monk Eastman) Osterman, Arnold (The Brain, The Big Bankroll, A.R.) Rothstein, (Dopey) Benny Fein, Jacob (Gurah) Shapiro, Albert (Tick-Tock) Tannebaum, Harry (Pittsburgh Phil) Strauss, Jacob (Greasy

*Thumb) Guzik, Bernard (Who-Ah) Horowitz, Charles (The Bug)
Workman, Abe (Kid Twist) Reles, Otto (Abbadabba) Berman, Louis
(Lepke) Buchalter, Bernard (Lulu) Rosenkrantz—most of whom were
members in good standing of that erudite but effective organization known
as Murder, Inc. One would be remiss to leave out (Peg Leg) Lonergan or
(Two-Gun) Crowley and, last but not least, the Bronx Bad Boy of all time,
Arthur (Dutch Schultz) Flegenheimer. Now, crime figures in other
ethnic groups cannot boast such colorful nomenclature??? Really,
Mr. Safire, I think you are quite remiss in this category.*

*Thomas Vasti
New York, New York*

COUNTERFACTS

What if Bill Clinton, after his reelection, had decided to settle the
Paula Jones lawsuit? The titillating tintinnabulation of the belles that
occurred would not have taken place.

That's a *what if* that will intrigue historians and novelists who like to
explore alternative scenarios. Jeffrey McQuain is the coauthor of *Coined
by Shakespeare*, a fascinating romp through the words first used by the
Bard. He first tackled the nomenclature of the burgeoning art form of
virtual history three years ago, with labels ranging from the Greek-
prefixed *allohistory* to the derogation *suppository story*. McQuain reported
one other possible denotation: *counterfactual*.

This month William H. Honan wrote in *The New York Times* that
"such speculations, long disparaged as parlor games by sober-minded historians, have recently become a fashionable new discipline known as
counterfactual history. . . . Last month a group of *counterfactualists* con-
vened at Ohio State."

Counterfactualism is hot and marketable. (In *As You Like It*, Celia—as if
fattened by good news—uses a freshly minted word to Rosalind: "We
shall be the more marketable.")

CRATER

Secretary of State Madeleine K. Albright sent a message to Serbian
strongman Slobodan Milosevic via Charles Gibson on ABC's revitalized
Good Morning America: "Whichever side *cratered* the talks would be held
responsible." The use of that verb was surely planned and tested: The

same night, the Queen of Foggy Bottom repeated that high-impact figure of speech on Jim Lehrer's *News Hour* on PBS.

For a decade, we in the language dodge have been watching the new
verb, *to crater,* undergo what we like to call "sense deterioration" (much as
cunning, which originally meant "knowledgeable," slipped in sense to
"slyly clever").

At first, the verb *crater* (originally a noun from the Latin word for
"bowl," from the Greek "to mix") was intransitive, meaning "to form a
hollow." In World War I, it learned how to transmit action to an object,
as "scores of mine explosions had *cratered* it." In World War II, Cecil Day
Lewis gave the terrifying term a poetic twist: "Yet words there must be,
wept on the *cratered* present."

The verb, still associated with the pits and pockmarks left by bombs,
then gained its metaphoric extension. Following the Persian Gulf War,
during the 1992 presidential campaign, President George Bush used the
word to describe Saddam Hussein's grudging compliance with U.N.
inspection requirements: "I'm glad that he *cratered* once again."

Now it means "collapse." In today's diplolingo, talks *crater.* In base-
ballese, pennant hopes *crater.* In mutual fund management jargon, "sales
lately have *cratered.*" With constant use, the disastrous sense of a huge
meteor slamming into Earth has deteriorated; its slang sense shows signs
of fading from "collapse" to merely "abandon" or "cast aside," as in, "We
cratered the project." I await the Arnold Schwarzenegger movie *The
Craterer.*

Like Judge Joseph Force Crater, who disappeared into a New York City
taxicab in 1930 and was never seen or heard from again, the monosyllabic
verb that this vogue usage has replaced—the simple but powerful *fail*—has
been all but lost to the public lingo of movers and shakers. And to think how
powerfully moving that little verb once was. Words *crater* me.

And while we're at it, whatever became of the famous search for the
vanished jurist? According to a Detective Burns at the New York Police
Department, "There has never been an arrest made on the case, so it is
not closed." For those still on the lookout, he's a little, dignified guy with
glasses, and he would now be 113 years old.

*One source of "to crater" is climber's jargon. In the early 1970s, my climb-
ing partner, fresh from a summer in Yosemite, warned me not to climb too*

*high above my last piton (without putting in a new one) for fear of crater-
ing on the ledge below.*

> *Willard Wood*
> *Norfolk, Connecticut*

CRONY CAPITALISM

The Washington Post finds South Korea's economic distress troubling,
"particularly its outmoded form of *crony capitalism*."

The Japanese call it *keiretsu;* the Koreans say *chaebol;* the Russian word
is *semibankirshchina;* and the Americans label the cozy arrangement
among industrialists, bankers and government officials *crony capitalism.*

No matter what you call it, the system now roiling Asian finances is
seen as a perversion of the open market that is the essence of real, trust-
busted, unfettered free enterprise.

If you've been stuck in an emerging-market mutual fund, you want to
know: What's the difference between a Japanese *keiretsu* and a Korean
chaebol?

"Family-owned conglomerate" is the meaning of the Korean *chaebol,*
pronounced *chay-bol.* Sometimes as many as two dozen companies in varied fields belong to one family; the managers are brothers and cousins
and in-laws who steer business one another's way and cover up mistakes.
Korea, which was a Japanese colony for most of the first half of this century, took the family-network practice from Japan, where it was called
zaibatsu until the holding companies were disbanded by General
MacArthur at the end of World War II.

After the occupation ended, Japanese businessmen took the conglom-
eration concept a long step further to *keiretsu,* pronounced kay-RET-soo.
Family members were replaced by professional managers, directorships
interlocked and the companies owned pieces of one another, making
them invulnerable to hostile takeover. At the core of the *keiretsu* is its
nationwide bank, facilitating the mutual back-scratching and under the
indirect but tight control of Japan's Ministry of Finance. The result is
more self-protective than any corporate clique, and *keiretsu* was a process
much admired in the United States until impregnability lost its luster.

The Russians drew on their czarist history for a term to describe a
financial oligarchy with political connections. *Semiboyarshchina* means
"rule of the seven boyars" and refers to the group of seven nobles who

traded favors for influence with the Kievian princes until Czar Peter I broke the boyars' power and abolished their rank in the seventeenth century.

Today, the boyars are replaced by bankers; seven bankers are said to run the Russian economy. Having made fortunes from their political connections during the breakup of the Soviet Union, they are now helping politicians friendly to them get air time on their media to win elections. Their system, modeled on that of the U.S. "robber baron" monopolists of the nineteenth century, is called *semibankirshchina*, "rule of the seven bankers."

"China has not lagged behind these other countries in the practice of *cronyism*," noted *The Wall Street Journal Europe* last month. "The word that best encapsulates the whole process—*guanxi*, or connections—is, after all, Chinese." That word is pronounced gwan-SHEE and often goes beyond "personal connections" to describe a form of extreme networking. The *South China Morning Post* quoted a Singaporean businessman, Ho Kwon-ping, condemning "cronyism and pork-barrelling" in East Asia, adding, "In place of good management, many relied on *guanxi*."

In the United States, *keiretsu, chaebol, guanxi, semibankirshchina*— similar in meaning but with subtle cultural shadings of difference—are lumped together under the American phrase now in heavy vogue: *crony capitalism*.

The earliest use I can find of this alliterative gem is in the August 24, 1981, issue of *Time* magazine, in an article about the financial predations of President Ferdinand Marcos. "*Crony capitalism* is thus turning into crony socialism" was its last line, and "A Case of *Crony Capitalism*" was its headline. The writer, John DeMott, disclaims coinage, suggesting that it may have come from a correspondent in the field or from an insertion by his editor at the time, George M. Taber.

Taber, now editor of *Business News New Jersey*, recalls how "everyone was talking about Marcos and his 'cronies,' and I probably came up with it for alliterative reasons." *Time* editors then wrote the headlines, and "we spent an awful lot of time on the last paragraph, trying to make that loop from the headline to the last paragraph."

Let us now follow the track of *crony*, college slang at Cambridge in the seventeenth century, rooted in the Greek *khronios*, "long-lasting," from *khronos*, "time." (The slang term they used at Oxford for this was *chum*.)

The chronic diarist Samuel Pepys, in his entry for May 30, 1665, wrote of "Jack Cole, my old Cambridge school-fellow . . . who was a great *chrony* of mine."

In politics, *crony* took on a pejorative connotation as the sinister side of "friend"—more of a hanger-on, the recipient of favors for old times' sake. In 1946, when President Harry Truman's poker-playing friends brought disrepute on his administration, the *New York Times* columnist Arthur Krock wrote that "New Dealers and Conservatives found themselves together in opposition to what a press gallery wit has called a '*government by crony.*'"

Soon afterward, Secretary of the Interior Harold Ickes (the memorable father, not the forgetful son) resigned from the Truman Cabinet with the well-publicized blast, "I am against *government by crony.*"

When I first went to work at *The New York Times* in 1973, Krock still had an office at the Washington bureau. I went down the hall and introduced myself, explained that I was a political lexicographer on the side and asked—for history's sake—if he could reveal the name of the anonymous "press gallery wit" who coined the phrase made famous by Ickes.

"I was referring modestly to myself," Krock said.

I had suspected as much. In the same way that "Western observer" was often used as the source for piquant quotes dreamed up by foreign correspondents, "press gallery wit" was an attribution often used by reporters who came up with a good line but could not quote themselves. I pressed for the source: Was Arthur Krock the actual coiner of the phrase encapsulating the stream of petty scandals?

"I couldn't document that I am the originator," said my predecessor pundit conservatively, adding with justifiable pride, "but I, too, have seen no previous use of the expression in the public prints."

DAM UNTOWARD TINKERS

"I DON'T THINK a censure resolution would be worth a tinker's damn," said Senator Arlen Specter about a trial balloon floated out by the Senate majority leader Trent Lott. "It would be regarded as a highly political, untoward matter."

The Washington Post spelled it *damn*. I waited for the inevitable call, and it came from Gar Joseph, an editor for the *Philadelphia Daily News*, who noticed that the *Inquirer* spelled it *dam*.

The controversy is a century old. The 1890 *Dictionary of Slang*, by J. S. Farmer and W. E. Henley, contains an entry on "not to be worth a dam," akin to "not to care a fig." The early slanguists noted that "the *dam* or *dawm* is an Indian coin worth barely the fortieth part of a rupee." (A rupee is now worth two cents.)

A second theory backing up the *dam* spelling is in Norman Schur's 1973 *English English*, dealing with tinker's cuss and tinker's *dam*, based on an 1877 dictionary of mechanics. To spell it *damn*, Schur holds, "is an error of folk etymology. The term is properly *dam*, the small clay guard that a tinker [an itinerant mender of household utensils] puts around a hole that is to be sealed with solder, to prevent the solder from running off the rounded surface of the pot until it has cooled. The hot solder dries out the clay, which is then thrown away. Thus there is hardly anything in the world worth less than a *tinker's dam*."

However, a hellfire-and-damnation set exists that spells it *damn*, led by the *Oxford English Dictionary*. Etymologists there argue that the 1877 mechanics dictionary offered "an ingenious but baseless conjecture" and conclude that *tinker's damn* is rooted in "the reputed addiction of tinkers to profane swearing" and cite an 1839 entry in the journals of Henry David Thoreau that says, "Tis true they are not worth a '*tinker's damn*.'" I'd go with the *OED*.

But what did Specter mean by *untoward*? That is not now the opposite of *toward*, "in the direction of," though *untoward* originally meant "disinclined to go or do." The word now means "unseemly, improper" or "unfortunate, ill-starred." Though surely not intended toward his distinguished colleague, it can also mean "foolish."

DANGLE

I asked Representative Chris Cox if the Chinese *walk-in* was a *dangle*, and he *waved me off*. Thirty years before, I asked Jim Angleton of the CIA if the Nosenko *walk-in* was what he called a *dangle*, and he *waved me on*.

Times change, adversaries shift, but spookspeak—the inside lingo of the intelligence trade—lives on. Those who confuse a *drop-dead* dress with a *dead-drop* address have not come in from the cold and are unable to cope with delicious nuances of espionage.

In the three volumes published by the House Select Committee on U.S. National Security and Military-Commercial Concerns with the People's Republic of China, a.k.a. the Cox Report, this drama is teased: "In 1995, a '*walk-in*' approached the CIA outside of the PRC and provided an official PRC document classified 'Secret' that contained design information on the W-88 Trident D-5 warhead."

The report helpfully cited the definition of *walk-in* in *Spy Book: The Encyclopedia of Espionage*, by Norman Polmar and Thomas B. Allen: "An unheralded defector or a *dangle*, a '*walk-in*' is a potential agent or a mole who literally walks into an embassy or intelligence agency without prior contact or recruitment."

Note those *or*s: If the *walk-in* is a true defector, the spy becomes a potential agent for the side walked in on; if he or she is a *dangle*, the spy is seen as a potential *mole*, a word coined by the novelist John le Carré to mean "penetration agent."

Dangle is a Danish verb meaning "to hang so as to swing freely." In its espionage sense, a *dangle* is like a delicious morsel swung in front of the nose of a slavering animal. The *dangle* is a tempter, much like the serpent in the Garden of Eden, offering an apple of discord to the spy agency that welcomes and trusts the *walk-in*.

Representative Cox, a buttoned-up attorney not given to colorful language, apparently felt the need for a cooler term for *dangle*. He chose *directed walk-in*, "purposefully directed by the PRC to provide this information to the United States." (The specific *purposefully* means "with intent to carry out a given purpose"; the general *purposely* means "on purpose, not accidentally.") Spy novelists hope the compound, formalized Cox synonym for *dangle* does not catch on.

Although the earliest printed citation in the Dow Jones database for *dangle* in the specialized sense is from 1985, I heard it in 1970 from the lips of James Jesus Angleton, the legendary counterintelligence chief of the CIA. He was deeply suspicious of the bona fides of Yuri Nosenko, a Soviet *walk-in* who transmitted to the United States information about Lee Harvey Oswald dissociating Moscow from the Kennedy assassination. Angleton, an orchid-raising fishing enthusiast and poetry lover nicknamed Mother, talked of Nosenko as "a probable *dangle*" and what he brought in as "feed material," both phrases taken from fishing. To this day his supposition that Nosenko was supplying disinformation is fiercely disputed within the agency.

When I asked if I would be wise to think of Nosenko as what Angleton called a *dangle*, he replied only that he would not *wave me off.*

To wave off, in hockey, means not to count a goal even though it looks as if the puck went into the net. In auto racing, a driver has the chance to *wave off* his qualifying laps if he doesn't think his car is making good enough time. On aircraft carriers, it is to abort a landing. In general colloquial use, it means "to disregard or dismiss."

In journalingo, akin to spookspeak because of their commonality of snooping, to *wave off* means "to suggest a hypothesis is mistaken without denying it." The earliest citation I can find, unfortunately, is in a column of my own in 1981: "As columnist Jack Anderson was about to write of the Secretary's incipient [I meant imminent] departure, the Secretary of State [Al Haig] panicked to the point of begging the President to call the newsman to *wave him off* the story. Mr. Reagan complied."

If the reporter is not *waved off* a story by a source, is the source tacitly confirming it? No. In 1990, Attorney General Dick Thornburgh deplored the fact that "the media on occasion interprets the fact that we will not deny information or *wave them off* of a story as confirmation of an unauthorized disclosure." However, when a source, worried about confirming a leak, *waves a reporter off* a story that is true (as Cox did with my early query about a *walk-in*), that is considered by the inquirer to be a misstep in the symbiosis minuet.

DAY OF INFAMY

The day the Japanese attacked Pearl Harbor, President Franklin D. Roosevelt—who could have turned to his great speechwriters, Robert E.

Sherwood and Samuel I. Rosenman, for his speech to Congress calling for a recognition that "a state of war has existed"—chose to write the message himself. He dictated this to Grace Tully, his secretary:

"Yesterday, December 7, 1941, a date which will live in world history," went the first draft of his six-minute message, "the United States was simultaneously and deliberately attacked by naval and air forces of the Empire of Japan."

FDR was not satisfied with that. *Simultaneously* dealt with the naval and air forces operating as a unit, which was not his central point; besides, it was a six-syllable word. He changed *simultaneously* to the more dramatic *suddenly*, which went to the surprise nature of the combined attack.

What about "a date which will live in world history"? That seemed to credit the Japanese with a historic act and carried with it no condemnation. He reached for a word that expressed "shame, disgrace, evil reputation, obloquy, opprobrium." His choice: *infamy*.

It was an unfamiliar word to most people; few recalled the passage in Ezekiel in the King James version of the Bible: "Ye are taken up in the lips of talkers, and are an *infamy* of the people." Because the adjective *infamous* is within the periphery of understanding of most English speakers, the noun *infamy* was a better choice than, say, *obloquy* or the more bookish *opprobrium*.

History has a way of editing phrases to make them more memorable. Just as Churchill's "blood, toil, tears and sweat" has been shortened in memory to "blood, sweat and tears," FDR's "date which will live in infamy" has been cut to "FDR's *day of infamy* speech." (*Day* is not as puissant as *date* in this case, as FDR was marking the date with great specificity; however, I would have substituted *that* for *which*.)

Looking over the drafts supplied by the archivist Raymond Teichman at the Franklin D. Roosevelt Library in Hyde Park, I note that the President added and then crossed out "without warning"—why should an attacker give warning?—and handled the duplicity of Japanese negotiations with "was continuing the conversations," which he shortened to "was still in conversation."

FDR, reading what he had dictated, evidently felt the message needed a lift. He wrote an insert: "No matter how long it may take us to overcome this premeditated invasion, the American people will in their righteous might win through to absolute victory."

Every President can make use of good writing help. Lincoln used a suggestion of his Secretary of State, William Seward, in developing "the mystic chords of memory" peroration to his first inaugural address. In the final draft of FDR's war message, the student of perorations in speech-writing can see the handwriting of Harry Hopkins, the President's closest adviser. Under the word *Deity*, he suggested an insertion, reminding the President that a reference to God was called for.

To lift the spirit of a stunned nation, Hopkins, not noted for his writing skill, wrote in the line that subtly evoked Lincoln's wartime "with firmness in the right" and combined it with an adaptation of the final few words of the presidential oath: "With confidence in our armed forces— with faith in our people—we will gain the inevitable triumph—so help us God." (Hopkins had added another phrase, "with assurance in the righteousness of our cause," but that must have seemed excessive to him, and he crossed it out of his insertion.) FDR then escalated "faith in our people" to "with the unbounded determination of our people."

Sherwood, the dramatist who had won a Pulitzer Prize for *Abe Lincoln in Illinois*, might have been understandably grumpy at being shut out of such a historic speech. He did not hear the echo of Lincoln's triple-*with* construction in his second inaugural ("With malice toward none, with charity for all, with firmness in the right") in Hopkins's insertion. Sherwood later called Hopkins's insertion "the most platitudinous line in the speech," but he was mistaken.

FDR scrapped his own insertion about winning through to victory and, making emendations, chose Hopkins's line instead. All this is why, as Americans remember Pearl Harbor, speechwriters remember the Pearl Harbor speech.

Contrary to your assertion that Sherwood "might have been understandably grumpy at being shut out of a historic speech," the facts underscore that Sherwood served a key role in the history of that fateful message.

Jimmy Roosevelt in his 1976 book, My Parents: A Differing View, *tells us that regarding the Declaration of War Against Japan speech, his father "turned it over to Bob Sherwood."*

Moreover, Sherwood in his own Roosevelt and Hopkins: An Intimate History *reports that after the President dictated to his secretary Grace Tully . . . "a first draft of his message to Congress," he, the Presi-*

dent, and Tully then "had dinner together in the Oval Room." Sherwood goes on to say that he and FDR "went over the speech again briefly, and the President made a few corrections and decided to read it to the Cabinet."

At the very least, Sherwood proved to be the final sounding board for FDR's famous infamy speech.

Miles Beller
Los Angeles, California

As a kid, I, too, was impressed with FDR's improvement of "history" to "infamy"—for its weight and strength.

Now, as a poet, I notice not only the in *alliteration, but the beautiful chain of short i sounds which bind the dependent clauses "which will live in infamy." Notice, too, the double* ins *forcing the voice to emphasize the second one. So I think FDR got it just right.*

Judith Saul Stix
St. Louis, Missouri

DEAD TIGER BOUNCE

A puzzled zoogoer sends in a clip from the *Financial Times* about a possible recovery of Asian stocks headlined, with no explanation, "Dead Tiger Bounce."

In 1985, the same newspaper quoted Singaporean investment advisers warning of a *dead cat bounce:* False hopes are stirred when a stock rises slightly after a crash but turns out to be lifeless. This odious variation of a bounce, or temporary upturn, is being applied here to other cats—the "tigers," symbolizing formerly ferocious Asian economies, now turned by adversity into bruised pussycats.

Thus, a temporary rise in the stock of an Asian company that has recently plummeted is a *dead tiger bounce.* By this analogy, any agreement to limit the fluctuations of currencies of Asian nations will be called the *dragon in the tunnel.*

"DIRTY" WORDS

"(Warning: pun ahead)," writes Walter Kirn in *Time* magazine, and then writes of a presidential passion for lawyerly phraseology that the writer calls "cunning linguistics." The pun is on *cunnilingus,* counterpart to *fellatio* in oral sex.

As scandal is revealed or rebutted, we are sure to be exposed to words or allusions not previously used in what was once called "mixed company" or in the presence of children. As the *dimes are dropped* and the dirt gets *dished,* we should remember that the words themselves are not dirty, but it is the behavior described or accused that can be scandalous or *tawdry* (from "Saint Audrey," a Norwich church fair at which cheap lace was sold).

Shakespeare's King Henry IV worries that his son, the hot-blooded Prince Hal, is picking up gross terms through his youthful association with the dregs of society, and this carousing might lead to "unguided days/And rotten times." The Earl of Warwick reassures the King, "The Prince but studies his companions/Like a strange tongue." Warwick then extends his word picture, sending a message to those today who feel queasy about salacious terms used to describe actions at the seat of power: "to gain the language,/'Tis needful that the most immodest word/Be look'd upon and learnt."

> *At least you got the correct country. Saint Audrey is a corruption of Saint Ethelread (d. 679), founder of the double monastery at Ely (Cambridgeshire). So "tawdry" is a second-generation corruption. Norfolk (in Norwich) has a perfectly lovely cathedral and its own fair.*
>
> *The goods in general that were sold at the fair were shoddy, not simply lace.*
>
> [The Reverend] Larry Bailey
> New York, New York

> *In the movie* Tomorrow Never Dies, *M's secretary, Miss Moneypenny, is briefing James Bond on a mission to the Orient where he is destined to meet an old flame. The question arises as to whether Bond can speak Chinese, and Miss Moneypenny states, "James has always been a cunning linguist."*
>
> *All of the Bond movies contain double entendres which are entertaining and often missed in the action.*
>
> Saul S. Schiffman
> Verona, New Jersey

DISMILITARIZE?

Few people are for unilateral *disarmament.* Most Koreans and Americans are familiar, after four decades, with a *demilitarized* zone, or DMZ. Now, from the war that brought us *nonpermissive environment,* we have a distinction drawn between *disarm* and *demilitarize.*

The former chairman of the Joint Chiefs, Gen. Henry H. Shelton, said on ABC's This Week: "We never said that we were going to *'disarm'* the KLA. We used the term *'demilitarize.'"* *The Wall Street Journal* editorialized on its meaning to the Kosovo Liberation Army: "This distinction apparently means they can keep their hunting rifles, relying on a U.N.-supervised force to protect them from Serbian tanks."

The distinction, more finely put, is this: *Disarm* means "to divest of weapons; to deprive of the means of attack." *Demilitarize* means "to close a military organization; to remove the military power or potential."

Now we're into the trickiest kind of semantics. How *disarmed* do you have to be to call yourself *demilitarized?* I think it depends, first, on the power of the weaponry: If you carry a rifle or a pistol, you are armed but not necessarily militarized; if you are in an armored personnel carrier or in a choppering gunship, You're in the Army Now. But how about an automatic rifle, a small mortar or a light machine gun? If that's not *militarized,* what about a little howitzer or a heavy machine gun or a shoulder-mounted missile? This has yet to be determined.

The second part of the meaning of *demilitarized* deals with organization. Can a *demilitarized* group call itself an army? (The Salvation Army would say yes.) Are a buncha guys hanging around in civvies and calling one another "mister" *demilitarized* if they practice maneuvers and draw a table of organization in the sand?

A Pentagon spokesman, Ken Bacon, informs me: "*Disarm* means to take weapons away from an army. *Demilitarize* means to disband the army." As I get it, the KLA will be disbanded but not *disarmed,* which suggests its members can keep all their arms as individuals but may not assemble or otherwise get organized.

The current meaning will be worked out at the negotiating tables and on the field, then passed to lexicographers. Meanwhile, we are in a gray area. I asked a top soldier-diplomat if he would like to set me straight on the latest specific meaning of *demilitarize.* I am not sure if he replied, "No, thanks," or "No tanks."

DISMISSALESE: MOVIN' ON

"Our country has been distracted by this matter for too long," said President Clinton in his brief speech after his grand jury appearance. "Now it is time, in fact it is past time, to *move on.*"

Commerce Secretary William Daley quickly agreed: "I wish the situation was what he said in January. But it isn't. So let's *move on.*"

The phrase soon became the mantra for those supporting the President. Some, like Senator John Glenn, preferred "Let's *put it behind us,*" but *move on* was the dismissal of preference by those who objected to the sex revelations. Senator Tom Harkin used both: "It's in our best interest to *put this behind us and move on.*" (In 1992, *Newsweek* quoted his wife, Ruth Harkin, saying of the incoming First Lady, "One of the things about Hillary Clinton is she *moves on.*")

Seekers of the President's impeachment could not effectively counter with "Let's stay with this" or "No moving on," because a call for stasis is hardly rousing; they chose to counter a different dismissal, "It's just about sex," with the bumper-sticker slogan "It's the Perjury, Stupid."

The imperative dismissal was first recorded in 1831, as a direction given by a London policeman to loiterers. In a 1978 song, Paul Stanley, of the vocal group Kiss, recalls advice from his mother not to be tied down to one woman but to "Move on."

Curiously, few supporters of Mr. Clinton used the phrase hurled by the mayor of Washington, Marion Barry, at those who objected to his election comeback: *"Get over it."* That formulation of dismissal is too confrontational. Indeed, some saw *move on* as insufficiently contrite: "Nothing sets a woman off faster," observed Janis Spring, a Yale psychologist, than *move on.* "The idea of *moving on*—men have a tendency to use that expression. You can't *move on.* You can only move through."

Perhaps the White House damage controllers included a psychologist, because both the President and the Vice President subtly modified their phraseology soon after the speech. "It is very important that our nation *move forward,*" Mr. Clinton and Mr. Gore said at various times. "It is time to *put this matter behind us* once and for all and *move forward.*"

Cannot spend too much time in close analysis of this propelling locution. Time to get on with the business of lexicography. (Unlike the command *get over it* or the exhortation *move on,* the brisk *get on with it* is a more neutral dismissal.)

Regarding "moving on," I'd like to point out the moving song "Move On," from Sondheim and Lapine's moving 1985 Pulitzer Prize–winning Sunday in the Park with George. Among the lyrics are:

Move on . . .
Stop worrying where you're going—
Move on.
If you can know where you're going,
You've gone.
Just keep moving on.

Allen Mogol
New York, New York

DIVINE PROVIDENCE

When Donald G. Higdon of Ridgewood, New Jersey, received a letter from E. Gordon Gee, president-elect of Brown University, addressed to "Women and men of Brown," the member of the class of 1958 sent it on to me with a few corrections.

"Brown values the concepts of thinking and of scholarship," wrote the new boss, ". . . under the guidance of one of the nation's most distinguished faculty." Although the "concept of thinking" makes one think twice about concepts, it was "one of the nation's . . . *faculty*" that Higdon found troubling.

While I had the University of Chicago's Jim McCawley on the phone, I ran Gee's curious usage past him. "The most charitable interpretation that I can put on 'one of the nation's most distinguished faculty' in President-elect Gee's letter," replied McCawley, who is not so charitable when it comes to my mistakes, "is that *faculty* is an error for *faculties*. In a different context, *faculty* could be used as a collective noun (like *personnel*), but surely the new president is not claiming that Brown's *faculty* is the nation's most distinguished and that one of its members guides Brown's valuing of the cherished concepts."

Gee's string of solecisms concluded with "Brown is already connected to the world by a bridge of ideas and opportunities, and I intend to deepen that connection." Higdon, who learned from professors of English at Brown never to mix his metaphors, wants to know, "How do you deepen a bridge?"

As a father of a Brown graduate, I can attest to the Providence, Rhode Island, school's reputation for self-reliant scholarship. And I recognize my own geezerly vulnerability in putting a comma after "Providence" contrary to the Postal Service's new usage. But as they say in professional football when the newest whiz is first slammed to the AstroTurf, Welcome to the NFL, President Gee.

DON'T CALL ME "NEAR ELDERLY"

"I'm the oldest of the baby boomers," President Clinton told a fundraising gathering in Miami. "I'm what you'd call *near-elderly*."

That locution was evidently being bruited about the White House at the time, because the President announced a proposal to extend government health insurance to people as young as fifty-five. "The three million uninsured people in this group," wrote John M. Broder in *The New York Times*, "known by insurance statisticians as the '*near elderly*,' are too young for Medicare."

This means that another age euphemism—one aimed at junior seniors—has reached maturity. It was first cited in an Associated Press dispatch in 1978 to describe those, in addition to the already elderly, urging additional Social Security benefits. Now *near-elderly* (usually hyphenated) is the fatalistic term embraced by *middle-aged* demographers—those from forty to sixty or so.

Headline writers are not altogether happy about it. *The Washington Post* has tried the slightly shorter noun *almost-old* to refer to people aged sixty-two to sixty-four, but this confers *old* on everybody above that, which causes great codger unease, especially when life expectancy for Americans jumped from forty-seven to seventy-one in the twentieth century.

Old is a dysphemistic no-no (unless you're *oldest-old*, in a category of those over eighty-five, and wishing you were eighty again). That's a pity; the root of *old* is the Latin *altus*, "high, deep," and the word's provenance ought not to put off the vulnerable venerable.

Women who bridle at being put down as *no spring chicken* or *long in the tooth* prefer the arch *of a certain age*. Men stretching their sideburns over their bald spots resist such sports terms as *losing a step* or *past his prime*, preferring *mature*, which has the connotation of deliciously ripe fruit.

"We prefer that the word *elderly* not be used at all," reports Tom Otwell at the American Association of Retired Persons. "And we try to avoid *senior citizens*, which, if not pejorative, is stereotyping." So what would be near-perfect? "We prefer *older Americans* or *mature Americans*." The AARP sends applications to people turning fifty, a chilling reminder to recipients that their days of wine and roses may be passing, and accurately considers them "older" than most of the population (though "mature" is not based on chronological age). MetLife includes *baby boomers*, now over fifty, in the *mature market*.

Near-elderly, despite its White House use, is not an official classification. "The term *elderly* has a common definition, because of repeated and relentless use," says Greg Spencer, chief of the population projections branch of the Census Bureau, "of meaning sixty-five or older. So *near-elderly* might be fifty to sixty-five—but I'm just making this up."

A near-irate Robert Spero of New York noted in an Op-Ed article in the *Times* that his Supplemental Security Income notice carried this admonition: "To get SSI, you must be elderly, blind or have a disability. Elderly means 65 or older!" Spero objected especially to the government's near-gleeful exclamation mark.

"It doesn't have the record of use that *near-poor* does," says Richard Coorsh at the Health Insurance Association about *near-elderly*, which the insurers don't use as a category.

The near-observant reader will note my frequent use of *near*, a most flexible word that can function as an adverb modifying an adjective (this is a *nearly* lucid piece), an adjective modifying a noun (my *nearest* and dearest friend), a preposition (don't come *near* me) or a verb (I *near* the end of this subject to turn to the grammar).

With this vogue use of the word, I can see a bearded sandwich-sign man, attuned to the latest lingo, advertising: "Repent! This is the *near-end*."

What is it with *near* as a trendy substitute for *nearly?* Isn't *nearly elderly* what we mean? Doesn't the clipping of the *ly* result in a grammatical *near-miss?* (Yeah, I know *near-miss* is semantically cockeyed and really should be *near-collision*, but it's an idiom now and there's no use fighting it.)

Near is called a "flat adverb," with the *ly* clipped off and morphing into the same form as its related adjective. "Drive *slow*, think *different*, do *right*, hang *tough*." Don't let this dual use get you down; the flat adverb is one of English's little confusions, and it sure (or surely—pick one) doesn't worry usagists.

Now we're going to get tricky and lose everybody. *In the elderly*, the article *the* transforms *elderly* from an adjective to a noun. (The same happens with *the rich*.)

Since *near* is an adjective meaning "close to," it works as a modifier of the functional noun *elderly*. Now here is what I get from Sol Steinmetz, the great lexicographer: "This would not be true of *nearly*, which is an adverb and would therefore modify *elderly* only if the latter were used as an adjective, as in 'Many of them are *nearly elderly*.'"

Get it? Sol also likes the *near-elderly* because the two *ly* endings in the *nearly elderly* fall discordantly on the ear: "The grammatically and euphonically suitable phrase is the *near-elderly*, not the *nearly elderly*."

Learn grammar, baby boomers. Fire off those synapses in your brains. Keeps us pre-geezers young.

Near doesn't "function as an adverb modifying an adjective," as your column says it does, in "this is a nearly lucid piece." There it functions as the root from which the adverb nearly *is derived. Your description applies rather to examples such as "You damn near killed me!" Nor does it function as "an adjective modifying a noun" in* my nearest and dearest friend, *where it is not* near *but its superlative* nearest *that modifies the noun. This last point isn't at all trivial, in view of the odd property of superlatives that they are acceptable as prenominal modifiers in many cases in which the corresponding simple and comparative forms aren't: You can say* the closest bank to my house *but not* a close bank to my house *or* a closer bank to my house than the Deadwood Trust. (With postnominal modifiers there is no such restriction:* a bank close to my house, *etc.) Near has a remarkable property of behaving like an adjective and a preposition simultaneously in sentences such as* His house is very near the beach: *It has the adjective-like property of taking* very *as a degree modifier (prepositions instead take* very much: *very much in keeping with local customs,* not *very in keeping with local customs) and the preposition-like property of combining directly with an object rather than through the mediation of a preposition (cf.* very close to my house, *not* very close my house).

Professor James McCawley
Department of Linguistics
The University of Chicago
Chicago, Illinois

I will give you "drive slow" and a partial on "think different," but I disagree that "do right" or "hang tough" qualify as examples of what you call flat adverbs (a term new to me).

"Do right" is not a clipped form of "do rightly." "Right" in this case is more likely used as a noun itself or as an adjective modifying an implicit noun—e.g., "do right actions" or, more colloquially, "do the right thing." It is essentially the same as "do good," which famously is not the same as using the adverb, "do well."

"Hang tough" likewise is not a clipped form of "hang toughly." It describes a way of being, not a way of doing. It is linguistically equivalent to "be tough" or "remain tough."

"Think different" could be interpreted either way. It could, as you suggest, be a clipped form of "think differently." Or it could be a shortened form of "think different thoughts," in other words it could refer to what you think rather than how you think.

David Ewing
East Dover, Vermont

My reason for writing is to protest/correct your misinterpretation (albeit a common one) of "near miss." (Note that "near-miss" is not the correct form.) This does not mean, nor was it ever intended to, "nearly a miss." It means a shot, throw, or other action/event that, while it did miss, was close (near) the goal, target or some other object. A miss is as good as a mile, but a near miss can be as frightening as a hairy escape (which I have heard explained as an escape by a hair's breadth).

Suzanne S. Barnhill
Fairhope, Alabama

What do you call old people? The French don't go in for all the stuff we do: golden years, old codgers, sixty-five years young (what a grotesquerie), senior citizens, chronologically gifted, and other oddly contrived terms to avoid at all cost elderly or old. Leave it to the French, though, to originate the most fitting, warm and genteel expression in their inimitable and elegantly euphemistic way: le troisième âge. *Perfect! Doesn't say too much, but just enough to be ever so satisfactory in its ambiguity.*

William B. Dunham
Annapolis, Maryland

DROP THAT DIME

"When you hook a wire to somebody," complained Paul Begala, an aide to President Clinton angry at the investigative techniques of the office of independent counsel, ". . . and then you turn and drop the dime in a phone and call the press, that's not the kind of investigation people need."

Most people under forty would find that reference to a coin baffling. One does not get a dial tone with anything less than a quarter; in Washington and environs, the price of a local call from a coin-operated phone has just gone up to thirty-five cents. Is the President's defender unaware of the ravages of inflation over the past generation?

No; he was speaking metaphorically, and metaphors do not take seasonal or even generational adjustment. *To drop a dime*, in underworld lingo, has meant "to inform the police," with the *squealing* being done over the telephone, often anonymously by the informer, who is referred to by the squealed-upon as a *rat, fink, snitch* or *tipster.*

The recipient of the call refers to the fink as a *whistle-blower.* Different figures of speech for different folks: A bad guy doing good inserts a coin to make a surreptitious call, making himself a *dime-dropper,* while a good guy blows a piercing whistle, making himself a much-admired (though sometimes prosecuted) *whistle-blower.*

Mr. Begala has extended the coin metaphor from an informant calling the police to a police source calling the press. In so doing, he takes the shadiness attached to the *dime-dropper* ratting on his underworld buddies and imputes it to the police source speaking to the press. In his extension, however, the spinmeister has not spoiled the trope by trying to update it by saying something as awkward as "the manipulative investigator *dropped a dime plus a quarter* to leak to the media." That would spoil the effect.

That's how we intentionally preserve anachronisms. Feel free to have your dialing machine leave a message on my answering machine about all this; it's your nickel.

THE E-LANCER
EATS A BAGELWICH

HOW ARE NEW WORDS created? What's the logic behind neologisms? How can you, working at home, coin your own words for fun and profit?

Here is how you can amaze your friends and dismay your derogators by displaying your hidden ingenuity. The secret: knowing your combining forms.

Take *-ware*. This started out in the Sanskrit *vasna*, "*price*," and came to mean, in English, things of value—"goods." We used this combining form for articles made of clay (*earthenware*) or a range of tools (*hardware*). Then, in 1960, as computers came on the scene, we had the need for a word to describe the programming needed to go with the hardware. Coinage: *software*, the opposite of "hard" with the combining form *-ware*. That was only the beginning: If a company promises new software and doesn't meet its deadline, the nonproduct is derided as *vaporware*.

Last month, in a harangue against gloom-and-doom economists wringing their hands about a global crisis, I had the need for a name for what ailed them. What's the combining form for an ailment? Often it's *-itis*, as in *sinusitis*. So I blazed away at those afflicted with *global crisis-itis*. Strictly a nonce coinage, but it fit the moment's vituperative need.

In the spring 1998 issue of *American Speech: A Quarterly of Linguistic Usage*, Adrienne Lehrer of the University of Arizona had an article about "Scapes, Holics and Thons: The Semantics of English Combining Forms." She described how "source words" like *Watergate* get splintered, with a portion becoming a combining form, from Carter's *Billygate* to Reagan's *Irangate* to Clinton's *Monicagate*. In the same way *alcoholic* spawned *workaholic* and *chocoholic*, as *-holic* became a combining form meaning "hooked on."

Take a familiar word like *sandwich*, a culinary creation named after the fourth Earl of Sandwich in 1762. Say you are a bagel baker and you want to use your product instead of bread to purvey smoked salmon and cream cheese. You put up a sign: *bagelwich*. Everyone instantly knows you are pushing a sandwich made on a bagel. Across the street, a Francophile competitor puts up his own sign, *croissantwich*, and your customers desert you, mouths fixed for croissants stuffed with the filling of their choice.

The same with hamburger, originally chopped meat enjoyed by residents of Hamburg, Germany. Using the *-burger* combining form, we come up with *cheeseburger* and now *veggieburger*, with a score of variations in between. You get the meaning instantly with no explanation needed, even if you've never seen or heard the word before. Quick: What is a *turkeyfurter?* (It could be wurst: Would you like to wash one down with a *vodkatini?* You need no help to make the leap to these neologisms based on *frankfurter* and *martini*.)

Jargonauts (a play on *Argonauts* and an example of the *-nauts* combiner used by *Reaganauts*) like to use *-speak* as their combiner. The source word is George Orwell's *newspeak*, and it spawned everything from my *Haig-speak* (Al Haig's "Snakecheck that" and shades-of-gray *nuancal*) to the San Fernando Valley girls' *Valspeak* ("grody to the max").

Let's leave behind the *-holics* and *-thons*. (Just as a *television marathon* blends to *telethon*, an unending stream of faxes becomes a *faxathon*.) We can also skip the *-scapes*. (*Landscape*, the source word, led to coinages of *seascape*, *moonscape*, *cityscape* and *Xeriscape*, "parks created with little need for water.")

Turn to the fifth letter of the Roman alphabet for the combining form now most in vogue: I've been keeping a fair weather eye on the letter *e*.

"More of us will work as *E-lancers*," said Snigdha Prakash, an NPR reporter, in the course of an interview, defining the term as "free agents who are electronically linked to other soloists for specific projects, and move on when the work is done." These are the unaffiliated employed ("drifters," we used to call them), and the term is a rhyming play on *free-lancer*, originally a mercenary soldier of the Middle Ages, now often a middle-aged soloist.

When *electronic mail*, coined in 1977, was shortened five years later to *E-mail*, it became the combining form of the Information Age, muscling aside its competition on the prefix menu, *cyber-* (from the Greek *kyber-nan*, "to govern"). In short order, the capital *E* was lower-cased.

Now we have *e-text* published in an *e-zine* (often shortened and pronounced "zeen"). You can buy an airline *e-ticket* with *e-money* or *e-bucks* (terms that have bankrupted *cybercash*), unless you want to use *e-credit*, a form of Internet dealing known as *e-commerce* or *e-tailing*. That last is a play on *retailing* and, as in *e-lancer*, the letter *e* does not stand only for "electronic."

Dr. Wayne Glowka, an editor of the "Among the New Words" section of *American Speech*, reports that *e-gifts* of *e-bouquets* are often given by members of the *e-generation*.

All of this, plus generations of new terms as yet uncoined, will be sneered at as *e-speak*, a product—just think of it—of two combining forms, which I have just coined this instant unless some *e-reader* of my *e-text* beat me to it.

> *Probably the most common use of* ware *as meaning goods comes from the child's rhyme Simple Simon: "Said Simple Simon to the pie man/Let me taste your wares." I assume that warehouse refers to goods as well.*
>
> *One more recent example is "shelfware," i.e., software that a user does not install or otherwise use.*
>
> Gary Muldoon
> Rochester, New York

> *I got the term "e-lancer" from an article called "The Dawn of the E-Lancer Economy" in the October issue of the* Harvard Business Review. *The authors are two MIT academics, Thomas Malone and Robert Laubacher. I thought you'd like to know.*
>
> Snigdha Prakash
> National Public Radio
> Washington, D.C.

EACH OTHER

"The two were not only made for each other," wrote *The Washington Times* about star-crossed lovers, "they deserve one another."

The editorialist, grappling with the rules of correctness, was undoubtedly torn. Question: When writing about a relationship between two people, is it proper to use *each other* or *one another*? The writer refused to choose, and the editorial went both ways.

At *The New York Times* we have firm guidance to keep us from such pushmipullyu style. Our *Style Manual*, now embedded in software so that century-old judgments can be amended in a flash, is sternly prescriptive:

"*each other, one another:* two persons look at *each other*; more than two look at *one another*."

It's a comfort to have a rule. That's our style. If you write for *The New York Times* (or the Associated Press or *The Wall Street Journal*, whose stylebooks present a united front and follow one another on this), that's the way it is, like it or lump it. If I were to write, "Two stylebooks disagree with *one another*," an alert copy editor would demand I change it to "two . . . *each other*." Sometimes a kindly copy editor will call to say, "Are you deliberately trying to slip this egregious error into the paper, thereby generating mail from infuriated grammarians and giving you a subject for your language column?" (I don't do that, as a rule.)

What if I were to respond to the corrector in chief at my newspaper: Samuel (Dictionary) Johnson once wrote about "six ministers who meet weekly at *each other's* houses," breaking the rule. And Bishop Robert Lowth, the eighteenth century's high priest of grammar, instructed that "two negatives in English destroy *one another*," breaking the rule the other way. In 1926, Fowler—Saint Henry himself—wrote that "the differentiation is neither of present utility nor based on historical usage," and in his recent revision of Fowler, Robert Burchfield declares that the belief of the rule makers is "untenable," citing recent breakings by classy writers like Anita Brookner and Nadine Gordimer. E. Ward Gilman, editor of Merriam-Webster's indispensable *Dictionary of English Usage*, often unfairly dissed by me as "Dr. Roundheels," assembles these authorities and concludes about the *each* rule: "There is no sin in its violation," adding from his loosey-goosey perch, "It is, however, easy and painless to observe if you so wish."

I so wish. If I did not, and instead chose to break the stylebook rule, a great contretemps would take place. Citations all over the floor. [*No sentence fragments!—Ed.*] In the end (at the denouement of the contretemps but never *at the end of the day*), a Sanhedrin of copy editors might permit my dissenting usage, but only if accompanied by an explanation for my departure from the Stylebook Team, including their punchy rebuttal and my stinging surrebuttal. (Sometimes they let me win; that's why *Times* style is now to spell Rumania *Romania*.)

In the same way, the three newspaper stylebooks stand foursquare for the *between/among* rule. The A. P. cites "the maxim that *between* introduces two items and *among* more than two." Thus, it's "between you and me" and "among the three of us." But here comes Dr. Roundheels again (Mr. Gilman is honorably retired but comes out swinging at my request), trotting out a parade of authorities who disagree, and denouncing as a waste "the enormous amount of ink spilled in the explication of the subtleties of *between* and *among.*" And no doubt he has common usage on his side.

But not good usage. [*You really ought to do something about those sentence fragments.—Ed.*] What's wrong with an obeisance to sharp edges in a world of fuzz? If we adopt as a rule the practice of using *each other* and *between* with two, and rigorously apply *one another* and *among* to three or more, our world of words is a little more tightly organized. We're operating comfortably within agreed guidelines. We have a Style.

A style is a set of conventions, not a fundament of grammar fixed in our brains like subject-verb agreement. A stylistic rule is not a law. No cellblock in Reading Gaol is reserved for those condemned for using *between the three* (and indeed a medal is pinned on writers careful to use *between* when expressing a relationship of several items considered a pair at a time).

But when you play by the rules of grammar—that is, when you agree to adopt a style that befits a certain level and tone of discourse—and then stick to the rules you've learned, you get a subtle intellectual kick that the anything-goes crowd never experiences. And when you break any rule for effect, as when you use a sentence fragment now and then for emphasis, or begin a sentence with *and* to foster an illusion of spontaneity or afterthought, you are like an actor playing a drunk and performing an exquisite stumble.

The respecter of the rules of an adopted style becomes a member of a club so determinedly inclusive as to be truly snooty. You're in, and nobody can cancel your membership as long as you consult the rule book. The secret handshake and the code ring are yours. With these symbols comes the sense of belonging, of serene security, of smug noninferiority that suffuses all those who clothe themselves voluntarily in the golden chains of good usage. (I learned psychology from *The Story of O.*)

If you take language as a metaphor for life, your respect for the gently arbitrary rules of style signifies your willingness to respect the rules of civility in the way you behave. Breaking a rule of style or even of civility gains force and meaning only when you know what code you are violating and why.

Imagine, two centuries ago, the copy editor for the Committee on

Style of the Constitutional Convention going up to Thomas Jefferson and pointing to the last line of his proposed Unanimous Declaration of the Thirteen United States of America: "We mutually pledge to each other our lives, our fortunes, and our sacred honor."

"Not only is *mutually* redundant, Tom, but you're referring to more than two people, so it should be *one another.*"

And Jefferson would reply: "We're the Committee on Style, right? Leave it the way it is."

Among you, me, and the lamppost you are almost right most of the time.
                                              Emilio Venezian
                                Whitehouse Station, New Jersey

EDGY

"Everyone in this room," wrote Mark Leyner in *The New York Times*, quoting a composite TV network executive, "is committed to developing adventurous, *edgy* material."

"Risqué Reading" was the headline in *The Wall Street Journal*, subheaded "Books for young adults take on *edgier* themes."

"There was a move toward more *edgy* comedy," Will Miller, the therapist-comedian, sadly told New Jersey's *Record* about a shift in audience tastes, "and I was just this yuppie with no *edge* at all."

A new sense of an old word was born about a decade ago, went through its nonce phase, has gained vogue status and bids fair to shove the old sense over the edge of the linguistic cliff.

Back in the 80s, when someone said, "I feel *edgy*," the response was a soothing "There, there—nothing to be nervous about." Or if you heard "The boss seems a little *edgy* today," you were not likely to hit him up for a raise. The adjective meant "nervous, irritable, apprehensive"—three different but similar states of tension—derived from the phrase *on edge*. The metaphor was that of a cliff, with a person standing at the very brink, or grimacing in irritation, showing teeth *on edge*, or balanced precariously in a narrow space, as on a *razor's edge*.

That nail-nibbling sense began as the adverb *edgily* in an 1837 letter by Cardinal Henry Manning: "Newman did not like my joking letter. He answered rather edgily and defensively." Novelists moved it ahead as World War I began: "Do you mind if I come in here for a little?" Rudyard Kipling had a character plead. "I'm a bit *edgy.*" In 1915, in *The 39 Steps,* John Buchan wrote: "Then I could see that he began to get *edgy* again. He listened for little noises."

Originally, *edgy* meant "sharp," as in this 1775 use: "Walking over broken rocks, either ragged, or cleft, or *edgy.*" The poet Leigh Hunt wrote in 1820 of a razor, "How cold, how *edgy,* how hard!" This is the sense that is making a comeback on the cusp of three vogue phrases.

One is *hard-edged,* first used ringingly by the novelist J.R.R. Tolkien in 1954: "Long slopes they climbed, dark, *hard-edged* against the sky." In Britain in the early 60s it was used as the name of a school of abstract art—crisp, geometric and unemotional. Its severe certainty was picked up in 1976 by *New York Times* correspondent John Darnton, who extended the metaphor with "there is no *hard-edged* sense of impending disaster in Rhodesia." That meaning goes somewhat beyond "sharp." Darnton, who became the *Times's* culture editor, recalled, "I used it to mean 'clear-cut' but with a sense of violence behind it." A generation later, Senator Joe Lieberman of Connecticut, searching vainly for consensus during the Year of Monica, shook his head and said, "The partisan differences have become *hard-edged.*"

A more likely source of the current sense of *edgy* is *leading edge,* which the *OED* notes since 1877 has meant the forward side of a moving object, like the blade of a propeller screw or a wing, and the more recent *cutting edge.* This has replaced the old *state of the art.* Funny how that popular phrase fell into desuetude; it was once right out there *on the cusp,* which has also been overtaken by events. Not even *modern* stays modern, as *postmodern* becomes passé. It's hard to keep up with, much less stay ahead of, words that define a state of being ahead. You think that *leading edge* is all that *with-it?* Jesse Sheidlower, Principal Editor of *Oxford English Dictionary,* North America, pointed me to this use of computer jargon in a 1996 *Wired* magazine article: "experience that combines *bleeding-edge* graphics with old-school gameplay." See what happens when you play around with *cutting edges?*

Here we are, then, with the old-new *edgy.* Its first use is derived from *hard-edged,* connoting "with an attitude." Jim Lowe of Merriam-Webster has a citation from the May 1990 *Elle* magazine in which Mark Schapiro writes of the white rappers Peter Nash and Michael Berrin as "brazen, *edgy* street poets."

For the sense of the new *edgy* that is more upbeat—"innovative, precedent-shattering" or "avant-garde," as the French have been saying for about 150 years (you'd think they'd find a new expression for this)—the earliest citation I can find is this November 1993 use in the *Orlando Sentinel* in which Andy Meisler, a reporter, quotes the animator John Kricfalusi about fuddy-duddies at Nickelodeon: "The network hated all the *edgy* stuff. That's why it's not on the *cutting edge* anymore. Which is too bad."

Even as you read this, that sense is endangered in this high-velocity semantics. The finger-snapping reader will note a recent citation above from *The Wall Street Journal* suggesting a meaning of risqué, French for "off-color, verging on indecent." Phil Mushnik, a columnist for the *New York Post* and *TV Guide*, says: "*Edgy* is a euphemism for 'profane.' It's a dodge for 'obscene.' We've seen the steady inclusion of words with sexual connotations or profanity on television and radio. Now this language is no longer described as 'colorful' but as '*edgy.*' It's a word in the pop culture that means 'vile.' It's a very convenient little word, *edgy.*"

The problem with this vogue word is that it means (a) confrontational, (b) ultramodern and (c) lewd or profane. Because the meaning is in flux, I don't use the word; it makes me feel, as nervous Nellies used to say, *edgy.*

As a twenty-three-year-old woman living in New York City, I will assign myself the role of ambassador of my generation and attempt to respond to your article discussing the word edgy. *I would like to point out one additional usage, the term* straight edge. *In street vernacular, this term describes fellow youths who lead a drug- and alcohol-free existence. It does not describe the naive who do not delve into the realm of the forbidden, but rather those who are enlightened. At times this term is (was?) used to describe a certain street style (borderline punk) that has pretty much disappeared in the late nineties, but was very popular in the late eighties especially in Washington, D.C., where I was raised.*

Anyway, today's terminology of the word edgy *has become a bit extreme. To me* edgy *is a nod to the new and obscure, a blanket adjective for the not-yet-classified product of a younger generation.*

Morgan E. Goldberg
New York, New York

EDITOR GORE

To show that Al Gore personally participated in the writing of a TV spot blasting the Senate rejection of the nuclear test ban, his campaign made available the script with his handwritten editing. Let's see how he did:

A line in the draft read, "I want to ensure [the drafter meant *assure*] our nation and the entire world that this vote does not speak for the majority of the American people." Gore changed that to "I believe in my heart that this vote does not speak for the American people."

Another line went, "Campaigns should be about the important issues, and there's none more important than stopping the spread of nuclear weapons." Gore's fix: "I believe campaigns should be about the future, and there is no more important challenge than stopping the spread of nuclear weapons." Note (1) the insertion of the self with *I believe*; (2) the substitution of *the future* for the dull *the important issues*; (3) the replacement of the ungrammatical *there's none more important* with *there is no more important challenge*, a correct use of the singular that avoids repeating *important*.

The weak draft: "I will ask the American people for a clear mandate. And if elected president, my first act will be to resubmit the test ban treaty." The erstwhile Vice President's handwritten redraft rolls along with greater strength: "I ask for your support and your mandate if elected President to send this treaty back to the Senate with your demand that they ratify it." *Demand* beats *resubmit* any day, and by making it *your* demand, rather than his own, he avoided arrogance.

A careful TV-spot writer would not use the plural *they* with the singular *Senate*, but that's nitpicking. The drafter erred in not capitalizing *President*; when referring to a particular office, like President of the United States, my idea of correct usage is to uppercase the *p*. Editor Al Gore knew that and rightly corrected the error, and I believe in my heart that everyone else working in the Gore campaign should get that straight.

EMERGING NATIONS

First they were *undeveloped nations*. That was a put-down, so they became LDNs—*less developed nations*. Still patronizing. Finally emerged *emerging nations*. Now they're still undeveloped and nobody has emerged, but everybody's happy.

Who dreamed up this latest name? The answer can be found in *Commanding Heights: The Battle Between Government and the Marketplace That Is Remaking the Modern World*, by Daniel Yergin and Joseph Stanislaw. (My own next opus will be titled *Subtitling Books: The Desperate Need for Publishers to Explain Everything on the Front Cover.*)

In 1979, a Dutch banker named Antoine van Agtmael went to New York to launch what he wanted to call a *third world investment fund*. Back in bipolar 1952, the sociologist Alfred Sauvy coined *tiers monde*, "third world," to describe nonaligned nations that wanted to position themselves between the Soviet and Western blocs. (*Tiers* was chosen rather than *troisième* on the analogy of the French *tiers état*, "third estate," referring to the commoners.) In time, *third world* gained a connotation as much economic as political and was made up mostly of *have-not* nations.

"No one wants to put money into the *third world investment fund*," the banker recounts he was told. Write Yergin and Stanislaw: "*Underdeveloped markets* was a complete nonstarter. *Third world* wouldn't do. Nor would the World Bank's favorite, *developing nations*. 'I knew we needed something positive, uplifting, not negative,' van Agtmael said. And by the time he came to work on Monday morning, he had the answer: *emerging markets*." In 1984, he wrote a book and titled it *Emerging Securities Markets*, which didn't sell too well because it had no exhaustive subtitle, but did establish his claim to the coinage (which will stand until I get an earlier written citation).

Commanding heights, by the way, is a military term that was adopted by Lenin. Attacked by militant Communist comrades in 1922 for the New Economic Plan that seemed to turn back toward capitalism, Lenin assured them he was not backtracking. Why? Because the Bolshevik state would still control the strategic sectors of the economy—what the Marxist leader called the *commanding heights*. From that we got the *command economy*, since replaced by the despised *market economy*.

An earlier example of emerging nation appears in the Third Barnhart Dictionary of New English (1990), which dates this sense of emerging to 1975.

The dictionary's entry on emerging includes the following citation from The New York Times Magazine of April 18, 1976: "The white racist attitudes that are part of the problem at home have also been an often unconscious element in the policy of the white leadership vis-à-vis the emerging nations, most recently in Africa."

Hugh Rawson, Director
Penguin Reference Books
New York, New York

I suspect that it is not fair to cast all of your aspirations upon publishers— desperate or otherwise. At the very least, they are following a time-hallowed tradition. I am certain that you do not need to be reminded that Dr. Johnson's great work was entitled* A dictionary of the English language: in which the words are deduced from their originals, and illustrated in their different significations by examples from the best writers. To which are prefixed, a history of the language, and an English grammar. *And the novel at its birth can claim* Richardson's Pamela, or Virtue rewarded: in a series of letters from a beautiful young damsel to her parents, and afterwards in her exalted condition, between her, and persons of figure and quality, upon the most important and entertaining subjects, in genteel life.

Nancy Freudenthal
Newton, Pennsylvania

I suggest you name your next book The Colon of Oedipus: The Never-Ending Battle Between Academic Writers (who wish to give their articles and books short titles comprehensible only to the extremely sophisticated) and Editors and Publishers (who wish the titles of articles and books to describe the subject matter in manner understandable to the average reader).

Richard Hall
New York, New York

THE EMERGING WORD, ACTUALLY

"I have noticed a proliferation of the word *actually* in telephone conversations," writes Richard J. Durbin, the junior senator from Illinois. "Without exception it is surplusage and often used to mask deception,

---

*I believe that I have shown great and commendable self-restraint by not saying here, "You of all people. . . ."

as in 'Senator, I'm sorry Mr. Jones cannot come to the phone to discuss your fund-raiser, but *actually* he is away from his desk on safari.'

"Next to inane voice-mail messages," continues the Senator, "and unconscionable delays before the tape recorder engages, I find this use of the word *actually* to be the latest scourge of telephone life. Sincerely (*actually*), Dick Durbin."

He is not asking about the real *actually*, an adverb meaning "truly, in reality," as used by Thomas Hobbes in his 1651 *Leviathan:* "Christ shall come to judge the world, and *actually* to govern his owne people." Instead, he wonders about what the philologist John Algeo calls a "discourse signal—a device to relate what the speaker is saying to what someone else has said, or to the situation in which the conversation is carried on." Americans pronounce it with all four syllables and place the discourse signal in the front of a sentence; Britons use it either at the start or, more typically, at the end.

H. W. Fowler called it a meaningless word, similar to *of course:* "The superior-indulgent *of course*. It seems absurd to tell you but he half-hopes you do not know."

Alistair Cooke calls them tics, filler words as ubiquitous and unnecessary as *I mean* and *y'know*. (Cooke has been named chairman of Olbom, On Language's Board of Octogenarian Mentors, though he insists on calling it OGPU, Octogenarians Guarding Proper Usage, because his acronym recalls an old Soviet spy organization.)

But it is not always meaningless. "The British tic," Cooke explains, "can also be used to show that all alone, the speaker has come through a rather difficult personal conflict and made a positive, mature decision, e.g., 'What would you like to drink?' 'I'd like a Scotch, *actually*.'"

The proper use of the word—in its true, actual meaning—would go, in Cooke's second example, like this: "What would you like to drink?" "I'll have a Scotch. No, *actually*, I'd like a martini."

Sometimes the tic is used in mock modesty. To "Do all women succumb to your charms?" the answer might be "They do, *actually*." Norman Schur, in *British English*, notes that the word—pronounced EK-chill-ee—may also be used in veiled reproof, as if the speaker feels forced to say it: "*Actually*, we don't do things that way," or "I was coming to that, *actually*."

It can be used to mark a contradiction of what the other person has just said. Algeo supplies this: "The director doesn't seem to understand what the play's about." "He's a very good director, *actually*." Or it can mark the unexpected, vouching for what may seem surprising: "Who won?" "Well, I did, *actually*."

The senator from Illinois has asked for a vote. Should we condemn *actually* as meaningless, overworked and obfuscatory, an affected form of *y'know?*

No. In its nonliteral form, and when not interjected as mere filler, *actually* is a subtle device, used differently in British and American English. E. Ward Gilman, editor of Merriam-Webster's *Dictionary of English Usage*, argues that "words like *actually* often improve the rhythm of a sentence and help set off the more important words effectively." I disagree and would not use it to smooth the flow of a sentence, because that is "surplusage," to pick up Senator Durbin's legal usage. But I would readily use *actually* (more in speaking than in writing) as a signal conveying a shade of meaning outside the normal semantic rules.

Like a raised eyebrow, a shrug or a pleased wriggle, *actually* contributes to understanding the speaker's meaning. For example, what's another way to say "Come to think of it"? *Actually* . . .

EMPOWERING OUT, ENABLING IN

"Tobacco is an addiction which should not be *enabled* by public funds," writes Mike Harman of St. Albans, West Virginia. Although his argument would be strengthened by using *that* instead of *which* to introduce a restrictive clause, he uses a verb that is gaining great popularity.

"*Enabling* Bad Behavior" was the headline over the letter to the *Times* from another reader, William Frago of Lake Forest, Illinois, who objected to a leading feminist's vigorous defense of President Clinton: "I am afraid that Gloria Steinem has become an *enabler* to the very behavior the women's movement once sought to punish."

Especially in its noun form, *enabler*, this word has made a quantum jump from hero to villain. (In physics, a *quantum jump* is tiny but sudden. In general use, *quantum* means "huge and sudden"; it is used here to mean "sudden.")

Some people still use the word in its positive sense: Pastor Thomas Kilgore of the Second Baptist Church of Los Angeles says his task is "to be an *enabler* to the people who are farthest down and getting the bitter end of life." But many are substituting *facilitator* for that positive sense of "helper" and are using *enabler* to mean "one who by ignoring, appeasing or condoning makes possible the continuance of wrongdoing."

This sense has its origin in the group therapy that is now called *the recovery movement*. Bill Pittman of Alcoholics Anonymous, coauthor of the 1989 *AA: The Way It Began*, says that its use of "the word *enabling* first appeared in Al-Anon literature in the early 60s." Al-Anon is an organization of groups of family and friends of alcoholics. A 1965 book reads: "There are many occasions when we all engage in *enabling* destructive or inappropriate behavior in other people. . . . Most instances are not so obvious or dramatic as the *enabling* that may have gone on with the alcoholic."

Wendy Kaminer, author of *I'm Dysfunctional, You're Dysfunctional*, defines *enabler* as "someone who makes it easier for another to pursue an addiction, one complicit in bad behavior—like the wife of an alcoholic helping him hide the bottles from the kids." She says: "The word *enable* can be contrasted with the word *empower*. You *empower* a person to do something good, and you *enable* someone to do something bad."

Though a lexicographer would disagree (a dictator can be *empowered* to invade a neighbor and a surgeon *enabled* to save a life), usagists understand that latest connotation. A 1987 book published by the Johnson Institute was titled *The Family Enablers*, and a 1994 book by Carol Remboldt further darkens the connotation with the title *Violence in Schools: The Enabling Factor*.

That new sense is no longer limited to families of alcoholics or drug abusers, as indicated in usages by critics of a defender of Mr. Clinton in his friendship with an intern. Michael Curtin, a trust attorney in Washington, was quoted by *The Washington Post* on how to give siblings with disabilities a feeling of self-worth and independence: "Whatever you do, you have to be careful not to be an *enabler*."

I tried the word on an Internet search engine and triggered this response. "I play in the *Enablers*, the Dallas band with the Web site you visited," writes Bart Chaney from Texas. "I came up with the name when we put our combo together about four years ago. I had the noun in mind from the world of therapy. There was some irony here, but it was not meant darkly. Some addictions—one to cool music in a dark room, for example—are not all that bad." The musician added, "Hey, if you mentioned us, that would be a thrill."

Having just adjusted to the change from "writer" to "content provider," here am I, a *thrill-enabler.*

You write that "in physics, a quantum jump is tiny but sudden." Sudden is not really the right word here; tiny and discontinuous might be better. The defining aspect of quantum physics is that it is quantal, *i.e., the energy changes can occur only in certain fixed quantities, as "packets" of energy are ejected or absorbed. One can readily imagine a set of tiny but sudden (indeed, instantaneous) leaps of energy, where those leaps of energy would be, in your phrase,* tiny but sudden, *but would certainly not be quantal since any degree of shift in energy along a continuum might occur.*

So your phrase is, I think, inadequate as a definition of a quantum jump, because of the dual meaning of sudden. Sudden may be taken to mean either "instantaneous" or "discontinuous," and it would be better to use the latter word specifically in order to convey more fully and correctly the nature of a quantum jump. At least your example, "hero to villain," is a good example of a discontinuous jump; I do deplore the general usage you mention in which quantum *means "huge and sudden."*

Bart K. Holland, Associate Professor
New Jersey Medical School
Newark, New Jersey

ENOUGH ALREADY!

"What red-blooded American hasn't surveyed the muck and mire of our national politics," writes Mark Jurkowitz of *The Boston Globe,* "and said, '*Enough, already*'?"

"*Time* magazine reports that Clinton's woes have left U.S. foreign policy adrift," writes the *Guardian* of London, "though Garrison Keillor says, '*Enough already!*'"

Howard Fineman of *Newsweek* asks, "Is there any way out of this mess?" leading to an inch-high, 102-point, block-letter headline: "ENOUGH ALREADY."

The stylistic issue raised is: Should there be a comma between the first and second words of this increasingly important phrase? The publication that pioneered in its popularization is *The* (Toronto) *Globe and Mail;* of the nineteen thousand entries in the Dow Jones database, the first twenty-two uses (from 1977 to 1983) were in that newspaper. According to Warren Clements, style editor, "We abandoned the comma in 1979 because *enough already* was considered one of those expressions that is almost one word. It rips rollingly off the tongue; the comma would slow it down." Adds Michael Kesterton of that newspaper, "I know it's a Yiddishism, but it just fits the Canadian soul—you know, 'I've had it and I'm not gonna take it anymore.'"

The origin is the Yiddish *genug shoyn*, literally "enough already." It is part of an array of phrases using *shoyn* for emphasis, from the similar *gut shoyn*, "All right already!" in the sense of "Stop bugging me," to *shvayg shtil shoyn*, "Shut up already!" one calibration more irritated than *genug shoyn*.

"This use of *already* began to appear early in the century," says Sol Steinmetz, the lexicographer who has taken the place of the late Leo Rosten as my primary Yiddish adviser, "among immigrant Yiddish speakers living in New York who were just starting to talk English. By the 1930s it had become common usage among their children who no longer spoke Yiddish—a development that enabled it to entrench itself in the American language."

Another scholar, Lillian Feinsilver, in her *Taste of Yiddish* (1970), notes that "English would normally use the mild now, as in 'Come, now,' or the stronger 'Come on, now.'"

Now is an adverb of time that can be used as an admonition before a statement ("Now, I want you to listen to this . . ."). Similarly, *already* and *yet* are adverbs of time that can be used to intensify a statement when used at the end. ("Were you bitten by a mad dog?" "And the dog is mad, *yet*.") Thus, *already*—in standard English, "beforehand; by this time"— can be used in this idiomatic sense to mean "without further ado" or "and you'd better believe it."

We have seen how this Yiddishism has been thoroughly assimilated and is now an Americanism. Because other American English expressions have been adopted in many other languages—*O.K.* and *no problem* are examples—does this mean that this particular emphasis of exasperation is taking root elsewhere?

Some evidence exists that it does. Here is a letter to *The Washington Post* from Robert Hill, an American working in a large Saudi hospital in Riyadh, Saudi Arabia: "The overwhelming—by nine to one—response to the Clinton affair varies among 'What is the very big deal?' to 'What about the problems in the rest of the world?' to '*Enough already!*'"

When a Yiddishism takes root in Riyadh, that's saying something. Have we exhausted this subject? The reader may now vent exasperation at a surfeit of data by expostulating the very phrase being so minutely examined.

Can you imagine Macbeth's final words in the play spoken in the American idiom? "Lay on Macduff; and damn'd be him that first cries, Hold, enough already!"

Paul S. McCaig
Dana Point, California

EYE ROLLER

"The numbers came in high," a senior administration official told John Harris of *The Washington Post*, about an estimate of NATO troops needed to protect Kosovo. "No one said yes, no one said no; it was taken off the table. . . . It was a complete *eye-roller.*"

This is an example of an unfamiliar word that is immediately understood. To "roll one's eyes" upward (the usual direction is *heavenward*) is to visibly express astonishment, dismay or disbelief. An *eye-roller* is the compound noun that describes a situation or remark that causes such a reaction.

The useful word apparently has a Pentagon origin or association. On December 1, 1987, Edwin M. Yoder Jr. reported in *The Washington Post* that at a breakfast meeting Caspar Weinberger, then Defense Secretary, was "cheerfully rattling on, and some of his listeners are rolling their eyes upward in an unmistakable 'oh, brother' expression." Yoder described Weinberger's claim that record defense budgets had nothing to do with high deficits in the Reagan era as "the big *eye-roller.*"

The defense jargon spilled over, as it often does, into sports: "the Bills' winning score in the fourth quarter," wrote Nick Cafardo in *The Boston Globe* in 1996, "was a head-shaker and an *eye-roller.*"

One synonym is *stunner*, connoting "a revelation that leaves one thunderstruck or dumbfounded." Another is *mind-boggler*, from something that "*boggles* the mind" (originally "frighten," from the sixteenth-century *bogle*'s dialect root in *goblin*, but now denoting a high degree of amazement rather than fear). However, these synonyms do not carry the connotation of skepticism in *eye-roller*; that new term's *heavenward-*

looking association suggests "Lord, save us from this baloney."

The *Post's* Harris, on a linguistic roll in his report of the troop estimate that so staggered Pentagonians, went on to write: "NATO's analysis, officials said, was not a comprehensive study. Instead, it was an initial review that some officials called a 'SWAG'—military parlance for a 'scientific wild-ass guess.'"

The *Chicago Tribune* reported in 1984 that Col. John Stewart, testifying in a libel suit brought against CBS by Gen. William Westmoreland, recalled admitting to his commander years before that an estimate of enemy strength was based on "the SWAG principle" and that the courtroom erupted in laughter at the explanation of the acronym.

The U.S. Army's home page lists the acronym merely as *swag*, defining it as "a gross estimate or guess." This is in error; when not printed in all capitals, *swag* is an old slang term for "money, booty." Only when printed all uppercase does SWAG become an acronym for "scientific wild-ass guess."

Other Army phrases defined on its home page include *ankle biters*, "people who criticize one's position but offer no constructive alternatives"; *readahead*, "material sent to officials to prepare them for upcoming visits"; *shotgun coordination*, "sending duplicate packages to several offices simultaneously to save time"; and *wrapped around the axle*, "lacking progress because of immersion in details or inability to see the big picture." Presumably concerned about the third word in SWAG, the Web page warns readers to "avoid using these terms in official correspondence, at formal briefings, when dealing with outsiders."

At ease; the attributive noun phrase *wild ass* is not a vulgarism. On the contrary, the juxtaposition of words (as adjective and noun) can be found five times in the King James version of the Bible, most famously reflecting well on donkeys in Job 24:5: "Behold, as *wild asses* in the desert, go they forth to their work."

McGraw-Hill published my Dictionary of Development Terminology *in 1975 in which I defined scientific wild-ass guess (SWAG): "Frequently used term denoting that while an estimate is 'educated,' it is not to be interpreted as necessarily a good one."*

I came across the term in the 1960s and 1970s in the vernacular of community development.

This use of SWAG seems to predate the Pentagon's; however, I readily concede that their SWAGs are probably much "wilder."

> *J. Robert Dumouchel*
> *Nassau, Bahamas*

Another definition of SWAG is "Stuff We All Get." This usually refers to a company's product samples or marketing materials made available to employees; for example, at a record company, free CDs, T-shirts and concert tickets are SWAG.

> *David R. Maxwell*
> *Chappaqua, New York*

The piece on "Eye-rollers" reminded me of an instance I should like to share with you. It is slightly older than those you cite and has always amused me. It is the interlocution in the Phil Harris song "That's What I Like About the South": "When you tell me that you love me/How come you roll them eyes?"

> *James M. Kennedy*
> *New York, New York*

EYEBALL HANG TIME

Say "computer lingo" to most people, and they'll rattle off their rudimentary knowledge of the meaning of *byte, hacker* and *cybersex gritch* (the last marries *digiporn* to the portmanteau of *grouch* and *glitch*, producing a phrase meaning "hacker's complaint about the encryption of dirty pictures").

In the same way, say "management jargon" to an old-fashioned CEO in Buggywhip Industries, and that executive will slip into an archaic patois of *dotted-line responsibility* or the oxymoronic *structured competition,* taking you down a critical path overgrown with *zero-based weeds.*

But that's yesterday's talk. As my with-it colleague Maureen Dowd likes to sigh, "It's so *over.*" The new jeaniuses working for IPO options at the profit-free start-ups—intensely laid-back execugeeks who never trust anybody under $30 million—have a language all their own.

I have a lexicographic spy in their midst. He is Edward Bleier of Warner Bros. (in a lifelong battle against *The New York Times's* insistence on spelling out the *Brothers*), who has just been elected to the board of

RealNetworks, one of the many modern companies whose names were created in a tightly packed elevator (and which the *Times* rightly resists). Ed was my Syracuse University classmate, thus no spring chicken, but he refuses to let the new lingo close down his communicativeness. At his first board meeting, he jotted down some examples of the new code of "E-lingo," with his guesses at their meanings.

Does this company have *management bandwidth?* In computerese, nothing can beat the *bandwidth*, which used to mean "a range of radio frequencies" and came to mean "the data-transfer rate of a communications system," among other things. However, *management bandwidth* means "the strength and depth of senior executives." It is what football coaches call a *deep bench*, rested and talented reserves who impatiently watch the marching *bandwidth* at halftime.

Nobody says *now* anymore; it's all in *real time.* What is the *full stop?* It's a deadline for a meeting or a phone call to end.

What do you demand when you need measurements, standards for evaluation? *Metrix.* Do not confuse this with a matrix, the grid on which data is shoveled for three-dimensional planning. (Back when I was a writer, I thought a *matrix* was a mixture of "matronly dominatrix," but now I am a content provider and know better.)

Don't run when you hear *run rates;* they are the vector (never say "direction") and speed of the *metrix.* But stop when you come to the *inflection point,* which is what used to be known as a *crossroads,* as in the sage advice of the Old Managers, "When you come to a *crossroads,* take it."

If you make the right decision, you will *vector* right to a *power point.* This is "activity that provides added leverage to improve another aspect of the service or business." I think this used to be called "synergy," but don't use that word because it's *over.* (*History,* as in "He's *history,*" is also *over. Over* is not yet over, but will soon be.)

Nor should you seek the old *consensus,* which used to be the Holy Grail of the other-directed; instead, seek *mind share.* Don't worry about being *hardcore;* it used to apply to porn, but now it is a killer-app adjective meaning "intense, dedicated, tough-minded."

Environmentalists will be dismayed to learn that their favorite word, *ecosystem,* has been spirited away by the e-speakers. According to Bleier's hurried notes (written by ergonomic pencil on paper, not even scratched on a screen with a stylish stylus), an *ecosystem* is "a matrix of suppliers, sites and users that relate to an Internet enterprise."

The trick is to step back and look at this data *longitudinally*. As Ed tentatively explains it (after all, it was his first meeting), this means "examining an issue from side to side, as opposed to top to bottom." (Some newly noir Raymond Chandler will arise to write, "He looked at her *latitudinally*.")

And what if some RealNetworks executive reports to the board, "This place is a *beehive*"? In olden times, that would have meant "active," as in "busy as a bee." Now, however, if it's *beehive*, it's "not working because elements are swarming about aimlessly."

The word *improvement* has itself been improved; it is now *next generation*. *Transfer?* Out. Use *port to*. And when information has been not merely *transcoded*—that is, put into another format—but ported to a wholly different source, as from a music CD onto a computer hard drive, it has been *ripped*. (Shakespeare liked "untimely ripped.")

Though most of us worked out Y2K, the year 2000 problem, the question that the boys in the *bandwidth* are asking is "Is the new secretary *24/7?*" This is no lascivious reference to anybody's bust-and-waist metrix. It has to do with the employee's willingness to be on cell call twenty-four hours a day, seven days a week.

You can always tell if the Internet company management has *next-generation bandwidth* by its ability to achieve *stickiness*. This is a measurement of how long an individual Internet user—you, for example—stays on the particular Web site without hypertexting off to some other seductive site like a faithless wanton. Holding you as the user fast to the site—making you *hardcore*—is what used to be called the name of the game. Are you ready? In the new Internet boardrooms, this Web site loyalty is referred to reverently as *eyeball hang time*.

A "vector" represents velocity and direction, so to make a distinction between vector and speed is not appropriate, I think.

Michael Alcamo
New York, New York

The word is metrics, not metrix. Metrics is the plural of metric, a fave here at Lucent Technologies and, I'm sure, at many of the other organiza-

tions you wrote about. Now, to a mathematician (and I am one of those), a metric is a nonnegative function of two points in a metric space (so-called because it is a set on which a metric is defined) that tells something about how far apart (often in quite nonintuitive ways) the two points are. However, in the modern industrial state, a metric is simply any quantitative description of some phenomenon currently in vogue. For instance, the number of inventory turns per year is a metric. The total time it takes for a product to go from the idea stage to "first ship" is a metric. I could go on and on (and sometimes do). An appropriate suite of metrics is a powerful talisman because, in theory, a quick glance at their current values is supposed to give the savvy observer a quick snapshot of the state of the business and where it's headed.

Michael Tortorella, Distinguished Member of Technical Staff
Bell Laboratories
Middletown, New Jersey

Longitudinal means "over time," not side to side; it refers to the analysis of a process as it develops, rather than the comparison of the same process in two companies or two divisions, which is a cross-sectional analysis. Similarly, a vector gives direction and speed, and the inflection point is a "crossroads" that means an accelerating process is not decelerating, or vice versa. The term bandwidth, in my experience (which is similar to Bleier's), has many different meanings; in my company, it means the range of products offered.

James Geiwitz
Victoria, British Columbia, Canada

FAITH-BASED

"GOVERNMENT should welcome the help of *faith-based* institutions," Governor George W. Bush of Texas said in 1996. In April 1999, a spokesman for his brother, Governor Jeb Bush of Florida, told the *News and Record* of Greensboro, North Carolina, "The Governor supports *faith-based* initiatives."

"For too long," said Vice President Al Gore to the Salvation Army in Atlanta last month, "*faith-based* organizations have wrought miracles on a shoestring." He welcomed "the voices of *faith-based* organizations."

In covering Gore's speech, John Harwood of *The Wall Street Journal* noted "both political parties' growing acceptance of *faith-based* solutions since Republicans began promoting the idea several years ago." But Kevin Sack of *The New York Times*, though reporting Gore's usage in direct quotation, did not use the suddenly popular phrase in his own writing; instead, he used the more traditional noun in discussing "government financing of *religion-based* welfare-to-work initiatives."

Faith-based is hot enough to be enshrined in the official canon. In Wisconsin, the Joint Legislative Council established the Special Committee on *Faith-based* Approaches to Crime Prevention and Justice. Assembly Speaker Scott Jensen's legal counsel defines those approaches as "the acknowledgment of and faith in a higher power," the belief that social pathologies include "conditions of the soul" and that treatment involves "a fundamental transformation of character."

The earliest use of this modifier now so in vogue was in criticism, not affirmation, of religion in public life. In 1981, Clarence Martin, a lobbyist for the Association for the Advancement of Psychology, wrote that scholars of the social sciences, heirs to Darwin, Marx and Freud, "are the empirical left who may challenge the views, or more importantly reject the *faith-based* values, of the creationists, the moral majority, the laissez-faire industrialists, the economic determinists, the sexists, the militarists, the coalition who put Reagan in office."

The linguistic mystery: Why are political figures all using *faith-based* rather than *religion-based* or, more simply than that adjectival compound, the old-fashioned adjective *religious?*

Religion (probably from the Latin *religare,* "to restrain") is a set of beliefs; *faith* (from *fidere,* "to trust") is the unquestioning trust in the truth of those beliefs.

American political tradition, following its metaphor of "a wall of separation between church and state," shies away from "religion in politics" but not away from religious values in public life. By substituting *faith* (trust in the truths) for *religion* (the organized set of beliefs), the new compound adjective gets around the traditional objection. The Reverend Bill Callahan of the Quixote Center in Hyattsville, Maryland, says, "The language of *faith-based* signals to people our motivation while separating us from the institutions."

-Based is a hot formative suffix. Though *broad-based* is two centuries old, *zero-based* took off around 1970, and missile lingo gave us *land-based,* *sea-based* and *space-based.* A discussion of this particular parasynthetic derivative is *based-based.*

I was glad to see the piece, not just because you spelled my name right, but also because I deliberately chose to use religion-based *in that Gore story specifically for the reason you describe. My feeling was that the faith-based euphemism lets folks get away with masking their intent, which is, rightly or wrongly, to chop away at the wall of separation between church and state, at least as it is currently constituted. After all, virtually all of us have faith in something or other. What could be objectionable about being faith-based? Now religion-based, that's a different matter.*

Kevin Sack
The New York Times
New York, New York

FAREWELL TO SINO

At a White House briefing, Samuel R. Berger, the national security adviser, was asked about a statement by China's President, Jiang Zemin, and replied, "It's not a new formulation in the theology of Chinology."

He was interrupted by raucous laughter from Sinophiles in the press corps, one of whom shouted the correction, *"Sinology."*

Meekly, the National Security Adviser began to accept the correction, but then—suddenly—a wave of hawkishness overtook him. "*Sinology*—no, *Chinology!* I'm inventing a new term."

It's about time. For centuries the combining form *Sino*—from the Greek *Sinai*, akin to the Sanskrit *cina*, meaning "Chinese"—has been used in lieu of *Chinese*. Why? *Sino-Soviet* had a smooth, sibilant sound, but now that we're back to Russia, what's so sacrosanct about *Sino-Russian relations?* Why not *Chinese-Russian relations?*

This may upset the Foreign Policy Establishment, the legion of U.S. *Sinologists, China-watchers* and *Beijingologists* everywhere, but I'm getting on the Berger bandwagon to dump *Sino*, which only confuses people. If the national security adviser uses it, and I use it, and you use it, the dictionaries will have to record it—and then the word will be in. The *New York Times* stylebook urges reporters to avoid *Sino-* in adjectival references to *China*, preferring *Chinese-American*, but sticks with *Sinologist*. C'mon, fellas—time to go all the way.

Now, about the name of the newly assertive coiner. His name is Samuel R. (for Richard) Berger. He likes to be called Sandy, which is fine for a nickname, especially when a line is being drawn in the sand, but I do not believe in substituting warm, cuddly nicknames for real names in standard newspaper writing.

Chinologist. Play it, Sam.

FATIGUE UNIFORM

"*Clinton fatigue* is not a myth," wrote Jack W. Germond and Jules Witcover in *National Journal.* "It may be the greatest obstacle between Gore and the presidency."

Myth or not, the phrase bids fair to be the political thumb-suckers' pontification of choice for the run-up to the pre-primary preliminaries. Who coined it and when?

In the *Congressional Quarterly Weekly Report* of June 2, 1990, the journalist Dave Kaplan filed a dispatch about the Arkansas primary with this pregnant line about the governor's reelection chances: "Clinton's closer-than-expected renomination touched off speculation that Arkansans may be tiring of Clinton's rule. (He will have served 10 nonconsecutive years at the end of this term.)" The zingy subhead over this not overly prescient line read, "Clinton Fatigue?"

Three days after Clinton was sworn in as President of the United States, James Morgan of the *Financial Times* declared, "One thing the papers shared this week was *Clinton fatigue*." This was not the voters' weariness with his time in office—only three days—but a reflection of the media's displeasure with their own saturation coverage of the transfer of power. The old meaning returned toward the beginning of his inevitable lame-duckiness in an article about Hillary Clinton's senatorial prospects: "The Mayor Rudy Giuliani may also be helped," wrote Bob Herbert in *The New York Times* in June 1999, "by the so-called *Clinton fatigue* factor."

However, a former pollster for Ross Perot, Frank Luntz, warned Republicans that the general tiredness with the folks in the White House might spill over to the GOP officeholders: In addition to *Clinton fatigue*, he found *congressional fatigue*.

What lies at the root of this lingo of lassitude? The Latin stem *fati*, "enough," probably referred to "yawning." Its first use in that sense was by Daniel Defoe, whose Robinson Crusoe complains of "it having been a Day of great *Fatigue* to me."

Soon more than people felt it. *Mental fatigue* was noted in 1854, *muscular fatigue* a generation later. A century after that, the term *war neurosis* was rejected and *combat fatigue* was adopted.

As the comedic linguist George Carlin was to observe, in World War I the syndrome caused by the sustained stress of fighting was called *shell shock*; in World War II, it was *combat fatigue* and *battle fatigue*; in the Korean conflict, it was *operational exhaustion*. But it took the Vietnam War to take it down the pompous path of vainglorious terminology: *post-traumatic stress disorder* (PTSD). Before we degenerate to *post-Clinton stress disorder*, the yakketing class is likely to cause viewers to fall victim to pre-primary analysis regurgitation syndrome (PPARS).

Meanwhile, despite all the talk of the voters' *Clinton fatigue*, Clinton remains indefatigable. (Yop—same Latin root, meaning "untiring.")

FIGHTBACK

"Once we get the right leader, and the right chairman," wrote the Lord Feldman to *The Times* of London after the political debacle of the Conservatives, "we can then start our *fightback*."

There's a lively Britishism for Americans to adopt. *Fightback* is a verb form first used as a compound noun in 1953, hyphenated in a book about polo in 1960, and now found as a familiar one-word description of a losing side's surge in cricket.

The neologism was formed on the analogy of *kickback*, "a sometimes corrupt return of a portion of money paid"; *fallback*, "a prepared retreat," as in "*fallback* position"; and especially *comeback*, which can mean either "a snappy retort" or "a return to power," as in President Clinton's description of himself as "the *Comeback* Kid." *Fightback* is a more active form of *comeback* and is a noun for lexicographers to watch.

English word coinage is not exclusively an American trait, as recent visitors to London can attest. Although the modernized Claridge's is no longer the grand hotel it used to be, the language does its own refurbishing, often by squeezing old words together. The BBC's Sir David Frost recently took a three-word phrase popularized by W. Somerset Maugham—*The Summing Up*—and compressed it to the one-word *upsumming*.

Don't know if that one will fly.

FILM CLICHÉS

The quotation anthologist Nigel Rees's "Quote . . . Unquote" newsletter takes up the topic of film clichés.

No movie comes close to *Casablanca* (screenplay by Howard Koch, Julius J. Epstein and Philip G. Epstein) for the coinage of what later became clichés: *Play it, Sam* (without the "again") has been extensively studied here, as have *shocked, shocked* and *the usual suspects*, later the name of a rock group and now the title of a movie.

But consider the phrase *What a dump!* This was quoted by Elizabeth Taylor in the 1966 film version of Edward Albee's play *Who's Afraid of Virginia Woolf?* as derived from a line delivered by Bette Davis in the 1949 film *Beyond the Forest*. But Jean English, a newsletter correspondent, found it in Otto Preminger's 1945 *Fallen Angel*. Dana Andrews holes up in a fleabag hotel and expostulates, though without Miss Davis's diction, "*What a dump!*" This phrase has been the bane of real-estate agents ever since.

"*What do we do now?*" "*We wait.*" This staple of TV crime series can be found in a 1967 episode of *The Champions* and was repeated in films like *Beverly Hills Cop* in 1984 and *Ghost* in 1990. No stakeout can be filmed without this exchange.

"*We'd better call the police.*" "*I am the police.*" Richard Hollinshead did the research on this classic dialogue, finding it in Clint Eastwood's 1971

Dirty Harry and in his 1973 *Magnum Force*, antedated by the Dana Andrews line in the 1944 *Laura*. (If anyone ever says to me, "We'd better call the language police," I'm ready.)

FILM NOIR IS MY BÊTE NOIRE

Whatever happened to gloomy Gus, the downcast brother of Fred Opper's 1904 cartoon character Happy Hooligan?

On the comics pages, that pioneering symbol of misery and despair was succeeded, in a failing way, by George Baker's "Sad Sack" and later in "Li'l Abner" by Al Capp's bleakly unpronounceable Joe Bftsplk, who was followed everywhere by a dark cloud.

But the Gloomy Guses have found a bright, new future. They are now the *auteurs, producers, stars* and *critics* of *film noir*. These days, if a film isn't *noir*, it's nowhere.

In Canada last year, Butch Vig, of a musical group depressingly named Garbage, told *The Vancouver Sun*, "We had Werner Herzog movies running in the studio all day, so we felt that noir ambience." About the same time in London, *The Independent* wrote that "Kim Brandstrup's Arc Dance Company dances his ballet *noir*, 'Crime Fictions,' . . . inspired by Raymond Chandler."

Chandler was a master of metaphor ("She was blond enough to make a bishop kick a hole through a stained-glass window") who competed with Dashiell Hammett and James M. Cain in the heyday of the hard-boiled detective novel. He wrote in Los Angeles in the 40s and 50s, a locale of sunshine and deep shadow recollected through a glass darkly as an era of *noir*.

The new movie set in that scene of crime, prostitution, glitz and dreary fun, *L.A. Confidential*, based on the 1990 book by James Ellroy, has occasioned a spate of citations of the French word for "black."

"Imagine a film set in the exotic past," wrote Richard Schickel in *Time*, "Los Angeles in the *noirish* 50s." *Daily Variety* called it "Warner Brothers' period *noir* thriller." *Newsday*'s Jack Mathews called it "an often funny pulp *noir* that grabs you by the throat."

Where did the vogue use of this word—now surpassing *luminous, gritty, unsettling, riveting, stylish, steamy* and *resonant* in the ambience-chasing vocabulary of film criticism—have its origin?

The earliest use found so far of *film noir* in the *Oxford English Dictio-*

nary is from a 1958 review in *The Spectator* about a play that "tries to be a parody of a *film noir.*"

In the 70s, the French adjective appeared in *pied noir,* a disease that attacks grapevines, and in the plural *pieds noirs,* Algerian refugees settled by the French in Corsica.

But the meaning of *noir* that took hold in the 80s departed from the color black to the metaphor of blackness, as in *black comedy,* amusement in morbidity that goes one step beyond mordant wit. (*Black comedy* has been updated to *comic-noir.*)

Mark Kernis caught the new meaning in a 1978 *Washington Post* review of a Tom Waits recording: It is "the aural equivalent of a Raymond Chandler novel. . . . He draws scenes from dark alleys and pool halls, and the ambience he creates forms a type of *music noir.*" A decade later, *The New Yorker* film critic Pauline Kael wrote of Kenneth Branagh's *Henry V,* "He's trying to make it into an antiwar film, an *epic noir.*" In 1986, the novelist James Robert Baker had a disk-jockey character say: "This is Scott Cochran, macho superstud, male feminist and untreatable schizophrenic. You're listening to *Radio Noir.*"

In the 90s, the French word took off. The Ellroy novel was blurbed as "not imitation *noir,* but neo-*noir.*" The Thomas Berger retelling of *The Oresteia* was reviewed in *The Times* with "His Clytemnestra is a classic nympho of the *noir* imagination."

What's the meaning of the new *noir?* One sense is "gloom inspired by fatalism," a characteristic of Chandler's private eye, Philip Marlowe; a more recent and less profound sense is "overtones of menace and criminality."

That scary sense is embodied in *boudoir noir,* described by the *Toronto Star* as "the newly mainstream leather-fetish-consensual S/M lobby." (When did sadomasochism become mainstream? Is nothing kinky anymore?)

In the old days, the villains in the sagebrush epics were the *black hats;* now, thanks to the reviewing community, they are the stars of *cowboy noir.*

Reading the future is easy. We can trust the critics of the next generation to look back on our prosperous *fin-de-millénaire* period as a time of *blanc.*

Your remarks on the vogue for the term film noir *seem to imply that it was casually created by a bunch of movie critics operating in their pretentious twit mode. That's not quite the case.*

As Alain Silver and Elizabeth Ward tell us in their literate and defin-

itive encyclopedia of the genre, in the years immediately after World War II a French publisher reprinted a group of novels mostly by the American hard guy school (Chandler, Cain, Horace McCoy) under the overall title Série Noire. *At the same time American films influenced by, and often adaptations of, work by this group began arriving in France.*

Silver and Ward say that it was a cineaste named Nino Frank who invented the phrase in 1946; they also cite an article in La Revue du Cinéma *by Jean Pierre Chartier published later that year. It was entitled "Americans Also Make 'Noir' Films," which seems inferentially to prove the literary-movie link. Obviously the term made its way to English via the work of French movie critics whose regard for American genre films of all kinds influenced some of their American counterparts to start taking seriously a body of work that most middlebrow critics had previously dismissed as impossibly lowbrow.*

Be that as it may, I join you in deploring the vague and trendy application of the term to other modes of expression. When I use it I have a very specific movie style and attitude in mind.

Richard Schickel, Film Critic
Time *Magazine*
Los Angeles, California

O.K., I don't care that you gave the Twilight Zone *origin to Tony Thorne instead of me. But you misquoted the master! Never misquote the master!*
The actual bishop line is:

It was a blonde. A blonde to make a bishop kick a hole in a stained glass window.

—Farewell, My Lovely, *ch. 13*

Note also the -e spelling of blonde.
P.S. O.K., while we're on great Chandler lines about blondes, esp. lines that are examples of truly great writing but that, like Hemingway, are often palely imitated:

The blonde was strong with the madness of love or fear, or a mixture of both, or maybe she was just strong.

—The Big Sleep, *ch. 15*
Jesse Sheidlower, North American Principal Editor
Oxford English Dictionary
New York, New York

According to Raymond Brode and Etienne Chaumeton in the seminal study of this kind of film, Panorama du Film Noir Américain *(Paris: Editions de Minuit, 1955), the phrase first appears in a review written by Nino Frank in* Ecran Française *No. 61, dated 28 August 1946.*

Following the end of World War II, French audiences discovered all at once what Hollywood filmmaking had been like during the war years when no Hollywood films could be exhibited. On the basis of viewing The Maltese Falcon; Laura; Murder, My Sweet; Double Indemnity *and* The Woman in the Window *within the space of a few months, Frank sought to describe the films' darkened, cynical tone by likening them for his readers to the hard-boiled American fiction they knew that had been published in French translation before 1940. Since these novels were published in a series called* Série Noire, *Frank adopted the series' title to describe films of a similar tone, hence "film noir."*

> *Marshall Deutelbaum*
> *West Lafayette, Indiana*

The first French book on the subject, Panorama du Film Noir Américain, *by Brode and Chaumeton, appeared in 1955, but it cites magazine articles going back as far as a November 1946 essay by J. P. Chartier in* La Revue du Cinéma *entitled "Les Americains Aussi Font des Films Noirs."*

It may not be true, but I've heard that one reason the French came up with the term is that they saw American films all in a rush after World War II (the Vichy government having apparently forbidden their exhibition during the war) and noticed a general darkening of tone. Also, some people connect the term to the famous yellow-and-black Série Noire *series of translations of American hard-boiled writers like Chandler and Hammett published by Gallimard.*

> *Kenneth Turan, Film Critic*
> The Los Angeles Times
> *Los Angeles, California*

As a French-born film critic and historian, I think I can enlighten you somewhat on the French origin of the phrase film noir. *It was coined by French film buffs/critics in the late forties to describe an American kind of crime thriller that had appeared during the war years and had not been identified as a separate genre by either the profession or the critics in the States.*

In 1947, Gallimard, the prestigious publisher, launched a series of mystery novels called La Série Noire *which introduced Chandler, Hammett, Cain and dozens of other hard-boiled detective writers to French readers and became enormously successful. Those novels were popularly known as* romans noirs *(although the phrase has been earlier used by academics and literary critics to designate nineteenth-century British Gothic novels). But why* série noire? *Partly because the cover of the book was black, but also as a pun on a journalistic phrase of the time—*série noire *(as in* La série noire continue . . .*) was used to refer to what was perceived as serial accidents (a number of plane or car crashes happening within a short period of time). Obviously, all this must have had some influence on the coinage of the phrase* film noir.

Jean-Pierre Coursodon
Lynn, Massachusetts

FIRST THINGS FIRST

Subtly, stealthily, almost subliminally, a political slogan has been drummed into our heads all year long. The rallying cry was never shouted; the insistent phrase was never capitalized in speeches or printed on buttons. But it has quietly gripped the nation and is doing its job of persuasion.

Speaking of the budget surplus in his 1999 State of the Union address, President Clinton said: "We should not spend any of it until after Social Security is truly saved. *First things first.*" He had inserted that phrase during a rehearsal on January 16, 1999, in the White House theater at the suggestion of Gene Sperling, a domestic-policy aide. Michael Waldman, the speechwriter, seized on it as an easy-to-grasp way out of the anticipated GOP charge that Mr. Clinton was opposed to tax cuts.

The noun in the phrase (infinitely better than "Let's prioritize") had the added advantage of being plural. That meant it could cover not just Social Security but a range of other outlays. But how could all of them be "first"? Answer: Taken as a group, they were first in contrast to the one proposal that was designated to come last. Throughout the year, Mr. Clinton resolutely repeated the familiar phrase whenever asked about tax cuts: "*First things first.* When we've met our obligation of showing what we need for debt reduction, for Medicare and Social Security and education, then we'll be in a position to know how much is left for a tax cut."

Press releases followed the line in lockstep: "The President will urge Congress to work with him to enact a responsible budget that puts *first things first.*" John Podesta, the White House chief of staff, was programmed to use the phrase at least twice at every Sunday talk-show appearance when asked about the GOP tax bill: "Send it down to us so that we can veto it and then move forward, putting *first things first.*"

By September, Mr. Clinton was able to work the three-word agenda prioritizer into almost every appearance, no matter what the subject: "I want America to say," he told elementary school pupils in Olney, Maryland, "Let's put *first things first,* nothing is more important than our children."

The familiar phrase was first popularized first in 1894. (Nope; the redundancy works best with a noun in the middle, not a verb.) The Reverend George Jackson titled his collection of sermons *First Things First: Addresses to Young Men,* which included his ringing harangue on "modern idolatry."

It was taken up early in 1992 by David Wilhelm, the Clinton campaign manager: "*First things first,* and the first thing is winning.*" (But that was set aside for James Carville's "It's the economy, stupid.") Mr. Clinton, meeting later that year with Israeli Prime Minister Yitzhak Rabin, told reporters he had explained that his emphasis on the economy "was not a symbol of isolationism, but a necessary commitment to putting *first things first.*"

Part of the brilliance of Mr. Clinton's relentlessly repeated slogan putting everything else behind is that it resists argument or parody. How can Republicans respond? With *last but not least?*

FOLLOW THAT SUPPORTER

During his televised joint news conference with China's president, Jiang Zemin, in Beijing, President Clinton corrected himself in a way that demonstrated a concern for precision in the meanings of words.

After Jiang raised the subject of Tibet's Dalai Lama, Clinton said: "President Jiang pointed out that he, the Dalai Lama, has a few *followers* of Tibetan Buddhism even in the United States and Europe. But most of his *followers* have not given up their own religious faith. He has *followers* who are Christians—*supporters,* excuse me, not *followers, supporters*—who are Christians, who are Jews, who are Muslims, who believe in the unity of God and who believe he is a holy man."

A *follower* is one who accepts a master or guide; for eight hundred years the word has connoted spirituality, as in an adherent to a religious cause or a disciple of a charismatic leader.

A supporter (*portare* is Latin for "to carry," as in *portable* or *porter*) is one who upholds another person's principles and authority. Its overtones are more political than spiritual: "So was Thomas Becket," wrote Hobbes in *Leviathan*, ". . . supported against Henry the Second, by the Pope." A religious group *follows* its leader; a political party supports its leader.

Clinton's point was that the Dalai Lama's Buddhist *followers* had not given up their religious faith, but that in a larger group he also had political *supporters* in other religions who respected him as a "holy man."

To lump together those who are Buddhists and those who promote the free exercise of Buddhism as *followers* would have been a mistake. The President moved quickly to correct himself and in so doing drew a nice distinction.

FOLLOW THE PROFFERING DUCK

"Follow the money. Always follow the money." That resounding phrase, coined on the analogy of the French *cherchez la femme*, has become the rallying cry of a generation of reporters investigating corruption in high places. It has echoes, of course, in the pursuit of the Asian connection to Clinton campaign finance; the title of PBS's series on the subject is *"Follow the Money,"* and CNN calls its coverage of the Senate hearings "The Money Trail."

Who first said *"Follow the money"?* Everybody knows the answer: "Deep Throat," the anonymous source quoted by Bob Woodward and Carl Bernstein in their book *All the President's Men.* Those three words from a mysterious administration official whose identity is unknown even today impelled the young journalists to money laundered in Mexico and ultimately to payments to burglars and a Nixon White House slush fund.

But wait: Thanks to Daniel Schorr, the National Public Radio commentator whose investigative credibility includes the credential of a place on the notorious "Enemies List," we now have a new and disconcerting take on the origin of the famous phrase.

Schorr searched for the phrase in the journalists' book. It wasn't there. Nor was it in any of the Watergate reporting in *The Washington Post. Fol-*

low the money first appeared in the movie *All the President's Men*, spoken by Hal Holbrook playing Deep Throat.

The screenplay was written by William Goldman. When Schorr called him, the famed screenwriter at first insisted that the line came from the book; when proved mistaken about that, he said: "I can't believe I made it up. I was in constant contact with Woodward while writing the screenplay. I guess he made it up."

Schorr then called Woodward, who could not find the phrase in his exhaustive notes of Watergate interviews. The reporter told Schorr he could no longer rely on his memory as to whether Deep Throat had said the line and was inclined to believe that Goldman had invented it. (Woodward, now in the forefront of those journalists pursuing the Asian-influence scandal, confirmed that to me one recent Sunday morning as we bolted down the tasty brunch NBC offers guests on *Meet the Press*.)

"Whoever said that inspired line," Schorr told *Los Angeles Times* readers, "which has entered the political and journalistic lexicon, it was an invention."

If the line was indeed a fiction, as it seems to be, what does that portend for its nonfictional source? Schorr only poses the question, but the irony is this: When recently asked on *Meet the Press* what the lasting legacy of Watergate was after a quarter century, Ben Bradlee of *The Washington Post* (brilliantly portrayed in the movie by Jason Robards Jr.*) replied with the words of William Goldman: *"Follow the money."*

Shortly after I started covering the Justice Department for Newsweek *in March 1973, Henry Peterson, then assistant attorney general for the criminal division, gave me an extensive update on the Watergate investigation he was heading. (Archibald Cox was named special prosecutor in May 1973.)*

In describing the work of his key legal eagles, Earl Silbert and Seymour Glanzer, Peterson told me that "from day one, I told them to follow the money. If they followed the money, they'd get to the bottom of the case."

Peterson, of course, was a principal source for all of us on the Watergate story; he also was one of the oft-mentioned candidates for Deep Throat, his name having been placed in nomination by John Ehrlichman. However,

*Jason Robards Jr. died on December 26, 2000.

Peterson died in 1991 and that, presumably, would have permitted Woodward to identify him as such. If Peterson used the "follow the money" expression with me, who was new to the story, he certainly must have used it with other reporters who, like Woodward, had been there from the start.

Stephan Lesher
Katonah, New York

I'd like to call your attention to a Chinese equivalent to the now-famous phrase "follow the money."

Ever since the late Deng Xiao-ping opened up communist China to market economy, get-rich-quick has been everybody's goal in that country and the watchword is Xian qian kan. *The phrase started out to be a rallying cry for a New China, meaning, "Look forward!" or "Look toward the future!" It so happens that there are two Chinese words with identical pronunciation,* qian: *one meaning "forward" and the other, "money." The Chinese, never a people to miss a good pun, have rewritten the slogan and made it read: "Look money-ward!" or "Look toward the money!" It has been widely employed but especially against officials and their offspring who use their influence to profit in business.*

It is interesting to note that "Follow the Money," the American-English approach to "corruption in high places," also has something to do with Asian (and Chinese) influence.

George Kao
Kensington, Maryland

FOR SHAME

Shameless, reckless and *indefensible* were adjectives used in first reports of a censure resolution early this year. When Senator Dianne Feinstein submitted her resolution (which was never voted on), a key word was changed: *shameless* became *shameful*. What's the difference?

The difference lies in the word that is modified. If it is the agent who lacks shame—who observes few constraints of modesty or morality—then that person is *shameless*. If the word being modified is the action itself rather than the person, then the action is filled with shame, or is *shameful*.

If I danced drunkenly through Times Square in the nude on Millennium Eve, I would be *shameless*. You, if you were clothed and sober, might find my celebration *shameful*.

FRIENDS WITH

"Senator John Kerry has an affinity for the Vice President's positions," writes Carey Goldberg in *The New York Times*, "and is friends with him."

That locution grates on the ears of Kenneth Smith of Newark, Delaware. "Since we have never met," he writes, "it follows that I am not *friends with* you." He finds his singular *I* ill fits the plural *friends* and prefers to put that as the all-plural "we are not friends" or the all-singular "you are not a friend of mine."

I checked with the usagist Jacques Barzun, who is a friend. He is untroubled by the number disagreement of this spreading idiom but finds a shade of difference in meaning: "*Friend of* refers to an established relationship. *Friends with* gives the connotation of 'friendly toward,' referring to the attitude rather than the firm relationship."

There is also the element of abstraction. *Friends with* is an outgrowth of *friendly with*, implying interaction between people. You can be a *friend of* the Constitution or a *friend to* man, but you cannot be *friends with* either abstraction.

"I'm *friends with* her" is not incorrect, in my book, but is informal. "We're friends" or "she's a friend of mine" is unassailable in any company.

THE FULL MONTY

How do you describe "everything"? I don't mean a few cosmic items or a bunch of stuff; I mean *the whole shootin' match, the works, the entire kit and caboodle, the whole ball of wax.* Everything including *the kitchen sink.*

For nearly a century the collective slang of choice by such writers as Walt Whitman, Bret Harte and Mark Twain was *the shebang*, a term meaning "a hut, shed, tent or dilapidated dwelling," perhaps from the Irish *shebaan*, or "lowly tavern"; by metaphoric extension, the whole shebang came to mean "the entire setup." After a good run, *the shebang* seems to be closing its tent.

Its replacement in the past generation had been *the whole nine yards.* No, this had nothing to do with football (you need ten yards, not nine, for a first down) or material for a wedding dress. Diligent research, buttressed by many letters from construction workers, points to the cubic contents of a cement truck. (I say it's a cement truck; they call it a concrete truck. Whatever you call the conveyance, a full rotating load supposedly contains *the whole nine yards.*)

Now a new challenger has entered the lexicon of surfeit. "Buy a simple package of fourteen channels," advises Britain's *Daily Mail*, and it will cost about $10, but it will cost you triple that if you take sixteen channels, a movie channel and Sky Sports, and in the newspaper's figure of speech, "go for *the full Monty*." In 1993, the *Glasgow Herald* described a diner "tucking into *the full monty*—bacon, sausage, eggs and black pudding." It was the title of a 1993 book by Jim Davidson, a TV comic, and the name of a horse in 1990. (For a century, a *monty* has been racetrack slang for "a horse certain to win.")

On this side of the Atlantic, *The San Diego Union-Tribune* ran a story about the Carlsbad City Council's zoning restrictions to avert garishness: "Carlsbad has reached the point where it can afford to go *the full monty*— full frontal snobbery."

That metaphoric reference to nudity is repeated in the movie section of the *Boston Herald:* "Apparently Tinseltown is atwitter over *Boogie Nights*, the New Line Cinema flick where Mark Wahlberg does *the full monty*, snorts coke and God knows what else as porn star Dirk Diggler."

The phrase is being spread around the world by the success of a low-budget British comedy-drama from Fox Searchlight Pictures titled *The Full Monty*. In it, the main character says, *"The Full Monty . . .* don't think I relish the idea of pulling off my kegs and showing my lunch box to the world." Fox publicity defines the phrase this way: "(1) naked, nude, (2) to go *the Full Monty*, vb., to take all one's clothes off, to go the whole way, to be totally naked."

The etymology of the term is in dispute. One school holds that it comes from a card game, either *monte bank* or *three-card monte*, the phrase derived from a pile, or mountain, of cards. Another points to a Liverpool haberdashery selling arriving sailors an entire shore outfit. Michael Quinion, who writes a lively Web page about new words (http://clever.net/quinion/words), reports the speculation that it may have to do with Field Marshal Bernard Montgomery, Monty to his troops, who cut a splendid figure in full regalia.

The origin has to be considered obscure, but the meaning is "the totality," with a special sense of "nakedness." The phrase is already spawning puns; *Entertainment Weekly* refers to *Wuthering Heights* as "the full Brontë."

I have always heard that "the whole nine yards" referred to the length of ammunition belts that World War II Spitfires carried and that when you used up the whole nine yards you were out of bullets. If this is true, the phrase would have added poignancy and certainly more urgency than receiving a dumptruck load of concrete.

Albert Huerby
Cambridge, Massachusetts

Yes, William, there is a cement truck. In fact, there are two kinds of cement trucks (a.k.a. "bulk carriers") plying our highways. One carries portland cement (sometimes called hydraulic cement because it demands water to work, as do most of us); the other kind carries asphalt cement (sometimes called bitumen, which needs no water, only heat, to become workable).

Neither of these useful carriers is what you describe: "the conveyance [that carries] a full rotating load." That's a transit-mix truck. It conveys concrete, a conglomerate of portland cement, water, sand, stone and a brew of new-age additives worthy of a two-day seminar. Only about 10 percent of most concrete is cement; the rest, as you already know, is, well, rocks—dust, even air. Air occupies almost as much space in concrete as cement does. Calling concrete "cement" is to salute the marketing expertise of the Portland Cement Association, a group of adroit and creative friends of mine who may excoriate my balloon picking.

A few years ago the Pennsylvania Supreme Court put it this way: "Cement is to concrete what flour is to fruitcake."

"Cement trucks" (portland cement, that is) deliver a talcum-fine gray powder in dry-sealed, nonrotating, sausage-shaped trailers into concrete plants all over the place. Out of those plants rumble "concrete trucks" with a full rotating load of wet, rocky mud to various construction sites.

I think it was Louie Prima who did most of us in with his silly song "Cement Mixer, Putti, Putti!" a half-century ago. Fagetaboutit! Louie got it wrong. As do you.

Orrin Riley, Editorial Director
The Concrete Industry Board
New York, New York

I suggest you look for the derivation of the phrase the whole nine yards *in the nose of a World War II fighter. Each of the four machine guns in the*

Lockheed P-38 Lightning was armed with five hundred rounds of .50-caliber ammunition. A .50-caliber bullet is, of course, half an inch wide. Adding the width of the cartridge case and the metal links that join them together, a full load would be just about nine yards long. Returning from a mission with ammunition boxes empty, a pilot would have fired off the whole nine yards.

Tony Peters
New York, New York

FULSOME APOLOGY

When Senator-elect Charles Schumer of New York told the Judiciary Committee that the President had already made a "fulsome apology"— intended to mean "copious, complete, full"—usagists such as Alistair Cooke winced. Throughout nine decades of speaking good English, the BBC commentator knew that the word meant nothing of the sort. On almost the contrary, he and other incensed hearings-watchers told me on voice mail, *fulsome* means "excessive, cloying," even "disgusting."

Centuries ago, the original meaning of "full" in that word had been influenced by *foul*. Surely the Clinton defender could not have intended to leave the impression that the apology reeked. Had the Senator-elect erred?

Two great dictionaries disagree. *Webster's New World*, now published by Macmillan, has as its first definition "disgusting or offensive, especially because excessive or insincere (fulsome praise)." But then it reports a second meaning: "(apparent revival of the original sense, obsolete since 16th century) full; ample; abundant: usage objected to by some."

Now to Merriam-Webster, whose patron saint, Noah himself, defined it in 1828 as "gross: disgusting by plainness, grossness or excess; as *fulsome* flattery or praise." In the tenth collegiate edition, M-W turns the tables. Its first definition is "characterized by abundance: copious." Only in its second sense do we get "esthetically, morally or generally offensive." It then gives other pejorative senses as "effusive" and "overdone" before swinging back to "generous in amount." A usage note is added: "Unless the context is made very clear, the reader or hearer cannot be sure whether such an expression as '*fulsome* praise' means *copious* or *offensive*."

This commentator says: If you mean *full*, say *full*, or if you want to put your thumb on the upscale, *copious*. But if you mean *gross*, say *gross* or *yucky*, or try an expletive like *feh!* Never refer to a *fulsome* bosom unless you want to get slugged by an intelligent woman. Indeed, cross *fulsome* off your list entirely. Phooey on ambiguity. Never be of two minds about ambivalence.

FUMBLERULES

A few years back, I collected a bunch of "fumblerules" that illustrated mistakes in English by using them. For example, "don't use no double negatives," "avoid run-on sentences they are hard to read," "place pronouns as close as possible, especially in long sentences—such as those of ten or more words—to their antecedents," and "a writer must not shift your point of view."

Rich Maggiani of Burlington, Vermont, found a few more on his e-mail. My favorites: "Foreign words and phrases are not apropos." "Be more or less specific." And finally: "Who needs rhetorical questions?"

GAM(BL)ING

THE COMMITTEE TO RESTORE AMERICAN VALUES, reports Richard L. Berke in *The New York Times*, has been asking presidential candidates to take a kind of *litmus test*. Every Bronx High School of Science graduate knows that litmus is a paper covered with the coloring matter from lichens that stays blue when dipped in an alkaline solution and turns pink when dipped in an acid solution. (Or is it the other way around? I did poorly in chemistry but got through because the kid next to me, who ultimately was awarded a Nobel Prize, let me crib. Some may call that cheating; we called it "helping a flunking friend," a Value that needs Restoring.)

That scientific meaning of *litmus* test has been extended to "a criterion that overwhelms all others." To get an illustrative usage of this, I just used my mouse to highlight the phrase and punched the dictionary symbol on my Microsoft QuickShelf. Here's what came up: "The word 'hopefully' has become the *litmus test* to determine whether one is a language snob or a language slob." (Cribbing from yourself is unsettling; what if I made a mistake?)

The testing questions from C.R.A.V. ranged from "Would you support a removal of the words 'under God' from the Pledge of Allegiance?" to "Do you believe gun control reduces crime?" Presumably, a "yes" answer to either would turn the paper a hot shade of pink. But the tester that struck me as insightful—a subtler guide to moral-political orientation—was "Do you normally call games of chance *gambling* or *gaming?*"

Frank Fahrenkopf is president of the American Gaming Association. As the lobbyist for the casino industry, he prefers *gaming*. "It's all wagering," he tells me. He knows I am an antigambling zealot but is willing to take a chance on my redemption. "Around the sixteenth century, the distinction came about between games where personal skill is involved and games of chance. For example, playing poker is *gaming* because it takes personal skill. *Gambling* is where there is no skill involved—like picking a horse.

"When Nevada legalized *gaming* in 1931," Fahrenkopf, a native Nevadan, continues, "most of the games involved skill: table games, like cards and dice. From the start it's been the Nevada *Gaming* Commission. But a change has come about in the last ten or fifteen years because the big games are games of chance—that is, slot machines. Now, that's *gambling.*"

It's all *gambling*, says Tom Grey, executive director of the National Coalition Against Legalized Gambling. "The use of the word *gaming* is our *litmus test.* When legislators use it, that shows us they're in the pocket of the casino operators, and they've bought the party line or PR guy's package. The word gaming puts 'foo-foo dust,' as we used to say in the Army, on a business that bilks the poor and traps the unwary with 'something for nothing.' That's how you make the wrong disappear. The use of the word *gaming* is an attempt to make a serious business seem like fun."

Both sides agree: *Gambling* has a negative connotation; *gaming*, a positive one. Opponents of lotteries denounce "*gambling* as public policy"; proponents say "*gaming* is an entertainment medium."

Five will get you ten that *gaming* came first. Rooted in the Old English *gamenian*, "to sport, play," it appeared around 1510 to mean "playing at games of chance for stakes," and the person who did it was a *gamester.* In Shakespeare's day, the activity was frowned upon as immoral: Hamlet, thinking about murdering King Claudius, thought the best time to consign him to hell would be not while he was trying to pray, but when he was engaged "at *gaming*, swearing, or about some act/That has no relish of salvation in't."

Not until the eighteenth century did *gambling* roll upon the scene. Its earliest slang sense was "cheating at *gaming.*" In 1726, "the *Gambling* Fraternity" was said to be a term used by those "with a just Derision of their own Vileness." *Gentleman's Magazine* in 1747 updated the earlier term: "*gamesters*, commonly called *gamblers*, players, women of the town." The lexicographer Samuel Johnson wrote that *gambler* was "a cant word, I suppose, for *game* or *gamester*" and defined it as "a knave whose practice it is to invite the unwary to *game* and cheat them." It was, as the *Oxford English Dictionary* later concluded, "essentially a term of reproach."

No wonder the casino operators and lottery advocates scrupulously avoid the word, while the moralists, joined by liberals who see it as regressive taxation, try to jam the pejorative word down the burgeoning industry's throat.

C.R.A.V. is right: The word is a surefire *litmus test.*

NO UNCERTAIN TERMS   121

The elite high school you attended must have been entirely peopled by pro-
totypical nerds for the prototypical mnemonic acronym for litmus testing
never to have taken hold. My high school chemistry teacher, Donald Burn-
ham, told my shocked coed class of 1940s rural teenagers to think BRA—
blue turns red in acid—and we would never again forget who does what to
whom.

John Strother
Princeton, New Jersey

GEEK PIQUE

Under a green, bucolic photo of a farm in Minnesota, a state that likes
to think of itself as the land of ten thousand lakes, *Newsweek* ran this caption: "The land of 10,000 *geeks?*" The story had to do with the Minnesota
High-Tech Association's ads to attract technical workers from California's Silicon Valley.

In the same way, the *Daily Oklahoman* wrote about Vice President Al
Gore as one who "dreams not of carnal conquests but of technological
breakthroughs" and is thus "the nation's No. 1 *geek.*"

This word's meaning has wandered far from its roots. "He is a foole, a
sotte, and a *geke,*" wrote Alexander Barclay in his 1515 *Certayne Egloges,*
using the lively words of the time to denounce a simpleton. Shakespeare
chimed in twice, first in *Twelfth Night* about "the most notorious *gecke*
and gull" and later in *Cymbeline* as a ghost denounces a rogue who made
Posthumus "the *geeck* and scorn o' th' other's villainy."

The old synonym for "fool" took a sinister turn in American carnival
slang to describe a "wild man" in a sideshow whose revolting act often
included biting the head off a live snake or chicken. Despite this specialized sense, and notwithstanding World War II military use in the form of
gook as a slur at Asians, the word continued to have a central sense of
"fool." In 80s slang it became a generalized term of contempt, like *dork*
(perhaps from the cutting-edge *dirk* influenced by a nickname) and the
too-studious student *grind* or *nerd* (probably from the earlier "*nerts* to
you," based on *nuts*).

How, then, did the derogatory *geek* become the self-description of
choice for hackers and computer technocrats?

It all began when bad, pronounced b-a-a-a-a-d, became synonymous
with "good—really good." The inversion of meaning swept through
groups eager to "out" their unpopularity, much as *queer* was adopted by

homosexuals to challenge their stereotyping by others. Hence, the term *geek*—the "fool" from five centuries back, later disdained in circuses as the lowest of the low—has become the badge worn proudly by the virtuosos of the Virtual Generation.

In 1969, I became a freshman at Rose Hulman Institute of Technology ("It's a RHIOT") in Terre Haute, Indiana. There were two labels which the freshmen of Speed Hall applied to ourselves. Anyone who partied a lot was known as a drunk. *A studious type was the opposite, that is, a* k-n-u-r-d *(pronounced nerd). I don't know who thought it up, or when, but by 1969* drunk *and* knurd *were firmly entrenched on that campus.*

Gregor Hartman
Ridgewood, New Jersey

With respect to your column on geeks, I would like to set the record straight. The GI slang term gook *has no connection to* geek *and, at least initially, was not an intended slur on Asians. When American troops arrived in Korea, in the summer of 1950, the locals pointed at them and said, "Miguk," a Korean variation of the Chinese word* Meiguo, *meaning American. The GIs heard* Me Gook *and decided that the term was used by the Korean language community to designate its members. Only later, when fear had been replaced by boredom, did the term acquire a derogatory shading.*

Richard H. Howarth
Reston, Virginia

GENDERESE

Hypersensitivity to sexism in language can pull the punch out of a good sentence.

In *All Too Human*, his revealing and riveting White House memoirs, George Stephanopoulos tells of his attempt to soften a line that Dick Morris wrote for the 1996 Clinton State of the Union address.

The line that stole the Republicans' clothes was "The era of big government is over." A poll presumably taken by Morris showed those words approved by 80 percent of Americans. But Stephanopoulos thought that such a potently illiberal line, unqualified, would make President Clinton a prisoner of conservative oratory. He and Michael Waldman, a White

House speechwriter, wanted to balance it with "but the era of every man for himself must never begin."

Wrote the memoirist: "Morris, surprisingly, didn't object; but our political-correctness police did. . . . They argued that 'every man for himself' was a sexist insult, and they appealed directly to the President." Clinton neutered the sentence: "But we cannot go back to the time when our citizens were left to fend for themselves."

"Not the same," noted Stephanopoulos correctly. "In a political speech, it takes a cliché to counter a cliché."

In wiping away the undoubted masculine tilt to a thousand years of English, and in attempting to imbue our language with gender equality, are we going too far too fast? Contrariwise, in making our language reflect a belated sense of fairness, should we tell tradition-bound male chauvinists, "Sorry, buddy, but you can't make an omelet without breaking eggs"? (Or contra-contrariwise, should we use an egg metaphor at all in this discussion?)

In some cases, the advocates of linguistic sex neutrality have indisputable logic on their side. If women are going to be firemen, policemen and mailmen, then we're better off with *firefighter, police officer* and *mail carrier.* If the boss of your company is a woman, you can't call her a *businessman;* she's an *executive,* and if she's tall and runs a small business, get a hyphen to help you out: she's a *tall small-business executive.*

In other cases, some have sought to unsex a word but found resistance: *chairman* went through *chairperson,* which sounded labored, to *chair,* which sounded four-legged, and then to *chairwoman,* which sounded too much like *charwoman.* Accordingly, some presiding women, in a display of security, preferred to go back to *chairman.* A more satisfying solution was found to *congressman/congresswoman/congressperson:* We now give all members of the House of Representatives the neutered title *representative, rep.* for short.

Humankind has triumphed over *mankind* among the many to whom the male does not automatically embrace the female. Thus has the *century of the common man* become the *time of the average person* or the *era of ordinary people.* Somehow *century of the common man* has more of a ring to it; unsexing has its drawbacks. (The replacement of the verb *man* with *staff* suggests the order "*Staff* the lifeboats!" and might encourage anti-P.C. types to go down with the ship.)

Some gender-diktats make it; some don't. At some colleges, *freshmen* were supposed to be called *first-year students;* that struck most *frosh* as a little stiff, but *freshman week* was replaced in many places by *orientation week.* (First-year Asian students did not object.)

I have long enjoyed the search for female equivalents to other masculine words: *avuncular,* for example, meaning "genial, kindly, familial," is rooted in the Latin for "maternal uncle." *The Nonsexist Word Finder,* a sternly prescriptive dictionary of gender-free usage, by Rosalie Maggio, directs readers to avoid the word. O.K.; why can't we have a new adjective that calls up the qualities of an aunt? (I took a crack at this coinage years ago, rejecting the hesitant *tantitive* for the smiling *amital,* based on the Latin for "father's sister." It went nowhere.)

Finding the appropriate feminine alternative to masculine words is not easy. How about *womanizer?* For a promiscuous female, *loose woman* sounds dated and *slut,* overly harsh; *temptress* and *seductress* deal with technique rather than state. My preference is *philanderer;* although based on "love of man," it imputes enjoyment of playing around to both sexes, on the analogy of *representative.*

Pronouns need special handling. By constantly personifying nouns like judge, author, critic and executive with *he,* notes the National Council of Teachers of English, we subtly condition ourselves against thinking of women in those roles. One way to avoid that is to recast into the plural: "Give each student *his* paper as soon as *he* is finished" can be desexed with "Give students *their* papers as soon as *they* are finished." In the same way, "The average judge is worried about *his* opinion being overturned on appeal" can be fixed as "Most judges are worried about *their,* etc." When desperate, fall back on the space-consuming *his or her.* (Why don't we use *her or his?* Relax; it's because the *s* elides more easily than the *r.*)

Curiously, one of the hottest new words in the computer world is resolutely sexist. *Webmaster* is "one who designs, develops, markets and/or maintains one or more sites on the Internet."

According to Bill Cullifer, executive director of the World Organization of *Webmasters* (WOW) in Fulsom, California, "the word originally came from *postmaster.* The early *Webmasters* were those academics who routed electronic stuff." (*Stuff* is a big word among *Webmasters.*)

But *master,* from the Latin *magister,* "chief," has always been associated with males, especially controlling, dominant, insensitive fellows. Its female counterpart is *mistress*, sometimes pronounced "gerfren." Many of WOW's seven thousand members are women; what to do?

"At the World Wide Web conference in Australia," Cullifer says, "some guy asked why we didn't use more inclusive language. A female *Webmaster* got up and said, 'If you don't like it—too bad.'"

In your discussion of pronouns, you suggest that the following example, "The average judge is worried about his opinion . . . etc.," be replaced with "Most judges are worried about their, etc." While I am aware that your point lies with the pronoun his *versus* their, *you have changed the meaning of the entire sentence by substituting* most *for the word* average. *Average, as I understand it, means a norm representing a middle point, while* most *changes the meaning of the sentence to one of quantity rather than value.*

Roz Goldstine
Beverly Hills, California

GETTING IT RIGHT

At the embattled White House . . . (Stop there. *Embattled* now means "under attack, being assailed," with the feisty connotation of "engaged in battle"; *beleaguered*, rooted in the Old English *leger*, "camp, bed, lair," means "besieged, blockaded, surrounded, beset by foes" and is more defensive than embattled. Its first use was by John Milton in his *Areopagitica:* "In defense of *beleagured* truth.")

Start again. At the beleaguered White House, Joseph Lockhart, a spokesman for President Clinton, lectured hectoring reporters with "I understand the competitive pressure that everybody is under, but I do think it's a significant lowering of standards when getting it first supersedes getting it right."

This was an allusion to a journalistic adage that was taken up in the 1940s by *Hearst's International News Service:* "Get it first, but first get it right."

In 1950, Seymour Berkson, then president of INS, told a young interviewer from the *New York Herald Tribune* that he had made that motto the guiding light of his agency. Accordingly, the reporter handed in his copy with a picture of Mr. Berkson attached and the suggested caption: "Berkson of the INS: 'Get it first, but first get it right.'"

At the same time, the cub also handed in a profile and picture of Min-
nie Guggenheimer, the beloved impresario of concerts at Lewisohn Sta-
dium in New York. Unfortunately, the pictures mixed themselves up, and
the article about the stern Mr. Berkson appeared under a picture of the
grinning Mrs. Guggenheimer. That might have gone relatively unno-
ticed but for the caption about accuracy.

As the papers hit the street near midnight, the reporter received his
first and only call from Helen Rogers Reid, owner of the *Herald Tribune*.
The redoubtable dowager was a good friend of both Guggenheimer and
Berkson, who did not look alike and who both had awakened her in high-
dudgeoned protest. The cub reporter and the night editor were told to
stop the presses, replate (at considerable cost) and never to forget the second part of the motto.

I was that cub and found a message from the composing room on my
typewriter the next morning: "Get It Last and Get It Wrong." That lesson has been impressed on my mind ever since, and I was pleased to see it
cited, in its original form, in the press room at the White House nearly a
half-century later.

GIMME THE OL' WHITE SHOE

"She is a lawyer in a white-shoe firm," wrote Randy Kennedy in *The New
York Times* about Tiffany Palmer, an attorney at a prestigious law firm.

In *The American Lawyer* last month, Jim Schroeder quoted an unidentified recruit who described the Chicago firm of Kirkland & Ellis as "hip
people of the 90s who have shed the old stuffy *white-shoe law* firm attitude
for an open, work-hard-and-play-harder lifestyle." That footwear modifier is not limited to law firms. "Price Waterhouse typically is considered
a conservative, *white-shoe* type firm," said Suzanne Verity of *Public
Accounting Report*, "while Coopers & Lybrand is more on the cutting
edge." And in 1990 the *Independent* of London asked, "Is Michael Milken
the victim of a vengeful plot by the *white-shoe* boys of the securities business, all those nice Harvard graduates in loafers who sit in the more conventional brokerage houses?"

You can track it back in print to the mid-70s. Here's a 1975 usage from
Forbes magazine quoting a syndicate operator, the first use I can find of
the compound adjective: "The flies go where the honey jar is. Every con
man and every *white-shoe* man in the world is there trying to tap Middle

East money!" A year later, *Business Week* wrote: "First Boston had let its *white-shoe* image and big-name client list go to its head. They simply vegetated."

What does it mean? The *Oxford English Dictionary* defines *white-shoe* as "slang (chiefly U.S.), effeminate, immature," but those great lexicographers just don't get it on this one. The word is better defined in *Webster's New World Dictionary* as "designating or characteristic of a business company, esp. a law firm or brokerage, in which the partners belong almost exclusively to the WASP upper-class elite and are thought of as being cautious and conservative."

The source is white "bucks," the casual, carefully scuffed buckskin shoes with red rubber soles and heels worn by generations of college men at Ivy League schools. Many of these kids, supposedly never changing their beloved footgear, went on to become masters of the universe on Wall Street and in the best-known law firms.

In its early days, the adjective was used in an envious, resentful way by those with less-privileged backgrounds; now it is either a dispassionate description of elitism or a passionate derogation of old-fogeyism. However, some of the nouveau-riche derogators of the old-line firms are classed by a different and more expensive shoe, the loafer with a brass link ornament made by the Gucci firm in Italy. In Washington, K Street, where many lobbyists make their headquarters, is known as "Gucci Gulch."

Many women think of white shoes in another sense. "It used to be simple," writes Diane Lacey Allen in *The Lakeland* (Florida) *Ledger.* "Labor Day rolled around and the white shoes went to the back of the closet." In San Francisco, Julie Hinds writes in the *Examiner:* "Everyone wants to typecast the tourists as a bad-shirt and white-shoes-after-Labor-Day crowd." Letitia Baldrige, author of *More Than Manners,* informs me that stepping out in white shoes between Labor Day and Easter would be a faux pas, "except, of course, if you lived in Florida or a tropical climate and it was hot. If it was cold in Florida, then no." Ivory is O.K.

A lesson can be drawn from this that goes beyond linguistics: Never appear in white buckskin footwear at an egalitarian office party, especially after Labor Day.

In the USN, white shoe refers to those personnel, especially officers, whose administrative and strategic responsibilities are fulfilled on the upper decks, while black shoe *refers to below-deck personnel, particularly those with engine room responsibilities.*

Peter Piven
Philadelphia, Pennsylvania

In the early 50s, friends of mine and I picked up from somewhere a bit of verbal play which involved categorizing almost everything and everyone as shoe *(short for buck shoe) or* unshoe. *As new alumni of an Ivy League university, we obviously considered being* shoe *a compliment.*

I remember that in clothing, button-down shirts, striped ties and gray flannel suits with narrow lapels were shoe. *Anything less conservative was* unshoe. *The Ivy League and kindred schools were by definition* shoe. *State colleges were definitely* un. *Professional careers were generally* shoer *than business ones.* Shoe *people were confident and casual,* unshoes *insecure and overeager.*

We grew up and less smug, of course, but for a short time, with our whole adult lives before us, we felt unafraid, undefeatable, immortal and very, very shoe.

Winifred G. Newman
New York, New York

With respect to lawyers' expensive shoes, the reference I have seen more is "tasseled loafers."

Daniel Knight
Philadelphia, Pennsylvania

GLOBALITY

Globalization was a hot word at the World Economic Forum in Davos, Switzerland. Forget it; the world has passed it by. This year's theme was "Responsible *Globality.*"

Coinage was attributed to Daniel Yergin, author of *The Commanding Heights* (appropriate reading in a ski village), who wrote in the May 18, 1998, *Newsweek,* "We are now beginning to see a reality beyond *globalization*—the world of *globality.*"

Reached in Boston, Yergin further explained the term: "What bothered me about *globalization,*" he said, "was that it describes a process. We needed a word to carry it into a state of being. *Globality* suggests a condition of community and interconnection."

Few feelings are as exhilarating as the thrill of coinage. Some unknown diplomat involved in the normalization of relations smacked his forehead one day and cried, "I've got it—we've reached *normality!*" Someday, a soldier denied fraternization with the local girls will long in print for *fraternality*, an uncoined word to shorten the equally sexist "brotherhood of Man."

Globality is not yet in the dictionaries, though it will be sooner rather than whenever. But sorry, Dan, coinage cannot be claimed; somebody almost always crops up to claim first use of a noun formed from a common adjective.

The correspondent Frank Gervasi wrote in 1943 of "a sense of the *globality* of the war." The Merriam-Webster files also turn up "even in 1942 a final obstacle to complete *globality* remained," in the 1942 *Global War*, by Edgar Ansel Mowrer and Marthe Rajchman. Econometricians liked it, too: Kiyoshi Kuga observed in the July 1972 *Econometrica* that "the problem of *globality* is always important in this topic" of the factor-price equalization theorem, my copy of which does not come readily to hand.

But cheer up, Dan; aside from a 1988 use by an explicator of a papal encyclical (a holy ghostwriter?) and a few murmurings by Eurocrats, *globality* was awaiting a push. Yergin was the unchallenged popularizer in its current politico-business sense. Globalization, panting, has at last arrived; here we are in a state of doggy-dog *globality*.

GO FIGURE

The editorialist at *The New York Times* was scratching his head in unabashed puzzlement at the conflicts within the Reform Party.

Donald Trump, the real-estate tycoon campaigning from his penthouse suite, was the favorite of Governor Jesse Ventura of Minnesota—a free trader—while the protectionist Ross Perot tacitly supported Pat Buchanan. Meanwhile, the liberal actor Warren Beatty had been making noises about seeking the party nomination as a way of pressuring the Democrats to move leftward.

"To borrow a phrase from those younger voters the Reformers are trying so desperately to attract," noted the *Times*, "go figure."

That phrase is indeed attracting youthful usage as a result of its popularization on recent TV situation comedies. It is borrowed from the Yiddish *gey rekhn*, literally, "go reckon," meaning "go and figure it out."

"In English, two verbs would normally be linked by *and*, as in 'go and eat something,'" says Sol Steinmetz, who has stepped into the late Leo Rosten's shoes as my maven in this fertile linguistic area. "But Yiddish immigrants early on dropped the conjunction *and* from English imperative constructions and would say, for example, 'go eat something,' translating *gey es epes*."

That is why we do not say, in English, "go and figure." But where does the *figure* come in? "The Yiddish *gey rekhn* may originally have been used in trade, meaning 'go figure out how much it will cost.' Then it came to be used metaphorically in English in the sense of 'I can't figure it out—can you?'"

Rosten considered it a variation of *gey vays*, "go know," which also means "How could anybody be expected to know that?" But *go figure* has the more specific sense of feigned helplessness in the face of contradiction, accompanied by a shrug, a spread of hands with upturned palms and a sigh: "There is no rational explanation for this anomaly." Few short phrases encompass such graphic expression of exasperated wonderment.

Among those that do are several also derived from Yiddish. *Bite your tongue (bays dir di tsung)* means "pray that what you just said doesn't come true." The gloater's favorite, *Eat your heart out (es dir oys s'harts)*, means "be jealous, see if I care." The emphatic *Enough already! (genug shoyn)* has become as much a part of the English language as *Look who's talking! (kuk nor ver s'ret)*.

But consider this: In the past half-century, the proportion of Jews in the U.S. population has dropped from 5 percent to 2½ percent. The number of Yiddish speakers, a tiny portion of those, has declined precipitously. And yet, Yiddishisms (*Big deal! For sure! I'll give you a for-instance—money, shmoney!*) flowing into mainstream English have proliferated. They are now such a part of the American lingo that it's easy to attribute them to "younger voters."

Go figure.

Figurati! *("Imagine that!") is a common Italian expletive, second person singular present imperative of the verb* figurasi—figurare a se, *which is not reflexive, but rather uses the pronominal particle, deriving, as in English obviously, from* L. figura, *in turn from* fingo, *as* finxi, fictum, fingere, *meaning to fashion, imagine, conceive, invent, devise, etc. (which leads us on to* fictio, factor, fictrix, fictilis, fictura *and their English cognates), all of which you probably know.*

At any rate, friends and I will occasionally exchange words in Italo-Anglo speech, in particular "figure thyself" which, of course, is an improper translation of figurati *(a more proper translation would be "imagine—create—for thyself"). Anyhow, it is our version of "go figure" as it indeed is for Italians.*

Michael Billingsley
Rome, Italy

THE GOVERNESS

"Au Pairs Are Not Nannies, Care Givers Insist."

There was a *New York Times* headline that covered the linguistic waterfront. It had to do with the trial of Louise Woodward, the young British woman who was convicted in Massachusetts of manslaughter in the death of a baby she was hired to watch.

The reporter, Sara Rimer, explained that the French term, *au pair,* "is the designation for young foreigners who are brought to this country under a program overseen by the United States Information Agency—a cross between a cultural exchange and a relatively low-cost child-care service."

A Concord, Massachusetts, reader extended the definition: "*Au pair* is an abbreviation of *'etre au pair dans une maison,'* which the French dictionary Larousse defines as 'free board and room without salary.' Therefore, young women who take care of children and receive a salary in addition to free room and board are not *au pairs.*" The term originated in 1897 to mean one who entered a European school to teach English while learning French or German.

Time magazine entered the synonymy dodge with a more current differentiation: "Americans tend to use the terms *'au pair'* and *'nanny'* interchangeably, but there is a difference. *Nannies* are formally trained in child care and are paid upwards of $300 a week. *Au pairs* (the term roughly translates as 'equal' in French) are teenagers who receive small salaries and expect to be treated as quasi family members in exchange for some housework and child care."

An *au pair* is thought of as a young person, from late teens to mid-twenties, who is given an "allowance" or stipend similar to that given a dependent youth in a family. A *nanny* is older and is more often considered a domestic employee—a professional instructor as well as a minder. The name comes from the pet name of a person named Ann; perhaps some English child in the late eighteenth century had a governess of that name. A. E. Newdigate-Newdegate (who apparently was involved in a dispute about the spelling of the family name) published in 1898 a letter written by Lady Newdigate a century before: "Nanny Ashcroft got me ye most delightful & perfect Warm Sea Bath last night . . . after wch I ate my Bason of Milk & went to Bed." The most famous Nanny, spelled *Nannie*, was the British Mary Poppins, a fictional creation of Pamela L. Travers in 1934.

In our time, *nannies*—especially the British women who came to eastern United States cities to take charge of children of well-to-do families—became known as members of the *nanny mafia*, on the analogy of the "Irish Mafia," an affectionate description of intensely loyal aides in the Kennedy White House. At the beginning of the Clinton administration, the discovery that two prospective nominees for attorney general had employed domestics without proper documents was dubbed *Nannygate*.

Women in this set used to be called *governesses*, a word coined in 1483 about a king who made his daughter "maystresse and gouvernesse of moo than two hondred Vyrgyns." That challenging task was later reduced to caring for children in a single family by a woman often derogated for her stern visage. "I think good looks are rather out of place in a *governess*," wrote Mary Hawker in *Mademoiselle Ixe* in 1890; a generation later, the French author Colette wrote: "I look like a molting bird. I look like a *governess* in distress."

This unfair physical characterization of *governesses* helped cause the term to fall into disuse; that, and the resistance of children to governance. The replacement ranged from the 1937 *baby sitter* (young person hired to "mind" children but not to instruct them) to the more professional *nursemaid* for taking care of infants.

Then *care* took over. In *The New Yorker* last month, Stacy Schiff, writing of "the stranger who is looking after your children," toured the horizon: "Enter the *nanny*, the *baby sitter*, the *au pair*, the *child-care provider*, the *nonbiological care giver."* (*New York Times* style is two words, *care giver.*) Lisbeth B. Schorr, author of *Common Purpose* (Doubleday), a shibboleth-shattering take on ways to strengthen families, devotes a chapter to *child protection*, a more active form of care.

How do you advertise creatively for someone who shuns labels to look after your kids? Wanted: *duenna* or *amah.* . . .

GRAMPS/GRANDPA/GRAMPA

"Dear *Grampa*" is the title of a chapter in Rabbi Steven Z. Leder's uplifting book *The Extraordinary Nature of Ordinary Things.* The ordinary thing that gets to me is the extraordinary disconnect between the spelling and the pronunciation of what we call our parents' fathers.

Most adults think they are saying *grandpa* when the sounds they make are *granpa* without the *d*. Most children, who use the word more often, say *grampa*, changing the *n* to *m*, which comes more easily before the *p*. (The dental *n* conflicts with the labial *p*, as Professor Peter Suber, a philosopher and semanticist at Earlham College in Indiana has shown, and it alters to *m*. *Amp* is easy; *anp* takes much too much effort.)

The first use I can find is attributed to Nelly Custis in 1799. George Washington's granddaughter was reported by a visitor to Mount Vernon to cheer up "the General, whom she always calls *Grampa*." The happiest use is in a 1957 poem by Ogden Nash: "How confusing the beams from memory's lamp are/One day a bachelor, the next a *grampa*."

I say it's time to spell the informal word the way it sounds: *grampa*. Got that, *gramps?* (All previous written usages are grandfathered.)

GREAT MOMENTS IN MOMENTS

"I'm always afraid I'm going to have a *senior moment*," jokes Hildegarde Mahoney of Palm Beach, Florida. She is quoted using this locution in *The Longevity Strategy: How to Live to 100 Using the Brain-Body Connection*, by David Mahoney* and Richard Restak, M.D., and her meaning is that she has forgotten something and figures that's evidence of growing older.

Dick Dougherty, columnist for the *Rochester Democrat and Chronicle*,

---

*David Mahoney, the creative philanthropist of the Dana Foundation and my longtime friend, died on May 1, 2000.

first reported the use of "I'm having a *senior moment*" in an article last year and says his source was a banker on vacation: "He said he heard it used in a geezer tennis match in Florida when one of them couldn't remember the score."

There are other *moments*. "For most photographers," John Hesketh told the *Los Angeles Times* in 1991, "the camera lets them know when an exposure is done. I have to feel it. That's a certain *Zen moment* for me." Five years later, *Newsweek* wrote: "Every athlete knows the feeling. The ball looks bigger. The game slows down. They have different names for it, of course: the zone, flow, harmony, the *Zen moment*."

John and Adele Algeo defined *Zen moment* in the summer 1997 issue of *American Speech* as a "state of altered consciousness in a sport when the athlete has a sense of wholeness with the activity and consequently of confidence and success." The association of *moment* with Zen Buddhism is rooted in *satori*, a Japanese word for "enlightenment," which can come as a sudden epiphany, as when the quarterback inexplicably senses a blitz and audibilizes a draw.

But there is another sense. When Barbra Streisand cooed about the tennis star Andre Agassi: "He plays like a Zen master. It's very *in the moment*," I mistakenly assumed she meant "up to date, *au courant*." Alan Alda set me straight: "You have to be acquainted with the concept of acting *moment to moment*. When you are playing a scene, you don't bring a predetermined attitude on stage. You don't pretend to be listening, you listen. You stay *in the moment*." That means, I think (not just think; I have this blinding flash of insight), that a *Zen moment* can be one disconnected from past and independent of future, just slam-dunk in the present.

Wait a minute. When did *moment's* time come? Maybe with the Spanish *el momento de la verdad*, which Ernest Hemingway translated as *moment of truth* in his 1932 book, *Death in the Afternoon*. Then in 1983, Howell Raines of *The New York Times* was the first to use *defining moment* in print, which captured the public fancy for more in-the-moment moments of truth and turned out to be the turning point for the word.

It spawned the *Maalox moment*. After the stock market mini-crash in 1987, the Rorer Group, manufacturers of the antacid, sent a man to Wall Street dressed as a Maalox bottle and wearing a T-shirt saying, "I'm having a *Maalox moment!*" Grey Advertising followed with a memorable television ad: a father, sitting in an overstuffed chair and eating an overstuffed sandwich, was introduced to his daughter's date—a fellow wearing punk clothes and sporting a large earring. The father was described as suffering from a period of heartburn suitable for the taking of the product.

That led to *Kodak moment*. Burt Manning, chairman emeritus of J. Walter Thompson, recalls that the phrase was used by customers in the late 80s and in 1992 was picked up for use by the ad agency to describe the customer's emotional need to take a picture at the right time. Last month, *Newsweek's* article about the corporate reign of Kodak's CEO, George Fisher, was headlined "Four Years of *Kodak Moments.*"

Recently, a television actress playing a ditzy-dame role said, "I'm having a *blonde moment.*" (What was the name of the show that illustrated the latest example of analogical word formation? Can't tell you; I'm having a *senior moment.*)

In Maine I heard "mature moment." It's more alliterative (a mature moment in Maine) and more euphonious than "senior." Who told me this? I forgot.

Norman F. Wesley
Pittsburgh, Pennsylvania

THE GREAT OBNUBILATOR

"Did you hear the President's answer on Russia?" a reporter asked the White House press secretary Mike McCurry at his daily briefing. "Sure did," he replied. The journalist, puzzled, said, "I couldn't tell whether he said that the Duma had to ratify Start II before he would go to Russia or—"

"He *obnubilated*," McCurry said coolly, "just the way I did yesterday."

Nobody demanded an explanation of the word, suggesting that everyone in the pressroom was familiar with it or was too shy to ask. Not me; I looked it up to find the Latin *obnubilare*, "to cover with clouds or fog." The only citation in my handy-dandy Dow Jones database is in the word column by James J. Kilpatrick, "The Writer's Art," reviewing a book by Eugene Ehrlich titled *The Highly Selective Dictionary for the Extraordinarily Literate*. "I intend to put in my album such collector's items as *patulous* (spreading, open, gaping) and *obnubilate* (cloud over, darken, obscure)," my brother Kilpo writes.

Apparently the press secretary is a reader of Ehrlich's elitist dictionary, or is a fan of Kilpatrick's delicious column, or—most fittingly for one working in his beclouded state—has been perusing Robert Burton's 1621 *Anatomy of Melancholy:* "So doth this melancholy vapour *obnubilate* the mind."

GREENFIELD, MEG

Mary Ellen Greenfield—her initials spelled the acronym MEG, which became the first name she was known by—died at 68. The *Washington Post* editorialist and *Newsweek* columnist, a Pulitzer Prize winner and later a Pulitzer board member, was long an inspiration to every opinionmonger in the nation. She was suitably eulogized by journalists and political figures for her incredibly good sense and zero tolerance for hypocrisy and pomposity.

Because Meg was often a secret source of "On Language," a word is in order here about her love of the political lingo. At a time when Washington colloquies were endangered by an outbreak of *watershed,* she drew a bead on that vogue word and effectively blasted it out of the shallow water of pretentious discourse. When, in 1968, *Newsweek* compounded the cliché with "a *watershed* in the quagmire," she responded with "I have become an incurable, even obsessive collector of printed *watersheds,* of which I believe I now have the best collection in town—*watersheds* perching on escalation ladders, *watersheds* embedded in arms spirals, *watersheds* wrapped (like chicken livers, perhaps) in an enigma. It is not, however, an expression I would dare to use myself. I came to that drainage basin two years ago and paddled left, into the sunset."

It was a turning point. She did the same thing to *virtually,* the cop-out modifier, and to *crossroads,* the pothole in the path of every headline writer. Miss Greenfield (no Ms. for Meg) insisted that words be used to transmit clear meaning, and rejected those that confused the reader or diffused her focus.

We shared a taste for arcane puns. A generation ago, in an article about the Palestine Liberation Organization and its leader, I used the title "That's My Baby" and wondered if someone, somewhere would catch the dim allusion. Silence for a day. Then in came the call from Meg, singing in her sweetly rasping voice: "Yassir, that's my baby. No sir, don't mean maybe."

It pained Meg not to be outrageous enough to do the same above her editorials. Though she may have been the first to consider "Between Iraq and a Hard Place" in a headline, she felt that the dignity of her editorial page would not permit really deep groaners. When her deputy Stephen Rosenfeld addressed a difficulty being faced in a Latin American republic, she called me to pass along his rhyming bilingual encapsulation: "Tsoris in Honduras." (She called again to object to my spelling of the Yiddish word for "trouble"; her version is *tsouris*, closer to Honduras.) And when Bhagwan Shree Rajneesh was arrested for some wrongdoing, Meg had the forgiving headline in type but could not bring herself to run it. So she passed it on to me: "Let Bhagwans Be Bhagwans."

Those of us in the world of words knew the little lady of towering stature to be serious and funny, astringent and wise. She leaves a void.

Tsoris is Litvac.
Tsouris is Galitziane.

Jerome Woods
New Hyde Park, New York

GUILT BY ASSOCIATION

A somewhat inflammatory phrase—one charged with political overtones—was used by President Clinton in defending the clemency he granted to a score of long-imprisoned Puerto Rican nationalists.

"None of them, even though they belonged to an organization which had espoused violent means," the President told a news conference, "none of them were convicted of doing any bodily harm to anyone. . . . And because I did not believe they should be held in incarceration, in effect *by guilt by association.*"

The phrase, popularized in what is sometimes recalled as "the McCarthy era," means "an unfair technique of an accuser to contaminate an innocent person with the wrongdoing of a friend or colleague." It is a specific type of *smear.* One charged with *guilt by association* is not guilty of a crime and is indeed a victim of unscrupulous accusers. One charged with using *guilt by association* is seen as an oppressor; the phrase has long been an effective verbal weapon used in counterattacks against investigators, prosecutors and muckrakers.

Who coined it? The earliest citation in the *Oxford English Dictionary* is from a 1942 book by the Harvard Law School professor Zachariah Chafee (uncle of Rhode Island senator John Chafee): "The doctrine of *guilt by association* is abhorrent."

However, the indefatigable legal phrasedick Fred Shapiro, editor of the *Oxford Dictionary of American Legal Quotations*, searched the Westlaw database and found a 1922 decision by Illinois chief justice Floyd E. Thompson. In affirming the conviction of thirty-nine members of the Communist Labor Party (the famed lawyer Clarence Darrow represented some of those convicted), Thompson wrote: "We do not wish to be understood as approving the principle of *'guilt by association,'* because it is not in harmony with American ideals. A fundamental principle of American jurisprudence is that 'guilt is personal.'"

Shapiro up at Yale says that Thompson's use of quotation marks suggests an earlier coinage. Thanks to the JSTOR database of scholarly publications, which Syracuse University lets me access, I am zeroing in on a 1920 decision by Federal Judge George Weston Anderson in a case of deportation of Communists. According to David Williams, in the December 1981 *Journal of American History*, that judge turned to the Harvard law professors Felix Frankfurter and the above-mentioned Zack Chafee to serve as friends of the court. In Anderson's Brookline, Massachusetts, home, the two professors helped draft the opinion. In historian Williams's maddening paraphrase: "*Guilt by association*, he declared, had no place in American society and ran counter to all Anglo-American legal traditions."

GYPSY RUN-THROUGH

"I recall the *Music Man gypsy run-through*," writes Stuart Ostrow in his new book, *A Producer's Broadway Journey*. He defines the phrase as "a private performance of a new musical attended by the cast members' family and friends on the last day of rehearsals before the out-of-town tryout." *Run-through*, or "hasty rehearsal," was coined by P. G. Wodehouse in his 1923 *Inimitable Jeeves*. And *gypsy* was defined in the 1973 *Language of Show Biz* as "a chorus member in a musical," specifically a dancer. But *gypsy run-through* was a new one to me, so I called Professor Ostrow at the University of Houston.

I knew the origin of *gypsy*—"Egyptian"—but was gypsy dancing the metaphoric source of calling members of a chorus line *gypsies?* No. "Bob

Fosse once told me," Ostrow said, "that dancers are the best soldiers. You tell them to jump into the orchestra pit, and they ask only, 'How many counts?' We call dancers *gypsies* because *gypsies* are known for always moving from place to place—and a dancer has to be constantly on the move." Real *Gypsies* rightly resent the use of the verb to *gyp* as an ethnic slur, but mobility is no derogation, and I wish I had a dancing relative to invite me to a *gypsy run-through*.

HAIR-RAISING FUND-RAISING

LANNY J. DAVIS, erstwhile White House senior spinmeister, used his favorite modifier: "We understand that the military office . . . may have *inadvertently* neglected to photocopy the first two sheets."

The hot word at the White House is *inadvertent*. The root is the Latin *vertere*, "to turn"; to *advert* is "to turn to," and an *advertisement* is a message to turn one's attention to. An *inadvertence*, contrariwise, is the result of a turning away of attention leading to what is invariably described as "an honest mistake."

The synonym of *inadvertent* is "accidental," but no government likes to use that word too often; the synonym of the noun *inadvertence* is the dread "oversight," a Janus word that means both "an innocent error" and "a bunch of slavering congressmen on a witch-hunt." (A favorite verb of mean-spirited pundits is *animadvert*, adding a snarling animus to the turning-to, meaning "to note with a sneer.")

A campaign finance scandal has at last turned up one of the great words in the lexicon of graft. Representative Dan Burton, former chairman of the House Committee on Government Reform and Oversight, fixed his sights on a "rather mysterious figure who had ties to Charlie Trie, the Lippo Group and John Huang. He was apparently the *bagman*."

A *bagman*, in underworld parlance, is "one who carries the *boodle*, or money, from the beneficiary of a corrupt deal to the grafter." First spotted in 1928, *bagman* was accurately defined as a New York criminal term by London's *Sunday Times* in 1952: "A *bagman* is one who administers the collection of graft money from either the underworld or the business world and its subsequent distribution among politicians and civil servants."

Though the carrier of the sack of cash from payoffer to payee is not as seriously culpable as his clients, the word, in both masculine and feminine form, is libelous; when the Harlem congressman Adam Clayton Powell labeled as a *bagwoman* a person he thought was a courier in the policy racket, she sued for libel and was awarded damages. (A *bag lady*, who lives in a doorway with her belongings in a large bag, has no course of legal action for being so called; even so, it is safer to refer to her as a *street person.*)

Finally, to a word carefully chosen by the former attorney general, Janet Reno. After she had been humiliated by being among the last to learn of the existence of White House videotapes of fund-raising coffees, she entered a news conference with a characterization of her reaction clearly in mind: "I was *mad,*" she said in answer to the anticipated question.

Mad, from the Old English *gemaedde*, has at least three senses: (1) "crazy," as in "Mad King Ludwig" of Bavaria; the diarist Samuel Pepys wrote in 1664 of a "*mad* freaking fellow" (which was probably the origin of *freaked out*), or (2) "wildly foolish," as in General (Mad Anthony) Wayne, who earned his sobriquet because of imprudent actions during the American Revolution, but who later became the father of America's Regular Army, or (3) "angry," from the Latin *angere*, "to strangle," first used by Chaucer in 1386, to mean "aroused to a state of ire." Its use in that sense in American politics was best exemplified by a family slogan attributed to the Kennedys, "Don't get mad; get even."

A week after the Attorney General said she had been *mad*, in the confines of a "greenroom" before a television appearance, I had the opportunity to ask Ms. Reno—"Mad Janet," as old fogies with memories of Mad Anthony promptly dubbed her—why she chose that particular word, a selection obviously premeditated.

"*Angry* is two syllables," said the nation's waste-not, want-not chief law-enforcement officer. "*Mad* is one. One is better."

HAMLET ENTERS WHITEWATER

The ghost of a melancholy Dane strode upon the Whitewater stage this month.

The audience will recall President Clinton's agreement with a question about whether he thought the independent counsel Ken Starr was out to get him: "Isn't it obvious?" countered the President. Starr believed that such public talk was a signal from Clinton to Susan McDougal to continue to resist testifying before a grand jury.

Such comments, the prosecutor wrote to the White House counsel

Charles Ruff, amounted to "a president publicly indicating his essential agreement with a convicted felon's asserted reason for her continuing contumacious behavior."

Alas, poor counsel: Starr was guilty, along with most commentators, of redundancy in *convicted felon.*

A *felony* is a crime long thought to be more serious than a *misdemeanor.* The root, *fell,* is a Latin noun for "gall"; one filled with *fell* is consumed by bitterness, envenomed by wickedness and hatred. As an English adjective, as in "one *fell* swoop" of a hawk, it means "cruel."

A *felon* is a person who has committed a *felony.* (Shakespeare's Paris tells Romeo he plans to "apprehend thee for a *felon.*") But you cannot call someone a *felon,* or even a lesser *criminal,* based on your own belief, unless you want to invite a libel suit (or in Paris's case, a sword). To be identifiable as a *felon,* the wrongdoer must first be convicted of a *felony,* having been found guilty or having admitted guilt.

Thus, *convicted felon* is redundant. It says "convicted convicted of a felony," which is as tautologous, pleonastic and repetitive as *revert back, general consensus, safe haven* and *sworn affidavit.* (Kill *tautologous* and *pleonastic;* they're repetitive.) Such usage treats the reader as an uneducated oaf unaware that an *affidavit* must be sworn and that the essence of a *haven* is safety. Strike out all such unnecessary padding. (And because *padding* in this sense is "unnecessary verbiage," lose *unnecessary.*)

But hark! What term doth our Redundant Counsel use to describe Susan McDougal's behavior? The perfect word: *contumacious.*

The Latin *contumax,* "insolent, obstinate; insultingly contemptuous," was first used by Chaucer in 1386 to describe one "against every authority."

And here comes Hamlet to bestride the stage, in the soliloquy that begins "To be, or not to be," listing the burdens of life: "For who would bear the whips and scorns of time,/Th' oppressor's wrong, the proud man's *contumely.*"

At the same time those words were written, Richard Hooker in *The Laws of Ecclesiastical Polity* used the adjective: "*Contumacious* persons which refuse to obey their sentence." Nathaniel Hawthorne, in his 1859 journals, observed, "*Contumacious* prisoners were put to a dreadful torture."

The word is defined in the *OED* as "stubbornly perverse, insubordinate, rebellious," and specifically in law: "willfully disobedient to the summons or order of a court."

Just as *convicted felon* is to be treated as a no-no in all cases, *contumacious felon* is indisputably apt in this case. (Hamlet, having denounced "the proud man's *contumely*," went on to complain in what now seems to be an evenhanded way about "the law's delay,/The insolence of office.")

I'm surely not the first to point out that the column "Hamlet Enters Whitewater" has a gaffe in it (I almost said "bad gaffe," but that would be like "convicted felon"). The noun corresponding to contumacious *is* con-tumacy—*not Hamlet's* contumely.

True, the words appear to be etymologically related, but you have to go back pretty far. Please don't think me contumelious in pointing this out.

Bryan A. Garner, Editor
Black's Law Dictionary
Dallas, Texas

HAMLET CONT'D:
SQUAD SQUAD STRIKES AGAIN

IN DEFENDING the mother tongue from redundancies, often at the behest of readers organized into "the Squad Squad," I recently hooted at the use of *convicted felon* (a person is not a felon until convicted of a felony) and *sworn affidavit* (which is a "written declaration upon oath" akin to *affiance*, "to pledge one's troth" to a cohabitant once known as a fiancée).

A *felon* is still a "convict," but Joseph Restifo, a lawyer in Philadelphia, sends me this selection from the *Pennsylvania Rules of Civil Procedure:* "*affidavit* . . . either (1) sworn to or affirmed before an officer authorized by law to administer oaths . . . or (2) is unsworn and . . . subject to the penalties . . . relating to unsworn falsification to authorities."

Therefore, *sworn affidavit* is no longer redundant. Remanded to usagists down the line for reversal.

Relatedly, I came across some fused words on the Internet that qualify as oxymorons: *found missing, working vacation* and—here's an unexpected one—*tight slacks*. Best is the throat-clearing oxymoron, used by lawyers for incipient felons to introduce summations to the jury: *Now, then. . . .*

Should you ever treat the subspecies trioxymoron, *I submit "Mount Desert Island."*

Michael Byrne
Media, Pennsylvania

Your final "throat-clearing oxymoron" reminds me of an oxymoronic hat-trick I heard on a tram in Edinburgh c. 1948. Some boys, playing on the platform, were addressed by the conductor, "Here, there. Now, then. Come on, get off." Try translating that into any other language than English!

Rutherford Aris
Bloomington, Minnesota

HE SAID, SHE SAID

"Americans have grown accustomed," wrote *Time*, "to weighing the word of one defendant against that of one plaintiff, the steadfast denial against the angry accusation: *he said, she said.*"

That was about the Paula Jones case. Turning to the accusation of Kathleen Willey and its denial by President Clinton, the columnist Richard Cohen compared the clash in sworn testimony to that of Anita Hill and Clarence Thomas: "Here we have the usual *he-said, she-said* differences."

That phrase now dominates the accounts of what lawyers used to call formally *material fact disputes*, and more colloquially *swearing matches*. The new form was given this extension by Susan Carpenter-McMillan, spokeswoman for Paula Jones: "It's no longer *she-said, he-said*," after the testimony of Ms. Willey and reports of the tapes made of Monica Lewinsky about Mr. Clinton, followed by his adamant denials. "It's now *she-said, she-said, she-said and he-said.*"

Let others fight their way through the maelstrom of charge and countercharge about low sex in high places; the duty of this column is to get to the bottom of the origins and development of the hot phrase.

Remember the big-band singer Marion Hutton? In 1948, she popularized the song *"He Sez, She Sez,"* by Roy Jordan. (If you have the 78 rpm record of the hit "Borscht" in your attic, it's on the flip side.) The lyric's intent was to recount a dialogue rather than a confrontation.

In 1976, a book by the sociolinguists Nancy Henley and Barrie Thorne was titled *"She Said–He Said."* They also wrote *Language and Sex: Difference and Dominance;* the phrase's meaning then dealt with what Professor Deborah Tannen, in her book *You Just Don't Understand,* later called "cross-gender discourse"—different understandings of the same words.

The idea was that when a woman says, "I have a problem at work," she means "Listen to my problem"; a man takes that same phrase to mean "Tell me how to solve the problem." That theme was picked up in the 1991 movie *He Said, She Said,* written by Brian Hohlfeld and given its title by the codirector Marisa Silver. "The phrase gained popularity during the Anita Hill–Clarence Thomas hearings," Hohlfeld recalls. "Our film was about gender differences, but now the phrase seems to be more about who is telling the truth and who isn't."

He's right. The latest meaning has nothing to do with dialogue (*he said* and then *she said*) and no longer refers to missed communication. Now the phrase most often means "testimony in direct conflict," with an implication that truth is therefore undiscoverable. That was its meaning in this October 7, 1991, account in the *Chicago Tribune* about Hill's accusation of the Supreme Court nominee Thomas for verbal impropriety: An FBI report "could not draw any conclusion because of the '*he said, she said*' nature of the allegation and denial."

Within two years the phrase popularized in the Thomas hearings found its way into judicial proceedings: "It was an error for the trial court," noted an Ohio appellate judge in a dissenting opinion, "to admit such *he said–she said* testimony."

Uniform punctuation would clarify the phrase's use as a modifier: by hyphenating the pronoun and verb on each side of the issue, we make them two units that can then be separated by a comma, which acts as a kind of referee. Treat it thus: "It's one of those classic, unresolvable *he-said, she-said* situations."

HELLMOUTH

"New York, which gave us a generation of female political superstars," wrote Gail Collins in *The New York Times Magazine*, "has turned into the *hellmouth* of women in politics."

What's a *hellmouth?* In the back of my head was Tennyson's "Charge of the Light Brigade": "Into the jaws of death,/Into the mouth of hell/Rode the six hundred." The image of the entrance to hell as the mouth of a horrifying sea monster is familiar to infernologists; the Book of Job's crocodilelike Leviathan has lips "ringed round with fearsome fangs" and "from his mouth flames leap like sparks of fire escaping."

Rudyard Kipling, in his 1891 *Tomlinson*, had the Devil taunt his hero, "Now ye wait at *Hell-Mouth Gate*," taking the word Spenser used three centuries earlier in his *Faerie Queene*. On the medieval stage in Metz, France, the mystery play employed special effects of a mechanical monster with what was called its *hellmouth* agape, sparks shooting out. Was this the derivation of my colleague's unfamiliar usage?

"*Hellmouth*, right now, comes most directly from *Buffy the Vampire Slayer*," Ms. Collins tells me, referring to the television series. "It's the place where all things evil sort of arrive on the scene."

That's a bit of an etymological letdown, but it's good to see writers for today's TV series drawing on medieval theatrical traditions. In the community of Sunnydale, the fictional "watcher" of Buffy—a high-school student with a knack for slaying the evil beings lurking at the local *hellmouth*—explains, "The Spanish who first settled the area called it Boca Del Infierno—roughly translated, *'Hellmouth,'* a sort of portal from this reality to the next."

Thanks to its rebirth in the TV series, the archaic word (it had all but abandoned hope) has returned to vogue in related contexts of horror. In the Kokomo, Indiana, *Tribune*, Todd Burlage warned: "They appear as *hell mouths* in the road and can sneak up on a driver about as subtly as a hurricane. They are potholes."

HEY, GENTLELADY

"How about letting Chairman Henry Hyde (and many other congressmen as well) know," writes G. Mackenzie Gordon of Lakeville, Connecticut, "that the correlative of *gentleman* is *lady*, not *gentlelady?*"

The use of *gentle* before *man* or *woman* has, for some six centuries, indicated noble birth or, more recently, good manners. According to Judith Martin, the syndicated "Miss Manners": "There is no such thing as a *gentlelady*. A *lady* is referred to in the third person as 'the *gentlewoman*' or 'the *lady*.'" (She notes that when used to address an individual, as in "Hey, *lady*, watch where you're going," the *lady* is less-than-respectful usage.)

Judy—an ol' pal, so I can call her that—is, as usual, correct. The only *gentle lady* I can find outside the halls of Congress is in *Macbeth*, when Macduff cries: "O *gentle lady*,/'Tis not for you to hear what I can speak:/ The repetition, in a woman's ear,/Would murder as it fell." But the two words were not joined.

Does this mean that the word does not exist? Certainly it exists: It was a favorite salutation of the chairmen Henry Gonzales and Gerald Solomon. It may not be in dictionaries, and some feminists may think its courtliness is excessive and therefore regard it as sexist, but the word is intended to be a mark of respect and is surely in the spoken language. What you cannot courteously say, however, is "Hey, *gentlelady*, watch where you're going."

HIT ON

Noah Webster, the political activist, journalist and educator who began his lexicographic career in the tempestuous Federal era, asked Basil Hall, a British naval officer, why he considered all American contributions to the English language unworthy. Hall's reply: "Because there are enough words already."

There are never enough words. That colloquy comes from a doozy of a book titled *Never Enough Words*, by Jeffrey McQuain, who has been both a researcher and an occasional bylined contributor in this space for fifteen years. (He teaches me grammar; I teach him *mavenry*. *Mavenry* is a new word, coined five seconds ago because I couldn't come up with a way to express aficionadohood, connoisseurship or state of specialized enthusiasm. Never enough.)

Interest in coinage, or neology, is closely akin to etymology, the history of coinage and semantic development. In today's future-oriented tummeling toward the millennium, you think this glance backward is *small potatoes?* McQuain points us to the first definition of that British phrase, from a Boston newspaper in 1831: "When a person is guilty of a mean action, or takes much pains to make himself ridiculous, it is often said in relation to the circumstance, '*small potatoes*—rather small potatoes, and few in a hill.'"

That led the language maven to the opposite meaning of a garden phrase, *some pumpkins* (with the gourd's name from the French *pompon*, "melon," usually pronounced *punkins*). During our Revolutionary times, *pumpkin head* insulted New Englanders obeying the Blue Laws that enjoined males to have their hair cut round by a cap. When a cap or bowl was not available, the shell of a pumpkin was used, and *pumpkin head* was a phrase of derision. With the addition in 1846 of *some*, however, the meaning was reversed, and the politicians so described were considered highly praiseworthy.

I called McQuain's book a *doozy*, meaning "a stunning example, a wow." I've speculated that its origin is in the Duesenberg automobile of the early 30s, but according to the etymologist Gerald Cohen, that word may be an alteration of *daisy*, influenced by the Italian actress Eleonora Duse early in the twentieth century (a chronological term that used to connote modernity).

Cohen, often collaborating with Barry Popik, publishes a mimeographed sixteen-page "Comments on Etymology" from the hallway outside his office at the University of Missouri–Rolla. He is a superb phrasedick, advertising for and reporting on origins of current slang expressions.

For example, *to hit on* takes the phrase *to come on to*, or "sexually approach," to an unwanted level; when a predatory male *hits on* a woman, he harasses her and she considers him a *lech* (pronounced "letch," from *lecher*, rooted in the Germanic *leckon*, "to lick"). What is the source of the expression? *Hit* in standard English is a verb meaning "strike," and in slang *hit up* has long meant "to seek a loan from," figuratively once removed from striking. But whence *hit on*?

One of Cohen's colleagues, a chemistry professor named Gary Bertrand, is a fisherman and provided a source of speculation. "If fish are nibbling or biting at the bait without taking the hook," reports Cohen, "the fisherman may say that the fish are *hitting on* the bait." Is the problem solved?

Could be. After citations come in from the Izaak Walton mavenry, we'll reopen that can of worms. Never enough words.

I first heard the term "hit on" in 1974 in the Washington bureau of NBC News. A black female coworker noticed me staring at another female coworker across the room. "Ever hit on her?" she asked. I had no idea what she was talking about. Before long she taught me what those and many other hip words I had been hearing from black Washingtonians meant.

David Ewing
New York, New York

HOLY LAND

In the course of research into the mild-mannered controversy of what to call the Bible (the designations "Old" and "New" Testaments have been running into some theological flak), I have received this compromise suggestion: *Holy Scriptures.* Jews can assume it covers the Hebrew Bible plus those scriptures that Christians consider holy; Christians, that it means the Old and New Testaments taken as one.

The compromise is rooted in the graceful way one quasi-geographical term can slip past the political passions of the Middle East. Jews call one area, including disputed territory, *Israel;* Arabs, including Muslims and Christians, call that territory *Palestine,* applying that name as well to an area many Israelis consider *Israel.*

The one phrase that seems acceptable to all is the *Holy Land,* translated from the medieval Latin *terra sancta,* and used in Shakespeare's *Richard II:* "Make a voyage to the *Holy-land.*"

The phrase is capitalized, but that does not confront the issue of whose capital is where. The title of a Muslim cleric is *Mufti of Jerusalem and the Holy Lands;* Christian tourists buy *Holy Land* tours that take them to sites administered by Israelis and Palestinians. Jews tend not to use the English phrase *Holy Land* (many say *Land of Israel*), but those words are in a Hebrew phrase, *Eretz* (Land) *Hakodesh* (Holy), perhaps derived from God's command to Moses in Exodus 3:5 of the Hebrew Scriptures, or Old Testament: "Put off thy shoes from off thy feet, for the place whereon thou standest is *holy ground.*"

More on this after I sort out the letters taking positions on B.C. (before Christ) versus B.C.E. (before the Common Era). Language is flexible; we can work these things out.

There is one appellation for the Old Testament I have not seen used and that I would like to suggest. How about calling it simply the Jewish Bible?
Mark Bender
Chappaqua, New York

HOLY FOLLOW-UP: B.C./A.D. OR B.C.E./C.E.

My claim to fame? Responsibility for the first mistake made by an earthling on an extraterrestrial body.

As a White House speechwriter, I had a hand in writing the text on the plaque marking the spot where Apollo 11 astronauts first set foot on the moon. To slip in an unobtrusive reference to God, I wrote, "July 1969 A.D." When some alien from a U.F.O. lands there in a few thousand years, it will surely know that the initials stand for the Latin *anno Domini* and get the point that our first explorers feared only God. My mistake was putting the A.D. after the date. Correct dating usage is to put B.C., "before Christ," after the year and A.D., "in the year of our Lord," before the year.

I may have goofed in more ways than one. In a recent column about what to call the Bible, I posed the question: Should it be B.C. or—in deference to Muslims, Jews and other non-Christians—B.C.E., standing for "before the Common Era"?

In the same ecumenical way, the question arises: Should A.D. or C.E., "Common Era," be used to signify the time since Jesus of Nazareth was born (in 4 B.C., for reasons of calendar error; it is not in my linguistic purview to explain)?

What a mail pull. From Professor Harold Bloom of Yale, my Bronx High School of Science classmate whose landmark book *The Western Canon* booms across the Kulturkampf battlefields: "Every scholar I know uses *B.C.E.* and shuns *A.D.*"

The shunning of *A.D.* (like the one that sits wrongly placed on the moon) goes clear up to the Supreme Court. Adena K. Berkowitz, who has both a law degree and a doctorate in Hebrew literature, applied to practice before the Court. "In the application," she wrote, "I was asked if I wished 'in the year of our Lord' to be included as part of the date listed on the certificate or omitted." She chose to omit: "Given the multicultural society that we live in, the traditional Jewish designations—*B.C.E.* and *C.E.*—cast a wider net of inclusion, if I may be so politically correct."

That application form reflects a new sensitivity in Washington; a Court spokesman said that the choice is only eleven months old. By nearly two to one, other scholars and some members of the clergy agreed with Bloom and Berkowitz. "Christians could be a little less triumphal," noted the Reverend Charles B. Atcheson, rector of All Saints Church in Waterloo, Belgium.

"Yes, the world has largely accepted the Christian calendar scheme that begins, a little inaccurately, with the birth of Jesus, but calling it 'the common era' is not a great loss and could be taken as a sign of acceptance of others. It will not be lost on anyone what happened shortly before the year 1."

Disagreement is sharp. "It is one thing to deny the divinity of Christ," observed Michael McGonnigal of Silver Spring, Maryland. "It is quite another to deny His historical existence, which is what is implied by the superfluous switch from the traditional *B.C.* to the *P.C. B.C.E.*"

David Steinberg of Alexandria, Virginia, called *B.C.E.* "a strained innovation requiring explanation in most of America." And James McInerney Jr. of Cleveland Heights, Ohio, said, "That this dating system has become accepted worldwide reflects the cultural importance of Christianity in world history."

A Muslim view from Khosrow Foroughi of Cranbury, New Jersey: "Jews and Muslims have their own calendars. Muslims have a lunar calendar reckoned from *A.D.* 622, the day after the Hegira, or flight of the Prophet Mohammed from Mecca to Medina. The Jewish calendar is also a lunar one and is the official calendar of the State of Israel. [This year is 5762.] The Christian or Gregorian calendar has become the second calendar in most non-Christian countries, and as this is the Christian calendar, I cannot see why 'before Christ' and 'in the year of our Lord' would be objectionable." Contrariwise, a leading student of Islam, John Esposito of Georgetown, said, "'Before the Common Era' is always more acceptable."

I turned to Hershel Shanks, editor of the *Biblical Archeology Review*, who helped break the scholarly monopoly on the Dead Sea scrolls. Two years ago his journal put out a delightful paperback—*Cancel My Subscription!*—with a section of letters on this controversy. As a result, the magazine let authors have their individual choice and published a careful note on style: "*B.C.E.* (before the Common Era) and *C.E.* (Common Era), used by some of our authors, are the alternative designations for *B.C.* and *A.D.* often used in scholarly literature."

Shanks told me, "It doesn't diminish the number of canceled subscriptions we get from people on both sides of the issue, but there are authors who will not allow their work to be printed unless they determine the time demarcation used."

Evidently many think *B.C.E./C.E.* is religiously neutral; others hold that the change is silly because the count remains from the birth of Jesus Christ and confuses those who think the *C* stands for *Christ* and not *Common*.

Here's my take: I'll stick with *B.C.* because *Christ*, in American usage, refers directly to Jesus of Nazareth as if it were his last name and not a title conferring Messiah-hood. For non-Christians to knock themselves out avoiding the word *Christ*, when it so clearly refers to a person from whose birth we date our secular calendar's count, seems unduly strained and almost intolerant. (If you're a tiny bit uncomfortable, just drop the periods and make it *BC*.)

A.D. is another story. *Dominus* means "lord," and when the lord referred to is Jesus, not God, a religious statement is made. Thus, "the year of our Lord" invites the query "Whose lord?" and we're in an argument we don't need.

Besides, if the year is not *B.C.*, who needs a demarcation of the year? If you're writing about the birth of Jesus, write "4 *B.C.*"; if you're writing about the year that *B.C.E.* was first used by Lady Katie Magnus, write "1881" without emendation.

I'm for giving John Glenn his wish to go to the moon (at the age of 75), provided he takes an eraser and gets to work on that plaque.

You inquired: "Should it be B.C. *or—in deference to Muslims, Jews and other non-Christians—*B.C.E., *standing for 'before the Common Era'? In the same* ecumenical *way . . ."*

Although "ecumenical" is sometimes used as a synonym for universal, it is not correct in this context. Because of the explicit reference to non-Christians, the proper term is interreligious. *In the religious context, "ecumenical" properly refers to relations among different* Christian *denominations, especially those promoting unity and cooperation. General-usage dictionaries may not refer to this distinction, but it is made by ecumenists and other religious scholars.*

Barbara A. Lee
New York, New York

Christ is precisely a "title conferring Messiah-hood." It is Greek for "the anointed one" (e.g., chrism). The Hebrew equivalent is Moshiach, *which is anglicized to Messiah. (His name was Jesus ben Joseph!)*

The term was applied, in general, to the sons of David's line who were kings of Israel. The Messiah is that one of the line who will herald the end of days.

This is another reason you should opt for B.C.E./C.E. *on this planet or elsewhere.*

Martin E. Cobern
Cheshire, Connecticut

You state that "I'll stick with B.C. *because* Christ, *in American usage, refers directly to Jesus of Nazareth as if it were his last name and not a title conferring Messiah-hood." This may be your own opinion rather than a widespread viewpoint. Without question, reference to Jesus Christ does associate with Jesus of Nazareth, yet as a last name, it is a reach. Christ is a title, bearing directly to* the *Messiah of Christian religious beliefs.*

Lawrence Levy
Houston, Texas

HOTSPUR!

"He must find a way out among moderate Republicans and Democrats," the *Times* editorialist wrote of the Senate majority leader

Trent Lott, "even if Republican *hotspurs* object."

Every dictionary worth its spurs notes that the word *hotspur* was the sobriquet of Sir Henry Percy, son of the Earl of Northumberland, killed in 1403 in the rebellion against Henry IV. (A *sobriquet* is a descriptive appellation, like Governor Jesse [the Body] Ventura, which geezers will fondly recall followed, by two generations, Marie [the Body] McDonald.) The earliest citation of *hotspur* was in a chronicle a half-century later: "Herry Percy the yonger, whom the Scottis clepid Herry Hatspore." Shakespeare then used the word in his *Henry IV*: "A haire-brained *Hotspurre*, gouern'd by a Spleene."

Tangent time: Those citations show us (1) that *Henry* led to *Harry* by way of *Herry*, or *Herry* was the progenitor of both, and (2) that the Shakespearean spelling of *haire-brained* is a source of the confusion about that word's meaning. It has nothing to do with hair found on the scalp on top of the skull that encases the brain. Rather, it is a hare, or rabbit, which was thought to have an especially small or weak brain. End of tangent.

But what is the metaphoric basis of *hotspur?* Why not *coldspur* or *hotsaddle* (as in the discomforting title of the Mel Brooks movie *Blazing Saddles*)? When an equestrian rides impetuously or cruelly, spurring his horse constantly, the spurs are seen to become hot from the friction—if not literally, at least figuratively. That's what harebrained Henry (not hairebrained Herry) did, and why they clepid, or yclept, or named him that. And that is also why profoundly literate editorialists still use *hotspur* to mean "a rash, impetuous, hard-driving person."

HOW NOW, VOYAGER

At the height of the travel season, as you look for a place to stay away from home, what do you call the business that caters to your needs?

The *hotel business* is too narrow. Thirty-four years ago the hoteliers changed the name of their association to include *motels* (coined in 1925 from "motor hotel"), but now we have places to lay your weary head from rural *bed-and-breakfasts* to luxurious *resorts*.

This need to spread out a category has produced the *lodging industry*, which includes *extended-stay lodging* (four nights or more at a place with a kitchenette) and *alternative lodging* (time-sharing arrangements and vacation condominiums). The origin of *lodge* as well as *lobby* is from the Latin for "shelter of foliage," which explains why so many hotel lobbies and atriums look like jungles today. In *The Spirit to Serve*, a new book by J. W. Marriott Jr. and Kathi Ann Brown, *lodging industry* is the preferred term, but the accompanying news release refers to Bill Marriott as a *hospitality industry* executive.

Now we're getting somewhere. The *hospitality industry*, according to Marni Dacy at the quaintly named American Hotel and Motel Association, includes both the *lodging industry* and the *gaming industry*. (Never say *gambling*, and *casino* has a sinister connotation; *gaming* sounds like fun and games.) Cornell University's School of Hotel Administration says on its Web site that it "has set the standard for hospitality management" and is "helping prepare the future leaders of the global *hospitality industry*." Florida International University in Broward County has a School of Hospitality Management.

If you're being *hospitable* (from the Latin *hospes*, "host," as are *hotel, hostel, hospitality* and *hospital*), you've got to feed the guest. Part of the *hospitality industry*, says the restaurateur-raconteur George Lang, is the *restaurant industry*. Lang—whose forthcoming autobiography, *Nobody Knows the Truffles I've Seen*, is a book to savor, relish, smack one's lips over and profoundly appreciate—includes in the *restaurant industry* everything from tablecloth manufacturers to vintners and interior designers. He cautions me, however, not to make that the *food and restaurant industry*, lest the sale of food and beverage on premises, which is the primary business of restaurants, slops over to the production and sale of food from farm to supermarket, which is the *food industry* and goes beyond what we're talking about here.

Hospitality's umbrella covers where people stay (*lodge*) and what they do there (play and eat), but not how they get there. Now you need a super-umbrella term to reach out over the method of reaching the hospitable place. *Leisure industry?* No, that huge field of determined recreation contains much that can be done at home, a place of habitation rather than lodging. The tie to, and subsumer of, *hospitality* is the *travel and tourism industry*.

We're there. The lingo of travel agents is worthy of separate study. Work is needed on the differentiation of *layover, stayover* and *stopover*; initial research from a nice lady who gives me a bagel and a schmear on the Delta shuttle suggests that *layover* is a term for a *stopover* by flight crews, but a *stayover* is a stay of any length by passengers. This department is prepared to entertain further analysis of the combining form *-over* from

5

flight attendants, formerly stewards and stewardesses, but why can't they substitute nut bread for the bagels once in a while?

Here are some neologisms culled by Thomas Wallace, editor in chief of Condé Nast's *Travel* magazine:

- *Back-to-back ticketing:* a technique business travelers use to take advantage of airline weekend fare offers. These Sneaky Petes buy two bargain round trips, each with a Saturday whatever-over, using only half of each ticket, which is cheaper than one Tuesday-to-Thursday round trip.
- *Leaf peepers:* "people whose vacations consist of seeing the country's fall foliage."
- *Open-jaw ticket:* a triangular pattern of air travel (like Toronto–London–New York) without completion of the return.
- *Affinity miles:* frequent-flier miles you get through your credit card, your long-distance telephone company or any other outfit that likes to throw a FIT, an acronym for "frequent international traveler." (*Affinity* is rooted in "related by marriage," as opposed to *consanguinity*, "related by blood." When an airline owns a hotel and the hotel offers frequent-flier miles, those should properly be called *consanguinity* miles.)
- *Red sea rig:* men's cruisewear having nothing to do with the Red Sea; a black-tie outfit worn without the jacket but with a red cummerbund.
- *Express checkout:* a columnist's quick way of leaving a subject.

The term Red Sea rig *does indeed have a reference to the Red Sea. As explained to me by British Colonial Office senior staff in the Solomon Islands forty years ago, who themselves adopted the "rig" in the evening, all such officials were expected to "dress" for dinner regardless of where they were stationed. However, even top officers refused to wear dinner jackets and black tie when in the tropics. Those serving in the British Red Sea colonies came up with the alternative of the* Red Sea rig: *tuxedo trousers and white shirt (without the tie) with the red cummerbund to offset the absence of a dinner jacket. Much more comfortable, and quite dashing in appearance.*

Judith Huggins Balfe, Professor of Sociology
College of Staten Island and Graduate Center, CUNY
Montclair, New Jersey

HOW TO BE GRUNTLED, KEMPT AND COUTH

In wordplay you can sometimes get word understanding. Phrases like "If vegetarians eat vegetables, what do humanitarians eat?" and "Why do we put suits in a garment bag and put garments in a suitcase?" have been knocking about the Internet.

Such *double-entendres* can be funny. For example, two meanings of *funny* are the basis for the line "Is it true cannibals don't eat clowns because they taste funny?" Because *season* has several meanings, we can ask, "If it's tourist season, why can't we shoot them?"

These one-liners, spuriously attributed to the word players George Carlin and Steven Wright, neither of whom claims credit, cause us to take another look at what we're saying.

The word to be examined today is treated in a similarly thought-provoking phrase: "How come you don't ever hear about *gruntled* employees?"

Those of us in the scandalmongering dodge rely heavily on "disgruntled former employees" for leaks, tips and other often-slanderous leads; in gratitude, we change their designation to the more upbeat *whistle-blower*. But they are surely in a state of disgruntlement, and the time has come to get to the bottom of the word.

It begins, as great armies and New England dessert makers do, with *grunts*. These are the short, deep, guttural sounds made by hogs, especially when eating. The word seeks to imitate the sound; a Roman farmer was probably responsible for the Latin *grunire*, "to grunt; to sound like a rooting pig or sickly cow."

Gruntle is what lexicographers call a frequentive, a verb that describes repeated or recurrent action. (Some call it "frequentative," but they need preventive, not preventative, medicine.) The frequentive of *wrest* is *wrestle*; of *prate*, *prattle*; of *spark*, *sparkle*; and the frequentive of *grunt* is *gruntle*.

The *Oxford English Dictionary* defines *gruntle* as "to grumble, murmur, complain," and cites a 1589 sermon by Robert Bruce: "It becomes us not to have our hearts here *gruntling* upon this earth."

Haynes Goddard of Cincinnati writes to suggest that the verb *disgruntle* means "to deprive of the opportunity to register dissatisfaction and complaint"—that is, to deny the release of a good, loud grunt, and thereby to make the would-be gruntler sullen. We don't know; the *OED* mysteriously lists *disgruntle* as appearing in 1682 and meaning "to put into sulky dissatisfaction or ill humor." You might think that if the old *gruntle* meant "complain," then *disgruntle* would mean "to stop from complaining," but language is not always logical.

However, thanks to a comic writer, *gruntled*—having died as obsolete—has indeed made it back into the dictionaries. P. G. Wodehouse, creator of Jeeves, wrote in his 1938 *Code of the Woosters*, "If not actually *disgruntled*, he was far from being *gruntled*." The *OED* and Merriam-Webster list that play on a word as a back-formation from *disgruntle*, and the word *gruntle* is born again—meaning "to put in a good humor."

Wodehouse has answered the comedic question. There are, indeed, *gruntled* employees. They're the ones with soaring 401(k) accounts, and those fat kittens rarely blow their whistles to scandalmongers.

While we're at it, and to save each other mail, let's look at the humorous use of *couth* and *kempt*, wordplay on *uncouth* and *ill kempt*.

As the second millennium began, *kempt* meant "combed." Such personal tidiness was not always taken to be a positive: "If a man have a *kempt* hed," John Wyclif warned young women in 1380, "thanne he is a leccherous man." (That same suspiciously slicked-down hair gave rise to the pejorative *city slicker*.) In the sixteenth century, *kempt* divided into *ill kempt* (slobs a girl could trust) and *well kempt*, as in James Joyce's *Ulysses*: "a *wellkempt* head, new-barbered" and still lecherous. Today, the seldom-used *kempt* is neutral, as if with hair hastily combed by the fingers.

Also a thousand years ago, *couth* meant "known, familiar" and *uncouth* was "unknown, foreign, strange" (as the admonition to young women later went, "uncouth, unkissed"). *Couth* faded out, but was back-formed and born again, thanks to Max Beerbohm in 1896. It was popularized in a funny line delivered by a shrewd dumb-blonde character, played by Judy Holliday in Garson Kanin's 1946 *Born Yesterday*. When criticized by her overbearing lover as uncouth, she replied, "I'm every bit as *couth* as you are!"

Thanks to the comic spirit of language, we still have *couth*, *kempt* and *gruntled*. Like a stand-up comedian on a sit-down strike, I am still working at 186,300 miles per second on the cosmological-linguistic question "So, what's the speed of dark?"

I agree with you on preventative, *but you should know that* frequentative *is still the standard term in teaching frequentative Latin verbs to Latin students.*

Don Buck
New York, New York

Speaking of Judy Holliday's persona Billie Dawn, you stated: "When criticized by her overbearing lover [Harry Brock] as uncouth, she replied, "I'm every bit as couth *as you are!"*

In fact, in the play itself, it's Billie that takes Harry apart for picking his teeth and taking off his shoes, and saying to him, "You're just—not—couth!" He responds, "I'm couther than you are!"

For some reason, in the 1950 movie, Harry responds, "I'm as couth as you are!"

Phil Wesler
Lake Worth, Florida

Your problem with the word disgruntle *(the problem being that it seems to mean pretty much the same as* gruntle) *doesn't take into consideration the pig factor. The* OED *as you quote offers a meaning of gruntling taken from Robert Bruce's sermon about people who gruntle and complain. But that's humans who do that. Or did that. Somewhere I read that the word less metaphorically applied described happy pigs rooting and eating, gruntling contentedly, and "disgruntled" was formed against that.*

Robert McCarty, S.J.
Jesuit Community
Saint Peter's College
Jersey City, New Jersey

IF TRUE

IF IS A SHORT WORD that covers several different senses: "in case that" or "granting that" or "whether." The "in case" sense is conveyed in the phrase heard so often in coverage of the Clinton sex charges: "if true."

But its wandering nature leads to ambiguity. In Robert S. Bennett's motion to advance the trial date of the Paula Jones case in light of the Monica Lewinsky firestorm, the President's attorney writes: "All the while, violations of the spirit, if not the letter, of the court's confidentiality order continue unabated."

Does the *if* in that sentence mean "although," thereby admitting that the letter of the order was not violated? Or does the *if* mean "possibly even," suggesting that the letter was likely violated as much as the spirit?

That *if* lacks precision. In coming weeks, this department will be on the alert for abuses of verbal power in this alleged wrongdoing. (*Allege*, along with *if true*, an all-purpose libel-averter, means "to assert without proof.")

IMPACTING STATUS

"You can now *status* your transfer request 24 hours a day," Fidelity Investments wrote Yvonne Freund of Bellevue, Washington. She immediately *statused* her vocabulary and wrote me, "Is this English?"

Not standard English. Rather, that new verbal status of *status* is in the jargon of finger-snapping brokerese. The purpose of making a verb out of the noun *status*, meaning "standing" or "condition," is seemingly to save space: The old way, *to learn the status of*, takes up valuable room that might be utilized for hot stock tips.

I say "seemingly" because the real purpose of most noun-verbing is to give the illusion of modernity. "This door is *alarmed*" zips along much faster than "An alarm system is affixed to this door that will make horrific noises and summon heavily armed police officers to haul you off to jail if you open it." And yet it conjures a mental picture of a door with an alarmed expression on its face, evoking a "There, there, maybe you need therapy" from passersby.

If the verb *statused* is too short-handed, and *alarmed* is ludicrous, what about *impacted?* Can you say, "That will *impact* an election" instead of "That will *have an impact on* it"?

Yes, because it has withstood the test of a generation-long derision. Remember *prioritize?* That squeezing of "give priority to" was subjected to withering fire from prescriptivists and other self-appointed guardians of good usage, and we won. When a government official uses *prioritize* today, he identifies himself as a raging bureaucrat and is hooted at by aesthetes who find that an "ugly" word. (The *-ize* do not have it.)

Impact, on the contrary, strikes me as losing its preceding *have an* and succeeding *on*. Although the past participle can be traced to 1601, purists will continue to object to any use of *impact* as a verb. My hat is off to them because they force the language change to go through a crucible, and in the case of *status* may stop its pompous-seeming verbification. But their objections do not always impact new usage.

Let's try another. "I am encouraging you to participate," wrote Donna Shalala, Secretary of Health and Human Services, pushing a departmental health outing, "by walking, running, spectating or volunteering."

Saul Rosen of Bethesda, Maryland, said, "Coinages are worthwhile only when they bring added value." (He means "when they add value.") "This one, not!"

I figuratively raced over to Health and Human Services, formerly Health, Education and *Welfare* before they spun off *Education* and before *Welfare* became a word to avoid. "My trusty Merriam-Webster Web site tells me," Secretary Shalala said, "that *spectating* is indeed a legitimate back-formation of *spectator.*" On second thought, she wished she had not used the gerund form and instead encouraged employees "to walk, run, volunteer or spectate."

I was ambivalent about *spectate* (and I'm of two minds about *ambivalent*) until I thought the new verb through in the light of *status* and *impact*.

There's no doubt that the verbal form is in the language: The *OED* has it coined in 1709. But its use has been rare, and we should apply Rosen's Value-Added Criterion. Does it supply a meaning not covered by the simple "watch" or "cheer"?

Although I like *commentate*, which has a more media-opinionated connotation than the noun and verb *comment*, I'd hold off on *spectate*. Too soon to buy in formal writing. Bears watching.

> *I was saddened to see you surrender to the verb form of* impact. *Your concession is a lost battle in the war against illiteracy.*
>
> *As an editor of Army directives, I work in a* impact *area that absorbs a continuous barrage of incoming strikes against the English language. One weapon launched by Army authors is the verb form of* impact. *Soldier-writers use it metaphorically in various forums, knowing that most of their readers have had some experience with incoming artillery and will therefore understand the impact of whatever is being said. When authors use* impact *as a verb, I challenge them by demanding qualification of the term. (After all, an impact can have positive or negative connotations.) Once the intent is understood, I usually change it to "affect" as in, "The level of risk affected the level of security." Is that not preferable to "The level of risk impacted the level of security"?*
>
> Dwayne J. Viergutz
> Heidelberg, Germany

IMPEACHMENTESE

"Even in survival," wrote Jim Hoagland of *The Washington Post*, "Clinton will emerge from this experience chastised if not chastened, humiliated if not humbled."

There is a serious challenge to synonymists by a serious foreign-affairs columnist (even though he uses the reader-friendly "Jim" in his byline, which would raise the eyebrow of a bygone era's Walt Lippmann).

Chaste is from the Latin *castus*, "pure," and *chasten* means "to make pure" by some mode of discipline, with the positive connotation of being strengthened by moral correction ("whom the Lord loveth he *chasteneth*"). *Chastise*, as well as *castigate*, comes from the Latin *castigare*, which adds the force of *-igare*, or *agere*, "to drive," to the purifying. Although both verbs mean "to correct by punishment or reproof," *chastise* adds coercion or severity to the moral instruction in *chasten*.

In the synonymy of censure, then, *punish* implies "to penalize for disobedience to authority"; the verb *discipline* suggests "to subjugate or bring under control"; *chasten* means "to strengthen by setting straight"; *chastise*, "to inflict some coercion in correction"; *correct*, "to straighten for the purpose of reform"; and *castigate*, "to tongue-lash or rebuke severely."

As I parse the subtle Hoagland, his *"chastised* if not *chastened"* means "corrected but not truly purified" or "punished but not made *chaste."*

What about *"humiliated* if not *humbled"*? If you're a gardener, you know what *humus* is: that deliciously decomposed plant or animal manure that, mixed with your backyard's flavorless dirt, gives an organic boost to the roots of your flowers. It is also the Latin word for "earth, ground" and is the root of both *humble* and *humiliate*, words that suggest the bringing of someone down to the ground, sometimes to the extent of figuratively grinding his face in the dirt.

The verb *to humble* originally meant "to make meek," as in Valentine's profession of awed affection in *The Two Gentlemen of Verona:* "O gentle Proteus, Love's a mighty lord,/And hath so *humbled* me, as, I confess, /There is no woe to his correction." Now, however, it is part of the lingo of abasement.

Merriam-Webster's Dictionary of Synonyms has an uplifting entry on *abasement.* After running through *demean* (loss of dignity), *debase* (deterioration in value) and the Pentagon's favorite new word, *degrade* ("conveys a strong implication of the shamefulness of the condition to which someone or something has been reduced"—take that, Saddam), *M-W* comes to *humble.*

"Frequently used in place of *degrade,"* synonymizes the philological hairsplitter, "in the sense of *demote* when the ignominy of the reduction in rank is emphasized . . . but often suggests a salutary increase of humility or the realization of one's own littleness or impotence." But *humiliate*, which used to be a synonym of *humble*, has gained a more forceful meaning of taking someone down: "comes closer to *mortify*, for it stresses chagrin and shame."

Therefore, when Hoagland writes that Mr. Clinton has been *"humiliated* if not *humbled,"* I think he's saying that others have *demeaned, debased, degraded* the President, but he remains neither *defeated* nor newly possessed of a sense of meekness and humility.

Whew! What a spectrum of meaning some columnists can pack in a single burst of alliteration.

IMPEACHMENTESE (CONT'D)

Great events turn unfamiliar words into household terms. Like a fish named the remora, or suckfish, which attaches itself to a whale and goes along for the exciting ride, the language maven latches on to the imposing subject and nibbles on the nourishing usages churned up in its wake.

Every schoolchild now knows the meaning of *impeach:* "to charge with misconduct," or more generally, "to cast doubt on." A few even know the Latin derivation, from *impedicare*, "to fetter, to fix shackles on the feet; to hinder." The root is *ped*, "foot," also the origin of *impede* and *impediment*. Mnemonic: The first step on the road to *impeachment* is putting your *foot* in your mouth under oath.

But less familiar words are churned up as well. Senator Daniel Patrick Moynihan regaled reporters in the Capitol corridors with a reading of *The Federalist* No. 67, by Alexander Hamilton. This Framer, a believer in "energy in the executive," derided worries about a too-powerful president and included this line: "We have been taught to tremble at the terrific visages of murdering *janizaries* and to blush at the unveiled mysteries of a future *seraglio*."

The *janizaries* were elite Turkish troops; the word now means "close aides, loyal supporters"; FDR's "brain trust" was mocked by Republicans as "the *janizariat*." *Seraglio*, spelled with two *r*'s in Italian, originally meant "Turkish palace" but came to mean "harem." Edward Gibbon wrote in his 1776 *Decline and Fall of the Roman Empire* that the emperor Commodus spent his hours "in a *seraglio* of 300 beautiful women." Hamilton was exaggerating the fears of a monarchic presidency, and Moynihan was deriding the interest in Oval Office goings-on as the salacious search for a harem, or *seraglio*.

Another Italian word, *imbroglio*, "a confused entanglement," was used by editors of *The New Republic* in a portmanteau coinage. The magazine took *bimbo*, Italian for "baby," and in English, "ditzy dame," and combined it with *imbroglio* to form *bimbroglio*, a description of the complicated mess President Clinton got himself into. The coinage didn't catch on, but the editors grimly stuck with it.

The New Republic ran a fine article by Walter Shapiro, a columnist for *USA Today*, about the way liberals have stayed with Clinton, which included the line, "Democrats were pantingly eager to excuse the President's *latitudinarian* campaign tactics."

Not only did the freethinking Shapiro make an adverb out of the participle *panting*, thereby providing an intensified form of "eagerly," but he also was first on the pundit's block to use *latitudinarian*, "liberal or broad-minded in standards of conduct or religious belief." (No, the opposite is not *longitudinarian;* the antonym is "like a hidebound stiff.")

Representative James E. Rogan, one of the most articulate impeachment managers, used a word familiar to bashers of textual deviates: "Ms. Lewinsky doesn't bother attempting to match the President's linguistic *deconstructions* of the English language."

Who says the Republicans don't read Jacques Derrida or go to Woody Allen films? *Deconstruction* is a philosophy that challenges the ability of language to represent reality. It holds that a reader is free to find meaning in a text that the writer did not intend and—in making the interpreter a partner in the creation of copy—seeks to replace the stability of logic with the fluidity of paradox. Derrida's late-60s antitheory theory, despised by orderly structuralists, has led to much scholarly wordplay and interdisciplinary whipping.

As used by impeachment managers, *deconstruction* means "Humpty-Dumpty language," taken from Lewis Carroll's line in *Through the Looking-Glass:* "When I use a word . . . it means just what I choose it to mean—neither more nor less." (Woody Allen, in the title of his 1997 *Deconstructing Harry,* used the word in its literal sense, to mean "taking apart," I think, but *deconstructionists* are free to read into his title anything they want and the dickens with the auteur.)

A word with a relatively fixed meaning was used by the Iowa senator Tom Harkin, who denounced the House case as "counterfeit" and "a sham," adding for emphasis on national television, "a pile of *dung*." The word was front-paged by *The Washington Post* and A-elevened by the *Times.* It is evidently a socially acceptable word that the *OED* defines as "excrementitious and decayed matter employed to fertilize the soil; manure." First spotted at the beginning of the second millennium in a Latin-to-Anglo-Saxon glossary under the heading "Concerning Tools of Farmers," it is now "a term of obloquy." In some translations of the Book of Job, the suffering protagonist is described as seated on a *dunghill.* Harland Braun, a Los Angeles criminal defense lawyer, told a *Times* reporter what he thought of the O. J. Simpson case in 1996: "You can't make a chicken salad out of chicken dung." (I sense a bowdlerization of that quote.)

The Democratic Senator Harkin's barnyard characterization of the case recalled a similar usage by the snake-checking Al Haig at the Republican convention in 1988. He compared the Democratic leadership to a bat, "flying erratically for brief periods at low levels and hanging upside down for extended periods in dark, damp caves up to its navel in *guano*." That is the Spanish word for seafowl dung.

Obloquy, used above to define *dung*, was used by the lead manager Henry Hyde. From the Latin meaning "speak against," the noun is less abusive than *calumny* or *slander* but much stronger than *blame* or *criticism*. The original sense of *obloquy* was "evil-speaking," but the current sense is the result of all the defamation, vituperation and invective: *disgrace*. The philosophic view: *Dung* happens.

> *You refer to a special type of symbiotic relationship known as* commensalisms. *It is the barnacle (not the remora) that attaches itself to the body of a whale in order to get a "free ride" through the ocean. The remora uses its sucker to attach itself to a shark. It eats the leftovers from the shark's meals. In commensalisms, one organism is benefited (i.e., the barnacle or the remora) by the relationship, and the other is not affected in any way (i.e., the shark or the whale).*
>
> Arlene Marin
> Orangeburg, New York

IMPEACHMENTESE III

In an earlier take on impeachmentese, I speculated that the ubiquitous metaphor "lowering the bar" might be derived from high jumping.

Lexicographic Irregular Coral Samuel of London called with a deeper etymon: "Try the Temple Bar." Jack E. Garrett of Jamesburg, New Jersey, agreed: "I believe this expression derives from the old English tradition centered on the Temple Bar at the entrance to the City of London."

From 1301 to 1672 a gateway, or bar, separated the cities of London and Westminster. When the sovereign wished to enter, goes the story, he or she had to stop at this boundary (now marked by a dragon on a pedestal at the junction of Fleet Street and the Strand) or a similar gateway to receive the formal assent of the Lord Mayor of London. The tradition is remembered today in the symbolic handing over of a sword or giant key, and American mayors copied this with the presentation of a "key to the city."

This raises (but does not beg) the question: If "lowering the bar" meant removing a barrier, how did it come to signify a lowering of standards? Answer: It became a symbol of welcome, or easement. Raise the frequency of lowering the bar, and anybody can get in.

I suspect the term lowering the bar *originated with the dance called the limbo. Remember? One danced under a bar, and if you made it without touching the bar, they lowered the bar and you tried again.*

The lower the bar got, the more erotic the maneuvers became which were required to get under the bar, hence: lowering the bar = lowering of moral standards.

Peter Huyck
Iowa City, Iowa

THE INCREDIBLE 'N' CREDIBLE

Beware the substitution of *'n'* for *and.*

What we hear is not necessarily what is said. In written English, *and* stands in front of us with a *d* at the end, but when it is placed between two words, we tend to clip it to *'n,'* as in *ham 'n' eggs* or robust, uninhibited *'n' wide open.* This smoothing out of sounds separates the written from the oral language, and confusion arising from the death of the fully pronounced *and* is nowhere better illustrated than in what happened at a recent *Larry King Live.*

Attorney General Janet Reno, appearing on the CNN program of her fellow former Floridian, was asked about appointments of independent counsel. She said, "What I've got to do is find if there is specific *'n'* credible evidence that a covered person . . . that there's specific *'n'* credible evidence that they may have violated the federal criminal law."

Larry King, whose ear heard *'n' credible,* interpreted that as *incredible* and said, "Define *incredible.*"

The Attorney General was uncharacteristically nonplussed. "Define 'specific'?"

King pressed: "*Incredible.*"

They never quite connected on that. Later in the show, I came on and noted that the phrase in the statute was not "specific and credible evidence" but "specific evidence from a credible source," which is different. Larry picked up on that and cleared up the earlier confusion: "She was saying *and,* but I thought she was saying *in.* And I swear she said *in.*"

Thus did two highly communicative individuals—who like each other and were speaking and listening carefully—miscommunicate totally. How does this happen? For a deep philological explanation of this phenomenon, I turned to James McCawley, professor of linguistics at the University of Chicago, who is regarded by most of his peers as the man who hits the longest ball in the language game.*

"The pronunciation of '*n*' involves two reductions," explained McCawley, "simplification of the final consonant cluster and reduction of the unstressed vowel." (Did anybody see where he hit that ball?) "There is considerable individual variation and dialect variation in the pronunciation of reduced vowels. An additional possible difference in the pronunciation of the two phrases is in whether the *n* is assimilated to the following consonant."

Could the professor give me a f'r instance (using *f'r instance* as a phrasal noun)? "Sure. I often pronounce the *in* of *incredible* with the velar nasal sound of *sing*, but I wouldn't generally pronounce *specific 'n' credible* with that sound."

Then would it make sense for those of us eager to facilitate human communication to leap to the ramparts and inveigh for the enunciation of *d* at the end of *and*?

"A wasted effort. Virtually the only case in which the *n* pronunciation could cause a misunderstanding such as occurred on the Larry King show," says McCawley, "is something so unusual that it isn't worth worrying about—in which *and* conjoins adjectives and the second adjective has a counterpart with the prefix *in* that would make sense in the given context."

I knew that I had been present with King and Reno at a rare linguistic confluence, while an audience of millions conjoined the fun. But isn't the death of the concluding *d* in *and* something to be mourned? "Dutch, the closest living relative of English, lost the *d* of what is etymologically the same word (*en*) centuries ago," replied the foremost modern interpreter of Denmark's grammarian and phoneticist Otto Jespersen, "and it gets along fine without it."

Incredible.

*See an appreciation of the late Professor McCawley on page 180.

The closest living relative of English is not Dutch, but rather Frisian, spo-
ken by several hundred thousand people in northern Holland and Ger-
many. You can look it up.

Arthur S. Goldberg, Professor of Economics
University of Wisconsin—Madison
Madison, Wisconsin

ISSUE ISSUE

In politics, *the issues*, plural, intoned with great solemnity, is a goo-goo's term for "subjects the political scientist thinks are important but the average voter doesn't really care about."

In law, *take issue* and *at issue* direct the listener to the opposite side, making clear the controversy in a case. The sense of "dispute" was illustrated when Greta Garbo, in the 1939 film *Ninotchka*, said, "Don't make *an issue* of my womanhood." From this flowed *the issue*'s meaning of "what is central to, or is the nub of, the case," neatly differentiated in a 1980 *New York Times* story about Vernon Jordan, then head of the Urban League, answering a reporter's question about a local league official who drove him to a hotel on the night an assassin attempted to kill him: "Mrs. Coleman is not *an issue*. The shooting is *an issue*."

But in recent years, an *issue* has spread across all walks of life to mean either "problem" or "disagreement."

Dr. David Forrest is a psychiatrist at Columbia-Presbyterian Hospital in New York who provided a dictionary for foreign-born psychiatrists in 1976. ("Buzz off, Buster—a direction said to someone bothersome to make him go away.") He told me last week that when he asked his niece recently about what was new at Bucknell College, she said, "I have *issues* with my calculus class" and "*issues* with my roommate." From these usages, he took the word to be a euphemism for "aggravation."

"I think it has a source in psychoanalytic psychotherapy," says Forrest, "and not in cognitive or behavioral psychology. Psychoanalysts might say their patient is having a 'transference *issue*' or a 'payment *issue*' or a 'termination *issue*.' It's a way of saying, 'I'm struggling with this.'" It's also why Jim Crotty, in his recent *How to Talk American*, defines issues as "deep psychological difficulties best resolved through hugely overpriced workshops or therapy."

An early citation with the meaning of "problem" in the files of

Merriam-Webster, which is tracking the new sense, is from a 1987 catalogue of the Society of Plastics Engineers: "Permeability is *an issue.*" In the same year, *Language Arts* magazine wrote, "The illusion of space is not *an issue* in sculpture." Fred Shapiro at Yale has a 1988 citation from the Illinois Supreme Court, as a hearing examiner said, "I really don't have much *issue* with that."

To *have an issue* is not to *join issue* or to *take issue.* In this vogue sense, *have an issue* with is a euphemism for *have a problem* with, which is a euphemism for *have a disagreement* with. To those who have an issue with that, I say: Buzz off, Buster.

JAMMED TOGETHER NAMES INC.

TYPO-POETRY is a treat for the eyes. John Kearney of Marina Del Rey, California, noted this from *Variety*, the weekly: "John Calley pointed to a number of high-profile pics that are thisclose to a greenlight."

A *greenlight*, as a single word, is a metaphoric step forward. When a traffic light turns green and the guy behind you splits a second by honking, that's a *green light*, two words. When a city designates a neighborhood for strip joints and porno parlors, that's a *red-light district*, with the red light hyphenated to become a compound modifier. But when the signal is an extension of the metaphor of the green traffic signal to a nodded approval of high-profile pics, an argument can be made for experimenting with a single-word noun, *greenlight*. It's not standard English, but I'd give the pioneering usage an amberlight.

What tickled me even more was *Variety*'s use of *thisclose*. You can just see the thumb and forefinger a half-centimeter apart. It's a typographical word-picture—visual prosody—especially apt for describing moguls in s t r e t c h limousines.

The imagist poet who delighted in this device was Edward Estlin Cummings, who determinedly broke the rules of capitalization and punctuation by styling himself e e cummings. In his classic 1923 "Buffalo Bill's defunct," he illustrated the rapidity of the Western showman's shooting with "onetwothreefourfive pigeonsjustlikethat."

Closing up words that are attracted to each other is a *neverending* process; something there is that doesn't like a hyphen, and there goes *never-ending*. When inveighing recently against run-on sentences (don't do it it's incorrect), I took a hard look at the attributive *run-on*. The dictionaries report it the hyphenated way, but you see it losing its hyphen in the press. Soon it will be *runon*. Pass the *gingerbread, greenhorn*. As the linguistic drill sergeant says, "Close it up."

This is a *windup* (formerly *wind-up*) to my pitch: We are in the grip of a fad that compresses proper names and ordinary words into visual identifiers.

Peter Osnos left the Times Books division of Random House to start his independent publishing company *PublicAffairs*. One word, with a capital in the middle. A big discount broker styles his company *CharlesSchwab*, a movie company calls itself *DreamWorks*, and an apostrophe-hating, space-saving adman changed the incomprehensible CNS-Sovran to *NationsBank*, not to be confused with *MellonBank*.

I used to think this trend started with companies that affected computer lingo—*CompuServe, DigiCash, WordPerfect, HotJava*—but the lexicographer Richard Weiner, who I suspect coined *inner-capped* on the analogy of the mafia's *kneecapping*, reminds me of the 1959 *TelePrompTer*. (That is still a trademark and requires initial capitalization, but few use inner caps to describe the reading device by which tongue-tied anchorpeople become hyperarticulate.) And *BankAmerica* must have saved millions by excising its *of* back in 1954.

Before *inner caps*, companies and products used hyphens. Sun-Maid, Star-Kist and Sani-Flush followed the 1925 Old Gran-Dad. In 1927, we had Kool-Aid; in 1994, Coca-Cola—which is keeping its hyphen—marketed its Gatorade-like PowerAde. (Every kid should have a lemonAde stand.)

O.K. How do we handle this manipulation of our media by marketers who want to catch our attention with tricky typography? With e e cummings, it was visual pyrotechnics raised to the level of art, but with corporate logomaniacs it's getting out of hand.

Wired magazine goes slavishly along with what it calls *intercaps*, though it draws the line at all caps. I prefer *The New York Times*'s solution. From the *Times*'s stylebook: "Contrived spelling in which the letters are capitalized should not be used unless the second portion of the name is a proper noun." Thus, *Pepsico*, not *PepsiCo; Compuserve*, not *CompuServe*. That means *BankAmerica* is O.K., but *NationsBank* is written *Nationsbank* because "America" is a proper name and "bank" is not.

It's a lucky thing we caught this in time. We came *thisclose. . . .*

I would like to add to your list of together words with "weeknight." That one (or two) always stops (or stop) me short.

Casey I. Herrick
New York, New York

Sani-Flush was developed by my grandfather Charles H. Schlabach (1867–1955); he also coined the name, which was copyrighted in 1909 and thus actually antedates Old Gran-Dad.

William Schlabach
Houston, Texas

KISS THE LAWYERS

I ONCE HEADED one of my harangues "Kill All the Lawyers." This alluded to Shakespeare's line in *Henry VI*, Part II, Act IV, Scene II: "The first thing we do, let's kill all the lawyers."

However, Robert Nylen of Ashfield, Massachusetts, points out that the speaker is Dick the Butcher, a know-nothing thug in Jack Cade's gang, and Cade, agreeing, adds: "Is not this a lamentable thing, that of the skin of an innocent lamb should be made parchment? That parchment, being scribbl'd o'er, should undo a man?"

Thus did Shakespeare use irony to ridicule anti-intellectuals who resent lawyers and writers. In the spirit of the season, let's agree not to kill all the lawyers and *scribblers*. (Only a few, and those metaphorically.)

LANG SYNE

"WE'VE BEEN *languoring* here in Washington," said TV's omnipresent attorney William Ginsburg.

Languor, a noun only, is "a state of weariness or listlessness." To languish is "to pine away" or "be neglected."

You cannot *languor away.* On the other hand, through such mistakes we grow the English languish.

LEXIMUTTS

No pet lover calls a dog of mixed breed a *mongrel* anymore. Although *mong,* from the Old English *gemong,* meaning "mixture," is still with us in the form of *among,* the word *mongrel* has gained an ugly, snarling connotation; for years *mongrelization* was a term used by racists. A century ago, *half-breed* was a derogation of the issue of aboriginal Americans and white newcomers.

Times have changed, and so have the words. Among humans who have pets, euphemism has its uses. Although *mongrel* is taken to be harshly judgmental, the nonstandard *mutt* has gained an affectionate, if still slightly derogatory, connotation. Among the animalistically correct, the favored term for dogs and bitches that cannot meet the standards of the American Kennel Club is *crossbreeds.*

There's much to be said for a pedigree, as my pet, Peeve, insists. But a promotional newsletter put out by the veterinarians at the Friendship Hospital for Animals in Washington offers some fun for the holidays with a piece about "Crossbreed Dogs We Would Like to See." These merry matches include:

- Pointer and Setter, resulting in *"Poinsetter,* a traditional Christmas pet"
- Labrador Retriever and Curly Coated Retriever, producing *"Lab Coat Retriever,"* convenient for workers at the National Institutes of Health

• Bloodhound and Labrador, sire and dam of *"Blabador,* a gossipy barker"

• Malamute and Pointer, generating *"Moot Point,* a dog owned by . . . oh, well, it doesn't matter."

LIKE, DO YOU LIKE LIKES OR LIKE?

There was the handsome face of the basketball superstar and footgear endorser Michael Jordan on the cover of *Time* magazine. Walter Isaacson, *Time's* editor, gambled that the iconic Jordan would astound the sports world in the coming week—and sure enough, the cover subject came through with a stellar performance that won the championship for his Chicago Bulls.

The copy on the cover identified the face merely as "Michael," on the assumption that if you didn't know the megastar's last name, you probably lived in a cave beyond reach of mass communication. Below that, a reverent comment: "We may never see his likes again."

Seventeen letters came in to *Time,* and several to me, questioning the use of *likes.* "Shouldn't that have read, 'We may never see his *like* again'?" asked J. A. Sullivan III of Caldwell, New Jersey. "I always thought that using *likes* had a bad connotation, as in 'I'm finished with the *likes* of you.'"

Time's copy editors say they looked it up beforehand in *Merriam-Webster's Third Unabridged Dictionary* and Eric Partridge's *Dictionary of Slang and Unconventional English.* James Kelly, *Time's* Saturday editor, preferred the plural and made the call. The magazine resolutely stands by its usage (look, this isn't nerve gas) and is braced for any assault by nit-picking readers or gotcha grammarians.

Partridge was one of the last of the one-man dictionary writers; that generous sultan of slang used to do his research in the great reading room of the British Museum, where he was available to help such aspiring lexicographers as the likes of me. He opined that *the like of,* as used by the English vituperator William Cobbett in the late eighteenth century, was "generally in the plural" today.

Time's other source, *Merriam-Webster's Third Unabridged,* accepts *the likes of* but lists first *the like of,* labeling both colloquial. In *M-W's Dictionary of English Usage, the like of* is described as "a variant phrase" well chosen when "the reference is to a single object and no disparagement is intended."

Time could take further solace from Robert Burchfield, editor of the *New Fowler's Modern English Usage,* who notes, "I was upbraided by a

Scotswoman for writing 'Who has not seen *the likes of* the following?' but found examples of the plural use in the *OED." (Upbraid,* "to criticize or scold severely," is rooted in the Old English *bregden,* "to snatch, move suddenly," which lives in modern slang as "put a move on." Where was I?)

O.K.; a case can be made that the plural *the likes of* is acceptable in spoken English. (Lexies don't use the word *correct* anymore.) This despite the usagist Ted Bernstein's condemnation of it as "a casualism that has no place in serious writing" at bastions of good grammar like *The New York Times.*

The question then becomes: Does *the likes of* carry a pejorative connotation? It does; even loosey-goosey usagists say that when it has a single object like *you,* "it typically carries overtones of disparagement." Even when it is used with *me,* it most often implies a gently self-mocking derogation, as used above with such lexicographers as *the likes of me.* Mr. Sullivan of New Jersey had it right.

But disparagement of Michael Jordan cannot be what *Time* intended. On the contrary, its comment "We may never see his *likes* again" is probably bottomed on the rumination of Shakespeare's Hamlet about his ghostly father: "He was a man, take him for all in all, I shall not look upon his *like* again." Or *The Odes of Horace:* "When shall we look upon his *like* again?" Or the King James version of the Book of Job, in Jehovah's whirlwind description of the twisty serpent Leviathan: "Upon earth there is not his *like,* who is made without fear."

You could say, with a sneer in your voice, "Thank goodness we won't be seeing the *likes* of him," because that plural of *like* is part of a colloquial put-down. But you cannot run somebody down with "the *like* of him," because that *like* is comparative, not pejorative; it means "we may not see anybody *like* him again."

Why are we breaking our heads over this seemingly insignificant issue? Because the headline troubled copy editors; because a top editor weighed their evidence and made a decision about its use on the cover; because a score of readers then wrote in that it looked funny to them, and because it also struck me as just a little bit off.

Moral: Native speakers have an instinct for the "correct." Norma Loquendi, trust your ear.

Your fabulous thing on never seeing his like/likes again *prompted me to search the column to see if you used the Vernon Duke/Yip Harburg example of the song "I Like the Likes of You."*

I suppose Time *did not err, but it doesn't sound good to me. I guess I prefer the* Hamlet *version of never seeing his like again.*

Liz Smith
New York, New York

LOOKIT

The Kennedy Library occasionally releases tapes recorded secretly by JFK of conversations with other political leaders. In his *San Francisco Examiner* column, the hardballing Chris Matthews reported a familiar but curious locution on one of those transcripts. It will be semantically examined here for the first time.

JFK called Mayor Richard Daley of Chicago to complain in salty language that one of his local representatives was "sticking it right up us" in not supporting him on a civil rights bill. Daley replied: "He'll do it. The last time I told him, 'Now look *it* . . . you vote for anything the President wants . . . and that's the way it's gonna be.'"

The tape's transcriber got it wrong. The admonition is one word: *lookit.* You won't find *lookit* in most dictionaries, though it is a widely used, if somewhat outdated, urban Americanism, on the order of *see here.*

Lookit began as a corruption of the transitive verb *look at,* as used by Theodore Dreiser in his 1925 novel *An American Tragedy:* "Oh, do look at those sleeves. . . . *Lookit* the collar." But the intransitive verb has a different meaning. In Philip Barry's 1939 *Philadelphia Story,* the character played by Cary Grant in the movie says to Katharine Hepburn, "*Lookit,* Tracy, don't you think you've done enough notes for one day?"

In the same way, Mayor Raymond Flynn of Boston told a conference of mayors in 1991, "*Lookit,* cities are tired of being portrayed as, quote, problem areas." (Democratic mayors are especially keen users of *lookit.*)

The meaning is not "look at it" or even "consider this." The syllable *-it* has nothing to do with the word *it.* The meaning ranges between the imperative "pay attention" and the more severe "look at me when I'm talking to you" (perhaps rooted in the medieval *look ye*). The closest one-word synonym is *listen,* punched up by the recent favorite of football coaches, *listen up!*

Hold still for a further nuance. (*Lookit,* we're nothing if not thorough in this column.) I posted a query about this unexamined Americanism on the American Dialect Society list-server. (I think *list-server* may be a non-sexist word for "somebody who waits on lists," unless it is "somebody who hands you a list," as in "My name is Rodney, and I am your *list-server* this evening.")

Dennis R. Preston from the department of linguistics and languages at Michigan State University, who says he is a midwesterner, contributes this contour to the introductory admonition: "The tone of *lookit* for me is usually exasperated (*Lookit*, I've been trying to explain . . .) or even aggressive (*Lookit*, I got me a knuckle sammich here you gonna hafta munch if . . .)."

Another citation from the golden age of steam radio from the Jack Benny show: He would signal his waning patience with "Lookit, Rochester. . . ."

Henry Steiner
Hong Kong, China

LOWERING THE RUSH

Two metaphors that Democrats and Republicans were able to agree on during the impeachment proceedings: We must not *lower the bar* and yet we must not *rush to judgment.*

What bar? Is there a nurturing tavern on Capitol Hill known as "the Lowered Bar"? No. Is this, as some congressional wags have suggested, a reference to the limbo, a West Indian dance in which the dancer bends backward and seeks to shuffle under an ever-lower bar? Again, no. The old figure of speech was introduced into recent hearings by Arthur Schlesinger Jr.: "The lowering of the bar . . . creates a novel, indeed revolutionary, theory of impeachment." Presumably—but not certainly—the metaphor is derived from the high jump, in which lowering the bar or pole makes it easier for a jumper to clear.

Whoa! What about the *rush to judgment?* Mark Lane, a Washington lawyer, immortalized the phrase in a 1966 book suggesting a vast conspiracy in the Kennedy assassination. His source was Lord Chancellor Thomas Erskine, speaking for the defense in an 1800 case about the attempted assassination of King George III.

"An attack upon the king is considered to be *parricide* against the state," said Erskine, using a word meaning "the murder of a close relative," and added, "There should be a solemn pause before we *rush to judgement.*" Being British, he used an extra *e.* When you consider the original subject, this year's use of the metaphor seems apt.

JAMES MCCAWLEY

OF ALL THE LEXICOGRAPHIC IRREGULARS who regularly instruct, correct, clarify, amplify and berate the author of this column, none carried the scholarly authority of James D. McCawley, the University of Chicago's iconoclastic professor of linguistics.

When Jim straightened you out, you could feel the wrenching-around for months. As a pop grammarian, I like to abide by, and pass along, simple rules of style. But as the father of generative semantics, which instills logic and meaning into the built-in grammar discovered by Noam Chomsky of MIT, McCawley liked to challenge those rules by showing the delicious complexity of our syntax.

Recently I noted the Associated Press rule for when to use *between* and *among*: "*Between* introduces two items and *among* more than two." Although I fuzzily warned about the trickiness of the relationship of several items considered a pair at a time, McCawley came thundering back with the vivid examples that bring his theories to life: "Only *between* is appropriate when you say, 'He held four golf balls *between* his fingers' or 'He has a fungus infection *between* his toes.'"

No arguing with that, even as I try the four-golf-ball stretch; it is not in the grammar that is hard-wired in our heads to say, "The golf balls are *among* my fingers." Jim then zinged home the lesson: "What determines the choice of the preposition isn't whether its object denotes two entities or more than two, but whether the entities are being referred to in twos or in combinations of more than two." Therefore, I will follow the simple rule of style (*between* two, *among* several), remembering the exception's complexity every time I feel an itch in my shoes.

In the same authoritative way, McCawley took apart the *New York Times* style manual's representation of how *each other* and *one another* work. ("Two persons look at each other; more than two look at one another.") Try this sentence for size, McCawley responded: *They spent the afternoon taking group photographs of each other.*

"If you were to follow your style manual's recommendation and replace *each other* with *one another*," he wrote, "the result would have the ridiculous implication that each of the group photographs depicted only one person. The difference that this example points to is that *one another* generalizes over something that is semantically singular, whereas *each other* does not specify the semantic number and is thus available for generalizing over things like 'He took a group photograph of *them*,' with a semantically plural element."

In case I didn't get that, he offered another sentence with semantic singularity: *Those children like to gang up on each other.* "Again, replacing *each other* with *one another* would make it sound ridiculous," McCawley instructed, "implying that a single child could gang up on another child."

O.K., so our rule doesn't always work. But it usually does, and if we did away with rules, how could language mavens ever correct anybody? The Gotcha! Gang would be forced to disband, and one of life's great intellectual pleasures would disappear.

McCawley, a handlebar-mustachioed libertarian gutsy enough to take on his testy teacher, Noam Chomsky, sometimes came to my defense. When I wrote, "He made a few calls and reported back" in a political column, Charles Barnard of *Modern Maturity* magazine wrote: "To *report back* is redundant, no? Doesn't the prefix *re-* mean 'back'?" I appealed to Jim, who reported back: "No, *report back* isn't redundant. *Report* has severed its connection to its etymology, and one can report to anyone who's interested in what one is reporting. *Report back* specifies a report to the person who issued the order."

In language study, nothing beats a good illustration. A precept without an example is like a verb without an object: pale, flat and intransitive. In a column on *short shrift*, rooted in the archaism of a prisoner's being hastily *shriven* (confession heard and absolution given) before his execution, I asked Jim for other "fossilized expressions."

"I understand a *fossilized expression* to be one that was once an instance of a productive syntactic construction," he reported back, "and which has survived even though either that construction or the words in the expression or the relevant meanings of those words haven't." As an example of old words now bereft of meaning but still in use, he suggested "*to wit*, where the word—*wit*, as a verb meaning 'know'—has been lost."

His example of a vestigial construction in a fossilized expression used his favorite technique of proving something about what is said by what the brain refuses to let the tongue say: "*Long live the King!* There the words survive, but the construction doesn't. You don't say, *Loud laugh the audience!*"

Although an early report said that Professor McCawley died at 61 "of an *apparent* heart attack," Margalit Fox, an obituary writer at *The New York Times*, apparently remembered the grammatical admonition of Stanley Walker, of the *New York Herald Tribune*, to his copy editors: "Nobody ever died of an *apparent* heart attack." Ms. Fox's sparkling obit reported, "The *apparent* cause was a heart attack, university officials said." The scrupulous McCawley would have approved.

ME, MYSELF AND I

Self used to be a dirty word. "The wretch, concentered all in *self*," wrote Sir Walter Scott in 1805, might get "power and pelf" but would wind up "unwept, unhonored and unsung." Not so, said Walt Whitman a half century later. "I celebrate myself," he sang in his *Song of Myself.* Since then, however, the notion of *self* as something to be celebrated has been taking a beating; Scott's sneer at *self* reverberates through the language. It is bad to be *selfish*, good to be *selfless*. People who are smug are *self-satisfied*, narcissists are *self-absorbed* and often *self-indulgent* and braggarts are *self-serving*. You can find a few uses that reflect well on *self*—like *self-reliant* and *self-possessed*—but most praise is lavished on the rejection of *self*, as in *self-sacrifice*. And *selflessness* is next to godliness.

Then *self* made a comeback. Showing some self-confidence, it became the name of a Condé Nast magazine aimed at women interested in their own bodies and minds. Its twentieth-anniversary issue faces some of the bad *self*s ("self-love, self-pity, self-delusion, self-aggrandizement") but dwells more on the good *self*s ("self-help, self-governing, self-made, self-respect, self-denial" and, for ovens, "self-cleaning"). Though a bit self-conscious about a decline in their publication's circulation, *Self*'s editors gutsily reprint a Mike Twohy cartoon showing a timid fellow writing in his diary, "Dear Diary, Sorry to bother you again," captioned "Low Self-Esteem." In that regard, what to do about *myself*?

This reflexive pronoun requires reflection. *Reflexive* means "turned back on itself," and a reflexive pronoun turns the action back on its subject: "I [pronoun as subject] perjured [verb] *myself* [reflexive pronoun pointing back to the subject "I"]." The correct use of *self* or *selves* attached to *my, your, him, her, them* or *our* is to turn the action back on the other pronoun in the sentence. The subject and the object are the same thing. But too many writers are using *myself* in an orgy of false modesty, fearing to make the squeakily assertive sound of the first-person singular accusative and dative *me*.

President Jimmy Carter did it in his farewell address (a speech he concluded with the word *farewell*, which is the proper way to end a farewell address). He said, "I will work hard to make sure that the transition from *myself* to the next president is a good one." When I popped him on this, E. Ward Gilman, editor of Merriam-Webster's *Dictionary of English Usage*—"Dr. Roundheels" himself—cited the use of *myself* instead of *me* by grammar-conscious authors from Dr. Samuel Johnson to E. B. White. He even found the abomination in a sentence—"No longer were Price, Buchanan and *myself* part of the innermost circle"—written in 1974 by me and in no way "written by myself." Even Homer noodled.

Myself is being used incorrectly in place of the first-person singular nominative. (I'm too shy to write *I*.) The new Uriah Heeps, wallowing in phony humility, eschew the use of *I*. Sometimes, blushing shyly and digging a toe in the dirt, they substitute *yours truly*. More often they replace the "perpendicular pronoun" with the horizontal pronoun *myself*. A generation ago I was astounded when my predecessor as a conservative *New York Times* columnist, Arthur Krock, titled his memoirs about growing up in the 1890s *Myself When Young*. Not until I plunged into the philological scholarship required for this article did I discover that he bottomed the title on Edward FitzGerald's translation of a quatrain in the *Rubaiyat of Omar Khayyam* (*ruba'i* means "quatrain"; *rubaiyat* is the plural): "*Myself* when young did eagerly frequent/Doctor and Saint, and heard great argument/About it and about: but evermore/Came out by the same Door wherein I went." Poets can get away with anything, *myself* included.

If you hate to begin a sentence with *myself*, as in "*Myself*, I could not care less," try *as for me* or *for my part*. A reflexive pronoun is fine, however, as an emphasizer. I used one a moment ago, as "'Dr. Roundheels' *himself*," above. Americans use *myself* to underscore a pronoun as often as the British use the superfluous *indeed*, which means "you bet; hear, hear," and the emphatically reflexive "If I do say so *myself*." Let us not become the *Myself* Generation. If you want to show submission, sew a large sign on the seat of your pants that reads "Kick me." Avoid "Kick *myself.*" The latter lacks *self-esteem.*

Distinguish between a reflexive *pronoun and an* intensive *pronoun. "The correct use of" the* reflexive *pronoun "is to turn the action back on the other pronoun in the sentence. The subject and the object are the same thing." Thus: I saw myself.*

The correct use of the intensive *pronoun is to* emphasize, *and when an intensive pronoun is used, it is used in* apposition *to another noun or pronoun. Thus: I, myself, saw you. Or, I saw you myself. There is no turning back of action on the other pronoun, no subject-object relationship.*

A pronoun in a sentence can either be reflexive or intensive, but cannot itself be simultaneously both.

Edward Fischer
Jersey City, New Jersey

MILLENNIUM BUG

When a batter fans, baseball scorers put down the symbol *K,* probably from the distinctive letter in strike.

Creators of GOP bumper stickers in 1952 sought to encapsulate three issues against the Democrats: Korea (an unended war), Communism (soft on) and Corruption (the "mess in Washington"). They came up with *K1C2.* (The notion of a quasi-chemical symbol as bumper sticker was used again in 1964 to denote the name of Goldwater: AuH_2O.)

In the years since, *K*—from *kilo,* Greek for *chillioi,* "thousand," or 10 to the third power—has most often come to mean *kilobyte,* strings of binary digits expressed by 2 to the tenth power, or 1,024. My son the E-commercialist says that if my computer doesn't boast a memory of 48 megabytes—that's 49,152 *kilobytes*—I should forget about it.

O.K. (coined in 1839): Here comes *Y2K* (coined in 1995).

"I plead guilty to journalistic incompetence," writes the unduly self-flagellating financial columnist Robert J. Samuelson, "for ignoring what may be one of the decade's big stories: the Year 2000 problem. Among technical types it is shortened to the *Y2K* problem."

As we content providers are aware, the world as we know it is coming to an end at midnight on December 31, 1999. At that moment, the Times Square ball drops; couples embrace; killjoy mathematicians insisting the new millennium does not begin for another year are drowned out in the clack of celebrants' noisemakers; the ghost of Guy Lombardo reappears to play "Auld Lang Syne" (which drunken etymologists explain is Scottish for "Old Long Since"); computers that have not been properly rejiggered assume with perfect binary logic that the Gay Nineties are over and that we're going into the year 1900 and that Diamond Jim Brady is canceling our credit cards. What a moment!

This column understands its scope: at the moment of earthly doom, for example, its subject will be the origin of *doomsayer* and the pronunciation of *Armageddon.* Therefore, I will leave the nerdy technical reasons for the breakdown of expiration dates to chat-room eschatologists. (It has to do with space-hungry programmers in the 1960s leaving the first two digits off the year, so that 1965 was written as 65, and now the computer can't find the 19 to turn it to 20.) We deal here only with the linguistic roots of *Y2K.*

On February 26, 1995, James Coates wrote in the *Chicago Tribune* about what was being called the Year 2000 *Holocaust* and the *millennium bug:* "Once the code that was compiled with the *millennium bug* written into it is decompiled, it must be fixed to allow four digits rather than two in what is called the date field."

On February 28, 1996, a *Y2K* bulletin board appeared on the Internet. Its existence was noted in the world of Old Establishment Media by *The Wall Street Journal* on July 26, 1996. Peter de Jager, coauthor with Richard Burgeon of *Managing 00,* helped popularize the term among the netties, as did Dan Rather of the broadcast network netties. They accepted the old-fashioned symbol of *K* as *kilo,* 1,000, not as 2 to the tenth power, or 1,024.

If you don't cotton to *Y2K* and don't have the space for the year 2000, there's always the Roman numeral *MM.* A candy company that produces M&M's (named after Forrest Mars and Bruce Murrie) has seized on this idea to appoint itself "the official candy of the New Millennium." If you don't want your fingers sticky with chocolate as the electronic balloon falls, grab a handful of those millennium bugs.

MINDING THE COURT'S LANGUAGE

Justices of the Supreme Court may hand down the final word on the law, but they cannot offer the final word on the words. That's for all of us to hash out (cf. *Marbury v. Safire*).

In concurring with the Court's decision to refuse to hear a case brought by unendowed "performance artists" against the National Endowment for the Arts, a testy Antonin Scalia took aim at the language of the statute controlling that federal agency.

The law reads: "Artistic excellence and artistic merit are the criteria by which applications are judged, *taking into consideration general standards for decency and respect for the diverse beliefs and values of the American public.*"

Scalia took a bead on the portion of the law I italicized. That, he wrote, "is what my grammar-school teacher would have condemned as a dangling modifier. There is no noun to which the participle is attached. . . ."

Could it be that our lawmakers erred in their draftsmanship? Yes. The solipsistic solons, in choosing to modify the first part of that sentence, should have recast it to provide a subject anchor. "Judges should judge applications using the criteria of artistic excellence and artistic merit, taking into consideration," etc. Justice Scalia's grammar-school teacher, whose strict constructionism apparently influenced the future jurist, was correct.

Later in this decidedly grouchy concurrence, Scalia directed attention to the meaning of a participle properly connected to a noun in the First Amendment: "Congress shall make no law . . . *abridging* the freedom of speech." (*Law* is the noun that is being modified; *abridging*, the participial modifier.)

"To *abridge* is 'to contract, to diminish; to deprive of,'" wrote the Justice, giving as the source for that definition "T. Sheridan, *A Complete Dictionary of the English Language* (6th ed., 1796)." He went on to opine that denial of taxpayer subsidy was no *abridgment* of speech, but the question to lexicographers is: Why did a justice in 1998 use a 1796 dictionary? Can't the Court afford a new one?

Answer: In examining the Founders' intent, you are wise to use the definitions they turned to at the time. In 1789, when James Madison drafted the Bill of Rights, Noah Webster had not yet produced an American dictionary. A school dictionary was in print that had no authority in terms of meaning, but the great, authoritative Samuel Johnson dictionary did not cross the Atlantic until 1818 in its eleventh edition.

"Scalia, or whoever did the research for him," says Fred Mish, editor in chief of Merriam-Webster, "chose from a group of four dictionaries from that period available here, all British, that all focused on pronunciation: John Entwick's, William Perry's, John Walker's and Thomas Sheridan's. Sheridan was an Irishman and a stage actor (as was Walker) and probably based his work on his stage elocution."

Today, *abridge* still has a sense of "diminish," but its primary meaning is "shorten, condense." The meaning of "deprive" is now considered archaic, but that is what the Founders had in mind. They may have found it in the dictionary at hand, which was primarily concerned with pronunciation, not meaning. More likely they took its sense of "constrain" from the works of John Locke, popular with Constitution writers and later cited by Johnson: "The constant desire of happiness, and the constraint it puts upon us, no body, I think, accounts an *abridgment* of liberty. . . ."

If you think that's splitting hairs, at least it deals with what to some of us is the most important word in the Constitution. Turn now to the lengths to which Justices Stephen Breyer, writing for the majority, and Ruth Bader Ginsburg, whose dissent was joined by Rehnquist, Souter and Scalia (presumably still thumbing his Sheridan), went in debating the meaning of a fairly common verb: *to carry.*

In *Muscarello v. U.S.*, the issue was whether the phrase *carries a firearm* meant only "bears on your person" or could be interpreted to mean "transports in the trunk or glove compartment of your car." The broader construction meant jail for the defendant.

"*Carry* is a word commonly used to *convey* various messages," argued Ginsburg (subtly using *convey* to make her point), which she illustrated with this multifaceted passage from the television series *M*A*S*H* in which Hawkeye Pierce, played by Alan Alda, proclaims: "I will not carry a gun. . . . I'll carry your books, I'll carry a torch, I'll carry a tune, I'll carry on, carry over, carry forward, Cary Grant, cash and carry, carry me back to Old Virginia, I'll even 'hari-kari' if you show me how, but I will not carry a gun!"

Only two were deemed relevant by Breyer. "When one uses the word in the first, or primary, meaning, one can, as a matter of ordinary English, 'carry firearms' in a wagon, car, truck or other vehicle that one accompanies. When one uses the word in a different, rather special, way," held Breyer, who is heavily into commas, "to mean, for example, 'bearing' or (in slang) 'packing' (as in 'packing a gun') the matter is less clear."

In my view, that is the meaning Mae West had in mind when she said, "Is that a gun in your pocket, or are you just glad to see me?"

He cited the *Barnhart Dictionary of Etymology* to show how the primary meaning includes conveyance in a vehicle: the Latin *carum* means "car" and "cart," and since 1896 we have used *car* to mean "automobile." He cited 2 Kings 9:28 in the King James Bible, "His servants carried him in a chariot to Jerusalem," and updated it with a *New York Times* clip about an "ex-con" who "arrives home driving a stolen car and carrying a load of handguns."

Only the twenty-sixth definition of *carry* in the *Oxford English Dictionary*, wrote Breyer, was directed to the special meaning that the defense used to narrow the meaning of the law: "to bear, wear, hold up, or sustain, as one moves about; habitually to bear about with one." In the opinion handed down by the Supreme Court of the United States, "the word 'carry' in its ordinary sense includes carrying in a car and . . . the word, used in its ordinary sense, keeps the same meaning whether one carries a gun, a suitcase, or a banana."

Your verdict about participles needing an attachment to a noun is in error. I am referring, of course, to today's article about Justice Scalia in the Magazine.

Consider these examples:

The teacher wrote the sentence on the blackboard, *using* cursive script.

He strode down the path, *veering* neither left nor right.

They left by the rear door, *making* sure that no one saw them.

These participles give meaning to the preceding verbs and need no noun. In the example you wrote about, "taking" gives information about the compound verb "are judged" and is used correctly.

Morton S. Krieger
Norwalk, Connecticut

You seem to have erred in characterizing as solipsistic those solons who dangled a participle in drafting the law controlling the National Endowment for the Arts. The near homophone for which you apparently reached is solecistic, *violating conventional grammar. Using* solipsistic, *a form of philosophic self-absorption, is* sciolistic, *i.e., shallow on understanding. What a catachresis!*

James L. Reynolds
Metairie, Louisiana

MISRULE OF THUMB

"We had to go by *rule of thumb*," said Louis Katz, vice president of George Washington University, explaining some funding problems to *The GW Hatchet,* an independent student newspaper.

This seemingly innocent figure of speech drew fire from a female student, Jess Brinn, who wrote: "For the unaware, in English vernacular, *rule of thumb* refers to an obvious solution of doing things the way they have always been done. However, the phrase originated in English common law, where a man was permitted to beat his wife as long as the rod he used was no bigger than the width of his thumb." She excoriated the "misogynistic connotations . . . disrespectful to women and men alike," and while assuming the university official intended no disrespect, noted, "We should all know what we're saying and where the phrases we use come from."

So we should. The president of GW, Stephen Joel Trachtenberg, sends me the student paper and asks, "Can this possibly be true?"

The irate student could point to a brouhaha that arose in 1782 when Francis Buller, an English judge, was said to have made a remark in public along those lines. He was promptly jumped on by several caricaturists, including the first great political caricaturist, James Gillray; on November 27 of that year, he depicted a berobed judge with an armload of sticks saying: "Who wants a cure for a nasty wife? Here's a nice Family Amusement for Winter Evenings." Meanwhile, a wife is shouting, "Murder!" and a husband is shouting back: "Murder, hey? It's Law, you Bitch! It's not bigger than my Thumb!"

In his time, Gillray set the standard for satiric savagery, making today's cartoonists like Paul Conrad and Pat Oliphant appear as gentle as Charles Schulz. The pioneering Gillray drew drawings that drew blood, taking on even the feared journalistic vituperator William Cobbett; by the time the caricaturist died insane in 1815, he had forever saddled the eminent jurist, Buller, with the name "Judge Thumb."

Thus, the notion that *rule of thumb* has its roots in the subjugation of women has a history. But a UCLA professor of English, Henry Ansgar Kelly, in the September 1994 *Journal of Legal Education*, titles his lengthy scholarly investigation "*Rule of Thumb* and the Folklaw Pun Intended of the Husband's Stick." His conclusion about the origin of the phrase in wife-beating: "*Rule of thumb* has received a bad rap."

That's because its first appearance in print is cited in the *OED* as 1692, nearly a century before Gillray's *Judge Thumb*. Sir William Hope, in *The Compleat Fencing Master*, wrote, "What he doth, he doth by *rule of Thumb*, and not by Art."

It was reported in 1721 in Kelly's *Scottish Proverbs:* "No Rule so good as

Rule of Thumb." The meaning is "a roughly practical method, or an assertion based on experience."

Origin? Could be that carpenters used the width of their thumbs to approximate an inch, or that artists held up their thumbs to gain perspective on a distant object, or that gardeners used their green thumbs as guides to depth of seeding.

The idea that *rule of thumb* is derived from an early form of spousal abuse is in error. It's "folk etymology," amusing, even plausible with its first citation two centuries old, but inaccurate. (The gender-sensitive will not, however, denounce it sexistly as an *old wives' tale*.)

> *You seem to suggest that there is little actual source in law, especially American law, for the notion that the phrase* rule of thumb *stems from a legal doctrine permitting men to beat their wives. In fact, an American court did hold that a husband may beat his wife "with a switch no larger than his thumb."* State v. Rhodes *61 N. Ca. 453 (Phil. Law 1868). Although this rule was rejected by the reviewing court, that court nonetheless refused to hold that wife-beating was subject to judicial sanction.*
>
> *While it is certainly possible that the phrase* rule of thumb *does not stem from this case and its predecessors, I think the fact that the notion that husbands were permitted to beat wives with a stick of certain size did exist in American courts (and not only early British common law) is probably the more salient point at the root of this debate. Scholars debate the degree of acceptance of such a rule, and certainly it was neither universal nor long-standing. However, it did exist.*
>
> *Joan S. Meier, Professor of Clinical Law and Director*
> *Domestic Violence Advocacy Project*
> *The George Washington University*
> *Washington, D.C.*

MISS PRISON OF 1998

"There is substantial and credible evidence," charges the majority staff of the House Judiciary Committee, "that the President may have engaged in *misprision* of Monica Lewinsky's felonies. . . ."

Minority counsel fired back that "allegations of lying under oath, obstruction and tampering—or even as counsel renames them as *misprision* of a crime"—did not rise to historical impeachment precedents.

Where is this *misprision*, and how is it pronounced?

The word has nothing to do with *prison*, though it can send you there. The last syllable begins with the same sound that begins the name *Zsa Zsa Gabor*.

The root meaning is "mistake"; misprision comes from the French *mesprendre*, with *prendre* meaning "to take." It was Shakespeare's meaning in *Love's Labour's Lost:* "sweet misprision!"

A more sour sense was already in use, that of "concealment." In 1533, Henry VIII beheaded Sir Thomas More for refusing to acknowledge an annulment of his marriage to Catherine of Aragon, calling his crime *"misprision* of high treason."

Today, the legal meaning is still spelled out in a treason statute. Title 18 of the U.S. Criminal Code: "Whoever, owing allegiance to the United States and having knowledge of any treason against them, conceals and does not, as soon as may be, disclose and make known the same to the president [or other legal authority] is guilty of *misprision* of treason" and faces a jail term of up to seven years.

Setting treason aside, and ignoring its application to all outdated sedition, *misprision* means "neglect of duty"; all citizens, especially government officials, are duty-bound to report knowledge of serious crimes.

The noun was thrust into the nation's vocabulary in 1974 during the Nixon impeachment hearings. White House attorney Leonard Garment, drawing on his familiarity with a 1649 poem by Richard Lovelace ("Stone walls do not a prison make/Nor iron bars a cage"), offered this amelioration to those accusing the President of obstructing justice: "Stonewalling does not *misprision* make."

Although I admired most of your explanation for misprision, *I think it important to observe that you provided only one of the root meanings of the word. If you'll check the second entry for* misprision *in the* Oxford English Dictionary, *you'll find a derivation, not from the French* mesprendre, *but from the English* misprize. *When the word is employed in the sense that enters our discourse by that route, it usually refers to a "contempt" or "scorn" that results from a "failure to appreciate or recognize as valuable." One of the illustrations the* OED *supplies is* All's Well That Ends Well, *II.iii.159, "That dost in vile misprision shackle up My love, and her desert."*

John F. Andrews, President
The Shakespeare Guild
Washington, D.C.

MORAL HAZARD

Sometimes a financial phrase kicks around the news, and we all act as if we understand it.

Did we bail out Mexico, and will we now rescue financially distressed Brazil and Russia? Watch out for the *moral hazard*. Forming a consortium to prevent a collapse of a hedge fund that is "too big to fail"? Careful— moral hazard. As we tut-tut at Treasury Secretary Robert Rubin and Fed Chairman Alan Greenspan for their not-to-be-worrying-about *moral hazard*, the question nags: What's the *hazard* and what makes it *moral?*

The Wall Street Journal describes it as "the distortions introduced by the prospect of not having to pay for your sins." Bengt Holmstrom, a professor of economics at MIT, defines it as "dysfunctional acts induced by a contract or law. If you have a contract with me that says heads you win, tails I lose, this type of a contract can induce you to take on inordinate amounts of risk." Burton G. Malkiel, professor of economics at Princeton, agrees it involves "cases where the existence of risk insurance alters the behavior of the insured toward taking more risk." Because depositors in savings-and-loans were insured by the government, the owners were induced to roll the dice on investments in the 1980s; heads the savings-and-loan lenders won, tails the government lost.

The phrase, which you can now astound your friends by readily defining, was born in the insurance industry early in this century. It was extended by Kenneth J. Arrow, the Nobel laureate in economics, in a 1962 scholarly journal and popularized in his 1971 book, *Essays in the Theory of Risk-Bearing*. Professor Arrow was asked by the Ford Foundation for a theorist's impression of the economics of medical care. Here's the story straight from the Arrow, now at Stanford:

"It struck me immediately," he tells me, "that one problem with insurance was that the user (the patient) was not required to pay the full cost (indeed only a relatively small fraction of it). Therefore, according to usual economic principles, the patient would use medical care excessively."

Makes sense; whenever a disk in my back starts to crumble, I greedily demand an MRI; if I weren't insured, I'd settle for a cheaper X ray. "It came back to me," notes Professor Arrow, "that the insurance industry had already recognized this problem and had used the term *moral hazard* for it. The simplest example is burning down one's house to collect insurance, an act that might clearly be regarded as immoral—less immoral if one had been slightly less careful in putting candles out."

(Morally hazardous executive says: "Business was terrible last year, but we had this fire and I was insured, so I'm O.K. You?" His friend: "Same— was losing a bundle, but there was this flood and I was covered." First crook: "Good, but tell me—how do you start a flood?")

Arrow's extension of the old insurance industry term was taken up quickly. "Now it's applied in a wide variety of fields," he reports, "including in the last fifteen years to the behavior of banks when they have reason to believe that they will be bailed out if they get into trouble."

Bail out, by the way, began as a verb meaning "to clear water from a boat by throwing it overboard" and developed a new overboard sense in 1930 as "to parachute from an aircraft." Since 1951, as both noun and verb, it has referred to financial rescue of an institution or nation, a practice that has led some critics to think we have all gone overboard.

The term moral hazard *in economics and now more generally throughout society muddies the precision of two distinct terms in the insurance industry:* moral hazard *and* morale hazard. *The first hazard generally refers to the inherent character of the insured. The second hazard refers to the fact that the existence of insurance can lead to indifference to risk. Therefore it is a* moral hazard *when someone's character can cause that person to be inclined to burn down a building to collect insurance money. On the other hand, a* morale hazard *exists when someone decides to build a house in a known flood plain while having government flood insurance. The current usage in economics lumps these together.*

Ozan Gurel
Cambridge, Massachusetts

MOTHER WIT

"No, it had nothing to do with ethics," said President Clinton's friend Vernon Jordan, originally from Georgia, explaining to Asa Hutchinson of Arkansas why he would have no hand in the destruction of evidence, "as much as it's just good common sense, *mother wit*—you remember that in the South."

In another answer, Jordan used the phrase in a way that defined it: "If you had been sitting where I was . . . I think just *mother wit*, common sense, judgment would have suggested you would be interested." Representative Hutchinson took the dialect cue and began another question with "Let's put it in the realm of *mother wit.*"

These gentlemen were using a phrase unfamiliar to many in northern and eastern linguistic regions but easily understood by "country" talkers and especially black Americans; it is deeply rooted in the usages of some of the great contributors to the English language.

The phrase was defined by E. Cobham Brewer in the 1894 edition of his *Dictionary of Phrase and Fable* as "native wit, a ready reply; the wit which 'our mother gave us.' In ancient authors . . . courteous but not profound." In the deliciously scholarly *Dictionary of American Regional English (DARE)*, this 1973 definition by Alan Dundes can be found: "A popular term in black speech referring to common sense . . . not necessarily learned from books or in school. *Mother wit* with its connotation of collective wisdom acquired by the experience of living and from generations past is often expressed in folklore."

First recorded in 1440, it was attributed to Mother Nature by Edmund Spenser in his 1596 *Faerie Queene:* "For all that nature by her *mother wit*/Could frame in earth." Shakespeare picked it up in his *Taming of the Shrew*, with Kate asking mockingly, "Where did you study all this goodly speech?" and Petruchio replying, "It is extempore, from my *mother-wit.*" In *Growth of Popery* (1677), the poet Andrew Marvell of coy-mistress fame immortalized the phrase in an apothegm: "An ounce of mother-wit is worth a pound of clergy."

This century, William Butler Yeats gave it a romantic twist: "I had the wisdom love brings forth;/I had my share of *mother wit.*" More recently, the phrase has been appropriated by black writers. Ralph Ellison, in *The Invisible Man* (1952), has a Harlem blues singer rhymingly opine that "all it takes to get along in this here man's town is a little . . . grit and *mother-wit.*"

In her 1969 memoir, *I Know Why the Caged Bird Sings*, the poet Maya Angelou wrote of advice to be "intolerant of ignorance but understanding of illiteracy," noting the intelligence of those unable to go to school: "She encouraged me to listen carefully to what country people called *mother wit*. That in those homely sayings was couched the collective wisdom of generations." More recently, several books have used the phrase in the title, including Ronnie Clayton's *Mother Wit: The Ex-Slave Narratives of the Louisiana Writers' Project* and *Folk Wisdom and Mother Wit: John Lee, an African-American Herbal Healer,* by Arvilla Payne-Jackson.

This raises (but, I regret, does not beg) the question: Are there any other words, rooted in mid-millennium English and preserved in dialect, that appear in the speech of southerners, especially African Americans?

Airish is one; Chaucer used it in the fourteenth century to mean "aerial"; in Scotland it developed a sense of "cool, chilly" and is preserved in a kind of dialectic amber today in the sense of "haughty, snooty," from one who "puts on airs." In the same way, *dry* as a modifier was used by the playwright Ben Jonson in 1637 to mean "meager, colorless," as he gave us some good advice: "As wee should take care, that our style in writing, be neither dry, nor empty." According to *DARE*, published by the University of Wisconsin, that sense persists among black speakers today, meaning "plain, without accompaniments," like "dry, without lemon or milk" in tea. Similarly, *nature* was used by Chaucer in a sense of "sexual vigor," and that special sense is retained, but only in regional dialect.

Here's another Old English phrase much more often used by blacks than whites today: *make haste,* first used as *"Make haist* (O Lorde)" in Coverdale's translation of the Bible's Psalms, and taken up by the novelist Henry Fielding in *Tom Jones* in 1749: "It was necessary for him to *make haste* home." Today, *DARE* counts it as "formerly widespread, now especially South and South Midland, especially frequent among Black speakers."

Why this preservation in black speech? Says Michael Montgomery, of the University of South Carolina, now writing a Smoky Mountains dialect dictionary: "Popular speech is really quite conservative. Things hold on in settings of social isolation." Why should specific Scots-Irish English dialect usages be the ones to hold on? "Most overseers who ran the slave plantations were not very well educated white men. We can tell from their surnames that most were Scots-Irish, or came from places like Ulster but had a Scottish heritage. The dialect they spoke was not London English, but was the English language the slaves heard."

Anyone with a modicum of *mother wit* should know that. If I were not so overeducated and had a little *horse sense* (1832) or *common sense* (1543, from the 1398 *common wit*) or *dry gumption*, I would have been able to figure that out for myself.

MY OFFENSE IS SKANK

Nancy Gibbs of *Time* magazine wrote that President Clinton was "accused of *skanky* behavior toward a young employee."

Skank is a locution coming on strong. In the 1996 film *Swingers*, a male character expostulates, "Some *skank* who is half the woman my girlfriend is is gonna front me?" Reviewing *The People vs. Larry Flynt* in 1997, Jay Carr wrote in *The Boston Globe* that Flynt's bisexual wife, played by Courtney Love as a compassionate libertine, was "a *skank* with heart." At about that time, the singer Toni Braxton complained to *The Washington Post* that black performers who posed nude were unfairly "considered *skank* whores or sluts."

The word is both noun and adjective, with the modifier either *skank* or *skanky*. Its meaning is in the process of moving from exclusively one sex ("slut, sluttish") to both ("immoral"). A related sense deals with odor: *Skanky* can be synonymous with "funky, stinky." A less-related British meaning is "to pass off other substances as hard drugs, such as aspirin for crack cocaine."

David Sullivan of Washington informs me that the word originated as Jamaican slang, "common in the musical cultures of *ska*, a related word, I believe, and *reggae*. The meanings range from 'hang out' to 'smoke pot' to 'dance.'"

The *OED* agrees, defining skanking as "a style of West Indian dancing to reggae music" with hands clawing the air in time to the beat. Richard Allsop's valuable *Dictionary of Caribbean English Usage* suggests that *ska* comes from American jazz's *scat* (why not spelled *skat?*), Louis Armstrong's word-sounds imitative of instruments, and that *skank* originally meant "to loaf, be shifty . . . to steal and slip or speed away," and by extension "to dance in the particular free style associated with *dub* or *reggae*."

What accounts for the word's sudden emergence in slang, accompanied by a wrinkled nose? Both its sound and its associations. The *sk* recalls *skunk*; the *ank* ending has resonance in *dank*, *stank* and *rank*. ("Oh, my offense is rank!")

Good word; keep your ear peeled for a *skank moment*.

Your description of scat singing as "Louis Armstrong's word-sounds imitative of instruments" is somewhat misleading. Scat singing is characterized by the use of vocal sounds that do not form words. For example, in his famous recording of "Hotter than Than" Louis sings, "Rip dad u dad u da du-ya dad it dip bah!" The New Grove Dictionary of Jazz *defines scat singing as "a technique of jazz singing in which onomatopoetic or nonsense syllables are sung to improvised melodies." You are correct that scat singing is usually considered to be a vocal imitation of instrumental melody.*

Michael Cogswell
Louis Armstrong House and Archives
Queens College, The City University of New York
Flushing, New York

When I was growing up in Brooklyn, in the middle 50s to late 60s, skank *was part of our street slang.*

In Brooklyn, skank *referred to a profoundly ugly girl of our age group. A typical* skank *would be very skinny (always flat chested); have long, stringy, oily, mousy brown hair; thick-framed glasses; and a pimple.* Skank *might also be used by one boy as a "rank" on another boy's date, even if that girl did not meet the "objective" test for a* skank.

Perhaps it was a combination of skinny *and* rank.

Philip M. Perlah
Westport, Connecticut

NAME THAT NATION

ON INDEPENDENCE DAY WEEKEND, it is fitting and timely to ask: Who coined the name *United States of America?*

In the year before independence, many in the colonies went with the name used by Benjamin Franklin in his July 1775 draft of an articles of confederation: *United Colonies of North America.* Another name, however, most famously appeared in print on July 4, 1776, in the Declaration of Independence, which was drafted by a committee that assigned the task to Thomas Jefferson: Its last paragraph referred to "the Representatives of the *United States of America,* in General Congress assembled."

In our first exploration of this mystery, it was reported that the widely accepted Jefferson coinage (written by young Tom between June 11 and June 28, 1776) might have been antedated by two other citations: the first in a letter from the Continental Congress member Elbridge Gerry to Gen. Horatio Gates dated June 25, and the second in a letter to the *Pennsylvania Evening Post* published June 29, from the pseudonymous writer Republicus.

This is important; it's our country we're talking about, and we ought to try to pin down its namer. Two letters have come pouring in. One is from a biographer of Thomas Paine, Professor Jack Fruchtman Jr., of Towson University in Maryland, who insists that Paine's usage two years after the Declaration in his widely read *American Crisis* publicized the name. Call me a summer soldier or sunshine patriot, but common sense tells me that a popularizer is not a coiner.

Comes now Ronald Gephart, last of the editors of the Library of Congress's twenty-five-volume *Letters of Delegates to Congress, 1774–1789.* He searched his new CD-ROM of all that correspondence, then dug around in the *Journals of the Continental Congress,* and alerted me to his findings just in time for the nation's 222d anniversary.

Richard Henry Lee of Virginia was the Founder who made the motion on June 7, 1776, to declare "that these United Colonies are, and of right ought to be, free and independent States." His resolution led to the formation of three committees: one, starring Jefferson and John Adams, to draft a declaration of independence; another, including John Dickinson, the conservative Pennsylvanian, and Roger Sherman, to draft articles of confederation, and a third, including Dickinson, Adams and Franklin, to draft a treaty plan.

"All three committees began deliberating simultaneously," writes Gephart, "and continued to do so until the end of June. Jefferson accepted the responsibility for drafting the declaration, Dickinson the articles, and Adams the treaty plan. But as many as eighteen members of the three committees were working together to create these three fundamental documents in which *United States of America* was used for the first time."

So who came up with the catchy name for which the initials are not U.C.N.A. but U.S.A.? We know that Dickinson had by June 17 prepared a second draft—all that survives—of the articles, which includes the flat statement "The name of this Confederation shall be the '*United States of America.*'" Nothing tentative about that.

"Jefferson, on the other hand," writes Gephart, "did not ask Franklin to review his draft of 'A Declaration by the Representatives of the *United States of America*' until June 21. It is not known when Adams drafted the preamble to the plan of treaties."

The historian concludes cautiously, "The term was first coined by one or more members during the early deliberations of the three committees—between June 11, when Jefferson's committee began work, and June 17, when it appeared in the second draft of Dickinson's Articles."

Coinagists would give the edge to the conciliatory Dickinson (who refused to sign Jefferson's Declaration), partly because the first recorded surfacing of the phrase was his, and partly because he's not as famous as Jefferson and can use the recognition.

I'd still like to see Dickinson's first draft, with date. Keep looking, historians; it's not as if he was working on a word processor that obliterates first drafts. It would be of great interest to all of us here in the good old U.C.N.A., or whatever.

You request historians to keep looking for information as to who coined the name "The United States of America." Being descendants of Oliver

Ellsworth, one of the framers of the Constitution, members of my family have accepted, as fact, he is the individual who deserves the credit.

In *Carl Van Doren's* The Great Rehearsal: The Story of the Making and Ratifying of the Constitution of the United States, *the events of the Federal Convention of 1787 are detailed. Mr. Van Doren says, "On the motion of Ellsworth of Connecticut on June 20 it was unanimously agreed to change the words 'national government' in the first Virginia resolution to 'government of the United States.' From then on the name was used in later resolutions."*

Another source I refer to is a book compiled by Donna Siemiatkoski, sponsored by the Ellsworth Memorial Association and the Connecticut Daughters of the American Revolution, Inc., printed by Gateway Press, Inc., in Baltimore, 1992. In describing his involvement during the summer of 1787 at the Federal Convention, she refers to Oliver Ellsworth and his Connecticut colleagues, William Samuel Johnson and Roger Sherman, crafting the Connecticut Compromise, which created two houses of Congress. She says, "He was also one of five people on the drafting committee. As such, he coined the phrase, 'The United States of America.'"

Molly DePatie
New Canaan, Connecticut

NEED NOT TO KNOW

At that memorable moment when the State of the Union message and impeachment trial of President Clinton converged, Senator Arlen Specter was heard to remark: "This is schizophrenia at its highest."

Though alienists might be alienated by the common use of one of their terms to mean "split personality," the fact is that *schizo* is Greek for "split." In the *Christian Science Monitor,* Francine Kiefer called that moment "the ultimate example of Bill Clinton's 'split screen' presidency." What the Senator and the reporter were getting at was Mr. Clinton's ability to *compartmentalize.*

As the President made a practice of appearing detached from his pursuers, Maureen Dowd wrote in the *Times,* "the White House euphemistically calls it *'compartmentalizing,'* and *The New York Observer* wrote about *compartmentalization chic* among boomers juggling busy schedules." She then delivered the sort of ukase that only certified pundits can issue: "All this prattling about *compartmentalization* has got to stop."

Although I am quite able to set this word out of my mind as I write this column, let me prattle awhile (from the Low German *pratten*, "to pout," and then "to prate, babble, talk idly").

The word, now a defining Clintonism, means "the act of dividing into separate sections" and was coined in 1923 by the biologist Julian S. Huxley in his *Uniqueness of Man*. He was comparing our ability to think and act in a unified way with "the much more rigid *compartmentalization* of animal mind and behavior."

In the age of multiculturalism and interdisciplinarianism (there's a new one), most of the nonscientific uses of the term have been pejorative. But in the military, the word found a home: "These scientists had worked for the Manhattan District," wrote *The New Yorker* in 1946 about our early atomic research, "and the Army, temporarily abandoning its policy of '*compartmentalization* of information,' had recently brought them together."

Espionage then took up the word and shortened it. *Compartmented* meant having "access limited to a 'need to know.'" If you're a spook and want to examine our satellite photographs of Saddam Hussein's favorite seraglio, you need a "Talent Keyhole" clearance. But that's *compartmented*; if you have no need to know, it matters not how much talent you have. They won't let you near the keyhole.

In the Clinton years, the word in its long form became his admirers' favorite description of his mind's ability to focus on specific business no matter what the distraction. On *Good Morning America*, when the former Clinton aide George Stephanopoulos told ABC's Elizabeth Vargas that "he always talks in the State of the Union under strange circumstances," she picked up the jargon and replied in awe, "He has a remarkable ability to *compartmentalize*."

Then, as usually happens, the word began to be used against him. "This is the same President renowned for his ability to *compartmentalize*," charged the impeachment manager Ed Bryant, ". . . and pleads that he simply wasn't paying attention . . . during his own deposition." Another manager, Lindsey Graham, said, "That's what this case is about—equivocation and *compartmentalizing*." And asked about the complexity of the arguments in the Senate trial, Senator George Voinovich of Ohio replied mischievously, "As someone has said, we'll just have to *compartmentalize*."

This word that will enter the political lexicon under his name is frequently used about him, but apparently not by him. It's nowhere to be found out of his mouth on the White House Web site. If ever given the opportunity to ask Mr. Clinton a direct personal question, I would unhesitatingly put the hot one to him: "Mr. President, what would you call your ability to focus on the issues of interest to the American people while scandalmongers wallow in Monicagate?" Or something to that effect.

NET: ON OR OVER?

Two headlines from the same issue of the *Times* came in from Omar Gharzeddine of New York. One read, "After a Delay, Text Gets Out *on* Internet," and the other, "Apple to Offer Custom Orders *over* the Internet." He asks, "What's the difference?"

One moves, the other sits—that is, one deals with transmission, the other with storage. "*Over* refers to transmission," says Harry Newton, author of *Newton's Telecom Dictionary*. "The Internet is really a transport mechanism, just a method of getting from A to B. When you get where you are going—and for most people this is the Web or another computer—you are *on*."

Here am I, with my column available *on* the Internet (at www.nytimes.com). There it sits, *on*. You can get it, or access it, *over* the Internet.

I'm doing my best to keep up. I don't say "w, w, w" anymore—just a breezy "Web." Saves eight syllables.

NEW OID WOID

A *syllogism*, from the Greek for "summing up," means "the drawing of a logical conclusion from two premises." In current use, the deduction may be deceptive: "All politicians and pundits are venal; Safire is a political pundit; therefore, Safire is doubly venal." The reasoning is seemingly logical but may be false.

In a footnote to his recent dissent from the Supreme Court decision on *Steel & Pickling Co. v. Citizens for a Better Environment*, Justice John Paul Stevens used a syllogistic construction: "If A . . . can be decided before B, and if B . . . can be decided before C . . . then logic dictates that A . . . can be decided before C."

Justice Antonin Scalia, pickling Stevens for the majority, observed that his brother Justice's argument was "replete with extensive case discussions, case citations, rationalizations and *syllogoids*."

"I've heard of factoid," writes Stephen L. Wasby, professor of political science at the State University of New York at Albany, "but where did *syllogoid* come from?"

The *-oid* suffix, rooted in the Greek for "shape," creates a noun or adjective meaning "similar but not the same; having the characteristics of." A *factoid*, coined in 1973 by Norman Mailer, is an imagined or simulated fact.

The noun *syllogoid*, therefore, means "an argument having the form but not the logical force of a syllogism." To Professor Wasby's point: Whence *syllogoid*?

An exhaustive search of databases and legal tomes reveals that we have here what the Greeks called a *hapax legomenon*—a word of which only one use is recorded in all literature. (It happens a few times in the Book of Job, making that biblical text so hard to translate.) In other words: (A, major premise) the word didn't exist; (B, minor premise) Scalia used it; (C, logical conclusion) Scalia must have coined it.

"There are only three possible responses to your note," Justice Scalia responds to my written query, "none of which is satisfactory. The first displays illiteracy ('You mean *syllogoid* is not a word?'), the second confesses incompetence (since a coinage that has to be explained is a failure) and the third risks giving offense. I pick the last and shall not respond at all, which I hereby do. Best regards."

I am a little confused about the need for a new word to express "an argument having the form but not the logical force of a syllogism." What happened to sophism?

Lenir Drake
New York, New York

NEW PAVING FOR
THE MIDDLE OF THE ROAD

A specter is stalking world politics, as Karl Marx might have manifested it—the specter of the *third way*.

"The *third way* is part of the politics of the center and center left," said Tony Blair, the British prime minister, last month. "In Britain, it means

New Labor." He defined his *third way* as a place where "economic dynamism and social justice can live together."

"European governments spend and tax heavily," noted Laura D'Andrea Tyson, former chairman of the Clinton Council of Economic Advisers, "but the architects of the new Europe see them as a human *third way* between old-style socialism and the supposed divisive social consequences of the American way."

Her former boss saw the way more benignly. In Bill Clinton's 1992 campaign, he said, "I thought we ought to have a *third way*," and in his 1998 State of the Union declared, "We have found a *third way*." Last month he told the Economic Club of Detroit: "We are working with business to use technology, research and market incentives to meet national goals. Some have called this political philosophy 'the *third way*.'"

Those "some" can also be found in Moscow. "Former Deputy Prime Ministers Anatoly Chubais and Boris Nemtsov accused Moscow mayor and born-again centrist Yuri Luzhkov of 'economic illiteracy,'" wrote Harry Kopp of the Jamestown Foundation's *Monitor*. "Luzhkov, who recently returned from Tony Blair's Britain, said Russia must choose 'a *third way* between total socialism and vulgar liberalism.'"

Where there's a way, there's a will; in this case, Will Marshall, head of Washington's Progressive Policy Institute, who says that Mr. and Mrs. Clinton "think a *third way* approach to governing is his legacy."

Of course, left and right take their pops at it. Liberals see self-contradictions in such a "slippery center." "The *third way* assumes a basic political symmetry," wrote Jonathan Chait in *The New Republic*, "an unreconstructed left, a radical right and a *third way* nestled in between." But this is self-defeating: "When the *third way* takes power, it alters that equation and no longer sits between the two poles of the political spectrum; it is the left pole. The calculus has changed, and, in order to retain the center, the *third way* must shift right again."

The Republican Lamar Alexander, of the Campaign for a New American Century (its onset is getting ever more likely), slams the way from the right. "The *third way* is no way," he claims. "Supposedly, this is an alternative to free-market capitalism, on the one hand, and socialism, on the other. When you peel the layers off this particular onion, however, what you get is 'social democracy'—the ever-expanding, cradle-to-grave welfare-state programs that hobble most European countries."

Where did the latest moniker for the middle of the road come from? You can find the phrase in theology (between the second and fourth ways of Saint Thomas Aquinas) and among the ways of phenomenology. In politics, the historian H.A.L. Fisher traced it to the French emperor Napoleon III, who steered between internal revolution and foreign war to choose a *third way* of liberalism. In the United States, early centrists working toward a third party between Federalists and Republicans were called *Quiddists*, from the Latin *tertium quid*, or *"third thing."*

NEW YORKESE

"If we hurry, we can make the light." Only New Yorkers say that to one another. Other Americans say in their whitebreadese, "If we hurry, we can start crossing the street before the green light changes." (They are more literal and probably not in that much of a hurry, anyway. That is why they, and not New Yorkers, define a split second as a *New York minute*.)

In a taxi, *making the light* can be raised to the art form of *checkerboarding*, a series of turns made late at night when there is little traffic and an adept cabbie can work his way both uptown and across town without having to stop at a red light.

Other differentiations in dialect go to the Apple's core and set it apart. Here are a couple few examples. (In New Yorkese, "two or three" becomes *a couple few*.)

Kids on the streets of other cities play *hopscotch*. You toss an object—it used to be a skate key, before skates became keylessly in-line, on plastic rollers—into one square of an oblong figure marked into the asphalt and then hop to it on one foot. (The *scotch* has nothing to do with whisky or people from Scotland; it is a variant of *scratch*, which is how you mark the boxes.) Kids in New York, however, don't know from *hopscotch*. (When *from* is added to *don't know*, it is a dialect emphasis for "what one means by.")

"I sat down for a while in a playground," wrote Saul Bellow in his 1956 *Seize the Day*, ". . . to watch the kids play *potsy* and skip rope." New York kids, like others in the northeastern United States, play *potsy*, the word derived from a marble of baked clay that the *Oxford English Dictionary* notes is "a fragment of pottery played with in hopscotch" when you don't have a skate key, which is now an antique.

Another example: To get away from the heat, people in Jersey (who consider themselves from New Jersey) go to the *shore*. No New Yorkers ever went there; they go to the *beach*.

In what New Yorkers call "the hinterland," which others call "the real America," incredulous people say, "You flipped your lid?" or "You gone ape?" New Yorkers, who once said, "What are you, crazy or something?" now shorten that to *"Whaddya, whaddya?"*

A more subtle difference can be found in how words are stressed in phrases. Philip Scheffler, a New Yorker and executive editor of *60 Minutes* on CBS, wrote me about how he and the late Charles Kuralt, from North Carolina, emphasized words differently: "I ordered 'APPLE pie,' to distinguish it from 'PEACH pie'; my Tarheel friend ordered 'apple PIE,' to ensure he didn't get 'appleSAUCE.' He dines on 'ham SAND-WICH'; I select a 'HAM sandwich.' Should an out-of-towner ask us to tell him where the New York Knicks play roundball, I would direct him to 'Madison SQUARE Garden.' Kuralt would send the visitor to 'Madison Square GARDEN.'"

These are *shibboleths*, a word rooted in the name of a place that was pronounced differently by Israelites and Ephraimites, and was useful in revealing spies. The Bible tells us that some forty-two thousand Ephraimites were slain because they got it wrong; in those days, stress had consequences.

Do not confuse New Yorkese with Brooklynese, where some sounds are often transposed. The *er-oy* transposition has long been noted: When the great Brooklyn Dodger pitcher Waite Hoyt was injured, fans said, *"Hert's hoit."* (Usually, the schwa feels schwach.) In the same way, the consonant *r* is dropped from some words and inserted into others: A reference to a girl named Brenda and her mother becomes *Brender's mudda*. Perhaps because of such television shows as *Seinfeld*, this transfer is less evidence of social stratification than it was in the sociolinguist William Labov's day.

The letter *d* also gets taken from one place and set in another. The contraction *didn't* in New Yorkese becomes the single-syllable *dint*. That lost *d* reappears as a substitute for *t* in the vocabulary of disgusted dismissal, as *fuggedaboudit* and *gedoudahea*. ("I dint do it, so gedoudahea." "Thanks." "Fuggedaboudit.")

Whenever pure-dialect Brooklynites take the subway to Manhattan (they get on at the glottal stop), they say they are *gawna Noo Yawk*, as if Brooklyn were not part of New York City. In all boroughs, however, there is a tendency to talk at times when people from other places would normally listen; this *conversus interruptus* is not considered impolite because it is an expression of interest. "Talking is a New Yorker's way of showing friendship, especially to strangers," writes Deborah Tannen. And Jim Crotty observes in his 1997 *How to Talk American*, "New Yorkers show they are listening by interrupting what you are saying and commenting on it."

I'd better explain the assertion above that "the *schwa* feels *schwach*." In the science of language that calls itself linguistics, a *schwa* is a neutral vowel sound, its symbol an inverted *e*, pronounced *uh* and usually unstressed, as the *a* in *ago* or the *i* in *easily*. The Yiddish word *schwach*, or *shvach*, means "weak, listless, enervated, slightly nauseated" and in my opinion is the way the *schwa* sound must feel amid all the more forceful vowels and consonants.

As a Marylander transplanted from New York three decades ago, I suppose some of my former neighbors would take note of this off-the-wall observation with *Whaddya, whaddya?* but I'll never know; they sprinted ahead to make the light.

I do not believe that New Jerseyans go "to the shore." Unless things have changed recently, New Jerseyans go "down the shore." In fact, some years ago there was a television show with that very name. Going down the shore is not to be confused with going down east in Maine, but I wonder if there is not perhaps some common denominator.

William Barnett
New York, New York

The entire phrase, as it is used in New Jersey, is "down the shore," as in "I'm goin' down the shore this weekend." This is in contrast to New Yawk City, where people go "out to the beach."

Walter Kent
Wyckoff, New Jersey

When I was on the New York Daily News *in the late 1950s, one of the comics was "Potsy," by Jay Irving (father of Clifford Irving, novelist who wrote the hoax autobiography of Howard Hughes). Potsy was an easygoing cop. I asked Jay where the cop's name came from. Jay, who collected cop artifacts, said that "Potsy" was a turn-of-the-century word for a cop's badge—and for a cop. And, as I remember, kids used a tin badge, also called a potsy, in the kind of game you describe.*

Thomas B. Allen
Bethesda, Maryland

Brooklynese—at lunch time this conversation often takes place among our students: "Jeet?" "No, diju?"

John J. Fallon
(Principal of Bay Ridge High School)
Bellerose, New York

Although swapping of er *and* a *in Brooklynese may be a demeaning social mark to a New York ear, I have often mistaken it for the similar "high-toned" Boston and Harvard accents. I was brought up in Manchester, New Hampshire, and said to mention a yacht race from "Bah Hahbah to Havaner, Cuber." Actually, it's not a swap, it's just a final* a *and a final* er *or* ar *are pronounced the same. It's the auditor who thinks he hears a swap.*

Charles L. Levesque
Blue Bell, Pennsylvania

As a little girl growing up in the Bronx up the street from the courthouse, my friends and I played both potsy and hopscotch. We used the same chalked sidewalk grid of boxes numbered one to ten for both games. In potsy, we tossed our keys (stones rolled too much) into the numbered square, then hopped around the grid and picked them up. In hopscotch, we started in square one and had to hop in numerical order, kicking the keys gently from squares one to ten as we went.

You probably didn't take note of the small differences in the girls' games, being occupied with stoop ball or stick ball.

Girls also played a lot of "A, My Name Is," a "turn-over" game, as we called it. Remember seeing the girls bounce a ball, turning one leg over it as they recited a rhyme?

And you must remember War, which we played on the grassless area around a tree trunk in Joyce Kilmer Park. We threw pocket knives at

*opponents' territories, which were marked off in a square in the clean dirt.
It amuses me to remember that no parent was the least bit alarmed that
her seven-year-old carried a knife around in his/her pocket. Mumbledy-
peg was a grass variation with complicated rules.*

Nancy Schuster
Rego Park, New York

*Dropped (or added) consonants indeed! For example, the r in drawring, as
in "what a nice pencil drawring." Now that's strictly New Yorkese!*

Roland Ginzel
Stockbridge, Massachusetts

THE NON-CRASH

Like the conservative New Year's Eve celebrator who wanted to purchase a noisemaker that wasn't too loud, headline writers were recently
faced with a challenge: how to deal with a *precipitous* ("steep," not *precipitate,* "abrupt, rash, headlong") decline in the stock market without
encouraging a panic. (*Celebrator* is *New York Times* style for *celebrant.*)

The onomatopoeic *crash* was a word that *Wall Street Journal* editorialists were unafraid to use, but the front page of that publication chose a
verb less evocative of 1929: "Stocks *Plummet* 7 Percent." (That verb was
formed in this century from the noun *plummet,* a weight used to sound, or
fathom, the depth of water; in Shakespeare's *Tempest,* Prospero says,
"Deeper than did ever plummet sound/I'll drown my book," a sentiment
quoted by excessively modest authors.)

"Massive *Sell-Off*" was the choice of *USA Today.* The adjective *massive* lent urgency to the stock-market term *sell-off,* a noun first reported
in 1937 by *The Baltimore Sun* and still specialized enough to retain its
hyphen in most citations. *The New York Times* disagrees; the bank, or
infixed subhead, of its Hong Kong article read, "The Hang Seng sets
the scene for a global *selloff,*" unhyphenated. *USA Today* also used the
noun *rout* (military origin) and the verb *dived* (from swimming, with
that past tense preferred *to dove*). Its columnist, Walter Shapiro, later
used a less-alarmist word picture: "Watching the Dow *snow-plow* down
the mountain."

Plunge (from a 1380 use about baptism by immersion) got a nice play
in *The Baltimore Sun* (but if I first reported the use of *sell-off,* I'd stick with

it proudly). In *Newsweek*, C. K. Binswanger and Lucy Howard noted the panic prevention in newspapers: *drop* (*International Herald Tribune*), *tailspin* (*Jiji Press Ticker* of Tokyo), *tumble* (*Milwaukee Journal Sentinel*) and *tremble* (*The* [Montreal] *Gazette*).

In the synonymy of the bears, *decline, sag, sink* and *slump* are mildest; *drop*, more sudden; *tumble*, not shocking; *dive* and *plunge*, precipitous; *plummet, precipitate, sell-off*, technical; *correction*, interpretive or euphemistic; *free fall*, alarming; *collapse*, sudden and steep; and *crash*, better lock that window.

Television journalists, who could immediately affect the market with their demeanor, were careful; NBC called it "the Big Drop" and Fox chose "Blue Monday."

Now we are into the color of the day. October 19, 1987, was called *Black Monday* on the analogy of *Black Thursday* of October 24, 1929, and *Black Tuesday* of October 29, 1929. These were antedated by *Black Friday* of September 24, 1869, when Jay Gould drove brokers into bankruptcy with his attempted corner of the gold market. It all began with *Blue Monday* in the Middle Ages, supposedly the first Monday before Lent, when revelers felt hung over from pre-Lenten flings; later, it became the day to feel depressed about returning to work after a weekend. Several commentators dubbed last month's *sell-off* (in retrospect, that seems the best word, but who knew at the time?) to have happened on a less-than-calamitous day: *Gray Monday*.

I confess to having used the euphemistic *correction* two months before October's financial fibrillation. My technical analysis went, "You're going to see a *correction* one of these days that will *curl your hair.*" This was an obscure allusion to a figure of speech that sent a shiver through the financial markets forty years ago. In a 1957 news conference (in those days called a press conference), Eisenhower's Treasury Secretary, a former steel executive named George Magoffin Humphrey, was asked if he saw any hope of cutting defense spending in the coming years. He replied that such spending was "a terrific tax we are taking out of this country" and that if we did not reduce defense expenditures "over a long period of time, I will predict that you will have a depression that will *curl your hair.*"

I enjoy making arcane allusions like that; a few in the codger crowd catch them. One such is Herbert Stein,* who once noted how a fellow economist, Sol Fabricant, described a period of less-than-robust expansion by calling it a growth recession. Stein satirized this at the time with an imaginary conversation:

Stein: That's a handsome dog you have there, Sol.

Fabricant: That's not a dog. It's a horse.

Stein: But Sol, it's so small.

Fabricant: It's a growth horse.

Since that time, just as brokers have eschewed the word *crash*, economists have avoided the word *recession*, especially those in which hair is curled to *depression* levels. In 1982, I asked a couple of economists how they would define *depression*. Alan Greenspan said, "A *depression* is either a 12 percent unemployment rate for nine months or more, or a 15 percent unemployment rate for three to nine months." Professor Alfred Kahn of Cornell defined it as unemployment above 10 percent with two quarters of consecutive decline in real GNP.

When serving in the Carter administration, Kahn was chastised for even using the word *depression* in public. He vowed to White House spin-meisters that whenever he had to refer to such a calamity, he would substitute the word *banana*.

I still think the market is due for a hair-curler one day, but not so severe as to lead to anything like the Great Banana.

NOODGE

In what must have been a very carefully written and edited story in *The New York Times*, Clyde Haberman wrote about the passing of leadership of the newspaper from Arthur O. (Punch) Sulzberger to his son, Arthur Sulzberger Jr. It included this paragraph:

"For the most part, he, Punch, left news judgments to his senior editors. 'He was not an absentee landlord, but neither was he a nudge,' said A. M. Rosenthal, a former executive editor, now a columnist."

As an English verb, *to nudge*—which first appeared in Thomas Hobbes's 1675 translation of Homer's *Odyssey*—means "to gently jostle, especially with the elbow, as a signal to pay attention, or a gesture of cau-

---

*Herbert Stein, an economist who served in the Nixon White House with the rare combination of a sense of history and a sense of humor, died September 8, 1999.

tion or sly merriment." It may be rooted in the Scandinavian *nugga*, "to rub," or the Old English *cnucian*, "to knock."

Now forget all that, because that is not the *nudge*, verb or noun, that Rosenthal meant. He had in mind a Yiddish word more closely represented as *noodge*, a verb that the *Random House Unabridged Dictionary*, second edition, defines as "to annoy with persistent complaints, criticisms, or pleas; nag." The noun is defined as "pest."

In *The Joys of Yiddish*, Leo Rosten spells the noun *nudzh*, pronounced in two syllables, NUD-jeh, to rhyme with "could ya." In his 1986 *Yiddish and English*, Sol Steinmetz derives the noun from the Yiddish verb *nudyen*, "to bore, pester," and cautions, "It should not be confused with the standard English noun *nudge*, meaning 'a slight push.'" Steinmetz reports spellings of the Yiddish word that range from *nudzh* to *noodge*, but prefers *nudge*, which is how it appears in those up-to-date dictionaries that include it.

I hate to be a pest, or even an especially pushy pest, but the sound of the *u* in the Yiddish word is the sound of the *oo* in *oof* or *look*. That is not the sound of the *oo* in *woozy* or *hooh-boy*. But neither is it the sound of the *u* in the English *nudge*, which is *uh*, close to the neutral sound of the schwa.

Therefore, I would spell the Yiddish word for "needling annoyer" *noodge*, not *nudge*. Remember: Pronounce the *oo* as in *look*, not as in *fool*.

I ran this past Abe Rosenthal, who was quoted in the article, and he said, "Yeah, I had to look at that word twice. It's a word you say, not a word you spell."

Language columnists have to make the hard decisions. I say spell it *noodge*.

NOT SO FAST!

It's relatively easy to find a label for a policy that involves the promise of action. Both "Fifty-four Forty or Fight!" and the more temperate "Speak Softly and Carry a Big Stick" carried messages of stern forewarning. Policy slogans beginning with *Remember*, with their pledges of vengeance, had a good run in wartime, with the outrages to be recalled ranging from the Alamo to the *Maine* to Pearl Harbor.

More recently, *containment* was George Kennan's somewhat more sobersided contribution to cold-war foreign-policy nomenclature, followed by the Clinton administration's *engagement*. These offered a sense of quiet but resolute policy action.

What do you label a policy that does not appeal to jingoism, adventurism, interventionism—or, indeed, commit you to any reaction whatever? Many statesmen find much in a philosophy that eschews escalation, arguing instead, "Don't just do something—stand there."

That was the challenge that faced Strobe Talbott, former Deputy Secretary of State, as he sought a catch phrase to define the Clinton administration's foreign policy in a multipolar but uni-superpower world. As a former correspondent and columnist for *Time* magazine, Talbott knew that a diplomatic word or phrase had to be conceived in quietude, preferably before an academic audience, and then be allowed to develop slowly over the months. Any more pretentious unveiling, or capitalization, would alert the legion of carping critics to strangle the label in its crib.

On September 19, 1997, he offered his conception to Stanford University: "We need to make sure we have a policy toward Russia that contains an indispensable feature: *strategic patience*. That means a policy not just for coping with the issue or the crisis of the moment or the week or even of the season, or for getting through the next summit meeting; rather it means a policy for the next century."

Few combinations of words are now wholly original. *Strategic patience* had been used two weeks earlier by a corporate executive, Jim Maxmin, in an article for *Industry Week;* a year before that, in *The Good Guys*, a book by Jules Bonavolonta and Brian Duffy, the phrase was used to describe the FBI plan to infiltrate major Mafia families to conduct long-term investigations. Earlier hits can be made in databases covering fields from music to the military.

But after Talbott slipped his diplomatic usage into the bulrushes, the Senate's authority on foreign affairs, Richard Lugar, picked it up in a January 1998 Harvard speech. "American policy toward Russia must contain a healthy dose of *strategic patience*," he said, accepting the Talbott definition but adding that it was today "particularly susceptible to Russian nonperformance."

By November, the conceiver was ready to incubate the phrase in a speech subtitle. In "Gogol's Troika: The Case for *Strategic Patience* in a Time of Troubles," Talbott—whose enthusiastic support of Boris Yeltsin has been tempered by disappointment—returned to Stanford to say,

"The policy that flows from realism is one of *strategic patience* and persistence." Lest he be accused of departing from previous policy, he added, "That means continuing engagement." After he reworked his thoughtful speech for *The Economist*, his phrase was picked up by his former colleagues at *Time*.

Because White House speechwriters have chosen no Clinton doctrine or catch phrase of their own and are not really married to engagement, Talbott's personal, long-suffering, tactical patience has paid off: His phrase is in play.

On what linguistic structure is this coinage bottomed? (As Henry Kissinger once shouted at a football referee who had just made an egregious interference call against a Redskins cornerback, "On vot theory?")

The use of an active modifier to qualify a noun that justifies not rushing into action has a grand history in diplomatic rhetoric. President Grover Cleveland, criticizing the seizure of Hawaii by the United States in 1893, wrote, "There seemed to arise . . . the precise opportunity for which he was *watchfully waiting*." Twenty years later, President Woodrow Wilson picked up that alliterative phrase and, refusing to be drawn into a war with Mexico, elevated it to policy status: "We shall not, I believe, be obliged to alter our policy of *watchful waiting*." The stern *watchful* gave a monitoring, almost monitory, cast to the feeble *waiting*.

This built on the tradition begun in 1791 by Sir James Mackintosh, a historian and member of Parliament, in *Vindiciae Gallicae*, a response to Edmund Burke's criticism of the French Revolution. "The Commons, faithful to their system," wrote Mackintosh, "remained in a wise and *masterly inactivity*. . . ." That phrase resounded among all who wanted to do little or nothing, and was soon followed by his equally stirring *"disciplined inaction."*

No ringing refutations or derisive slogans have yet met Secretary Talbott's sophisticated essay into the field of semi-oxymoronic phrase making. We will just have to let the dust settle. But those sensitive to the technique soon noted another, similar construction that offered a corollary to strategic patience. A White House spokesman seeking to substitute censure for impeachment used a highly active adverb to give backbone to a passive participle: "Officials publicly indicated more interest than before," reported *The Washington Post*, "saying they were *aggressively listening*. . . ."

Your stimulating article on semi-oxymoronic slogans reminds me of one I coined when I was an assistant secretary (for policy development and research) of HUD under President Reagan: purposeful inertia. *We used it so often that we began abbreviating it* P.I. *in meetings where we decided whether or not to include in our departmental budget proposal the latest ideas for new government programs that had gurgled up from below. As some ideas had even managed to gain support from one assistant secretary or another, I sought a term that would not exactly reject a dumb idea but would leave it floating ethereally in the bureaucracy, no doubt to be given new life the next year.* Purposeful inertia *filled the bill nicely. Usually upon my initiative, we made the firm, forceful decision to do nothing about the proposed program.*

> *E. S. Sava, Professor of Public Policy*
> *Baruch College, The City University of New York*
> *New York, New York*

NUKE 'EM

In a generally upbeat review of George W. Bush's maiden interview on *Meet the Press*, I zinged him on his pronunciation of the word *nuclear*. A half-dozen times he said "NU-ky-ler" rather than the correct "NU-klee-er" or "NYOO-klee-er."

"Because he can't pronounce *nuclear*," writes Joseph Friend from cyberspace, "he is a shoe-in in as much as neither can Carter and Clinton. Must be a requirement of office."

Lexicographers have noticed this phenomenon. "Though disapproved of by many," goes a usage note in *Merriam-Webster's Tenth Collegiate Dictionary*, "pronunciations ending in -ky -ler have been found in widespread use among educated speakers including scientists, lawyers, professors . . . and U.S. presidents (Eisenhower, Carter) and vice presidents (Mondale, Quayle)." Scholarly elucidations of the cause of this mispronunciation will be welcomed.

Mr. Friend's "shoe-in," by the way, is properly spelled *shoo-in*. The colloquial verb *to shoo* means "to gently urge in a desired direction." The racetrack term *shoo-in*, meaning "certain winner," is rooted in a fraudulent practice of corrupt jockeys: They agree to bet on one long shot, holding back their own mounts, and chase in or *shoo in* the horse they picked to win.

To mix political racing metaphors: *Dark horses* dispute that the *front-runner* is a *shoo-in*, no matter how he pronounces *nuclear*.

It is more demanding of the lingual neuromuscular system to change the shape of the tongue quickly from a k *sound (tongue closed at back of mouth in a glottal stop) to an* l *sound (tongue down in back, up in front with tip touching just behind central incisors) and then to an* e *sound (tongue up in the middle and way down at the tip behind the lower central) than it is to change the shape of the tongue quickly from the* k *sound we're starting out with to an* e *sound, which is the start of the yooler part of the mistake, and then to roll the tongue easily to the* l *sound to start the last syllable.*

See how much easier it is to say nu culer *than* nu clear. *Besides, everyone is used to that formation from saying* cellular *and* cellulose *and, before that,* celluloid. *(Maybe you don't remember* celluloid.*)*

Bob Earle
Ithaca, New York

NUTRACEUTICALS

A spelling controversy is about to explode about the word that means "a food or part of a food that has a medical or health benefit, including the prevention and treatment of disease." Plain bread supplemented with calcium, vitamin D, folate, dietary fiber and a shot of St. John's wort, or whatever, becomes a *nutraceutical*, unless you prefer to spell it *nutriceutical*, with an *i*, as in *nutrition*.

I checked it out with the coiner, Dr. Stephen L. DeFelice, now the head of the Foundation for Innovation in Medicine. His spokesman explained that the 1989 coinage is spelled *nutra*, with an *a*, on the analogy of *pharmaceutical*, with its Greek root *pharmak*.

Reached directly, however, DeFelice said, "To tell you the truth, I was drinking grappa in Rome one day and *nutra* sounded better than *nutri*."

That asserts "coiner's privilege," and the enhanced, enriched, jazzed-up food—as both noun and adjective—is spelled *nutraceutical*.

N.Y.T. STYLE

The president of the United States has lost his capital.

This is not about the burning of the Executive Mansion by the British on August 24, 1814, just after James Madison took flight from the nation's capital and his wife, Dolley, cut the Gilbert Stuart portrait of George Washington out of its frame and took it with her for safekeeping.

Rather, I refer to the recent Triumph of the Lowercase (or, as we are now encouraged to put it, the triumph of the lowercase). In the latest, eagerly awaited *New York Times Manual of Style and Usage*—subtitled (curiously, all in initial caps) "The Official Style Guide Used by the Writers and Editors of the World's Most Authoritative Newspaper"—the capital letter is decisively taken down.

We are guided: "It is *President Lamm* (without a given name) in a first reference to the current president of the United States." Note: not "the current President," with a capital *P*. From now on, even when referring to the specific person holding the highest office in the nation, *Times* style is to lowercase the *p*. The AP stylebook has been doing this for decades (which is why I sometimes refer to the *ap*), but I like the respect shown to the particular president marked by the capital *P*. My preferred style, no longer stylish: "'This is an attempt to bumfuzzle,' said the President."

The same lowercasing is in store for *founding fathers* (an expression coined by Warren G. Harding, the twenty-ninth president). The *Times* further suggests desexing the alliterative phrase to *founders*, though I can't think of any who were mothers. Inconsistently, the *Times* holds fast to the capitalization of *Fourth Estate;* that's got to go.

So it's "God save the king," not "the King." Speaking of God, the faithful will be happy to see that the Supreme Being retains his capital. But note that I just wrote "his capital"—lowercase *h*, not "His capital" or, as some would insist, "Her capital." The *New York Times* stylebook entry: "God (Supreme Being). Lowercase *he, him, his, thee, thou, who* and *whom* when the reference is to God, Jesus, the Holy Ghost (or the Holy Spirit) or Allah."

I go along with this judgment, though I may pay for it on judgment day, because of a parenthetical remark in a letter written in the last century by Herman Melville to his literary mentor, Nathaniel Hawthorne: "You perceive I employ a capital initial in the pronoun referring to the Deity; don't you think there is a slight dash of flunkeyism in that usage?"

Signs of the times can be seen in the entries dropped and added between editions of the stylebook. Gone are *Molotov cocktail, women's liberation, monkey wrench, Novocain* and *zymurgy* (a word for fermentation that hasn't been used or abused in decades). In are *voice mail, postmodern, euro* (that unified currency is lowercased, though *Eurocurrency* is not, to differentiate U.S. dollars held in European banks), *feng shui* and *into the breach.*

About that last: Apparently, too many reporters have been using that phrase instead of Shakespeare's "Once more *unto* the breach." And the Bard's usage is also neatly defended in the entry for *gild the lily:* "An accepted phrase for overembellishment, but writers who wish to delight the exacting reader will use Shakespeare's actual words, from 'King John': 'To gild refined gold, to *paint the lily.*'"

I think Allan M. Siegal and William G. Connolly, authors of the new stylebook, had this column in mind on *gilding the lily,* because an exacting readership is what I have.

In jocular jousting with the arbiters of style in New York, I win a few and lose a few. *Speechwriter* is now a solid word, and *catalog* no longer ends in *ue. Data* is now accepted as singular in nonscientific circles, and I'm thinking of starting a fight about *media,* which should be as singular as *fourth estate.* (If the copy editor has capitalized that, I've been sabotaged.)

The first entry I turned to was *American Indian.* For years I have been insisting that I am a *native American,* having been born in this country, and resisting the seizure of that compound by aboriginal Americans. The *Times* says that "American Indian(s) remains the most widely used term for the native people of North America" and notes that *Native Americans* is rejected by some Indians because the U.S. government uses the term to include Eskimos, Aleuts, Native Hawaiians and Pacific Islanders. The book's solution: Use the term preferred by the people written about.

Fights I have lost so far: *Ms.,* though not an abbreviation, takes a period. Nicknames, at least those for bad guys, are still in parentheses, not quotation marks, and so I cannot refer to Willie "the Actor" Sutton's nocturnal pioneering in automatic teller machine withdrawals. *Pee* is still disallowed (show me a little kid who asks to urinate), and *versus* is still preferred to *vs.,* though *v.* is O.K. for court cases. Even though my word processor defaults to *stories,* that word is frowned upon except at bedtime: "The preferred word for a newspaper or magazine report is *article.*"

Siegal and Connolly grimly insist on putting an apostrophe in decades: We're coming to the end of the 90's. They have a reason: Many publications omit such apostrophes, but they are needed to make the *Times*'s all-cap headlines intelligible and are therefore used throughout the paper for consistency. That means that you, dear reader, are free to drop that apostrophe if you don't use all caps in your headlines.

Style is not a set of rules; it is a group of conventions to reflect an attitude and set a tone. "In approaching the mechanics of usage and grammar," write Siegal and Connolly, "this manual reflects the *Times's* impression of its educated and sophisticated readership—traditional but not tradition-bound. . . . Throughout, the goal is a fluid style, easygoing but not slangy and only occasionally colloquial."

The best thing about this institution's language arbiters is their sense of place—neither on the ramparts nor on the cutting edge. For that reason I would cheerfully plunk down $30 for *The New York Times Manual of Style and Usage*, though I would capitalize a few of those words and put an apostrophe and an *s* after *Times*.

Siegal and Connolly do quite well, I think, in calling for lowercase pronouns for the divinity. I do not find the practice earlier than perhaps 150 years ago, and it appears to have originated in an overly pious and perhaps superstitious attempt to be respectful of divinity. It has never made sense to me. I have never used it in the manuscript of my articles or books, but some editors have style manuals that impose it on my writing. I find it curious that those who insist upon using the King James version (1611) are most likely to capitalize when KJV does not. In point of fact, they regularly capitalize KJV when quoting.

The practice flies in the face of grammatical reality: English knows nothing of proper pronouns. If there were any, it would be required of all pronouns whose antecedent is a proper noun. If one so capitalizes, is this to be done when the speaker quoted does not perceive Yahweh or God to be divine? If pronouns, why not verbs and adjectives? The best place to draw the line is where Siegal and Connolly prescribe. Too much capitalization destroys the effect of when it is necessary.

Wallace Alcorn
Austin, Minnesota

OCKHAM'S RAZOR'S CLOSE SHAVE

"OCCAM'S RAZOR is a principle that has served science well," wrote Charles Krauthammer in the *Weekly Standard*, "for about, oh, 650 years." The psychiatrist-turned-columnist, writing about the Middle East, served his readers well about, oh, immediately, with this definition: "It holds that the simplest, most parsimonious explanation for a phenomenon is likely to be the correct one."

A couple of months before, another conservative pundit, George Will, argued that the public could understand the rationale behind the year-long Clinton defense by its "intuitive wielding of '*Ockham's razor*,' also called the principle of parsimony. The principle is: When seeking to explain phenomena, start with the simplest theory."

Agreement on the meaning, if not the spelling, of *Occam/Ockham* is universal. The antonymic figure of speech is a "Rube Goldberg invention," after the cartoonist who drew up the most complex methods of completing a simple task. But it falls to this column to answer the question unasked by readers who do not want to appear unread: Who was Ockham, anyway, and what made him the Gillette of his day?

William of Ockham, the Franciscan logician known to his fellow friars as "doctor invincibilis," was born in England in 1280. His philosophic writing on the character of knowledge—the nominalist's difference between the name of a thing and the thing itself—made him a father of epistemology and caught the suspicious eye of Pope John XXII, then in Avignon. The monk further angered the Pope by supporting the spiritual Franciscans' defense of the vow of absolute poverty. And as readers of Umberto Eco's *Name of the Rose* recall, such a challenge to John XXII led to his being labeled a heretic and excommunicated.

Ockham and the mantra attributed to him, *entia non sunt multiplicanda præter necessitate*, "entities should not be multiplied unnecessarily" (which is a Rube Goldberg way of saying "Simpler is better"), became a favorite of later mathematicians and physicists. When competing theories came to the same result, the least complicated was preferred. However, Albert

Einstein observed that this shaving away by the Ockhamists could go too far: "Everything should be made as simple as possible, but not simpler."

But what about the razor? The function of a razor is to cut. Stephen Hawking, in his 1988 *A Brief History of Time*, noted that "it seems better to employ the principle known as *Occam's Razor* and cut out all the features of the theory which cannot be observed." The old Franciscan friar (probably bearded; shaving gear was hard to come by in the abbey) was figuratively cutting out details.

Why isn't the principle of this patron saint of editing called Ockham's scissors or knife or ice pick? "Philosophers and historians are generally puzzled as to why the principle of parsimony should be called *Ockham's Razor*," writes a trio of chemists in *Hyle*, a philosophy quarterly published by the University of Karlsruhe, in Germany. "We suspect that the association is due to the strength of the razor metaphor. . . . Scholastic and theological arguments were complex; to cut through them, to reach the remaining core of truth quickly, was desperately desirable. . . . Metaphor reaches right into the soul."

One of the authors, Dr. Roald Hoffman, a Nobel laureate in chemistry, helped track down the earliest reference to a razor in connection with our severely censured nominalist's parsimony pitch. He steered me to a July 1918 article in *Mind*, a philosophy journal, by W. M. Thornburn, in which that logician cited a footnote in a 1746 work of the French philosopher Etienne Bonnot de Condillac. In what Thornburn called "a flash of Gallic wit," de Condillac characterized Ockham's principle as the *Rasoir des Nominaux*, "the razor of the Nominalists." Almost a century later, in the 1836 lectures by Sir William Hamilton on metaphysics and logic, the man and the metaphor met: "We are, therefore, entitled to apply *Occam's razor* to this theory of causality."

From the barber chair of etymology, unwrapping the hot towel and splashing a little aftershave on the customer's newly unbewhiskered cheeks, we can safely say: The principle was Ockham's, but the metaphoric razor was de Condillac's. I cannot state this startling discovery more briefly.

You attribute the quotation "Everything should be made as simple as possible but not simpler" to Albert Einstein.

I'm the author of the book The Quotable Einstein *(Princeton University Press, 1996), and I have not been able to find the source of this quotation, so did not include it in my book. I get at least one call or e-mail a month from someone requesting the source. Since I haven't run across it in my readings (though I admit I haven't read everything the man said); since none of the Einstein experts I've asked know the source though they've often heard the quotation; and since no one else ever seems to document it, I had almost decided that someone made it up and put Einstein's name under it. This seems to happen often.*

Alice Calaprice, Senior Editor and Administrator
Einstein Translation Project
Princeton University Press
Princeton, New Jersey

Let me get to the point: Præter necessitate *in your definition of Ockham's razor,* entia non sunt multiplicanda præter necessitate, *is incorrect.* Præter *takes the accusative and not the ablative case and so should be followed by* necessitatem. *When I was chopping logic as a young Jesuit, I recall hearing variants of Ockham's razor that concluded* sine necessitate *as well as* sine causa rationabili—*which simply suggests Jesuits are more prolix than Franciscans.*

William B. Neenan, S.J., Vice President
and Special Assistant to the President
Boston College
Boston, Massachusetts

Your learned excursus on "Ockham's razor" mentions that "old Franciscan friar (probably bearded; shaving gear was hard to come by in the abbey)" shows confusion about the dwelling places of friars. Since the word is derived from fraters, *their dwelling places are properly called friaries or fraternities. Abbeys are for monks or nuns where abbots or abbesses preside. In the United States or perhaps the English-speaking world* convent *is reserved for women religious, but in Europe it is used for religious of either sex, and that is why one branch of the Franciscan friars are called* conventuals *(what Ockham was not, since he was a* spiritual*). The spirituals became an endangered species, along with his razor, at least within the Order. Perhaps that is why there are so many Franciscan* entia sine necessitate!

Fr. Stephen C. Doyle, O.F.M.
Franciscan Pilgrimage Office
Boston, Massachusetts

I am constrained to advise that the terms friar *and* monk *are not synonymous, and that a friar does not inhabit an abbey.*

A monk, be he a priest or a brother, is a member of a monastic order who joins an autonomous abbey, thus becoming subject to the abbot who presides over the house. In addition to the three vows taken by all regular clergy (i.e., poverty, chastity and obedience), a monk takes a fourth vow, that of stability; that is, he stays forever at his abbey except for the rare instance in which his abbot might direct otherwise. While, as just mentioned, a monk takes a vow of poverty, his abbey may be (and historically was) quite wealthy.

On the other hand, a friar, be he a priest or a brother, is a member of a mendicant order who usually lives in a friary (that said, I will admit that the Dominicans sometimes refer to their houses as priories while some houses of friars are referred to as convents). While a monk usually labors within the walls of his abbey, a friar's ministry might take him to the four corners of the world. Historically, orders of friars could not own property, and individual friars were beggars (hence the term mendicant*), although this was changed insofar as the orders were concerned by the Council of Trent. Still, an individual friar is bound by his vow of poverty.*

Thomas A. Brennan, Jr., Director
The Hearst Family Trust
New York, New York

FRIARING PAN

When competing theories come to the same result, the simplest is preferred. That cutting of complication is encapsulated in the metaphor of *Ockham's razor,* from the parsimonious work of the thirteenth century's William of Ockham, described here some months ago in this simple sentence: "The old Franciscan friar (probably bearded; shaving gear was hard to come by in the abbey) was figuratively cutting out details."

"Your reference to a *friar* in the *abbey* was a *non sequitur,*" writes the Reverend Thomas J. Paprocki, chancellor of the Archdiocese of Chicago, "unless the Franciscan's barber happened to be a Benedictine monk."

He explicates: "Franciscan *friars* usually live in a *friary,* defined as a monastery or place where friars live. An *abbey* is a monastery headed by an *abbot* or a *nunnery* headed by an *abbess.* The Benedictines are probably the best-known example of monks and nuns governed by abbots and abbesses, respectively. Franciscans, however, are not governed by an abbot. Saint Francis of Assisi preferred the term *guardian.*"

And this just in, as the TV newsies say, from the Conventual Franciscan Center in Toronto: "*Monks* are members of monastic orders," writes Friar Phil Kelly, "those who live in larger communities and follow some sort of monastic rule. Benedictines, Cistercians (as in Thomas Merton) or Carthusians are such groups. *Friars* are members of the four mendicant orders founded in the Middle Ages somewhat as a reaction to monasticism. They are the Augustinians, the Carmelites, the Dominicans and the Franciscans."

Although even I know that a *novice* lives in a *novitiate,* who lives in *a priory?* (All Cartesians live *a priori.*) "Some houses of friars, such as the Dominicans and Servites, are headed by a *prior,*" notes Chancellor Paprocki, "and some nuns, like the Discalced Carmelites, are governed by a *prioress,* all of whom are said to live in *a priory.*"

As Ockham would put it: Monks and nuns usually live in *abbeys* and *friars* in *friaries,* though some are in *priories.* "Your explanation of Ockham's principle was better than what we received in the seminary," notes Friar Kelly in the spirit of charity, "but whining is part of my nature."

OF HIGH MOMENTS

"This case is of *high moment,*" wrote independent counsel Ken Starr to the Supreme Court, because it involved "fundamental constitutional issues."

"We are fallen upon times," promulgated Pope Leo XIII in an encyclical a century ago, "when a violent and well-nigh daily battle is being fought about matters of *highest moment.*"

"Considerations of *high moment* call on the American," wrote the *Southern Literary Messenger* in 1839, ". . . to extend and disseminate every facility which our country can afford, for the promotion of information. Upon this pillar rests the question of man's capability for self-government."

Heavy stuff. In dealing with the voguish, momentary popularity of *moments* in this space recently (*senior moments, Zen moments, Maalox moments*), I neglected the essence of the word expressed in the adjective *momentous:* "of great weight; of major significance."

Moment, in this sense, seems like one of those Janus words with opposite meanings, like *sanction* (penalty; approval) or *sanguine* (bloody; optimistic). How can *moment* be both "fleeting" and "of consequence"?

Look to the Latin *momentum*, "movement." When you place a tiny particle on a perfectly balanced scale, you cause it to move; thus, even a time of incalculable briefness or the lightest weight of an argument, when added to one of the scales in equilibrium, breaks the balance and creates movement, which gains momentum, changes minds and moves the world. That's how a transitory moment can be of *high moment*.

High, in this phrase, means "significant"—more than in "high official," as much as in "high crimes" or "high dudgeon." Fred Shapiro, coeditor of *Trial and Error: An Oxford Anthology of Legal Stories*, tracks *high moment* back in legal usage to an 1861 opinion condemning a Confederate ship for violating a Union blockade.

At a time when *important* has lost its zip, *significant* is too lightly bandied about, and even *consequential* lacks gravamen, it's comforting to see *moment* regaining its moment.

ON THE LAM, WHO MADE THEE?

"Big-time Clinton-Gore donor Ted Sioeng," wrote *The Wall Street Journal*'s crusading editorialist, "poured some $250,000 into campaign coffers, and has recently been on the lam from nosy investigators."

On the lam means "running away" or "being a fugitive from the law"; bureaucrats would say "in escape status." The origin of the expression is in heated dispute among slang etymologists.

In *The Random House Historical Dictionary of American Slang*, J. E. Lighter defines the term as prison lingo for "an act of running or flight, esp. a dash to escape from custody." In his 1886 *Thirty Years a Detective*, Allan Pinkerton, the first "private eye," explains an operation of pickpockets: "After he secures the wallet, he will utter the word *'lam!'* This means to let the man go and to get out of the way as soon as possible." Lighter cites *do a lam*, *make a lam* and *take a lam* early in this century, finally emerging as the passive state of being *on the lam*.

Lighter speculates that it may be rooted in the dialect Scandinavian verb *lam*, as in the 1525 "his wife sore *lamming* him," meaning "to beat, pound or strike." Mark Twain used it twice: *"lamming* the lady" in 1855 and *"lam* like all creation" in 1865, both clearly meaning "to beat." The suggested connection is that to avoid a feared *lamming* (related to *slamming*), one *lams*.

At the University of Missouri at Rolla, Gerald Cohen, a professor of foreign languages currently at work on a slang dictionary, has another theory. He notes the cant *lammas* in Eric Partridge's *Dictionary of the Underworld*, the lingo of costermongers in London around 1855, alternatively spelled *nammou*, meaning "to depart, esp. furtively" and related to *vamoose* in the lingo of the American West.

"*Namase* with its variant spellings," Cohen says, "was the standard cant term for 'leave/make off/depart/skedaddle.' I don't know why *nam* became *lam*, but the meanings are the same."

The good news for investigators is that Yah Ling (Charlie) Trie is no longer *on the lam*. He has returned from his long sojourn in Macao to face the music (a metaphor first reported in the halls of the U.S. Congress in 1850).

ONE GUOJIA?

"We believe there is one *nation* and two *countries*," said Chen Chien-jen, chief spokesman of the Republic of China on Taiwan, speaking in English.

Seth Faison, *The New York Times*'s man in Beijing, asked him to say that in Chinese. Mr. Chen was stumped. "We are still looking for the right words," he said.

That's because in Chinese, *state, country* and *nation* are expressed in the same word: *guojia*, pronounced *gwo-jah*. But the Chinese leaders on Taiwan, which Beijing considers a renegade province of China, want to put a few degrees of separation between the two political entities. How to do this without declaring independence, which might start a war? "So they use the English words," writes Faison, "even though Taiwan is a Chinese-speaking country or state or nation—or whatever."

Though the Chinese language often uses pronunciation to express different nuances of meaning, the English language has a glorious range of synonymy.

Nation, from the Latin of the same name, stems from "breed, stock, race"—leading to the notion of "a people." When we speak of the Iroquois Nation or the Nation of Islam, we mean the culture, religion, race and/or language that binds people who may be dispersed. "He hates our sacred *nation*," says Shylock in Shakespeare's *Merchant of Venice*. (The

Chinese word for this racial sense is *minzu*.) Although that early sense is still in use, in the last two centuries the primary meaning of *nation* has shifted to "an independent political unit."

Is that later sense the same as a *country?* Yes. Its Latin root is *contra*, "against," originally the land or region separate from, or up against, other discrete areas. Though it has a second sense of "bucolic region" as in "I can't stand the beach; let's go to the country," the primary meaning is "an independent state; native land." (United States presidents traditionally began their inaugural addresses with "My countrymen" until it was desexed to "Fellow citizens.")

Sometimes the old meaning of *nation* can be used to make a contrast with the new meaning of *country*, as in: "The Kurds are the largest *nation* in the world without a *country*."

Note the use above of "independent state." The use of the modifier *independent* shows that *state* need not be wholly separate from a nation. The fifty American states are not sovereign, no matter what they say in Texas and Hawaii (the only states that were once sovereign nations). *State*, from the French *état*, "class, ranking," is a unit of government that may or may not be independent, which is why it requires a qualifier. Palestinians, for example, rarely say they want a state; they specify an independent or separate or "our own" state.

Now we can see what the spokesman for Taiwan was getting at when he said "one *nation* and two *countries*." He meant the early sense of *nation*—in this case, "the Chinese people"—with one part of that people on Taiwan set up against, *contra*, in a country next to but apart from the mother country.

Mainland China is not having any of this English linguistic hair splitting. It insists on "one China," a fiction of both sides that United States policy gladly acknowledged in the Shanghai Communiqué of 1972, provided ultimate reunification would be peaceful. The point here is that Chinese prefer their own language to gloss over differences but turn to English to introduce degrees of difference. Our language is as subtle as their minds.

Vermont (as well as Hawaii and Texas) was an independent republic from 1790 (when it purchased release of all claims by New York State for $30,000) until 1791, when it adopted the United States Constitution.

During Vermont's year as a sovereign nation, it carried on a foreign trade, coined its own money, maintained a militia, regulated weights and measures, and naturalized foreign citizens. May I say again that Vermont is a state, was a nation, and I hope will remain a mighty pretty country.

David A. Lord
Chester, Vermont

OPT IN

Dumpster-dipping is what advocates of privacy call "the act by information pirates of sifting through trash bins and garbage cans for credit-card numbers, Social Security numbers, and unshredded trade secrets."

Skip-tracers are the new breed of bounty hunters; they use their knowledge of databases, motor-vehicle license records (Texas and Florida drivers are most vulnerable) and credit-card purchases to track down deadbeats or forgetful consumers who have moved and left behind debts.

Header information is data that most people would consider confidential at the top of a credit report, which the Federal Trade Commission says may be disclosed by any credit bureau with no restrictions. This includes your name, address, phone number (listed or not), Social Security number and mother's maiden name. One credit bureau is demanding in court that even more personal data be included under *header information.*

Cookies, a term coined in 1703 and rooted in the Dutch for a small cake, has a meaning no longer limited to a product sold by Girl Scouts or lasciviously applied to older attractive women. "How can a company follow you all over the Internet without your knowledge?" asked Lesley Stahl of CBS on a recent *60 Minutes* privacy exposé. "By placing a tracking device called a *cookie* inside your computer while you're online."

That small file often surreptitiously created on your operating system is a kind of digital tattoo, enabling a company to create a dossier on your browsing history. It may then sell the track marks of your habits and interests to advertisers, prospective employers or—who knows?—outfits whose databases are easily penetrable by the basest stalkers. (One of these days a software genius will market a privacy program called *Cookie Cutter.*)

Spam—the canned luncheon meat so often derogated but which I found every bit as delicious as C rations—had its name lifted in 1970 by *Monty Python's Flying Circus.* The new sense—"unsolicited commercial e-mail sent far and wide"—was born in a skit in which a waitress tells a customer that the morning special is "lobster thermidor à crevette with a Mornay sauce served in a Provençal manner, with shallots and aubergines garnished with truffle pâté, brandy and with a fried egg on top and . . . *Spam!*"

When the customer asks, "Have you got anything without *Spam?*" the waitress replies, "Well, there's *Spam*-egg-sausage-and-*Spam*—that's not got much *Spam* in it." The breakfast customer's vain attempt to order something else is then drowned out by a group of Vikings in horned helmets chanting, "*Spam, Spam, Spam!*" That led to the current Internet sense of the term as "unwanted and oppressive advertising messages."

For these etymologies of privacy lingo, I am indebted to Robert Ellis Smith, editor of *Privacy Journal*. His Web site had better not have a *cookie* in it.

This brings us to the most critical and confusing term in the battle between those who would not intrude on individual privacy and those who see cookies and dossierization as a shopper's blessing: *opt in* versus *opt out*.

To opt is from the Latin *optare*, "to choose." But *opt* suggests a slightly more impulsive quality to the choice. In *Comfortable Words*, Bergen Evans described the subtle difference in a blaze of usagist brilliance: "Confronted with a choice between *choose* and *opt*, my impulse is to *opt* for *choose.*"

Now to the slight difference in a phrase—until recently considered slang, but now standard English—that could make a huge difference in our lives. "*Opt in* is the equivalent of giving consent," Smith says. "When *opt in* is required by law, the collector of information must seek and secure the affirmative approval of a person before disclosing it or using it for other purposes." The Privacy Act requires this with regard to federal records, with several exceptions, like criminal investigations, the Census Bureau or orders of the court.

"By contrast, *opt out* is merely a check off," the privacy maven points out. "The consumer must be given the opportunity—but must take the initiative—to say that he or she does not want personal information disclosed."

Opt in puts the burden on the collector to get the individual's approval. But *opt out* puts the burden on the individual to click on a box that says, "No—you cannot disclose my personal information." Most people don't know enough to care or are easily duped into not checking the box by offers of gifts or services—and thereby unwittingly make their purchasing decisions and their lives an open book. *Opt in* requires getting the customer to say yes, and positive approval is hard for the data collector to obtain; *opt out* merely requires giving the customer a chance to say no, which is harder for the mild-mannered customer to say.

In this year's act permitting the merger of banks, brokers and insurance companies, the few privacy advocates in the Senate, like the Republican Richard Shelby and the Democrat Pat Leahy, fought for *opt in*, but lobbyists for the banking industry blocked not only *opt in* but also the even more permissive *opt out*. In general political terminology, *opt out* has a wider meaning of "to withdraw from politics." It was first used in this sense by Kevin Phillips in a 1971 article about Vice President Spiro Agnew in *The New York Times Magazine*: "By next summer, if the Vice President is a political liability, he will *opt out* of a reelection bid long before anyone has to 'dump' him." This type of self-removal from the fray is exemplified by the prissy citizen who claimed that apathy was not the cause of refusing to go to the polls. "I never vote," the *opter-out* said. "It only encourages them."

Skip tracer is not a new term. The OED *has a first quote for it in 1953, but I recall it from about 1946, when I was combing the Help Wanted ads for a job (having been replaced at* Newsweek *by a man who—like me— was also a veteran, but had worked for the magazine before entering the service, hence had superseniority, a word not in the* OED *at all and misdefined in* The RHD Unabridged).*

It reminded me of another word I encountered wandering through the Help Wanted ads at the time: garde-manger. *As far as I know, The* RHD Unabridged *is the only English dictionary listing it (owing to my having put it there). The ad was, as well as I can recall over more than fifty years, for a garde-manger with the skill in ice sculpture from the Brown Swan Hotel in Denver. It wasn't as if I had any such skill or wanted to live in Denver, but I was sufficiently intrigued to try to find the meaning of the term. The best I could come up with from any of the sources available (French monolingual and bilingual dictionaries) was that it is "a cool room for storing foods and for preparing certain dishes, esp. cold buffet dishes," which is verbatim the first definition in the* RHD.

Typically, the second definition was much harder to find, for in those days, few dictionaries paid much attention to "words of art" in certain fields, and cookery was one of them. After much research, I finally came up with the sense still listed in the RHD *as "2. a chef or cook who supervises the preparation of cold dishes."*

Laurence Urdang
Old Lyme, Connecticut

OUT OF THE WHOLE CLOTH

When a young journalist embarrassed *The New Republic* and other publications by fabricating sources in articles, the columnist Richard Cohen wrote that the young man should seek another line of work after having filed articles *"made up out of whole cloth."*

About the same time, the independent counsel Kenneth Starr made a speech about the tendency of government lawyers to seek excuses like "executive privilege" or "protective privilege" to prevent witnesses from testifying. "The courts cannot be in the business of creating new privileges," Starr said, *"from whole cloth."*

This usage puzzles Elizabeth Hopkins in the editorial department of the *International Herald Tribune.* She writes that she has not been able to find the origin of *made up out of whole cloth.* Although the meaning is clear—"a story invented with no basis in fact; a complete fiction"—the metaphoric origin is obscure. Just what is the *whole cloth?* And what has any cloth to do with lying?

A *whole cloth*, or *broadcloth*, is material of the full size as originally manufactured—not the end bit or remnant or piece cut out of the whole for reuse in a quilt or smaller-size garment. Like a sense of the *whole person*— well balanced, "together"—*whole cloth* has integrity, akin to "all wool and a yard wide." Then, early in the nineteenth century, the phrase's meaning flipped. In 1840, the Canadian novelist Thomas Haliburton, in his dialect-rich *The Clockmaker,* had his Yankee character named Sam Slick say: "All that talk about her timper was *made out of whole cloth*, and got up a-purpose. . . . What a fib! . . . It's all *made out of whole cloth."*

In his 1972 *Hog on Ice,* Charles Funk speculated that tailors were suspected of being deceptive: "Instead of using whole material, as they advertised, they were really using patched or pieced goods, or, it might be, cloth which had been falsely stretched to appear to be of full width." The material presented as being of *whole cloth*, on that theory, had become suspect.

Come at *cloth* another way, through its synonym *fabric*, from the Latin *fabrica*, "workshop," a place or structure where things like clothing are made.

Fabricate means "to construct, manufacture, frame"; in the eighteenth century, it took on a sinister sense of "to make up a story, to invent a lie, to forge a document." In 1805, President Thomas Jefferson was accused of having cravenly fled from the state capital, Richmond, during the Revolution, when he was governor of Virginia. In helping his longtime aide, William Burwell, prepare his defense against accusations of cowardice, Jefferson wrote, "This *fabricated* flight from Richmond was not among the charges." That sense of "cooked up, untrue" continues.

Patricia Smith, a talented young columnist for *The Boston Globe*, was discovered by her editors to have made up quotations. In her departing column, the sadder and wiser journalist apologized to readers for committing "one of the cardinal sins of journalism: Thou shalt not *fabricate*."

Today, *fabrication* is most often used when *lie* seems too harsh. It's not too great a stretch to think of the *fabric* as *cloth* deceptively made up of patches and remnants to appear as *made of whole cloth*.

Fabricated material is not always considered sinister: A clergyman's distinctive garment has given it a good connotation in a *man of the cloth*. But six centuries ago, *cloth* was sometimes spelled *clout*, and in underworld slang, the original spelling has been preserved in its meaning of "cotton handkerchief." A thief in London in the nineteenth century would blow his nose in a *clout*. Then—perhaps because tossing a *clout* over a piece of jewelry was a way of stealing it—it became a verb for "to steal."

Eric Partridge noted that *to clout heaps* was twentieth-century underworld lingo for "to steal cars." From this slender thread I weave a speculation that *cloth*, or *clout*, has a history of nefariousness that may have influenced the whole phrase's semantic shift from positive to negative. Mine is a shaky theory, but at least it's made up of the partial cloth.

In German the word Fabrik *means factory. Thus, in the quest to search out the real from the false (fabrication)—the notion which obviously sprang from the early days of industrialization was that something made in a factory, i.e., machine made, was not the real thing. Real things were considered to be made by hand. Hence, my mother and grandmother would turn over a piece of cloth (particularly when it had embroidery) to see the stitching or weave at the back. For it was there one could always tell the real from the fabricated. Something manufactured or* fabriziert *was always considered not genuine, a substitute and cheaper version of the* "whole cloth."

Hannelore Hahn, Founder and Executive Director
The International Women's Writing Guild
Gracie Station, New York

You speculated how the word clout *came to mean "to steal." As a speaker of German (M.A. in history, Goettinger University), I instantly recognized the German verb* klauen *as a slang or colloquial term for "to steal." Whether there is in fact a connection between* clout *and* klauen *I cannot say. If* klauen *did enter English and become* clout *in the same sense that I suspect, then more than likely it came through Yiddish rather than from German.*

Michael R. Heydenburg
Jersey City, New Jersey

After your clear explanation of the literal meaning of whole cloth, *I think you got the metaphor backwards. If something is made up from whole cloth, it's made entirely new, not using anything previously used. In other words, a story made up from whole cloth is not an exaggeration or a coloring or a half-truth; it's completely fictitious.*

A story isn't a lie because it appears to be made from whole cloth; it's a lie because it is made from whole cloth.

John Hetland
New York, New York

OUT THERE IN RADIOLAND

What were the most memorable lines spoken on old-time radio?

I can hear it now: Edward R. Murrow, not just saying, "This . . . is London," but describing what he saw in a sortie over Berlin with the R.A.F.: "The small incendiaries were going down like a fistful of rice thrown on a piece of black velvet. The 'cookies,' the four-thousand-pound high explosives, were bursting below like great sunflowers gone mad."

And two years later, the equally familiar voice of his CBS colleague Bob Trout announcing on V-J day in 1945: "This, ladies and gentlemen, is the end of the Second World War."

Listen now to the opening line of the NBC science-fiction story "Knock" on the 1950 series *Dimension X:* "The last man on Earth sat alone in a room. There was a knock on the door."

A modern editor would have to make changes in all those lines. By "the last man on Earth" the writer meant "the last person"; now, because the male no longer embraces the female, he would have to write "the last person on Earth" because the listener would immediately assume that the source of the knocking was a woman, and not some subhuman or superhuman species.

Similarly, a newly spawned Trout would be less likely to say *ladies and gentlemen,* nomenclature so dated as to seem quaint and not even used on the doors of lavatories anymore. And the dramatic *this,* which used to be in fashion on radio to begin a sentence, has fallen into an innocuous desuetude.

Malapropisms, however, need no updating. "I don't object to President Roosevelt using the radio to inform the country on the state of the nation," said a man in the audience on the Blue Network's *Town Meeting of the Air,* "but I do object to his using it to propagate." And a character eagerly awaiting the arrival of the Lone Ranger shouts, "I hear a white horse on the way!"

These and other great moments in the broadcast world are taken from John Dunning's *On the Air: The Encyclopedia of Old-Time Radio.*

Comedy was based on carefully established character traits, a technique that carried over into television sitcoms. Jack Benny was the tightwad who, when held up by a thief demanding "Your money or your life!" answered with a long silence, interrupting the laughter only with "I'm thinking." The bandleader Phil Harris played his role with swaggering stupidity: "Phil is spelled with a *P?*"

The classic word-picture was Fred Allen's trope about NBC censors: "They are a bit of executive fungus that grows on a desk that's been exposed to conference." Groucho Marx's standard question for politicians who appeared as contestants on his quiz show—"How many times have you been indicted?"—would not be so funny today, but his regular query to baseball umpires—"Do you have any little thieves at home?"—is still apt.

But the humor most missed today is the flash of wit. When a young woman told Groucho, "I go to a college for girls," he riposted, "That's the reason I'd want to go, too." And when the Shakespearean expert and sportswriter John Kieran was stumped on *Information, Please* by a question that was sent in by his son, he said, "How sharper than a thankless tooth it is to have a serpent child."

Most people today think *Information, Please* is the name of an almanac. It was once a literate radio program, moderated by Clifton Fadiman, that was broadcast from 1938 to 1951. The title was based on what telephone users would say to smilingly live operators when an unknown listing was desired. Of time and the river of language: Now we pay for the information from a robot that dials it for us for an additional thirty-five cents, and nobody has to say "please."

> *Loved your "Radioland" column, but "we pay for the information from a robot that dials it for us"? Does the verb now in use in relation to telephones for more than a half-century apply?*
>
> *Keys it? Enters it? Transmits it? What should it be?*
>
> Fred Kerner
> Willowdale, Ontario, Canada

OVER AND OUTREACH

When he was first asked about his presence at a 1996 fund-raiser in a California Buddhist temple, Vice President Al Gore claimed he had no idea it was a *fund-raiser,* which has now become a politically dirty word. He thought the purpose of the gathering was *"community outreach."*

After the election, an aide put out word that Mr. Gore did know it was "a *finance-related event"* and added with fervent candor, "If he had the opportunity now to not say *'community outreach'* and to use a different term of art like *political outreach* or something like that . . . he probably would have done it." Another anonymous White House aide, after the derision directed at the euphemism *finance-related,* tried a different compound modifier: It had been understood to be a *"donor maintenance"* meeting.

In all this linguistic bobbing and weaving, the key word is *outreach.*

Officialdom embraces the word: "We care about the *outreach* to small business," says a Los Angeles small-business agent. So does the charity world: A new gymnasium "gave us greater *outreach* into the neighborhood," says a Memphis philanthropy. Churches get with it, too: "We want to see our church be the hub of evangelistic *outreach* to the community," says a Norfolk, Virginia, clergyman.

Where did its current popularization begin? In the labor movement: The "Apprenticeship *Outreach* Program" was begun by the AFL-CIO in 1969 to encourage the hiring of those who were then called Negro youths in the construction trades. Labor's Lane Kirkland and the Nixon Labor Secretary George P. Shultz put the government firmly behind the plan. Arnold Weber, then Assistant Secretary of Manpower and later chancellor of Northwestern University, recalls the word being bruited about heavily at the February 1970 labor conclave at Bal Harbor, Florida. "I was probably the passive conduit of some flack," he tells me. "The word was in the bureaucratic air at the time." The renowned educator (who used to send the White House memos stamped "Teeth Only") adds: "Your etymological question should be: Why was the word order reversed? Why wasn't it *reachout?*"

(Beats me, Chancellor; a related formulation, *takeout*, means food "to be consumed off premises," while the reverse, *outtake*, means "tape not used in a broadcast." No similar split took place with *reachout*.)

Politics—the business of involving voters in a party's cause—seized on the word. In their need to reach out and put the touch on someone, politicians have adopted and besmirched a word coined in its compassionate sense by the poet John Greenleaf Whittier in 1870: "No proof beyond this yearning,/This *out-reach* of our hearts, we need."

Or as the vice chairman of finance, Andrea del Sarto, never used to say: Man's *outreach* should exceed his outgrasp, or what's a fund-raiser for?

PADDLING YOUR OWN CANOODLE

SENATE JUDICIARY CHAIRMAN Orrin Hatch told *The New York Times* that if allegations concerning the President and the former White House intern Monica Lewinsky prove to be true, "we have perhaps the first presidential *canoodler* in history."

The Utah senator is a devotee of American slang; his 1996 use of *hissy fit*, meaning "temper tantrum," stimulated the speculation in this space that the etymon was *hysteria*.

Whence *canoodle*? Slanguists J. S. Farmer and William Ernest Henley in their 1890 dictionary defined the term as "to fondle; bill and coo; indulge in endearments," its synonym *firkytoodle*, a verb that seems to have slipped into desuetude. Their earliest citation was from an 1859 book by the English journalist George Augustus Sala: "A sly kiss, and a squeeze . . . known to our American cousins (who are great adepts at sweet-hearting) under the generic name of *canoodling*."

The derivation is in furious dispute. One school is influenced by H. L. Mencken's assertion that the word was an extravagant invention created by Americans in the Missouri-Mississippi basin, home of many German immigrants. The etymologist W. E. Umbach found the German verb *knudeln*, "to cuddle," which has a second, fondling-related sense of "to pat, knead," as in the making of dumplings called *Knoedel*. Samuel Jones of the University of Wisconsin informs me that the German *schmusen*, also meaning "to hold close," is defined in the 1980 *Collins German Dictionary* as "to canoodle."

The *knudeln* theory (with the *k* pronounced as *ca*) is knocked (with the *k* silent) by the school that argues that the word is not an Americanism at all. Drawing on the 1945 research of B. J. Whiting, James Rader of Merriam-Webster says that "Merriam files have nothing to suggest it is an Americanism. The British *Notes and Queries* for September 3, 1927, recorded it as 'Nottingham dialect for "to cuddle."'" Australia's *New South Wales Bulletin* in 1928 wrote, 'This fuss over the possibility of the Alsatian dog *canoodling* with his lady dingoes annoys me.'"

Merriam-Webster bases its judgment on an entry in Wright's *English Dialect Dictionary* that treats *canoodle* as a Somerset noun meaning "donkey. . . . Used also figuratively of one who makes love foolishly or 'spoonies.'"

Which side to believe? Is the origin in the squeezable German dumpling or the fumbling caresses of a lovesick English lass? Fair-minded readers are urged to disregard leaks from self-serving etymologists and to reserve judgment on *canoodle*.

I am now 87, but when I was a young girl, canoodling *was "heavy petting" in a canoe. The setting was romantic, but unless one were careful, the outcome could be disastrous. Ah! To be young again! Thought you needed another definition.*

Marguerite S. Buckley
Danbury, Connecticut

One of the great and repeated users of the word canoodle *was the mystery writer John Dickson Carr under his pseudonym Carter Dickson. Dickson's detective is Sir Henry Merrivale, baron, doctor, lawyer and all-around curmudgeon. A rather formulaic writer, Dickson also invariably has Sir Henry meet a young couple at some point during his investigation, and equally invariably, Sir Henry finds that young couple at some point during the novel engaged in what he is wont to describe as* canoodling. *To offer an example from the first Merrivale mystery I happened to take from the shelf: "It would have struck Chief Inspector Masters as odd that H.M. made no reference (for the moment, at least) to the subject of a canoodling. Canoodling is a subject on which he is apt to hold forth at length."*
—Night at the Mocking Widow.

Nancy Freudenthal
Newtown, Pennsylvania

PAINE IN THE NECK

A button man in the Gotcha! Gang, Jerome B. Agel of New York, was browsing through *Safire's New Political Dictionary* and let out a whoop: There, in the entry on "United States of America," was the assertion "coinage attributed to pamphleteer Thomas Paine."

Wrong. My source, the biographer of the author of *Common Sense*, had claimed that "to Paine also belongs the honor of naming our country 'the United States of America.' He was the first to use the name in print, and it was his own creation." Paine had written proudly in *The American Crisis II:* "The United States of America will sound as pompously in the world or in history as The Kingdom of Great Britain." (*Pompous* at that time meant "important"; it has since changed to "self-important.")

But Paine's prescient prediction was published on January 13, 1777. The year before, in *Common Sense*, the pamphleteer was still using the appellations "United Colonies" and "American states." Predating Paine's 1777 usage, notes Gotcha! Gangster Agel, "the last paragraph of the Declaration of Independence, signed on July 4, 1776, refers to 'the Representatives of the United States of America.' So nu?"

That slugs the supposed coinage by Paine in the neck.

Most historians now go with the scholar-novelist George Stewart, noted for his *Names on the Land,* who stated: "The theory that Thomas Paine invented the name is unwarranted. . . . The first recorded use was from the pen of Thomas Jefferson in the Declaration of Independence." The authoritative *Concise Dictionary of American History* concurs, noting that Benjamin Franklin in 1775 preferred *United States of North America.* (The Founders must have thought that was too long.)

Just to be certain, I checked the zingy new CD-ROM of the *Oxford English Dictionary.* It has a citation of Jefferson in 1774 writing about "the American states united" (we never did become the A.S.U.) and a simple *United States,* without the distinctive *America* added, from the *Journals of the Continental Congress* dated October 10, 1776. Curiously, this greatest of dictionaries didn't list the earlier use of the full title in the Declaration.

When my researcher at the time, Karen Goettsche Lubell, pointed out this oversight to the lexicographers at Oxford, they snapped into action. It seems they have a man—Jon R. Simon, an American—poking around full time in the musty recesses of our Library of Congress. Their challenge to him: Don't just accept the earliest usage as July 4, 1776, as others have said—dig around and see if an earlier use can be found that will burnish the escutcheon of the *OED.*

"Thanks for pointing out our oversight," Simon says by e-mail from Somewhere in the Stacks. "You may be interested in another, slightly earlier citation I encountered today. Pauline Maier, author of *American Scripture,* cites a letter on page 44 appearing in Peter Force's *American*

Archives (1846), Series 4, Volume 6, page 1131, column 1. The full *United States of America* is in a letter published in the *Pennsylvania Evening Post* on June 29, 1776, signed Republicus."

Simon checked the phrase in context: "As we cannot offer terms of peace to *Great Britain* until . . . we agree to call ourselves by some name," wrote Republicus, "I shall rejoice to hear the title of the *United States of America*, in order that we may be on a proper footing to negotiate a peace."

That was the week before the Declaration. As sobersided etymologists of historic phrases say, *hot dawg!*

But wait. When did Jefferson actually write the Declaration? According to Julian P. Boyd's 1943 *The Declaration of Independence: The Evolution of the Text*, the draft—written mainly by Jefferson, with Benjamin Franklin and John Adams—was delivered and read to the Continental Congress on June 28, 1776. And they didn't just knock it out that morning; Jefferson began working on it on June 11. We can reliably assume he used the name *United States of America* between June 11 and June 28.

So that settles it, right? Hold on—here's a last-minute entry dug up by Oxford's Jon Simon, in the great Sir James Murray tradition, and rushed breathlessly to my office in Washington. Elbridge Gerry (pronounced with a hard *G*, though the eponymous *gerrymandering* is with a soft *g*), a Massachusetts member of the Continental Congress, wrote a letter to Gen. Horatio Gates, George Washington's rival, giving him the good news that capital punishment was in store for all spies "or other enemies of the *United States of America*." That letter was dated by Gerry in Philadelphia on June 25.

So was the coiner Jefferson? Gerry? Or Republicus, whoever that was? In the game of Name That Nation, the controversy is yet to be resolved. I'll pledge my sacred honor to stay on top of it.

PAPA RAZZI

Who was the father of *paparazzi?*

The 1960 movie *La Dolce Vita* (The Sweet Life) was a drama directed by Federico Fellini illuminating the decadence, alcoholism, sex-satiation and other nonfamily values prevalent among a swinging set in postwar Italy. Marcello Mastroianni played a predatory gossip columnist and Walter Santesso a sidewalk photographer called "Signore Paparazzo."

An *Economist* magazine etymologist found that a Fellini writer, Neoennio Flaiano, took the name from a nineteenth-century hotelier in Catanzaro, Coriolano Paparazzo, mentioned in *By the Ionian Sea*, by George Gissing. But it was Fellini's character who gave birth to an eponym, a word derived from the name of an individual.

The most famous eponymous characters are Amelia Bloomer, a suffragist who wore Turkish-style pants; Captain Charles Boycott, the shunned British land agent in Ireland; and Samuel Maverick, the Texas rancher who didn't brand his cattle. Less well known are Thomas Bowler and John Batterson Stetson, the hat makers; Johannes Geiger, the counterman; Rudolf Diesel, the internal combuster; and King Mausolus of Caria, whose tomb was one of the seven wonders of the ancient world.

In our century, some leading eponyms are Ernst Mach, who predicted we would zip through the speed of sound; Maria Montessori, who came up with a method of teaching children; and Sun Myung Moon, whose Unification Church members are usually called Moonies. In current printed and spoken usage, however, Signore Paparazzo, camera in hand, outdoes them all.

Two years ago, Paul McCartney, the former Beatle, wrote a lyric titled "The World Tonight" that included the word in an aviary metaphor and concluded with a prescient shudder: "I saw you hiding from a flock of paparazzi./You were hoping, you were hoping that the ground would swallow you."

The description of Rudolf Diesel should be as a compression igniter, this more accurately being the type of motor he refined. The internal combustion power plant relies upon an external method of causing the fuel mixture to burn. The compression ignition type relied upon compacting the fuel mixture into too small an area for its volume until self-immolation occurs. This explains why diesel engines have no spark plugs, only glow plugs to commence the process from cold start-up.

Bruce Negrycz II
Lynchburg, Virginia

PARADIGM SHRIFT

The chastisement of the President continues to churn up quotes that call for correction or amplification.

"I for one would have very strong opposition," Senator Dianne Feinstein of California told CNN, as reported in *The New York Times*, "to any kind of star chamber proceeding that's held in private."

Members of the Squad Squad, spotters of tautologous redundancies, landed heavily on that one.

The *Star Chamber* was a room constructed in 1347 in the royal palace at Westminster, its ceiling decorated with "starres gilted." In the next century, Henry VII created the Court of the Star Chamber in that room, and its tyrannous abuses under James I and Charles I made it synonymous with oppression. Although some historians insist that it was as public as any other criminal court, the *Star Chamber*—abolished in 1641 by the Long Parliament—is now remembered for operating in secrecy. Therefore, the Feinstein formulation of "*Star Chamber* proceeding that's held in private" is indeed redundant, and needlessly verbose, superfluous, prolix and repetitive, too.

"My view is we need to commence the trial," said Senator Mitch McConnell of Kentucky. "Otherwise, it just completely makes short shrift of the action of the House."

What is a *shrift*, anyway, and aren't there any long ones?

To *shrive* is a religious term meaning "to give absolution to, after penance." *Shrift*, the noun, varies in meaning from the confession of sin to the penance offered or the absolution that results.

Short shrift was coined by Shakespeare to describe a brief confession before execution. In *Richard III*, Ratcliffe tells the condemned Hastings: "Make a *short shrift*," because the Duke "longs to see your head."

It has lost its confessional sense and now means only "make quick work of." Surely Senator McConnell could not have been thinking of his phrase's macabre origins.

PARSING FANCIES: SUBORN AGAIN

"This story seems ridiculous," said the President's attorney, Robert Bennett, "and I frankly smell a rat."

This somewhat odious metaphor was bottomed on the work of the British poet laureate John Skelton, tutor to Henry VIII, who wrote in 1520: "Yf they smell a ratt/They grisely chide and chatt." It was picked up, or independently coined, in the next century by the Spanish poet and novelist Miguel de Cervantes Saavedra, as he had his Don Quixote say, "I begin to smell a rat."

As the fare-free Staten Island ferry drags in behind it the flotsam and jetsam of the harbor, every major news event brings us metaphors, usages and vogue words that have echoes in our linguistic history. The controversy swirling around Mr. Clinton's relationship with a young White House intern has churned up its share of these; let us hang over the rail and examine what's floating around:

"I am not going to *parse* the statement," Press Secretary Michael McCurry insisted when reporters pressed him for the meaning of "improper" in a Clinton disclaimer of having an "improper relationship." He repeated *parse* twice in avoiding further interpretation, causing reporters to use *parse* in any subsequent examination of the President's remarks.

This has long been a favorite verb of grammarians. From the Latin *pars*, "part," *parse* means "to break a sentence into its components, to describe each part of speech and then to show how the words and syntax match a given grammar." I do that a lot in this column, especially to illustrate grammatical mistakes when awarding the Bloopies. Students of Latin answering the question *Quae pars orationis?* ("What part of speech?") have used the English word since 1553 (about the time Skelton began smelling a rat), when Prince Edward was said to have "learned almoste foure bookes of Cato to construe, to *parse*, and to say wythout booke."

The extended meaning of *parse*, as McCurry and his tormenters have been using it, is "to analyze critically," the current British usage, to which is added the American connotation of "to examine too minutely or laboriously." The verb was frequently used by lawyers in the O. J. Simpson trial.

To *parse* the press secretary's sentence: "*I* (pronoun)/*am* (auxiliary verb)/*not* (adverb)/*going* (present participle)/*to* (infinitive marker)/*parse* (infinitive)/*the* (definite article)/*statement* (noun)."

When reports of the tapes made it appear that the intern had been told to deny an affair in her affidavit in the Paula Jones lawsuit, the verb that arose was *suborn* (pronounced suh-BORN).

Back to the Latin: *sub* means "under," or in this sense, "secret." *Orn* comes from *ornare*, "to equip," related to a similar verb meaning "to order." Thus, the original meaning of the Latin *subornare* is "to secretly order," a concept snatched up by lawyers. In 1534, not fourteen years after Skelton smelled a rat, a statute of Henry VIII stated that offenders went to jurors "and have *suborned* them to aquyte dyvers murderers."

Today *Black's Law Dictionary* defines *suborn* as "(1) to induce (a person) to commit an unlawful or wrongful act, esp. in a secret or underhanded manner, (2) to induce (a person) to commit perjury."

Monica S. (for Samille) Lewinsky's lawyer, William H. Ginsburg of Los Angeles, depicted his client as a victim of either an overzealous prosecutor or a President who was "a *misogynist*, and I have to question his ability to lead." In a greenroom before a telecast, Mr. Ginsburg asked me: "Did I use the right word?"

A *misogynist* is a woman-hater. *Misos* is Greek for "hatred," *gyne*, "woman." This should not be confused with *misanthrope*, a hater of mankind, now called humankind, which includes both men and women. Mr. Ginsburg's choice of a word created some confusion, as it was not woman-hating that the President was possibly engaged in, though contempt for a young woman's virtue could be a form of misogyny.

In the former intern Monica Lewinsky's taped telephone conversations with her friend Linda Tripp, the word *shmucko* was reportedly used as a kind of sobriquet for what was assumed to be the young woman's highly placed inamorata. In a previous column, cleared by copy editors and other arbiters of editorial taste after great hair-tearing and teeth-gnashing, we explored the penile and ornamental origins of the German-Yiddish *schmuck*, which has lost its taboo and is now a slang synonym for *jerk, nerd, dork* and *creep*.

"The big creep" was another taped reference by Ms. Lewinsky that caused much wincing and not a few hoo-has. Let's cut the snickering and go directly to the etymology: *kreupan* was the Old Teutonic source for the intransitive verb defined by the *Oxford English Dictionary* as "to move with the body prone and close to the ground, as a short-legged reptile, an insect, a quadruped moving stealthily."

Things that crawl have been reviled since the temptation of Eve in the Bible. That quality of crawling stealthily is the basis of the slang noun *creep*. "What a stupid *creep!*" is a 1926 citation from a J. M. March novel, *Wild Party*, in the *Random House Historical Dictionary of American Slang*. *Creep* was cited a year later as meaning "worthless person" in the lingo used in Sing Sing Prison in New York and is slithering along strongly in today's slang.

I remember the word with a shudder. As a Nixon speechwriter, I suggested the name of the group to organize the 1972 reelection campaign:

"The Committee to Re-Elect the President." Senator Bob Dole cheerfully gave it the semi-acronym *CREEP*, which, after the Watergate break-in, gave that innocent name a connotation of stealth that lives with us today.

In your parsing of Mr. McCurry's sentence you identify going *as the present participle after the auxiliary verb* am. *I believe that* going *would be considered the main verb in a verb phrase rather than a present participle. The example given in the* Harbrace College Handbook *cites that "used with a form of* be, *all progressive verbs end in* -ing *as in 'was eating.'" This same reference defines* auxiliary verb *as "a verb (like be, have, do) used with a main verb in a verb phrase. An auxiliary regularly indicates tense but may also indicate voice, mood, person, number."*

Frederick J. Schroeder Jr.
Grosse Pointe, Michigan

INAM-ERRATUM

In an article that tried to treat with decorum and dignity a matter too often subjected to salacious snickering, I referred to the President as having been accused of being "Ms. Lewinsky's *inamorata*." I thought that was less judgmental than *paramour*, which imputes illicit sex, or *cookie*, which is both sexist and overly informal.

The Gotcha! Gang struck with the swiftness of a Ken Starr wirer-upper. An *inamorata*, I am informed by a legion of righteous students of Italian, is "a woman who loves or is beloved"; when used to refer to a man, however, the ending changes to the masculine, and the word becomes *inamorato*.

PHLOGGING IT

"The real writer is one/who really writes," writes the poet Marge Piercy. "Talent/is an invention like phlogiston/after the fact of fire."

In *Fooling with Words: A Celebration of Poets and Their Craft*, the TV documentarian Bill Moyers, quoting this poem, asked the author about the meaning of the unfamiliar word *phlogiston*.

"*Phlogiston* was a pre-nineteenth-century explanation for why things burned," Piercy replied. "People said things burned because they contained *phlogiston*. It always struck me as the perfect example of a false explanation."

For two decades I have awaited someone else's use of the word that was rendered obsolete by the discovery of the properties of oxygen. The unforgettable S. J. Perelman, in sending me his hefty collection of hilarious works that he scorned to title *The Best of*—he chose *The Most of S. J. Perelman*—inscribed it with his good wishes "together with a small jar of *Antiphlogiston* to rub on his deltoids should he read this compendium in bed."

POTUS AND FLOTUS

Controversy was bestirred by a memorandum dated November 20, 1995, from high officials of the Democratic National Committee to Harold Ickes, then deputy chief of the White House staff, asking for "18–20 calls by POTUS" and "10 calls by VPOTUS."

Muckraking political pundits and righteously reformist goo-goos were incensed by this fund-raising from the federal property that—in less populist times—used to be known as the Executive Mansion, but today's exercise in irenic scholarship focuses on the increasing use of an acronym: *Potus*, which stands for "President of the United States."

As a presidential aide in 1969, I first noticed this acronym on a label of an extension of a five-line telephone along the back wall of the West Wing's Cabinet Room. When the button next to that label lighted up, the phone was answered with special alacrity. A similar button labeled *POTUS* was on the telephone set of H. R. Haldeman, the President's chief of staff, and was used by him for calls both from and to Mr. Nixon.

Jack Valenti, an aide to President Johnson, recalls the initials appearing on phones in that administration but does not recall anyone's using the acronym in everyday speech, as in "What does *Potus* think?" Hamilton Jordan of the Carter administration also says the acronym was not bruited about in their day; its White House use began, it seems, in the Nixon era and then disappeared for a while.

Potus (acronyms of five letters or more are usually lowercased, sometimes with initial caps) was popularized to some extent in my 1977 White House novel, *Full Disclosure*, as the pet name adopted by the unmarried President's inamorata-photographer. She felt awkward calling the Chief Executive by his first name, and "Mr. President" was not appropriate for intimate moments; *Potus* was her solution.

In current practice, the acronym is not used in direct discourse with the president—nobody says, "How are you feeling this morning, *Potus*?"—but it is a handy, sassily insidish, behind-his-back reference to the individual in that office, as in "Is *Potus* in one of those moods where he wants to see teeth on the sidewalk?"

Bert Lance—reached in Rosebud, a suburb of Calhoun, Georgia—remembers the acronym was the Secret Service designation of President Carter on the "locator," the device that tells top staff members where the president and first family are at every moment. Secret Service agents were reported to have picked up the term in everyday use during the Reagan years, and added a dimension: "To their Secret Service shadows they may be '*Potus*' and '*Flotus*,'" wrote Donnie Radcliffe in *The Washington Post* in a 1983 citation. *Flotus* (pronounced FLOW-tus, to rhyme with *Potus*, and not FLOT-tus) is "First Lady of the United States," an informal designation first applied to Mary Todd Lincoln that has become a quasiofficial title.

In the Clinton administration, the usage was extended to *Vpotus*, pronounced VEE-po-tus, to refer to the vice president. Tipper Gore has not yet been labeled *Slotus*, though that acronymic designation of the "Second Lady" is possible because it has the advantage of brevity over *Sotvpotus*—"Spouse of the Vice President of the United States."

This rash of acronymese ending in "us" may have begun in wire-service coverage of a different branch of government. *Scotus* is "wirespeak" for "Supreme Court of the United States." Old newspaper skates can remember the "slug"—the quick name for an article that appeared on top of copy typed on cheap beige paper—for all High Court articles to be *Scotus*.

In 1983, as the Secret Service usage about the President began to appear in print, a *New York Times* editorialist took umbrage at the rampant acronymization: "Is no Washington name exempt from shorthand? The chief magistrate responsible for executing the laws is sometimes called the *Potus* (President of the United States). The nine men who interpret them are often the *Scotus*. The people who enact them are still, for better or worse, Congress."

This "nine men" error drew an amused retort from Justice Sandra Day O'Connor, who noted the need for updating *Times* files and tongue-in-cheekily added, "If you have any contradictory information, I would be grateful if you would forward it—as I am sure the *Potus*, the *Scotus* and undersigned (the *Fwotsc*) would be most interested in seeing it."

The first rule of acronyms, from *radar* to *NATO*, is that the initials must be easily pronounceable as a word. *Fwotsc*—First Woman on the Supreme Court—may be useful shorthand at the *Scotus*, but does not quite make it as an acronym.

And now to the etymologist's delight: discovery of first use, deep in American history, never before revealed to general lexicographers.

Richard M. Harnett, an old UPI hand ("Downhold expenses!"), is the author of *Wirespeak: Codes and Jargon of the News Business*. Part of this inspired lexicon—source of such vivid verbs as *eyeball* and *upstick*—is the full text of the Phillips Code, compiled in 1879 by Walter Phillips, a telegrapher and wire-service manager who worked for both the Associated Press and United Press International.

It was in that first edition that *Scotus* was first recorded. (Or "rkod," in the telegrapher's shorthand. A sentence meaning "The Secretary of War was shot and instantly killed" would be rendered in two acronyms, SOW SAIK.) Then, in the 1925 revision by E. E. Bruckner of Phillips's pioneering work, *Potus* found its way into print.

Some acronyms make it, some don't. In Phillips Code, WHU stood for "the White House"; not even *Potus* uses that anymore. (Coming soon, to replace U.S. Government—*Gotus!*)

While the New York Times *editorialist whom you have cited may have been technically correct that there was no acronym for Congress, a group of members of Congress traveling together has long been known as "Codel," presumably a "congressional delegation." My guess is that the acronym originated not with wire services, as in most of the cases you cite, but in State Department cables to warn embassies of impending visitations.*

Typically, the Codel would be described by the name of the House member who had organized the trip. Thus, when in the summer of 1991 I participated in a trip organized by then Speaker Tom Foley to review the U.S. aid program to Ireland, we were known as the Foley Codel, presumably to distinguish us from all the other Codels wandering the globe at that time.

Bill Green, National Chair
MODRNPAC
New York, New York

PREFIXATIONS

Stimulated by a recent piece about *couth*, *kempt* and *gruntled*, a new division of the Lexicographic Irregulars has formed itself: The Deprefixers.

My former *Times* colleague David Burnham, now with Syracuse University's Transactional Records Access Clearinghouse, is one. He notes the poet John Milton's use in *Paradise Lost* of "Not *nocent* yet, but on the grassy Herb," with *nocent* ("harmful") the near-opposite of *innocent*.

Norman Hyman of Milwaukee sends a 1994 *New Yorker* article by Jack Winter: "I was *furling* my *wieldy* umbrella when I saw . . . a *descript* person, a woman in a state of total *array*. Her hair was *kempt*, her clothing *shevelled*, and she moved in a *gainly* way." His reaction: "I was *plussed*. It was *concerting* to see that she was *communicado*, and it *nerved* me that she was interested in a *pareil* like me. . . . I acted with *mitigated* gall and made my way through the *ruly* crowd with strong *givings*."

Dorothy Berg of Madison, Wisconsin, and Barbara Scholl of New York directed me to the leading muse of the Deprefixers, the poet Felicia Lamport.* In both her "Scrap Irony" and "Light Metres," she deprefixed furiously.

Ms. Lamport graciously gave me permission through her husband to run her pioneering play:

> Life would be such a nice *broglio*
> Running so smoothly and *mok*,
> If I had a nice portfolio
> Full of negotiable stock.
> And if it were tax-exempt,
> I would be *gruntled* and *kempt*.

But that was only getting started. Then came such an outpouring of deprefixed delight not since matched:

"Nothing gives rise to such wild surmise/As the *peachable* widow with *consolate* eyes." And: "The *iquitous* girl often loses her balance/When wooed by a man with unusual *chalance*." And: "Men often pursue in suitable style/The *imical* girl with the *scrutable* smile."

*Felicia Lamport died December 23, 1999.

In my family we used to call them "obsolete positives"—OSPOS for short—and compiled a long list of them. Some of those I recall were ept, chalant, peccable, petuous, portunate, pulsive, pecunious, defatigable, choate, domitable, evitable, exorable, and so on and so on.

Annie Gottlieb
New York, New York

PRESENTISM

Here we stand, seized by *futurism*, back-formed from *futuristic*, meaning "an outlook imbued with the sense of tomorrow," sometimes drearily dystopian, but usually more upbeat and utopian.

In the midst of this millennial miasma, another word has come along to stir up historians. I came across it in the recent *Thomas Jefferson and Sally Hemings: An American Controversy*, a persuasive analysis of the close relationship between Jefferson and one of his slaves by Professor Annette Gordon-Reed of the New York Law School: *presentism*.

"It's when a historian sees events in the past through the prism of present-day standards," the lawyer-historian tells me. "For example, Thomas Jefferson is often judged harshly as a sexist even though the notion of complete equality between the sexes was almost unthinkable in his era." Gordon-Reed calls it the "why wasn't Jefferson like Alan Alda" question.

Fred Shapiro, the etymological hawkshaw who edits the *Oxford Dictionary of American Legal Quotations*, found the earliest use to date of this useful word in a 1950 article in *American Historical Review* by Chester Destler, a name not easy to say fast. Destler found that "subjectivist-relativist-presentism," along with a few other mouth-filling names of ideas, "constitute together [sic] the conceptual foundations of the new school of historical theory." This was pooh-poohed a year later in the same scholarly publication: "The concept of 'presentism' as it is described in Mr. Destler's article has no counterpart among serious philosophers."

The fact is (conventional historicists are into *facticity*) that Destler coined a useful word. When we apply today's morality to yesterday's mores, we indulge in *ex post facto* judgment. That's *presentism*, imposing the present on the past, which is usually unfair, so don't do it.

If both *futurism* and *presentism* are here, can *pastism* be far behind? That word was first used in 1921, "under the spell of *Pastism*," and again in 1962 in Britain's *Listener*: "The Jugendbewegung youth movement was sterile '*past-ism*' by contrast with contemporary futurism." Its meaning is "sentimental memory of an age gone by," which was best exemplified in the title of a 1978 book by Simone Signoret: *Nostalgia Isn't What It Used to Be*.

PROFFER PREFERRED

At the hearings led by Senator Fred Thompson into political funny money, the noun *proffer* keeps coming up. Senator John Glenn, referring to the possibility of getting the fund-raiser John Huang to appear, said, "I would think all this superbright legal talent we have represented on this committee can figure out a way to do it, to get a *proffer* for us to consider."

The word was born in romance. In the fourteenth century, an anonymous parish priest wrote in *Cursor Mundi* of a lady who "*porferd* him hir muth to kiss." Its Latin root melds *pro*, "for, in front of," with *offerre*, "to offer."

Now it's a legal term. "A *proffer* is an offer into evidence," said Bryan A. Garner, editor of *Black's Law Dictionary*, "and only such an offer. Lawyers wouldn't use the term as a verb merely to mean 'to offer a deal' in exchange for immunity. When giving a *proffer*, the petitioner must have something to give, that is, to offer into evidence."

Is there a difference between *offer* and *proffer*? Used as verbs, they have the same meaning; as nouns, especially in legal terminology, *proffer* has a narrower meaning. Bethany Dumas, editor of *Language in the Judicial Process*, explained that it can mean "I will summarize for you what I will testify to under oath if you grant me immunity." As Senator Thompson put it: "You don't buy a pig in a poke. You don't give anybody immunity unless you know their testimony will be helpful." (The dialect noun *poke*, akin to the French *poche*, means "bag.")

PUSHING IT

"Allergies, I am told, don't flare up the first time you come in contact with the offending agent," writes Tom Wolfe, author of the novels *Bonfire of the Vanities* and *A Man in Full*. "The allergens build up gradually over time until one day you can't take it anymore."

That's a writer's way of beginning a letter. None of this right-to-the-point e-mail stuff, or apologies for belatedness, or arch "anent: whatever." On the contrary, a letter that begins with an apt metaphor or an original turn of phrase causes the recipient to sit back and prepare to enjoy the vanishing art of correspondence.

"That happened to me when it came to the expression *pushing the envelope*," Mr. Wolfe continued, enclosing a clipping from *The New York Times* with the headline, "*Pushing the Bleeping Envelope.*" The article quoted Doug Herzog, president of the Fox Entertainment Group, about the sex talk and profanity in one of his television series: "Without question, it *pushes the envelope.*" The reporter, Bernard Weinraub, then observed, "Mr. Herzog is hardly alone in *pushing the envelope.*" This was fairly heavy pushing.

"Pushing an envelope isn't very hard," notes the novelist. "It's one of the easiest things in the world and one of the most pointless. The actual expression, which comes from a flight test, is '*pushing the outside of the envelope.*'"

There is a world of metaphoric difference between shoving a piece of stationery around and pushing the outside of a container from the inside. "Each type of aircraft has a certain envelope within which it can operate safely," writes Wolfe. "It can dive safely only up to such-and-such a slope or turn safely only beyond such-and-such a radius. Trying to stretch those limits is pushing the outside of the envelope."

In mathematics, the outer boundary of a family of curves has been known since the mid-nineteenth century as the *envelope*. Aeronautical engineers later applied the word to the limits of aircraft operation, from *gust envelopes* to *maneuver envelopes* to *flight envelopes*. When a test pilot presses against those outer limits, he *pushes the outside of the envelope*.

Wolfe helped introduce the metaphor and certainly popularized the phrase in *The Right Stuff*, his 1979 book about astronauts. "Perhaps that's why the allergens finally got to me."

When a test pilot exceeds the design limits described by the flight envelope, he pushes (against) the boundary of the envelope.

He does so from within a region of established response in order to expand the range of performance. He is thus pushing on the inside, not the outside of the envelope.

As an analogy, if you were to gain twenty pounds, would you say that you were pushing the outside of your belt?

Peter D. Klein

Houston, Texas

Surely Tom Wolfe is pushing the envelope of metaphor when he states that "the allergens build up gradually over time until one day you can't take it anymore."

In fact, it is the buildup of (IgE) antibodies in response to allergen exposure that causes allergic reactions. This buildup is determined more by the individual's innate tendency to form antibodies than by the frequency or intensity of allergen exposure.

Thus an allergic person can be bothered by just a little bit of ragweed while a nonallergic person can tolerate vast amounts without so much as a sneeze.

Likewise, Mr. Wolfe may be bothered by a few extra published references to "pushing the envelope," while another person, less inclined to produce linguistic antibodies, might take it in stride.

Carl Silverman, M.D.

Madison, Wisconsin

RATCHETING UP
THE PERISCOPE

ANTICIPATING TENSION among the heirs to Frank Sinatra's estate, Joshua Hammer wrote in *Newsweek* about Ol' Blue Eyes' will, "It's certain to *ratchet up* the family feud even higher."

A puzzled Marie Balandis of Houston writes: "My dictionary defines *ratchet* as a noun meaning 'a pawl, click or detent for holding or propelling a ratchet wheel.' Will be looking for your column on *ratchet*."

Here it is, and you need a newer dictionary.

Every mechanic knows that a *ratchet* is a toothed wheel or bar used to prevent a gizmo from moving backward. That sawlike catch is what gives us all confidence in elevators and the courage to jack up a car to change a tire. But this word (from the Old German *roccho*, "spindle") has been reborn with new senses.

The *ratchet effect* has seized economics, and to *ratchet up*—"to move upward in increments"—is a verb phrase that has thrust aside the previously voguish *escalate*. (*Raise* was long ago lowered, and *increase* has shrunk.)

Professor James Duesenberry of Harvard launched *ratchet effect* in a 1948 doctoral thesis that became a seminal macroeconomic book the next year: *Income, Saving and the Theory of Consumer Behavior.* He took the *ratchet* to be a device that enables something to move easily up but prevents it from moving easily all the way down, and applied that metaphor to the way we spend our money. In 1979, *Daedalus* magazine described the theory as beginning "with the common wisdom that prices go up more freely than they go down."

But that's only the beginning. I asked Professor William Doyle of the University of Dallas to simplify Duesenberry's theory for me, and it boils down to this: "It's easier for a household to adapt its expenditures to an increase in income than to a decrease in income. When income increases, consumption spending increases; but when income falls, consumers who have come to view their standard of living as 'normal' are very reluctant to decrease consumption spending." That's the *ratchet effect:* When you've been up there, you tend to spend as if you're still there—even when you can no longer afford it. Reached in Boston, Professor Emeritus Duesenberry recalls: "I think the *ratchet* I was familiar with was a car jack. I thought about the *ratchet* on a car jack and thought of it as an analogy to what was happening. It's an asymmetrical response."

According to Merriam-Webster, the editor of *Barron's* magazine, Robert Bleiberg, first used the phrasal verb *ratchet up* on April 10, 1972: "In a striking reversal of policy, the Fed in recent weeks has *ratcheted upward* the repo a collateralized short-term loan rate to 4 percent." Five years later, Britain's Margaret Thatcher, on her way to becoming prime minister, latched onto the image: "Britain is no longer in the politics of the pendulum, but of the *ratchet.*"

Economists still love the saw-toothed image, but came to use it in a broader sense. "If you build in wages and other benefits based upon an exaggerated Consumer Price Index," warned Paul Volcker when he was Fed chairman in 1981, "you *ratchet up* inflation."

Now it calibrates any rise. "Tension in the border war between Ethiopia and Eritrea," reported Agence France-Presse a few months ago, "*ratcheted up* a notch."

And Michael Kelly, in his column enlivening the weekly *National Journal*, dreamed up ways that Democrats would continue to try to embarrass Republicans with antitobacco bills, concluding, "The pain level *ratchets up*, and sooner or later, the theory goes, the GOP caves."

Needed: a phrase meaning "to lower by degrees, to decrease in increments." *Ratchet down* may be justified mechanically, but it doesn't do it metaphorically.

Consider "rappel down" as the counterpart of "ratchet up."
> Norman Cutler Smith
> Asheville, North Carolina

You say, "Needed: a phrase meaning 'to lower by degrees, to decrease in increments.'" We have a perfectly good word that means exactly that: decrement.
> Jack E. Garrett
> Jamesburg, New Jersey

REPREHENDING

"I felt the President's behavior was *reprehensible,*" said Representative James H. Maloney, Democrat of Connecticut. Feeling the need to save his constituents the time it takes to look up unfamiliar words, he added, "*Reprehensible* means 'deserving of rebuke.'"

He uses the *Random House Unabridged,* which defines the word as "deserving of reproof, rebuke, or censure; blameworthy." The synonym is *culpable. Reproof* is criticism administered gently; *rebuke* is sterner stuff, and *censure* is official condemnation.

RETRONYM WATCH

Used to be, your *partner* was the guy you were in business with. Now the word needs modification. We have *life partners,* people in a state of permanent cohabitation, straight or gay, connoting a more equal relationship than *companion* or *live-in boy-* or *girlfriend.*

That's why we see an article in *The New York Times* begin, "Mary Bidgood Wilson and her *business partner* of five years, Wendy Wilson. . . ." The modifier *business* is now needed lest the reader be forced to guess what kind of partnership the writer had in mind.

That's a *retronym,* a phrase with a modifier fixing a meaning to a noun that needed no modifier before: The shift to night baseball created *day baseball,* just as the invention of the electric guitar required us to call the old-fashioned instrument an *acoustic guitar.* To every water-skier, the crazies who slide down mountains are *snow-skiers.*

Some of my *ink readers* (a phrase now necessary to separate them from those who read this column on-line) have latched onto the semantic field day marked by retronyms as the best quick linguistic evidence of change in our culture.

Because I like to get letters and cards that are written by people who have no need for instant gratification, I noted here that I have happily resisted an e-mail address, which generated the question, "So what's your *postal address?*" Now I have a *postal address* to go with my *voice phone number,* a retronym caused by the rise of the fax machine.

Observant Jews celebrate Purim, a minor festival commemorating deliverance from the evildoer Haman (pronounced HOM-on). Professor Ranon Katzoff of Bar-Ilan University in Israel informs me that Queen Esther was presumed to have eaten "seeds," later specified as poppy seeds, in King Ahasuerus's court.

"Baked pockets of seeds filled with *mon* (Yiddish for 'poppy seeds')," Professor Katzoff writes, "are *mon-taschen*, and by a small punning step *hamantaschen*, 'Haman's pockets.' In their essence, they are made with poppy seeds."

Ah, but what about my favorite, prune hamantaschen? My local bakery also features apricot filling and is thinking about chocolate. "These are as off the mark as blintzes filled with blueberries," says the professor, a purist. "If a bakery on Purim advertises *poppy-seed hamantaschen*, that's a retronym just as much as *legitimate theater, analog watch* and, I claim, *cheese blintzes.*"

When hamantaschen go stale, they require the use of a cordless drill to penetrate them. "A few years back," writes James Bailey of Oak Lawn, Illinois, "a drill was either manual or electric. With the advent of battery power, some electric drills were labeled *cordless*, while the remainder were known simply as drills. Now that cordless drills have become so common, I notice an example of what you call a retronym: *corded drills.*"

(He adds parenthetically, "And shouldn't *battery-operated* be *battery-powered?*" Yes, and you can take that from a high-operated media biggie.)

"Sweet potatoes used to be light yellow," notes Paul Bruch of Southbury, Connecticut. "Then they started selling yams, dark orange in color, mislabeled 'sweet potatoes.' Recently our grocer began selling the original light yellow sweet potatoes, but now he calls them 'white sweet potatoes' (even though they're still yellow). Is this what you call a retronym?"

I tried it out on Frank Mankiewicz, father of the retronym, who waved it in. Frank also showed me three new gems in his collection: "In Los Angeles, there's 'the No. 1 *English-speaking radio station.*' And in this brave new single-parent society, we now have the need to refer to the *two-parent family.* Finally, a wine now made necessary by the presence of (I can hardly bring myself to say) blush wines: *red zinfandel.*"

Mr. Bruch's grocer is correct in telling his customers the color of the sweet-potatoes (not sweet potatoes) he sells. Sweetpotatoes range in color from white to purple, and I doubt that he sells many, if any, yams. Yams are not sweetpotatoes (Ipomoea batatas), but belong to the genus Dioscorea, which is not even a distant cousin of Ipomoea. The sweetpotato is native to the tropical Americas; the yam originated in tropical Africa.

The misnomer yam is applied to the soft, moist-fleshed sweetpotatoes of the Puerto Rico type that most commonly are grown in the South and are deeply pigmented; the dry, mealy types are the pale ones; but both types are sweetpotatoes.

I guess that the term yam, *as misapplied by growers and marketers of sweetpotatoes in the southern states, may have had its origin in the similar shapes of the roots of sweetpotatoes and the tubers (another basic botanical difference) of yams, the latter having been familiar to slaves from Africa. Thus,* white sweetpotato *definitely is not a retronym.*

Werner J. Lipton
Fresno, California

The use of the word yam *to refer to the orange one is at least as interesting an illustration of linguistic change as the retronyms you cite. As it happens, it was your correspondent, and not his grocer, who mislabeled that edible tuber. Both the yellow and orange forms are varieties of* Ipomoea batatas *whose species name is the native American source of our word* potato. *They were originally domesticated in pre-Columbia highland South America.*

Yams, on the other hand, belong to the genus Dioscorea *and were used as a staple in the Old World tropics all the way from east of New Guinea westwards to Africa. When West Africans were brought as slaves to the Caribbean and adjacent areas, they had not been allowed the privilege of bringing their own food crops with them. However, they did use a native West African word to describe the edible root crops they encountered in what perforce became their new home—hence the mislabeled dark orange "yam" which, botanically, really is a kind of sweet potato and not a yam at all.*

C. Loring Brace
Museum of Anthropology
The University of Michigan
Ann Arbor, Michigan

Is the newest retronym desk-top computer? Is the oldest retronym not-forbidden fruit (older than non-circumcised penis and kosher food)? Others (which I realize you may have already used): whole milk, stick shift, and black-and-white television.

Monroe H. Freedman
Howard Lichtenstein Distinguished Professor of Legal Ethics
Hofstra University
Hempstead, New York

Concerning "two-parent family," I am a divorced father with two children. When my fiancée, who has two children, and I marry, we won't quite be a "two-parent family" in the sense I take the phrase to mean (a family unit that is intact). We'll then be a "dual single-parent family" or a "double-headed household."

J. P. Riquelme, Professor of English
Boston University
Boston, Massachusetts

"Waved it in"? That may be okay for a third-base coach spotting the ball headed for the gap in the right field, but for an admissions officer, don't you think "waived" might be preferable?

Frank Mankiewicz, Vice Chairman
Hill & Knowlton
Washington, D.C.

The rise of the use of marijuana in the United States has brought about the use of the term tobacco cigarette.

John Fox
Austin, Texas

THE RETURN OF JOE SIX-PACK

"If I were just a private citizen—*Joe Six-Pack*," President Clinton told *Time* magazine after Paula Jones's lawsuit against him was dismissed by a judge in Little Rock, "I would have mixed feelings about not getting a chance to disprove these allegations in court."

However, Mr. Clinton explained on Air Force One, he did not "have mixed feelings" as president because he was not *Joe Six-Pack* and had to put the nation's interests before his own. This was not the first time President Clinton used the subjunctive mood, or presidential conditional, in speculation about what his reaction would have been had he not been a resident of 1600 Pennsylvania Avenue.

Two years ago, when a vituperative right-wing pundit had the gall to cast aspersions on the veracity of the First Lady ("congenital liar" was the outrageous calumniation), Mr. Clinton's press secretary stated, "The President, if he were not the President, would have delivered a more forceful response to that on the bridge of Mr. Safire's nose." Mr. Clinton, later that day, also used the subjunctive (from the Latin meaning "subordinate") to express a contingency contrary to fact, a grammatical device frequently used to express a suppressed emotion and one that requires a *were* rather than a *was*. "If I *were* an ordinary citizen," the President noted, "I might give that article the response that it deserves." His *if*, *were*, *might* sequence served as a model of correctness for this generation of grammarians.

In recently revisiting the presidential conditional, Mr. Clinton used a colorful modern locution to contrast his highly responsible chief executive position with that of the average person having plenty of time to spare, whose name was first *Everyman*.

In Dutch and English morality plays of the fifteenth century, *Everyman*—when called by Death—asked his fair-weather friends Beauty, Kindred and Worldly Goods to accompany him, but they turned him down. One friend, however, loyally agreed, and together Good Deeds and *Everyman* entered Heaven.

Only the Devil has more aliases than the average person. The Chinese call him *Old Hundred Names*, the Russians *Ivan Ivanovich*, the French *Monsieur Tout le Monde*, the Germans *Otto Normalburger* or *Jederman* and the Dutch *Elckerlijc*. As the *man in the street*, he made his appearance in 1831 and was popularized a decade later by Ralph Waldo Emerson in his essay on self-reliance, playing on John Bunyan's metaphor about the man with the muckrake: "The *man in the street* does not know a star in the sky."

He signs checks *John Doe* (on a joint account with *Jane Doe*); the editor William Allen White in 1937 called him *John Q. Public*, and in 1883 the Yale sociologist William Graham Sumner named him the *forgotten man*, a moniker that Franklin Roosevelt adopted while campaigning for president in 1932 (before beer was sold in cardboard containers of six bottles).

His first name soon changed to *Joseph*. The *average Joe* appeared as *Joe Blow* (1867), *Joe Doakes* (1926), *Joe College* (1932), *G.I. Joe* (1943) and, in Britain, *Joe Bloggs* (1969). Though *Joe Zilch* (1925, probably a play on zero) and *Joe Schmo* (1950, rhyming with hometown Kokomo) are derisive, *Joe Cool* (1949) gets respect. This assumption that *Joe* is average seems outdated because *Joseph* is a given name declining in vogue; if current averageness were the criterion, we might expect *the average Michael* or *Brian Six-Pack*. (The if, were, might succession, as above, uses the subjunctive mood to signify a condition contrary to fact.)

A *six-pack* (which still takes a hyphen, but not for long) is a half-dozen bottles or cans, often of beer, packaged to be purchased as a unit. Beer is traditionally *Everyman's* alcoholic beverage, slurped up noisily or chug-a-lugged breathlessly by those who sneer at effete elitists with "champagne tastes." Hence, the affinity of the plebeian *Joe* with the symbol of beer purchased in quantity, the *six-pack*, a word coined in 1952.

"Step aside, Geeks," writes Deborah Branscum in *Newsweek*. "Internet telephony is looking for *Joe Six-Pack*." (The writer contrasts the high-technology geek with the average clumsy person.) In the same way, Robert Luskin, a criminal defense attorney, was quoted in *The Washington Post* as saying, "You ought not to be indicting the President of the United States for things that you don't indict *Joe Six-Pack* for." Obviously, Mr. *Six-Pack* has bellied up to the bar of usage and elbowed aside *John Q. Public* and all the *Joes*.

Who invented him? The *Oxford English Dictionary* is silent; the *Random House Historical Dictionary of American Slang* has a citation in the *Los Angeles Times* from as early as 1977.

"Herewith *Joe Six-Pack's* birth certificate," writes Martin F. Nolan, the reporter and frequent writer on language at *The Boston Globe*. He attaches an article in that newspaper dated August 28, 1970, about Joe Moakley, then a state senator who was campaigning against Louise Day Hicks for the congressional seat held by Speaker John McCormack.

"Moakley plans to make Mrs. Hicks the major issue in the campaign," wrote Nolan, then at the *Globe's* Washington bureau, "talking about issues in the media and shouting in *Joe Six-Pack's* ear to wake up and face the unsimplistic facts of life." The headline over the Nolan story was "After the Soul of *Joe Six-Pack*."

"The guy I heard it from," writes Nolan, "now long dead, threatened to sue if I quoted him. He must have known something. The initial mail in 1970 was all negative, accusing me of using Irish (and Polish!) ethnic stereotypes."

And what happened to Joe Moakley? "He really does qualify as *Joe Six-Pack*. Joe does not follow Beltway couture or cuisine and seems the same as he ever was. He lost to Louise Day Hicks that year and had to run as an independent in 1972, winning suburban votes to defeat her by fewer than 3,500 votes.

"Thus, the heir to John McCormack, the protégé to Tip O'Neill and the future chairman of the House Rules Committee began his career in Congress as sort of a (gasp!) reformer."

Major coinage found, triggered by a president's use. A happy day.

RETURN OF THE LUDDITES

The lead attorney for Microsoft, the firm accused by the U.S. Government of seeking to monopolize the computer industry, strode into a Washington courtroom and told the judge that the proceedings had turned into "a return of the *Luddites*."

Bill Gates's lawyer, John Warden, explained to listeners unversed in English history that the *Luddites* were a band of workers who smashed machines "to arrest the march of progress driven by science and technology."

If I had been the judge, I would have interrupted to say, "If you're going to cite precedent, get specific."

In Leicestershire in 1779, a man named Ned Ludd broke into a house, and in what was reported to be "a fit of insane rage," destroyed two machines used for knitting hosiery. The breaking of such knitting frames—machinery invented two centuries before—had been going on for nearly a century. Ludd, however, did it with such gusto and flair that subsequently, whenever machines of any sort were found smashed, the excuse was given that "King Ludd must have been here."

What was Ludd's motive? Was he a lover of hand-knitted hosiery? Did he prefer going barefoot? Or was he making some sort of undarned social protest of deeper significance?

Revisionist historians say that Ludd and other frame-wreckers were protesting poor working conditions and low wages at the beginning of the Industrial Revolution. However, between 1811 and 1816, organized bands of masked men swore allegiance to "King Ludd" rather than the British sovereign, and waged a war against the serflike conditions spawned by the users of textile machinery. "If the workmen dislike certain machines," explained the *Nottingham Review* in 1811, "it was because of the use to which they were being put, not because they were machines or because they were new."

That living-condition claim was swept aside by commercial interests and officialdom, which hung the label *Luddite* on protesters not for demanding a living wage but for obstructing the march of technological progress. The historical revisionists argue that others attributed the anti-machinery "cause" to the *Luddites*.

Intellectuals and romantics such as the poets Blake, Byron, Shelley and Wordsworth picked up that antitechnology theme, but identified with its other side. In the "dark Satanic mills" of industry, they saw the human spirit being stifled. Lord Byron wrote an inflammatory "Song for the *Luddites*" in 1816. Its first stanza: "As the Liberty lads o'er the sea/Bought their freedom, and cheaply, with blood,/So we, boys, we/Will die fighting, or live free,/And down with all kings but King Ludd!"

Mary Shelley, daughter of the early feminist Mary Wollstonecraft and wife of the poet, gave the *Luddite* theme dramatic power in her 1818 novel *Frankenstein*. The danger of rampant technology is expressed by the monster, who says to Dr. Victor Frankenstein, "You are my creator, but I am your master."

Between the sweatshop operators and the romantic poets, the meaning of *Luddite* became fixed as "radical opponent of technological or scientific progress." The novelist Thomas Pynchon wrote in *The New York Times* in 1984, "The word *Luddite* continues to be applied with contempt to anyone with doubts about technology, especially the nuclear kind." But he foresaw the day when "artificial intelligence, molecular biology and robotics all converge" and found what Microsoft lawyers claim to be government barbarians at their Gates as "certainly something for all good *Luddites* to look forward to if, God willing, we should live so long."

From breaking knitting frames at the start of the Industrial Age to breaking into mainframes and PCs in the Information Age—you just can't keep old Ned Ludd down. Lord Byron and Frankenstein's monster would be proud.

It is best to view with suspicion stories about the origins of names used as rallying cries by violent, nineteenth-century protest movements. You will search in vain for an authentic Captain Swing who led the English agricultural rioters in the 1830s, a genuine Molly Maguire who fought Irish landlords in the 1840s or a real Rebecca who led rioters in Wales during that same decade.

I suspect that the same holds true for Ned Ludd. The OED says the story that he smashed machines in 1779 lacks confirmation. And Norman Simms, in a scholarly article entitled "Ned Ludd's Mummers Play" (alas,

I lack a better footnote right now), contends the 1770 story amounts to wishful thinking.

Mr. Simms explores a variety of other possible derivations, including lud, *a minced (and, as the* OED *says, mocking) form of* lord, *and* luds, *a term for buttocks. Either would seem to fit, given the links that Mr. Simms finds between irreverent mummers and rebellious Luddites (members of both groups were known to parade about disguised in women's clothing and black face).*

Mark Bulik
National Desk
The New York Times
New York, New York

REVELATION DISCLOSURE

In a reminiscence of the late Judith Campbell Exner, a put-upon paramour of President Kennedy, I wrote that "responsible newspapers subsequently revealed that [Sam] Giancana, the woman's Chicago lover, was also the Mafia don who took a contract from the CIA to assassinate Fidel Castro."

A careful reader questions my use of the verb *reveal.* Wouldn't a better choice have been *disclose* or *divulge?*

The root of *reveal* is the Latin *velum,* "veil"; to *reveal* is to strip away the veil. The early use of revelation had to do with the unfolding of divine will or the making-known by some supernatural agency. That meaning still clings to the central sense of the word today; to *reveal* is to allow a vision of what is beyond the range of ordinary human reason or sight.

Disclose is its workaday synonym; no heavenly choir is singing in the background. The root meaning is "to unclose," which means "to open"; the most common sense is "to make known what was previously unpublished, deliberately held back or kept secret."

Divulge can be tracked back to the Latin *vulgus,* "mob"; it means "to make known to the multitude," with the whiff of a suggestion that the informant should have kept his information to himself. It implies either a breach of confidence or other impropriety in the communication. (I like *Merriam-Webster's New Dictionary of Synonyms,* but will not divulge my source.)

"When I was a writer (called 'contributing editor') on *Time* magazine," notes Allan Ecker of New York, "the managing editor was T. S. Mathews, a brilliant man. He always struck out *revealed* ('The sergeant *revealed* that no gun had been found on the scene') and substituted *disclosed* or just plain *said*. According to Mathews, *revealed* was 'reserved for the five books of Moses and the poetry of William Blake.'"

I'll go with that. Not every full disclosure is a full revelation.

REVERSE DEFAMATION

The noun *defamation* means "an attack on the reputation of another person," whether spoken (*slander*) or written (*libel*). When the defaming succeeds, the attacked wretch is left in *ignominy;* the *ig* means "lacking," and if you cannot plumb the depths of *no-men*—the good name or reputation—you have been dozing off again.

Defamation comes from the Latin *diffamare*, with the *dif* meaning "spread" and the *famare* "report, fame," and the whole word meaning "to spread abroad by ill report" or "to dishonor." First use of the term was in a 1303 rhyme: "For to make hym be ashamede that he shulde be so *defamede*."

How do you go about *defaming* a woman? In olden times, you might cast aspersions on her virtue. Recently, however, the word was used in a context that set the old usage on its head.

In a report about the claim made by a Dallas woman to a long-ago affair with Bill Clinton, *Newsweek*'s Michael Isikoff and Evan Thomas wrote, "Dolly Kyle Browning says that Clinton's account in his deposition—that he never had an affair with her—is 'perjury' and that she intends to sue the President for *defamation*."

Can the denial of any adulterous affair—the assertion of virtuous conduct—be considered *defamation?* Meaning is elastic, but at some point the rubber band snaps. Ms. Browning's reasoning is that, in failing to support her claim of past sin, the President is "calling me a crazed liar," thereby damaging sales of her book.

Mebbeso, but it turns on its head the meaning of a word that has held firm for seven centuries. Perhaps a new word is needed: *unfamation*, "damaging refusal to spread a desired ill report." Its adoption would surely spawn an *anti-unfamation league*.

RIP-TOOTIN' POORBACKS

"Vice President Al Gore continued his efforts to put a new face on his presidential campaign," wrote Katharine Q. (for Quimby) Seelye of *The New York Times* from Nashville, ". . . promising supporters a *rip-tootin'* candidacy." His actual words were "a *rip-tootin'* campaign that is going to win in the year 2000."

I was not the only student of language who noticed that odd locution. Michael Kelly, editor of *The Atlantic Monthly*, wrote in his newspaper column, "He has moved his campaign headquarters from, as he says, K Street to Main Street, the better to run what he, God help us, called 'a *rip-tootin'* race.'"

This term may have an Australian origin. In a review of Genevieve Lemon's one-woman show in Sydney, Pamela Payne of the *Sydney Sun-Herald* wrote in 1997, "This first one is *rip-tootin'* great."

More likely, Mr. Gore took the first part of *rip-roaring* or *rip-snorting* and married it to the last part of *rootin'-tootin'*. In linguistics, the linkage of the first part of a compound with the second part of another compound is called a blend.

Rootin'-tootin' was adopted by American slang from England's Lancashire dialect. Nodal and Milner's 1875 glossary of the local patois cites, "He's a *rootin' tootin'* sort of chap." George Bernard Shaw, in his 1907 play *Neolith*, wrote, "The trumpet angel . . . *root-a-tooted* at the sky." The meaning is "noisy, boisterous, lively"; the *OED* adds *rip-roaring*. It strikes me as onomatopoeic, imitative of a trumpet sound, and was popularized in the United States by the 1924 song "*Roottin-toottin*-Lou from Kalamazoo." Since then, it has often been applied to cowboys: Russell Hayden was known in the 1930s and 40s as the "*rootin'*, *tootin'*, ridin' Romeo of the screen."

Rip, a verb meaning "tear," is rooted in the Flemish *rippen*, "to strip off roughly." In dialect, it is a combining form for expressions like *rip-stave*, *rip-snort* and the airheaded television presenter's *rip-'n'-read*. When not meaning "tear," notes Joan Houston Hall of the *Dictionary of American Regional English*, "*rip* can mean 'to let out a wild yell or expletive' and in these combinations usually has to do with noise." It also means "to start noisily, frantically or suddenly," as in *let 'er rip!*

Rip-roaring's first citation was from *The Kentuckian in New York*, by William Caruthers, in 1834: "There was a *rip-roaring* sight of sleight o' hand and tumbling work there." Two years later the *Yale Literary Magazine* noted, "What a *rip-snorting* red head you have got!"

Another dialectical variant presents itself: This bids fair to be a *rootin'-roaring* campaign. And now to the metaphor used by George W. Bush to dissociate himself from what he sees as less compassionate conservatives.

When Republicans in the House suggested distributing an earned income-tax credit to the "working poor" monthly rather than in a yearly lump, Governor Bush said, "I don't think they ought to balance their budget *on the backs of the poor.*"

This talk caused much anguish in conservative ranks, along with muttering about Clintonian centrist "triangulation," because the metaphor has a long Democratic history. The *Weekly Standard* found a May 1977 use by Senator George McGovern, charging that President Jimmy Carter was trying "to balance the budget *on the backs of the poor,* the hungry and the jobless." Soon after, Barney Frank, a disaffected liberal aide to Massachusetts governor Michael Dukakis, denounced his former boss for "balancing the budget *on the backs of the poor.*" A decade later, as the Democratic candidate for president, Dukakis threw the identical charge at Vice President George Bush.

The earliest use I can find about the poor's burdened back came from a far-left group led by Congressman Vito Marcantonio, the Committee to Defend America by Keeping Out of War. Until June 1941, its slogan was "Take the burden of war *off the backs of the poor.*" (After Hitler invaded Communist Russia, the rallying cry switched overnight to "For Victory Over Fascism.") Earlier uses, I imagine, will also spring from anticapitalist sources, which is why it so set Republican teeth on edge. Adding insult to rhetorical injury, Al Gore called for another increase in the minimum wage, adjuring the Republican-controlled Congress to "stop paying off their special-interest friends *on the backs of the working poor.*"

In his own speech, Governor Bush had also said, "Too often, on social issues, my party has painted an image of America *slouching toward Gomorrah.*" This phrase was an ironic play on a line in a 1921 poem by William Butler Yeats: "And what rough beast, its hour come round at last,/*Slouches towards Bethlehem* to be born?" The ironist was former judge Robert Bork, who titled his 1996 book about America's moral decline *Slouching Towards Gomorrah.* (In the Bible, Gomorrah and its twin city, Sodom, were destroyed with fire and brimstone for their *rip-tootin'* iniquity. The escaping Lot's backward-looking wife is revered by arms-control advocates for being turned into a pillar of Salt II.)

Responding with rhetorical zest to this blast at his work from the Republican front-runner, Judge Bork evoked the poorback metaphor in *The Wall Street Journal,* suggesting that Governor Bush "gives the impression that the *backs of the poor* would be safe in his administration, but that he intends to reach the White House over the dead bodies of conservatives."

Politicians have to be careful about figures of speech; they can hurt themselves. The best admonition to those who would blithely practice rope-a-trope came from the nineteenth-century vituperator William Cobbett, who told a rival in political pamphleteering, "When I see you flourishing with a metaphor, I feel as much anxiety as I do when I see a child playing with a razor."

> *My daddy's singing, dated from his youth: "He's a high falutin', rootin' tootin' son of a gun from Arizona. Ragtime Cowboy, talk about a cowboy, Ragtime cowboy, Joe."**
>
> *This must predate your 1924 "Lou from Kalamazoo" as it's from Albert Julius's very young days.*
>
> Coral Samuel
> London, England

---

*"Ragtime Cowboy Joe" was written in 1912 by the Brooklyn trio of Lewis F. Muir, Maurice Abrahams and Grant Clark. It is the traditional fight song of the University of Wyoming "Cowboys." (Of course, they say "son-of-a-gun from Wyoming.")

SCHLUMPING ALONG

A POLEMIC by a right-wing calumniator began with a story about a Jewish matchmaker. A character in the story, named Sammy, was identified as "a nebbish and a *schlumpeh*." My *Times* copy editor, Linda Cohn, asked, "Do you mean *shlump*?" I insisted on the long form.

This prompted a note from Sol Steinmetz, the lexicographer: "You spelled *nebbish* correctly, but *schlumpeh* is problematic, because actually there's no such word." He acknowledged the German word *Schlampe*, which means "a slovenly female or slut," but noted that I could not have applied it to Sammy because the word is feminine.

"In Yiddish, there's a related word, *shlumper*, meaning 'a slovenly, ineffectual person,'" wrote the ever-helpful Steinmetz. "The word I think you meant to use was the American English slang noun *shlump*, which derives from and means the same as the Yiddish *shlumper*." He cited Joseph Heller's usage in his 1979 novel *Good as Gold*: "an odious *shlump* who made war gladly."

As winking wonks say in Mel Krupin's Bethesda deli, I nonconcur. All my life I have had poor posture. This is not a source of pride; I can hear the voice of Ida Safir, my mother, saying, "Billy, stand up straight—why must you be such a *schlumpeh*?" She may have derived this from the Scandinavian *slumpa*, "to fall," the root of the English *slump*, as in "You call a thousand-point drop in the stock market a *slump*?" The pronunciation of the final syllable was more of a *schwa* than an *er*. The meaning was "one who stooped" but not necessarily "one who is stupid."

It could be that the picture of a person with shoulders hunched forward would lead to the extension of meaning of "slovenly, ineffectual," as Steinmetz now defines the Yiddish term. At any rate, the final syllable has been clipped in its adoption in American slang, and the meaning of *shlump* has become synonymous with *nebbish*, "a pitifully ineffectual loser."

The word once served me well. In Army basic training, a lieutenant snapped at me, "Why can't you stand straight at attention, soldier?" I remembered my mother's usage and promptly replied, "Because I'm a *schlumpeh*, sir!" He must have thought it meant membership in an esoteric band of fierce warriors, because he never bothered me after that.

SCHWONK?

In the nefarious tapings often churned up by investigations can be found the language as she is spoken.

Here is a passage from the tape recordings released by the House Judiciary Committee. Linda Tripp, the faithless friend, says to Monica Lewinsky about the President, "Right now I think he's a *schwonk*."

This qualifies as what biblical exegetes call a *hapax legomenon*, the only known use in print, which makes it difficult to define.

"Unfortunately, Ms. Lewinsky never addressed the *schwonk* word in response," writes Evelyn Brody of Chicago, "but it sounds to me like the Yiddish version of 'policy wonk'—preceded by whatever word starting in *sch* you prefer, from *schmuck* to *schlemazel*."

We have already defined *schmuck* in this space as having lost its original taboo sense to now mean "jerk." A *schlemazel* is a "loser." The shooshing sound at the beginning of a word has come to suggest derogation.

This brings us to *wonk*. The *Oxford English Dictionary*'s first sense from 1900 is "yellow dog," from the Chinese *huang* ("*yellow*") *gou* ("*dog*"). (No, we will not go into "yellow-dog Democrat.") *Wonk* was soon applied as a term of contempt for young naval cadets. In the 1960s, it replaced "meatball" and "grind" as a put-down of an excessively studious student.

Here's a touch of irony: The phrase *policy wonk*, now widely used to describe serious-minded politicians with too great a grasp of minutiae, was coined in a 1984 *New Republic* article, referring with scorn to Senator Walter Mondale's "thralldom to the *policy wonks* and wise men of the Washington establishment."

The coiner was Sidney Blumenthal, now the White House aide who reported that President Clinton thought of Ms. Lewinsky as being a stalker, meaning "relentless groupie."

Schwonk? *From the Yiddish? Yes, of course, but surely not* schmuck *or* schlemazel. *What my ear heard was* Schwantz *(with the W pronounced as V). In Yiddish—German, too, as I'm sure you know—it means "tail."*

Of course, that meaning "behind," "ass," etc., probably fit the context. Secondarily, I heard "vance," bedbug. Could be that also fit the context.

Leonard Borenstein
Brooklyn, New York

SCOT-FREE MUMBO JUMBO, TSK-TSK

For a generation after the Civil War, the national bloodletting was euphemized in the self-mocking phrase "the late unpleasantness." Instant historians have not yet come up with the phrase to describe the Clinton impeachment process, or the Monica Madness, or the Clinton *Kulturkampf,* but during this yet-to-be-labeled *annus incredibilis,* a couple of great old phrases that deserve examination were heaved around by both sides.

"Defense Challenges Impeachment 'Mumbo Jumbo,'" said a *New York Times* headline over one of R. W. Apple's memorable articles, which led with "A White House lawyer, Gregory Craig, accused House prosecutors today of resorting to 'word games' and 'legal *mumbo jumbo.*'"

The Mandingo peoples of the western Sudan were reported around 1740 to have a high priest who protected the villagers called the *Mumbo Jumbo,* an Englishing of *mam-gyo-mbo,* supposedly "magician who drives away troubled spirits of ancestors." Other accounts describe the *Mumbo Jumbo* as a grotesque idol used to scare women into subjection.

Perhaps because the reduplicated sound was similar to the English *mumble jumble,* the sense deteriorated from "frightened veneration" to "meaningless babble; gibberish" and further to "jargon designed to confuse." It is now an attack phrase often used by lawyers against lawyers, with the racial or sex-subjugating overtones long forgotten.

Those who grumbled about the acquittal of the President used a phrase with an accusatory overtone, *scot-free.* "I assumed this had to do with my own Scotch ancestry," writes a Scottish American, Duncan Steck, of New York, "but lo, it comes from Old Norse, meaning both a shot and a contribution."

Right. It has nothing to do with the slur on the proverbial tightness of the Scots or with their freedom. The *scot,* sometimes spelled *shot,* was a tax or required payment. It was also a bar tab marked or scored on wood (the root of "a *shot* of booze"). "Though I could scape *shot-free* at London," says Shakespeare's Falstaff in *Henry IV,* "I fear the *shot* heere: here's no scoring, but upon the pate." That meant he feared getting hit in the head in battle.

Whether *shot-free*, meaning free from either a tax or another kind of *shot*, or *scot-free*, the terms came to mean "unpunished" with a connotation of unfair escape from responsibility.

When President Clinton greeted the Pope in St. Louis, Alessandra Stanley reported in *The New York Times* that "many people throughout the world had been *tut-tutting* about the uneasy juxtaposition."

Tut, an interjection of disapproval or dismissal used by Ben Jonson in *Volpone* and in reduplicated form as *tut, tut* by Shakespeare in *Richard II*, is both a word in itself and an attempt to spell an unspellable sound.

The sound is a palatal click often represented by "tsk, tsk," although that attempt at imitating the sound in print often results in the mispronunciation "tisk, tisk." Place the tongue on the palate with lips apart and suck quickly; that's the sound of a *tut* or a *tsk*. We call that *tut-tutting* because it's awkward to make two palatal clicks and follow them with an *-ing*. Language has its limits.

I am writing this to humbly suggest another interpretation of Falstaff's line in Henry IV, *"I fear the shot heere, here's no scoring, but upon the pate." You suggested that he meant he "feared getting hit on the head in battle." Perhaps you were being facetious, but I believe the interpretation is that he fears drinking in a pub where they do not mark down the tab— keeping it by memory ("upon the pate")—either the barkeep or the serving wench! Falstaff felt more secure if there was a written tab.*

Joe McHale
Houston, Texas

SCRIBBLE

"Another damned, thick, square book!" said the Duke of Gloucester in 1781 to a hardworking historian, Edward Gibbon, whose *Decline and Fall of the Roman Empire* would ultimately run to six damned, thick, square volumes. "Always *scribble, scribble, scribble*, eh, Mr. Gibbon?"

That was the most famous use of a word that means "to write hastily, often illegibly," rooted in the Latin *scribere*, "to write." A *scrivener* is a public copyist, but that noun has fallen into disuse except among notaries public; a *scribe*, once "a copyist of biblical texts," is now used jocularly to mean "journalist," and a *scribbler* is a put-down of a writer. This eye-strained wretch, in the millennial winter of his discontent, can be found down in the subbasement of information architecture in a cubicle labeled *content provider.*

But the noun and verb *scribble* has been resuscitated by the Internet set and given a new command position. In *Wired Style*, by Constance Hale and Jessie Scanlon, the *scribble command* is a boon to *flame-throwers*—those intemperate types who post curses on bulletin boards and otherwise abuse the civility of computer intercourse: "*Scribbling* . . . the saving grace of flame-throwers on the Well, the *scribble* command lets posters delete their words after the fact. The original post is replaced by a [*scribbled*] notice. It lets you eat your words, but not without leaving some digital crumbs."

If you have second thoughts about some snarl you have posted on the Well, a members-only Sausalito, California, "on-line community," where this 1985 PicoSpan software was first used, you can delete it with the *scribble* command. The post time, date and user name will be listed, but the text of the heated message will be replaced by the word *scribbled.*

What a great idea. Our civilization would neither decline nor fall if only we could work out a mental eraser that would scratch out insults we wish we had never hurled. Thanks to Internetese, at last self-expurgation has a moniker—eh, Mr. Gibbon?

SINGULAR HEAT?

A full-court press is needed to straighten out the syntax of sports.

I see a headline atop *The Washington Post:* "Jazz Beats Bulls," with the verb construing the first team, from Utah, as singular. Had the game gone the other way, however, the headline would have read "Bulls Beat Jazz," construing the Chicago team as plural.

"Is (are) the Miami Heat singular or plural?" wonders Howard Kleinberg, a columnist for the Cox newspapers. His concern extends beyond one team: "The Colorado Avalanche? The Utah Jazz? That there are five men on the court for the Heat at all times would tend to support a decision that they are plural. But when referring to the team by the name of the city, Miami is singular no matter how many are on the court."

Previous generations of sports fans were never forced to deal with team-nominal singularity. The Brooklyn Dodgers were a team, all right, but we referred to Da Bums in Ebbetts Field as "they"; our Pete Coscarart would tag out their Mel Ott sliding into second for the Giants (a word pronounced in one syllable—"Jints"), but Brooklynites always thought of the invaders from the Polo Grounds not as a collective "it" but as an uncollected "them," as befitted a loose assemblage of individuals from Coogan's Bluff. Sometimes the Dodgers were referred to as "the flock," harking to the team's onetime name of Robins, but even using that obvious collective noun, the construction was often "the flock are in the cellar again."

Same anticollectivism in football; the Packers beat the Bears, the Bears put the rush on Ace Parker of the football Dodgers—it was all grammatically consistent and easy to follow. (Some of my sports allusions may be slightly dated—whatever happened to Joe Vosmik?—but when it comes to language change, I like to run my thumb along the cutting edge.)

Basketball's Jazz changed all that. Utah is not a state known for its jazz joints or jazzy way of life; however, when it attracted a franchise of that name from New Orleans, its owners wisely decided to keep it. Other teams picked up the notion of dropping the *s*.

"If I want to reflect on the Heat's series with the Chicago Bulls," asks my colleague in columny, "do I say, 'The Heat *were* crushed' or 'The Heat *was* crushed'? What is the dictum on teams that do not end plurally?"

Before formulating a dictum—a pronouncement that carries authority but not the weight of legal precedent—I consulted learned authorities. They do not agree. Martha Kolln, author of *Understanding English Grammar*, says, "I would treat 'the Utah Jazz' the same way as 'the Pittsburgh Pirates' and use a plural verb—the Jazz *are*." The former Penn State English professor adds, "You would never say, 'The Pirates *is* in town.'"

Contrariwise, Tom Jolly, an editor on the sports desk of *The New York Times*, says: "Because the team names are singular entities, we've elected to give them singular verbs. Sometimes it looks a little awkward—for example, 'The Bulls *are* playing much better than the Jazz *is* playing'—but we think we've chosen the better alternative."

But the *Sporting News* stylebook goes the other way, in grim consistency, on this matter of nomenclature: "Team names such as Magic (Orlando), Heat (Miami), Jazz (Utah), the White Sox (Chicago), the Red Sox (Boston), always take the plural verb"—that is, "the Magic *are*" and "the Sox *are*."

Enough dribbling; it's dictum time. To reach a decision, let us turn to the great guiding principle of English grammar, revered by linguistic sages, eminent lexicographers and the most useful usagists: "No matter how 'correct' it may be, if it sounds funny to the ear of the native speaker, it ain't right."

Words like *jazz*, *heat* and *magic* have long backgrounds of singularity in the language: "The jazz is cool"; "Stay lost, Looie, the heat is on"; "Sorry, my dear, the magic is gone." To say now "the Heat *are* losing" or "the Magic *are* gone" is to sound funny. If your usage causes your reader or listener to assume an expression that says, "What are you, some kind of grammatical nut?" then go with the natural sound of the language. If the team name ends with *s*, use a plural verb: The Bulls *beat* and *are*. If not, construe it as singular: The Jazz *beats* and *is*.

If you need an excuse, call it an idiom. Idioms get away with syntactic murder. Take your shot with a singular verb, treating the name of the team without an *s*, as you would a city. And there's no comma in *He shoots he scores!*

As the copy editor in The Washington Post's *Sports Department, I feel compelled to point out a mistake. Da home of Da Bums is Ebbets Field with one* t, *not two, as you had it, though I'd say that a plurality of all writers misspells da name.*

> Tony Reid
> The Washington Post
> Washington, D.C.

When I hear reference made to a team like the Heat or the Jazz, I think of the twelve who make up the squad, and therefore, to me, it "sounds funny" to use a singular verb.

I therefore would say "the Heat are coming to town" because the subject I have in mind is twelve players, who therefore take an "are."

So I guess I don't disagree with your general rule that one should use whichever version "doesn't sound funny." I just disagree with you on which version sounds funny in the particular situation you describe.

The ownership of the new Florida baseball team, the Florida Marlins, deliberately chose the plural form "Marlins" (a form that technically does not exist). I suspect that they did so because they feared that everyone would feel obligated to use the singular verb ("the Marlin is . . .") and would think it sounded funny.

Fred Hoogland
Houston, Texas

When you wrote "whatever happened to Joe Vosmik?" it brought back my boyhood memories of the Cleveland Indians and my favorite players Joe Vosmik, Hal Trotsky and their teammates Earl Averill, Mel Harder, Thorton Lee and Monte Pearson.

You may recall that, in 1935, Joe Vosmik had led the hitting in the American League with only one game remaining when his manager, Steve O'Neill, took him aside and told him to sit out the game and he would win the batting title. Joe replied that he did not want to win the title that way and that he would play. Joe, unfortunately, had but one hit while Buddy Myer of the Washington Senators went four for four and clinched the title by one or two points.

Whatever happened to Joe Vosmik? More important for us today is what happened to the class Joe Vosmik had?

Edward A. Tuleya
Millersville, Pennsylvania

SLOW BOAT TO JAPAN

Never underestimate the ability of dour business executives to come up with colorful word pictures. A system allowing interest rates to rise or fall only within a narrow range was called the *snake in the tunnel;* a stock rally doomed to be short-lived is a *dead-cat bounce.*

Japan has the *Gososendan-hoshiki.* To break it down, *Goso* means "shipped with protection"; *sen* is "ship"; *dan* is "group." *Hoshiki* is "system." English translation: "the convoy system."

When Treasury Secretary Robert Rubin decided to intervene in the currency markets to support the yen, he had just been assured that Tokyo would take action against the convoys. Last month David Wessel wrote in *The Wall Street Journal* that Japanese officials promised "that Japan finally will abandon what is called the 'convoy system,' which essentially involves strong companies bailing out weak ones—often under pressure from regulators—so that everyone stays afloat."

Vivid metaphor. A *convoy* is a group, usually of ships, organized to move in a way that best protects the whole group. In World War II "action in the North Atlantic," Allied convoys supplying Britain were assembled to ward off Nazi submarines, and it became a truism that "a convoy moves as slowly as its slowest ship."

In the current Japanese trope, the *Gososendan-hoshiki* consists of strong and weak banks; the strong banks hold afloat the weak ones. By breaking up the convoy, central bankers around the world hope to allow the Japanese banks weakened by bad loans to sink and the strong to survive.

The hero-villain metaphor has been reversed; in this case, the good guys are the U-boat commanders busting up the self-protective convoys and picking off the laggards. *Ratchet up* that periscope. Fire Vun!

THE SLOW-WALK ISSUE

"People *slow-walk* things, you know, especially if you've got a cutoff date," said Senator Fred Thompson of Tennessee, complaining to reporters last summer about the obfuscation he had faced from the White House in his investigation of campaign finance. He repeated the verb more emphatically as his hearings drew to a close: "We have been *slow-walked* and deferred and had objections every step of the way."

Another politician from the South, President Bill Clinton, used the same phrase at a Democratic dinner late last year, complaining of senatorial delays of his judicial appointments: "I had a four-year term; they still only confirmed thirty-five judges—*slow walk* and everything. It's like pulling teeth."

Slow-walk, the dialect verb, has two senses. The Tennessee sense, as used by Tennessean Thompson, means "delay." Citations are difficult to come by, but the Westlaw database, which covers all court proceedings, has several from Tennessee: "If I get the idea," one judge warned a mother resisting visitation rights to a child's father in 1989, "that you're dragging your feet or *slow-walking* the whole situation . . ." In a 1973 case, the U.S. Court of Appeals for the Sixth Circuit referred to testimony in a labor dispute that "many of the men were simply standing around and were purposely '*slow-walking*' the project . . . to stretch out the term of employment."

Then there's the quite different Carolina sense. Joan Houston Hall of the *Dictionary of American Regional English* at the University of Wisconsin found a report filed by a *DARE* interviewer in 1979 in central South Carolina, after a conversation with a black woman, the author Mary Meblane: "Her mother used to say: 'There's a dead cat on the line. I'm going to *slow-walk* you down.' She told her daughters that when she was sure that they were lying."

I have already reported on *a dead cat on the line*, used to express "a suspicion that somebody is trying to deceive you." (Fred Cassidy of *DARE* thinks that comes from a dead catfish on a trotline, evidence that a lazy fisherman has not been checking his poles.* Others insist the root is a dead feline blocking transmission on a telegraph line.) But if our Carolina source was suspicious of being tricked, what did she mean by "I'm going to *slow-walk* you down"? A clue is in a 1962 North Carolina trial: "Before he began hitting and stabbing his wife with a knife in the city of New Bern, he said, 'I'll *slow-walk* her.'" Judging by the context in the two citations, I'd say the phrase means "chastise, punish," or in its extreme form, "stab to death."

Etymology of the punitive Carolina sense is obscure, as the lexicographers say when they cannot puzzle out the root. The Tennessee sense—"delay"—may come from horse racing. Tennessee walking horses have three gaits: a flat walk, a running walk and a canter. A synonym for "flat walk" is *slow walk*, as used in Joe Webb's 1967 *Care and Training of the Tennessee Walking Horse:* "Whether you are successful or unsuccessful in getting the horse into a running walk, go back into the *slow walk* occasionally."

Will Senator Thompson *slow-walk* (in the foot-dragging Tennessee sense) those who want him to run for president? Will the President *slow-walk* (in the severe Carolina sense) the Senate blockers of his nominations? Consult your local dialect dictionary.

SOONERATHERNLATER

Whenever a president or other world leader uses a phrase in a highly charged situation, it echoes through the language. Sooner rather than later, it loses its referent and becomes a freestanding idiom; people use the familiar phrase out of voguish habit, forgetting the source that initially popularized it.

---

*Fred Cassidy, the greatest American lexicographer since Noah Webster, died on June 14, 2000.

On January 22, 1998, during a photo opportunity with a nonplussed Yasir Arafat, President Clinton told reporters inquiring about nonforeign relations, "I'd like you to have more rather than less; *sooner rather than later.*"

The phrase was repeated supportively by his press secretary as well as by his former chief of staff, Leon Panetta: "There is going to be a time, and I think it has to be sooner *rather than later,* where the President has to say to the country what the situation is." As lawyerly counsel was taken and this policy was abandoned, the President's critics used the phrase to beat him about the head. "The President himself states," argued the independent counsel before the Supreme Court, "in January of this year, that the American people are entitled to more rather than less, *sooner rather than later.*"

The phrase was quickly compressed in speech to *soonerathernlater* and spread far afield. Jane Brenner, a councilwoman from Punta Gorda, Florida, who is striving to save its 1927 courthouse from demolition, told the *Sarasota Herald-Tribune,* "We're hoping to get the courthouse worked out, and *sooner rather than later.*" A securities analyst in Fort Washington, Pennsylvania, asked by Dow Jones about the public offering of Goldman, Sachs, used the phrase as an adjective: "anticipating the *sooner-rather-than-later* offering of its stock to go public."

The phrase is an outgrowth of *sooner or later,* the lexicographer Sol Steinmetz informs me. In 1577, Barnaby Googe wrote in his translation of the Dutch author Conrad Heresbach's *Heresbach's Foure Bookes of Husbandry* that "the stones, stickes, and suche baggage . . . are to be thrown out *sooner or later.*" In 1933, J. M. Campbell, writing in *Speculum,* illustrated both root and branch: "But if efforts to overtake the meaning of a stubborn passage always include the Church Fathers *sooner or later,* then why not sooner than later?" The earliest citation I can find of S.R.T.L. is in an article from the journal published by the Royal Economic Society in June 1895. Referring to the "Boot War," W. B. Hoffman wrote: "The most we can expect is that repetition of the late disastrous war will not occur for some time to come, but even that hope may be shattered *sooner rather than later.*"

This followed the action of settlers who rushed into Oklahoma before April 22, 1889, to be ready to stake their land claims before the official opening date, and became known as the "Sooners." (Those who followed were called, presumably, the Laters, but left no impact on the language. I put this in as a service to readers in Oklahoma who may not know the origin of their nickname.)

The etymological analogy holds for Mr. Clinton's "more rather than less": That's based on *more or less*, from 1589, give or take a few years. *Give or take*, however, in its 1958 sense of "approximate," has not spawned "give rather than take" because it was not used in a crisis of the presidency.

In stretching out stock phrases resting on the fulcrum of *or*—from *one thing or another* to *here or there*—we must ask ourselves, Is this extension necessary? Does the redundancy detract from precision? Is S.R.T.L. any sooner than the unadorned *soon?* At the end of the day, are we slipping into the easy acceptance of a series of bromides as bad as *at the end of the day?*

Decide for yourself, one way rather than the other.

SPECIAL FOR TONIGHT

William Schaefer, former governor of Maryland and a lifelong bachelor, faithfully visits Hilda Mae Snoops, a divorced mother of three usually described as his "longtime companion," in her retirement home.*

In a warm and sentimental Valentine's Day feature, *The Washington Post's* Karl Vick wrote of the lasting quality of the friendship that included the time they kept house together during his two terms in the Governor's Mansion. However, no one was quite certain how to refer to her.

"This is his *girlfriend?*" said Nelson Sabatini, Schaefer's friend and former Secretary of Health, running through the usual options for the reporter. "This is his *close* friend? His *dear* friend? You know, *lady* friend?" Then he decided on what he felt was the perfect word: "His *special* friend!"

Special is a Rashomon word, gleaming with different facets of meaning. Rooted in the Latin *species*, "a particular group," the most common sense is "out of the ordinary," one step shy of the solitary "unique." That was its meaning in *The Economist* recently: "All this points to a relationship between President and intern which was in some way, sexual or not, *special.*"

---

*Hilda Mae Snoops died in June 1999.

But the special relationship is a phrase with its own historic connotation. Winston Churchill first referred to "our *special relationship* with the United States and Canada about the atomic bomb" in the House of Commons in 1945 and repeated *special relationship* in his 1946 "Iron Curtain" speech, meaning "the fraternal association of the English-speaking peoples."

During the 1980s, the adjective became a euphemism for "mentally or physically handicapped": *special* children were dealt with in *special ed* classes. A related meaning was "difficult."

Then there was the use of *special*, again with *relationship*, to describe gay males living together, which in the 90s is also applied to two men living together who are not lovers. The word was used against gay political activists seeking what they called *equal* rights by opponents who charged they were seeking *special* rights—using the adjective to imply more or superior rights.

This explosion of use, on top of the previous generation's *television special* and journalism's *Special to The New York Times*, caused a backlash. On *Saturday Night Live*, the comedian Dana Carvey, as "the Church Lady," derided her targets in a nasal twang with "Isn't that *special!*"

"The use of *special* in this way," notes Jim Crotty, author of *How to Talk American*, "is a hyperironic spoof of the way a Mr. Rogers-type might speak, or the way a kindergarten teacher might talk down to a 'young person.' The humor is in mocking the patronizing quality of another type of person's sincere use of the word *special*."

When too much use debases a word's currency, it becomes *specially priced*.

When gunmakers Smith & Wesson elongated their .38-caliber pistol cartridge at the beginning of this century, they gave the new round the name ".38 Special" to denote its extra power. Not long after, in the 30s (I don't work for The New York Times, *so I omit the decade's incorrect apostrophe), the shell casing was further elongated to create the even more powerful .357 Magnum. This relegated the "Special" designation to an inferior, "weak sister" position, so that by the time (the early 60s) a more user-friendly round was made by downsizing the sledgehammer .44 Magnum, it became known as the ".44 Special."*

Furthermore, the famous "Blue Plate Special" is a budget-priced com-

bination platter offered to the penny-wise. If, like me, you are (1) a member of the NRA, (2) a former rock musician, (3) an antique car buff, and you like to (4) eat in old-fashioned diners, then the term "special" first of all conjures up the meaning "economy job" or "cheap."

In the words of another famous TV comedian, Pee Wee Herman, "What's so special about it?"

John Wehrle, Editor
Graffiti *Magazine*
Charleston, West Virginia

STAKE IN THE GROUND

"I believe it is important to put a *stake in the ground*," said Governor George W. Bush, "and to say, '*Enough is enough*,' when it comes to trying to dig up people's backgrounds in politics."

Eight years before, a Democratic candidate, Paul Tsongas, used the same metaphor of determination in a Des Moines speech: "The Iowa caucuses are an integral part of any sense of American politics, and I intend to put my *stake in the ground* here."

This is a metaphor of determination, with a western flavor. It is rooted in, or has a stake firmly planted in, the laying of a claim to a piece of territory, owned by nobody, for mining or farm use. The rush for land after the Civil War popularized the phrase (along with doing a *land-office business*). The stakes driven in the ground were the markers used to post the boundaries of a homestead; this led to another phrase, *to pull up stakes*, which means "to move on" to greener pastures.

George Dubya's use of *stake in the ground* immediately called to mind a similar trope called up by his father, President Bush, after Iraq's invasion of Kuwait in 1990: "*A line has been drawn in the sand.*" This expression may have stemmed from the circle drawn in the sand around the Syrian king Antiochus Epiphanes in 168 B.C. by the Roman envoy Popilius Laenas, who ordered the king to agree to withdraw his forces from Alexandria before he could step out of the circle.

It is very unlikely that President Bush had this episode in mind. Despite the elder Bush's passive construction, the phrase evoked the Alamo legend, in which William Barret Travis, besieged by a Mexican army, used his sword to draw a line in the ground (or sand), saying, "Those prepared to die for freedom's cause, come across to me." One hundred eighty-nine did, and died. The President's son, George W., in a fund-raising letter opposing Ann Richards's election as governor of Texas in 1990, wrote, "When Colonel Travis *drew the line in the sand* at the Alamo, he discovered immediately who had the courage to stand and fight for the Texas Republic." Three weeks later, President Bush used that metaphor challenging Iraq's Saddam Hussein.

As a new political campaign approaches, metaphors of intestinal fortitude, or gutsiness—cool, courageous determination—will be at a premium. Not all are suitable in making the antiflinching point; for example, *stick to your guns*, first used in 1881 as a variant of *stand to your guns*, might backfire on a proponent of gun control. *Stand your ground*, however, has a stalwart image, especially because it was extended beyond military use in *On Liberty* by John Stuart Mill in 1859: "It is not easy to see how its individuality can *stand its ground*." (A similar construction, the seventeenth-century *stand to one's pan-pudding*, never caught on in America and is unlikely to be recommended by political debate consultants.)

Hold the line, however, has a nice connotation of military firmness with an overlay of college-football bravado. It is the same symbolic line as that *drawn in the sand*, as if between *two stakes in the ground*. The related *hold the fort* suggests that someone else act with fortitude until aid arrives; it is derived from a message that Gen. William Tecumseh Sherman of the Union Army sent to the garrison at Allatoona, Georgia, in 1864: "*Hold the fort*, for I am coming." They then *drew a line in the sand, put their stakes in the ground* and *stood to their pan-pudding*.

The opposite of all the above is to *shift one's ground*, sometimes a necessary maneuver but inviting the derogation *shifty*.

STOP ME BEFORE I APOLOGIZE AGAIN

"Being president," a wag said a generation ago, playing on a dreamy definition of love, "means never having to say you're sorry." That truism no longer applies.

President Clinton's "campaign of *contrition*" began in his ill-received expression of regret. That did not go down well because *regret* (though possibly rooted in the Old Norse *grata*, "to weep," also the curious source of *greet*) has become the mildest form of sorrow. *Regret* is what we express, often insincerely, in turning down an invitation. In diplomacy, it is the cool acknowledgment of error; in the acceptance of resignations, it is usually married to the adjective *deep* in a formal wave of farewell.

Deeper than *deep* is *profound.* In Moscow two weeks later, Mr. Clinton said, "I was expressing my *profound regret* to all who were hurt," adding that he had asked to be forgiven, though nobody could find that direct request in his previous remarks. That was not accepted widely as sufficient to express sorrow, either, perhaps because of its formal or bookish quality.

Then in Ireland came "I am very *sorry.*" That made front-page headlines. *Sorrow* is stronger than *regret,* though not as wrenching as *grief* or as tortured as *anguish.* In its adjectival form, *sorry* (from the 725 *Beowulf* as Old English *sarig,* "distressed, sore") can denote a general state of sadness and, in this case, was combined with an implied admission of wrongdoing. Though not as formal as an *apology,* the expression "being sorry" is considered synonymous with "being *apologetic.*"

Still, this was not considered a sufficient expression of *contrition.* That word, from the Latin *conterere,* "to grind, bruise," has a theological connotation, as a realization of a failure to respond to God's grace. To be *contrite* is a necessary state before the absolution of sin.

The President and his advisers saw the need to differentiate between *remorse,* the prolonged self-reproach often expressed in hopes of shortening the sentence after commission of a crime, and *contrition* and *penitence,* which deal with forgiveness after confessing a sin. Immorality is forgivable, illegality punishable; it was in Mr. Clinton's interest to focus attention on the sins of lying and adultery, which can be forgiven after confession and repentance, rather than crimes of perjury or obstruction of justice, which can result in impeachment and prosecution. That was why he adopted *wrong* rather than *unlawful,* accepting *indefensible* and rejecting *perjurious.*

Hence, "I don't think there is a fancy way to say I have *sinned,*" he told the national prayer breakfast, and "I have *repented.*"

And so we reach full linguistic circle. Both *penitence* and *repentance,* like *penance* and *penitentiary,* are rooted in the Latin *pænitere,* "to cause or feel regret."

The President's defenders came roaring back to attack the Starr report as *salacious.* This means "lustful, lecherous," from the Latin *salire,* "to jump or spurt," and originated in *Familiar Letters,* by James Howell, who noted in 1645 that Venus, goddess of pleasure, "was ingendred in the froth of the sea," which "makes fish more *salacious* commonly than flesh." (And I always thought it was brain food.) Synonyms like *lewd, lecherous, lustful* and *libidinous* (words disapproving of sex often begin with *l*) were rarely flung at the independent counsel's report; the chosen terms were *pornographic* (from the Greek *porne*, "whore") and *salacious.*

STUMP WORDS

When in California, you'll want to go to *SoMa.* Down in Florida, don't miss *SoBe.* And in Connecticut, the place to go is *SoNo.*

All these so-so names are a result of *stump compounding.* A *stump* is a piece of a word, the front or the back. Otto Jespersen, the great Danish linguist, noticed in 1922 that children tended to shorten names by using the ends: Albert became *Bert*, Arabella just *Bella* and Elizabeth, *Beth, Betty* or *Bess.* Adults, he found, liked to make the stumps out of the beginnings of words: a gymnasium became a *gym*, a kilogram a *kilo*, a photograph a *photo.* Exceptions abound, and the adults have adopted telephone's *phone* and caravan's *van.* But as language hurries up, the pressure is on to chop big words down to their *stumps.*

Geographers are leading the way. *Bosnywash* long ago triumphed over "Northeast Corridor," compounding the stumps of Boston and Washington with the initials of New York. In the nation's opposite corner is *SeaTac*, a community that has grown around the airport serving Seattle and Tacoma. (Next: *DallWorth?*)

The boom on *stump compounding* is in neighborhood nomenclature. The *So* is for "south"; hence, *SoMa* is south of Market Street in San Francisco, which old-timers looking at the cable-car tracks called "south of the Slot"; *SoBe* is South Beach in Miami, and *SoNo* is South Norwalk, Connecticut.

The grandpappy of these coinages (a play on London's *Soho* neighborhood) is *SoHo*, chopped down and put together in the early 70s to describe the neighborhood south of Houston Street in New York. In the current issue of *Beiträge zur Namenforschung* ("Contributions to the Study of Personal and Place Names"), published in Heidelberg (perhaps your copy is late in the mail), David L. Gold, a New Yorker, explains that stump-compounded neighborhood names in Gotham are "an expression of trendiness and gentrification." When the south Bronx wanted to assert itself as an arts colony, it adopted *SoBro.* In the 80s came *LoBro*, for Lower

Broadway. A refinement of *SoHo* is *SoSoHo*, which tells the visitor that the area is both south of *SoHo* and kind of middling. Such punning is popular: Gold points to *NoLiTa*, "a Nabokovian coinage for North of Little Italy."

TriBeCa, the name of the area bounded by Canal Street, Broadway, Chambers Street and West Street, is derived from the first syllables of the words *triangle below Canal*. (It's more a trapezoid than a triangle, but there's no longer a canal on Canal; a little poetic license is allowed in *stump compounding*.)

The annoyed reader will note that I am using the abomination of capital letters in the middle of words. Don't worry about this affectation, recorded here only to show the etymology of the compounds. Both in common usage and in telephone directories, the *stumpifications* are melded to *Soho*, *Tribeca* and the like.

English is not the only language that chops and jams its words. According to Rolf Bergmann, editor of *Namenforsch* (see? I just shrank the name of his publication), *Kripo* is the stump of *Kriminalpolizei* and *Juso* is short for *Jungsozialist*. The Germans call this formation a *Kurzwort*, "short word." The Russian *Komsomol* stumped *Kommunisticheskii soyuz molodezhi*, which means "Communist Union of Youth."

Do not confuse *acronyms*, which are pronounceable words made up of a phrase's initials, with stump compounds, which are shortened words glued together. *NATO* is an acronym, from the initials of the North Atlantic Treaty Organization; *KFOR*, from Kosovo Force, is an *initialized stump*, pronounced KAY-for. A pure *stump compound* is *Intelsat*, from *In*ternational *Tele*communications *Sat*ellite. Consortia and corporations like these herky-jerky names in the language of globalese.

Sorry to break the news to residents of a Brooklyn neighborhood where Walt Whitman sang the song of himself—and that now styles itself as the new Bohemia—that their *Dumbo* does not qualify as a *stump compound*. The name formed from the initials of Down Under the Manhattan Bridge Overpass is an *acronym*.

You surprisingly omitted what must be the most (in)famous such construction: Gestapo, *for* Geheime Staatspolizei *(Secret State Police). The underlying* Stapo *remains in use.*

Scott Monier
Alexandria, Virginia

North Hollywood has been known for a great many years throughout Greater Los Angeles as NoHo. *It's the preferred usage for headlines and captions. And don't forget* San Berdo. *It's not quite a stump, but it's useful, and it's been around since before World War II.*

William O. Felsman
Woodland Hills, California

THE SUMMER OF THIS CONTENT

In olden times, I used to file *copy*. A stack of cheap beige *copy paper* was on my desk for this purpose and to crumple up satisfyingly when I rejected my own lede or to make paper planes out of when the muse was absent. This was when *copy boy* was a coveted job for a kid and not a managerial slur. I used to get into arguments with the *copy editor*. ("I don't care if Shakespeare wrote *paint the lily*, people quote it as *gild the lily*.")

Now there is a movement among upscale copy editors to call themselves *language therapists*. Copy paper went out with carbon copies, and former copy-paper crumplers now float painfully through the carpal tunnel of love. And I no longer file copy, or even transmit data; ever at the cutting edge of the pointiest cusp, I *provide content*.

If any word in the English language is hot, buzzworthy and finger-snappingly with-it, surpassing even *millennium* in both general discourse and insiderese, that word is *content*. Get used to it, because we won't soon get over it.

"The accent is on *content*" is an advertising theme that Condé Nast publications has been running for the past eighteen months.

When Tina Brown, empress of buzz, left Condé Nast's *New Yorker* for a Disney affiliate to create a magazine that—living in synergy—would provide nonfiction material to become the basis of movies, she summed up her future with: "It's all about *content*."

This caused Maureen Dowd, the trend-sensitive *Times* Op-Ed columnist, to ask: "And what in heaven's name is *content?* Isn't it just a pretentious word for substance, which was, anyway, a pretentious word for ideas? Can *content* be synergized the way milk is homogenized?"

Only a few weeks before, a magazine about the media named *Brill's Content* burst upon the scene. "Steve Brill came up with the idea of *content*," says Bill Kovach, its external ombudsman and my former *Times* colleague, "to give the reader the understanding that the purpose of the magazine was to review the *content* of the writing of nonfiction journalism." To avoid litigation with another publisher threatening to seek an injunction to protect a trademark claim to *Content*, the proper name was added.

John P. Noon, who made the earlier claim (his Content World Publishing applied for the single-word trademark in 1991), says, "We named the magazine *Content* because it was going to be geared toward people in the content industry. It covers how different types of content can make it into digital media." (If you're planning a publication about questions, be careful—he has trademarked *Query*.) Another magazine, published in London, Ontario, that describes itself as "paving the way to the information superhighway," is titled *Content London* and has been in business since 1996, the same year *Canadian Content*, a review of software for educators, was born.

As used narrowly in the computer world, *content* means "the information on a Web site"; more broadly, it means "software rather than hardware" or "data or other material to be provided by on-line services." The phrase *on-line service provider* (OSP)—used to describe such firms as America Online, Fujitsu Niftyserve or CompuServe—led to the term *content provider* (which is not shorthanded as CP, because some of us remember the Communist Party). "A *service provider*—Earthlink, Prodigy, AT&T—gives you access, like a pipeline to a destination," says Paul Lewis, an on-line advertising pioneer. "A *content provider* is the outfit that offers the stuff you want at the destination."

The first use I can find is in the June 1, 1991, *Byte*, a McGraw-Hill print publication: "Compression will be handled primarily by the *content provider.*" The phrase still requires explanation to the Great Unwashed: Reporting in the *San Francisco Chronicle* about a Ziff-Davis venture, Jerry Carroll wrote: "ZDTV will create 300 new '*content provider*' jobs. In case you're wondering what they are, look no further. I'm a *provider* and what you're reading is *content.*"

Martin Nisenholtz, president of electronic media at the *Times*, recalls the predecessor phrase, *information provider*, in the days of videotext in the early 80s. "*Information provider* morphed into *content provider*," he says, "in the mid-80s, when it became necessary to include entertainment." (Martin uses verbs like *morphed*, zipping past the New Age types still mired in *evolved*.) The *content absorber* (that's you, formerly Dear

Reader) is undoubtedly experiencing the rush of insight made possible by the prism of lexicography. When *information*—the name of the highway, the society, even the era—needed a broader term to encompass or subsume entertainment, the carapace of *content* emerged.

And as the profit-making *synergy*—that combination of fact and fiction in which the entertaining whole is hoped to be greater than the informative parts—attacks the world of journalism, it has found its identity in the word *content*.

As a result, the old, narrow, truth-rutted information superhighway has morphed into nothing but a country lane, a tributary of the ever-widening channel of Original Synergy.

Access *content* before its stuff accesses you. But beware: This is no vogue word or Condé Nast usage. The darkly sweeping reach of *content* marks this coinage as a true millennialism. When every story is partly true, who can then be false to any man?

SWIFT ON CENSURE

What about *censure?* In the weeks after House impeachment of the President, censure promptly rented space in the halfway house between Senate conviction and acquittal.

Because this column's pristine purpose is to elucidate, not to calumniate, let's pull the politicized word out by its roots.

The Latin *censura* means "an assessment, a judgment, a reprimand." The title *censor* was given to magistrates in ancient Rome who supervised public morals and drew up the register, or *census*, of citizens. (Enumerating them one by one, of course, not using statistical sampling, although the related *censere* means "to estimate." But back to pristine purpose.) That Latin word for "judge" shot off in two directions in English.

One branch led to *censor*, as the judgment "to delete or suppress expression objectionable to those in authority." John Bellenden, in his translation of Livy's *History of Rome*, observed in 1533, "In this yere began the office of *censouris*," and *tsouris* (Yiddish for "trouble") is what writers have been given ever since. Shakespeare picked it up in *Coriolanus*, having Junius Brutus recall Coriolanus's ancestor as "twice being *Censor.*"

The other branch led to *censure.* That noun's early meaning of "opinion" soon gave way to "condemnation," the sense we use today. "Duke Robert justly *censured* stood," went a 1596 historical poem by Michael

Drayton, "For Disobedience and Unnaturall Pride." (The Duke of Normandy's full name was Robert Short-Thigh. The surname was quickly discarded by descendants.)

Shakespeare understood the meaning of both branches of *censura*. In *Measure for Measure*, he had Duke Vincentio opine that holders of high office cannot escape unfairly harsh criticism in this life: "No might nor greatness in mortality/Can *censure* scape; back-wounding calumny/The whitest virtue strikes. What king so strong/Can tie the gall up in the slanderous tongue?" White House aides might consider these words for placement in a stone carving over the entrance to the Clinton Library.

On the other hand, the satirist Jonathan Swift, in his 1726 *Gulliver's Travels*, had a Lilliputian tell the captured Gulliver, a giant they considered to be threatening their state, "The council thought the loss of your eyes too easy a *censure*."

The verb form paralleled the noun's meaning. Today, the verb *to censure* means "formally to find fault; to pronounce adverse judgment; to lay blame; to condemn as wrong." In general use, it need carry no penalty or other punishment.

SWIM SUITS

Usually respectable publications—from *Sports Illustrated* to *Vogue*—regularly fling modesty to the winds and publish annual best-selling *swimsuit* issues. Because most ogling readers are more interested in an ambience of prurience—that is, nearly nude women's bodies—than in sports or fashion, these issues sell gazillions of copies.

And so I ask: Why not an annual *swimsuit* language column? And when did they stop calling them *bathing suits*?

"Her petticoat, the most important part of her *bathing costume*, dropped off," wrote Frances Trollope in her 1830 *Domestic Manners of the Americans*, in what was one of the most intriguing lines of the English author's tart sociological study. It was also the first use of *bathing costume*. Four decades later, *bathing suit* came along and for a time competed with *bathing dress*.

Then Annette Kellerman, an Australian-born swimmer and diving star, announced before World War I, "I can't swim wearing more stuff than you hang on a clothesline," and appeared in a one-piece outfit with short sleeves, knee-length pants and a round high neck, which was basi-

NO UNCERTAIN TERMS   *291*

cally the underwear for the skirted *bathing dress*. Although Kellerman was arrested in Boston for appearing in public in the scandalous garb, in 1913 Carl Jantzen and his partners, John and Roy Zehntbauer, marketed a skirtless one-piece *bathing suit* for women.

In the Roaring 20s, just as *bathing beauty* was catching on, *bathing*—dipping or immersing oneself in water—began to give way to *swimming*, propelling oneself in water with the arms. In 1926, in *The Sun Also Rises*, Ernest Hemingway had a character say, "I found my *swimming suit*, wrapped it with a comb in a towel." That led to the clipped *swimsuit* and the more inclusive *swimwear*. In France in the 20s, the word *maillot*, possibly based on the name of the costumier of the Paris Opera, described a tight-fitting *bathing costume*.

In 1946, after the explosion of an atomic bomb at the Bikini Atoll in the Marshall Islands became synonymous with a great blast, the French lingerie manufacturer Louis Réard introduced a skimpy two-piece suit for swimming or sunbathing that he called the *bikini*. Eighteen long years of dreary skin coverage passed before the Austrian designer Rudi Gernreich interpreted the *bi* in *bikini* as "two" and introduced the *monokini*—one bottom, no top.

Lascivious lexicographers have closely examined *-kini* as a popular combining form. The *trikini* appeared briefly—very briefly—in 1967, defined as "a handkerchief and two small saucers." It reappeared a few years ago as a *bikini* bottom with a stringed halter of two triangular pieces of cloth covering the breasts.

The most recent evolution of the *-kini* family is the *tankini*, a cropped tank top supported by spaghetti-like strings. "The *tank* was the early term for 'indoor pool,'" recalls Steve Fritz, now president of Jantzen, "and you wore a one-piece suit when you competed in the tank." (Annette Kellerman, "the Diving Venus" in her one-piece bathing suit, splashed about in a huge indoor tank in the Hippodrome in New York City.)

An early *tank top* citation is an article in *The New Yorker* in 1968 about Suzanne Farrell, describing her as "a tall, pretty ballerina dressed in a purple *tank top* and baggy rubber warm-up pants." It has come to mean a sleeveless garment, often knitted, with deeply scooped armholes.

Stripping to essentials, if the *trikini* is three pieces, the *bikini* two and the *monokini* one, when will we see the *zerokini*? We have, and it is a practice, not a garment, called *skinny dipping*, from dipping one's naked skin in the water, a locution cited in the *Oxford English Dictionary* in 1966. (I remember it being used in Camp Copake, New York, much earlier, but will name no names.)

> *You omitted the factoid that the bikini was so named as it was a little nothing at all, like the geographical bikini which was a little nothing atoll.*
>
> Steven J. Halpern
> New Orleans, Louisiana

SHAPEWEAR

On a related subject, what's going on in underwear nomenclature? Remember *undies?* Or *unmentionables?*

They are now mentionable, sort of. These are euphemisms for *foundation garments*, or *corsets*. Ignored politicians complain that their story was "buried in the back of the paper with the *corset* ads," but has anybody recently seen an ad anywhere for a *corset?*

"*Shapewear—Bodyslimmers*—is the most prominent thing in the market today," says Tom Wyatt, a former president of Warnaco Intimate Apparel. In 1984, the Olga company of Van Nuys, California (there really is a Van Nuys), came up with *shapesuit*, which it also called a *Secret Hug.* (It was not to be confused with a *panty girdle*, which has legs.) *Shaping* in this context has a history; it was first used in 1564 in an English archdeaconry: "His *shappinge apparell* was a yowlowe sattanne dublet and a payre of housse."

Bodyslimmers, with the "emancipating *Hipslip*," are trademarks of Nancy Ganz, who is not only creative in the naming of her products but would—long ago—be hailed as "the Girdle Queen." More recently, she would be considered a leader in the field of *intimate apparel*. But as we all know, things formerly intimate have been outed, and intimacy has become outimacy. That is why we refer to Ganz, and to legions dedicated to helping men and women tuck it in and tighten it up, as *shapewear* executives.

TAKE MY QUESTION——
PLEASE!

THE FOLLOWING SENTENCE, in its entirety, appeared in *The New York Times Magazine* last month: "Which begs the question of whether Upper East Side residents might be wise to refrain from walking their corgis in the neighborhood for a while."

I tore it out to use in an excoriation of sentences without clear subjects. (Famous fumblerule: "No sentence fragments.") But the Reverend Darrell Berger, minister of the Fourth Universalist Society in New York, found a greater sin:

"This sentence fragment uses *'begs the question,'*" he writes, "in the sense of a question that begs to be asked, usually because it is obvious to all. However, I am plagued by my logic course of some years ago, which taught me that *begging the question* is nothing of the kind. Rather, *begging the question* is a logically invalid form of argument that uses the point to be proven as part of the argument for its proof."

Amen. Readers have been protesting this misuse of a term about a concept set down by Aristotle, a student of Plato Cacheris, in his book on logic written about 350 B.C. (Here comes mail on B.C.E.) His Greek term *en archei aiteisthai* was translated by the Romans as *petitio principii*, and rendered into English in 1581 as *begging the question*. In whatever language, it described the fallacy known as "the assumption at the outset."

In his 1988 book, *Thinking Logically*, Professor James Freeman explains: "An argument *begs the question* when the conclusion, in the same or different words, or a statement presupposing the conclusion, is introduced as a premise. The case for the conclusion ultimately depends on accepting the conclusion itself."

Judith Meyers, who taught logic at Hunter College in New York, gives an example of *begging a question*: "Lying is wrong because you shouldn't say things that aren't true." There's no logic to it; such an argument takes you around the barn, which is why it is known as "circular reasoning." You can argue that lying is wrong because deception undermines moral values, or even that lying is wrong because it can get you in trouble, but when you say that lying is wrong because it's wrong, you're nothing but a question-beggar, an illogical sidestepper of the issue and a corrupter of all that is precious in Aristotelian thought.

This demands that a question be asked: Since readers have sent me half a dozen examples of misuse of this phrase, in *The New York Times*, no less, can it be that common usage has changed the meaning? Put another way: When does an error become correct?

Let's say you argue: "Common usage makes it correct because that's the way most people talk." I say that *begs the question* because "the way most people talk" is the definition of "common usage." You could logically argue that "common usage makes it correct because language is changing constantly" or that "common usage makes it correct because rigid prescriptivists have been shown to be the laughingstocks of linguistics," but you cannot argue in a straight line that "common usage is correct because it's common usage."

Dictionaries have long reported that *to beg* no longer means only "to ask for a handout" or "to entreat humbly," as in "I *beg* to differ." It also means—especially in the phrases *to beg the question* or *to beg the point*—"to take for granted, to assume without logical proof." And beyond that, "to avoid the issue; to sidestep the argument." (Sentence fragments are O.K. when used for stylistic emphasis.)

"I wonder," wonders Ms. Meyers, not begging but asking, "has such frequent misuse of the technical term *to beg the question* made it somehow a proper use of the phrase? Or does such usage remain mistaken?"

Stay on those ramparts, logical thinkers—hold the fort for Aristotle, the English language and Saint George! To use *to beg the question* as a synonym for "to call for the question" is a mistake. Why? It's a mistake because it is in error. (That's *begging the question*.)

TCHOTCHKES

YOU PAY for good linguistic lawyering, you get it.

In the *Congressional Record* for February 4, 1999, following a transcript of the testimony of Monica Lewinsky, there is a corrective addendum from one of her attorneys, Plato Cacheris. Among the spelling corrections like "*Seidman* should replace 'Sideman'" is this: "*Tchotchke* should replace 'chochki.'"

The Cacheris partner who kept historians from slipping into spelling error is Preston Burton, who reports: "I used to date a Jewish girl in college, and she knew how to spell *tchotchke*. I verified it in *Webster's New World Dictionary*."

There, indeed, the Yiddishism is so spelled, and defined as "knick-knack, collectible, trinket." *Merriam-Webster's Tenth Collegiate Dictionary* agrees, adding the Polish etymology of *czaczko*. Ms. Lewinsky used the word to describe "a little box" she gave the President as a gift.

The problem is in the Anglicized pronunciation. Although it is *choch-kuh* in Yiddish, it is *choch-key* in English; Ms. Lewinsky gave it the proper English pronunciation, and the transcriber took the spelling of the final vowel from that.

I spell it *tchotchki*. Do I need a lawyer?

We were interested in your characterization of "choch-key" as the Anglicized pronunciation and "choch-kuh" as the Yiddish pronunciation. Actually, the Yiddish speakers of Galicia in southwestern Poland pronounced it "choch-key." They also said "pul-key" (not "pul-kuh") for chicken leg and "chal-ley" (not "chal-luh") for the braided Sabbath bread.

Our thought is that the "Galitzianers" comprised a large minority of the Yiddish speakers who emigrated to the United States from 1885 to 1921 (when American immigration laws changed to exclude eastern and southern Europeans). As Yiddish words were incorporated into English here, the pronunciation of the predominant group was adopted. Alterna-

*tively, the American ear confronted with a long-e ending ("choch-key")
chose that over the less-familiar "uh" (or "eh") ending of "choch-kuh."
Either way, the pronunciations are both of Yiddish origin, and the patterns
of adaptation which you point out are fascinating.*

Philipa Newfield and Phillip Gordon
San Francisco, California

THINKING TO MYSELF

Clifford Irving has just published the hoax he went to jail for a generation ago, *Autobiography of Howard Hughes*. Because no ordinary publisher would touch "the most famous unpublished book of the twentieth century," Irving is selling it through terrificbooks.com.

I thought to myself, How can he get away with it? And he replied:

"What other way can you think, other than to yourself? You can't think to someone else, and you can only think aloud in special fictional circumstances that are really not antithetical to *thinking to yourself*; thinking aloud contrasts only with thinking. Let's put a stop to this."

The Squad Squad, hunter of prolix tautologies, salutes him: *Think to yourself* is redundant. As the Cartesians say, "I think; therefore I *think to myself*." But still, I have to wonder, How does Cliff get away with it?

TMORRAS NGLSH

Bliss on þæm cumendum þusende ðeara, Eallum!

That's "Happy New Millennium, Everybody!" in the language that the residents of England were speaking in A.D. 1000. For this back-translation, which I have jazzed up only a little, I am indebted to Antonette diPaolo Healey of the *Dictionary of Old English* Project at the University of Toronto.

Though hard to understand today, that English wasn't gibberish a millennium ago. On the contrary, the somewhat guttural tongue spoken and laboriously written at the time of Aelfric's *Grammaticus* in 1000 was rich in vocabulary and complex in syntax. But we can now say—in the words they would have used then—*Nu we þus feorran common, cild* ("We've come a long way, baby"). Let us not derogate their mode of communication; that's when men were *menn* and women were *wifmenn*.

In the year 3000, will my clone—telepathically transmitting the content of this column to the *Times*'s Mars bureau—be using the same words as I do now? Of course not; even the word *evolve* will evolve, or evolute. (I just exhumed that back-formation from *evolution;* it's never too early to get a jump on the changes to come.)

Oxford University Press, preparing a book of *21st Century English*, has been surveying language mavens like me to get answers to questions like "Will English continue its progress to becoming a global language?" (An American ear would prefer "Will English continue to become" or "Will English continue its progress toward becoming," but perhaps I'm regressing.)

One future-fixated question engenders another: "What will happen to dialects?" (Fuggedaboudit.) And Alysoun Owen, a commissioning editor at Oxford, also wonders, in stiffly standard English, "How will language used in relation to the sexes develop?" (Human nomenclature has already been given a unisex haircut: "You, Leslie. Me, Alysoun. Who what?")

As it happens, I have for months been surveying Olbom—On Language's Board of Mentors—to get a fix on 3000's Earthlingo for today's millennial *Times* Capsule.

"Anything may happen to a language in a thousand years," says Jacques Barzun, whose House of Intellect is now in San Antonio. "Think of what befell Anglo-Saxon when William the Conqueror and fewer than a thousand men won a battle at Hastings: after a couple of centuries, a mixed English-and-French tongue with two words for the same thing."

Like *null* and *void;* for no good reason, modern lawyers cling to both. Language has no life independent of its speakers and does not change according to laws of its own. "The mass of new words born of cybernetics is no evolution but an eruption," Barzun notes. "English American may be subject to even more violent change. Suppose a coalition of other continents conquers North America and unloads here its surplus population. Or suppose illiteracy gets to be the prevailing mode, with only the relative few reading and writing. There would shortly be two languages spoken, as in ancient Rome and in England after the Norman Conquest."

But let's stipulate that the English-speaking world is not overwhelmed. What will we sound like then?

"The English of the year 3000 will sound like some strange dialect of current English," says Sol Steinmetz, the great American lexicographer. "It is impossible for any living language not to change. Edward Sapir, in his classic 1921 work, *Language*, called this inevitable change 'the drift of a language.'" Steinmetz predicts: "In this future language, the word *cents* might be pronounced as 'since' and the word *business* as 'bidnis.' Certain grammatical cases (like *whom* and *whose*) might disappear entirely." (No *who/whom* problem? Utopia beckons.)

Despite the braking action of schools and dictionaries, Steinmetz foresees a somewhat simplified spelling (as did Noah Webster two centuries ago, and he was *rawng*). Vocabulary? "A great expansion from the currently conservative estimate of half a million to well over a million words," he says. "This is not to say that 40 percent of our vocabulary will be replaced, a notion very hard to back up."

Howzabout slang, boyo? "Most of the current slang and argot will vanish," Steinmetz says, "but new slang, argot and jargon will continue to replenish the ever-growing vocabulary of the coming millennium." Presumably, this means "Man, that's cool" will give way to "Woman, that's warm." (I can do that; bring on the organ replacements.)

Will English and American English fuse into a great world language, understandable not only in Kansas and Liverpool but also in Kuala Lumpur and the Congo?

Robert Burchfield, former chief editor of the Oxford English dictionaries and the man who dared to revise Fowler's *Modern English Usage*, thinks not. "It seems likely that mutually unintelligible varieties of English will be distributed throughout the English-speaking world," says this New Zealander, now resident in Oxfordshire. "The two major forms of English, those of North America and the British Isles, will as languages be as separate from each other as, say, French and Italian and Dutch and Afrikaans are now."

This divergence is not what most of us expect, as Brits today embrace *mind the gap, humped-zebra crossing* and *bug jab* while Yanks adopt *watch your step, striped speed bump* and *flu shot*; on the other hand, a parallel political theory of "convergence," so confidently put forward only a generation ago by accommodationists between Communism and democracy, is discredited today.

But Burchfield has a solution to the problematic prospect of our parting: "Increasingly sophisticated electronic devices—the third-millennium equivalents of the mobile phone—will make it possible for intercommunication to occur, face-to-face or at a distance."

Here's how: "The message of Speaker A will be instantly translated into the language of Speaker B," Burchfield says. "Techniques now familiar to journalists interviewing people who speak, say, only Albanian will be familiar to English speakers throughout the world. No need for the presence of human interpreters—electronic translating aids will be no more remarkable than spectacles and/or glasses and hearing aids are now."

If this vision comes to pass, the uniqueness of national language and tribal dialect will be preserved, which will give societies the cohesion of tradition and a sense of cultural difference from the rest of the world.

At the same time—thanks to the tiny interpreter implanted in everybody's teeth—third millenarians will be blessed with instant understanding of what is being said in any language, which should convey a sense of worldly unity.

Think of it: Language in the third millennium will defend diversity, while translated communication will assert unity. "O brave new world, that has such people in't!"

Looking back a thou, we say, *Bliss on þæm cumendum þusende ðeara, Eallum!* Looking ahead to 3000, *Kant wate.*

TO THE MANNER BONE

"This move by the Independent Counsel is bone stupid," opined *The New York Times.*

"I've heard of *bonehead, bone china* and *bone dry,* but never *bone stupid,*" writes Ralph Palmesi of Trumbull, Connecticut.

Bone stupid. I was able to penetrate the wall of anonymity surrounding the *Times* editorial board to discover "it's Alabamian for 'extremely stupid' or maybe it's just a Rainesism."

No, the meaning of the attributive noun is more subtle than that. This intensifier combines the connotation of stupidity from the *bone* in baseball's *bonehead* play and its short form, *boner,* with the extreme tiredness of the *bone* in *bone weary*—exhaustion felt down deep in your bones. A star usage fell from Alabama.

TOPSY

"As the only African American in the United States Senate," writes Carol Moseley-Braun of Illinois, "I hope I am not overly sensitive to notice a tendency by Senate Majority Leader Trent Lott in statements on the Senate floor to allude to a fictional slave girl."

Senator Moseley-Braun notes with disapproval the majority leader's frequent use of the phrase "grown like Topsy" about the number of amendments added to bills. She points out that Topsy is a character in Harriet Beecher Stowe's 1852 novel, *Uncle Tom's Cabin*. When asked by Miss Ophelia, "Have you heard anything about God, Topsy? . . . Do you know who made you?" the child with twinkling eyes replies: "Nobody, as I knows on. I spect I grow'd. Don't think nobody never made me."

Is the widely used Americanism *grown like Topsy* to be marked off-limits as offensive, a racial slur to be expunged from the national discourse?

The word *topsy* entered the English language in 1528 as part of the assonant adverb *topsy-turvy*. At first it meant "in an inverted position" or "upside down" (originally *up-so-down*) and came to mean "confused or disordered." The novelist, Mrs. Stowe, may or may not have had that in mind when naming her character; the passage makes the point of an innocent child's lack of religious direction.

Uncle Tom's Cabin, with its character of Simon Legree as the cruel white overseer, was the most passionate abolitionist book of its era. No less an authority than Abraham Lincoln, when greeting Mrs. Stowe at the White House, said, "So you're the little woman who wrote the book that made this great war!"

An Americanism that arose from that antislavery source, and now used with the source almost forgotten, cannot be twisted into a racial slur, even in an election year. Even the dialect has been removed: *Grow'd* has been changed to the standard English *grown* in *grown like Topsy*. The *Oxford English Dictionary*'s definition is the clear meaning today: "something that seems to have grown of itself without anyone's intention or direction."

Just as *rule of thumb* was mistakenly seized on by feminists looking for controversy, Senator Moseley-Braun's concern is misplaced. She is indeed overly sensitive to this usage, and I suspect she knows it.

TOUCHING BASE WITH CUCKOLDS

We now inaugurate the Pundits Aid Society, committed to helping distressed columnists in search of roots.

In one of his occasional columns titled "Ask Mr. Language Person," the humorist Dave Barry purportedly received this question: "I am in the field of business, and people keep saying they want to 'touch base' with me. They'll say, 'I just wanted to touch base with you on the Fooberman

contract' or 'We need to touch base on the rental sheep for the sales conference.' But my understanding of the rules is that if you touch base *with*
somebody at the same time, at least one of you is out. So my question is,
Who the heck is 'Fooberman'?"

The answer from Barry's Mr. Language Person: "We decided to consult with William Safire . . . but his number is not listed."

It's my e-mail that's not listed.* But I bought a copy of the Sunday
Washington Post, turned to "Wit's End" in the magazine (as the Barry column is called there), and got the message.

It's a shortening of the baseball rule, *touch all bases.* Paul Dickson,
author of the *New Dickson Baseball Dictionary*, says: "The baseball term
means you have to make contact with the three bases in your way around
the base path to home plate. That's why coaches tell players to remember
to *touch all the bases.*"

That was extended to the general language in the sense of "to get in
contact with," as in "I'd better *touch base* with my mother; she gets sore
when I don't call." The more frequent sense is "to obtain the approval
of," as in "*touch base* with you on the Fooberman contract." Because the
metaphoric extension of the baseball term is not yet in the *Oxford English
Dictionary*, the "approval" sense seems relatively recent, with citations in
the late 70s.

The most memorable case of *base nontouching* took place on September 23, 1908. With two outs in the last half of the ninth inning, the
game tied 1-1, the Giants had runners on first and third. The Giant hit-
ter singled, scoring the man from third and apparently winning the
game. The runner on first, Fred Merkle, age 19, turned and gleefully
headed for the clubhouse celebration. But the Chicago Cub second
baseman, Johnny Evers (of the famed Tinker-to-Evers-to-Chance dou-
ble-play combination), spotted what he believed to be an infraction of
the rules. He called for a ball from the umpire and stepped on second
base, claiming to have retired Merkle on a force-out. The crowd had
poured onto the field, and play could not be resumed; the game was
called a tie. In the tiebreaking game two weeks later, the Giants lost the
game and the pennant.

This popularized the slang term *bonehead*, an American alteration of

*Now it is: onlanguage@nytimes.com.

the British *blockhead*. The *Chicago Tribune*, on September 24, 1908, wrote, "Then came the *bonehead* finish. . . ." The errant player, an otherwise intelligent first baseman, went through a sixteen-year career known as Fred (*Bonehead*) Merkle because he failed to *touch base*. It is a mild epithet for stupidity.

The second distressed syndicated columnist seeking help from the free services of the Pundits Aid Society is Richard Cohen of *The Washington Post*:

"I am enclosing Evan Thomas's review of the Nina Burleigh book on Mary Meyer. I direct your attention to the last graph, punditese for 'paragraph,' in which Evan says, 'Writing in his journal . . . shortly after he had been both promoted at the CIA and *cuckolded* by his wife. . . .' I thought it is the male lover, not the wife, who *cuckolds* the husband. I have turned to the *American Heritage Dictionary*, but without success. (The derivation of *cuckold* sure is interesting, though.) Please clear this up for me."

Gladly. The *cuckoo* bird is said to have the habit of laying its eggs in another bird's nest, leaving them to be cared for by the other, adoptive bird. That led to *cuckold*, "a derisive term for a husband who has been the victim of adultery, the party betrayed by an unfaithful wife."

All twenty-nine uses of the word in Shakespeare are directed at the husband betrayed, or at least believing his wife to be fooling around. Othello: "I will chop her into messes," he roars when the sly Iago unfairly accuses his wife, Desdemona. How dare she "*cuckold* me!"

In most citations of this word in the *OED*, first used around the year 1250 (this practice has been going on a long time), it is the wife who *cuckolds* the husband. This is etymologically consistent: The female *cuckoo* bird is the one who lays the eggs in the wrong nest. Male *cuckoos* just fly around and make a distinctive sound immortalized in clocks.

Thus the columnist Cohen has too narrow a focus: It is both the unfaithful wife and the seductive paramour, her male lover, who do the *cuckolding* of the husband.

But this leads to two other questions that cry out for answers. We know that the horns of the *cuckold* are worn by the deceived husband, but why horns? One answer in mythology: that cheatin' Actaeon, a hunter, was turned into a stag by Diana. The *OED* suggests that the horns come from the practice of planting spurs of a castrated rooster on the excised comb of another fowl, where they sometimes grew several inches long.

This free service to pundits does not cover research into why sixteenth-century poulterers did this, but the German for *cuckold* originally meant "capon."

The second question is more pertinent. Worldly-wise lexicographers know that adultery is not a one-way street. Is there a word to describe a wife who has been betrayed by her husband? *Wronged* seems weak. What is the cheatin'-husband equivalent of the noun *cuckold?*

"Your reader was wrong about there being no word for a female *cuckold*," Barry Rein of Azusa, California, wrote to the *Los Angeles Times* columnist Jack Smith in 1989. "It is *cuckquean*. Look it up in the *OED*." There it is: "Ye make hir a *cookqueane*" is the 1562 usage by John Heywood. In his 1922 novel, *Ulysses*, James Joyce retrieved it from antiquity: "her gay betrayer, their common *cuckquean*."

Once again, English shows itself to be an equal-opportunity language.

I am moved to comment on your reference to Actaeon being turned into a stag by Diana. In fact, Actaeon met his fate because of having seen Artemis (Diana's Greek counterpart) bathing naked or, variously, by having boasted of his skill as a hunter.

James E. Connors
New York, New York

You have written that the expression "touch base" with a person is a shortening of the baseball rule which requires a runner to touch all bases as he passes them. The Official Rules of Baseball state, "7.02   In advancing, a runner shall touch first, second, third and home base in reverse order, unless the ball is dead under any provision of Rule 5.09. In such cases, the runner may go directly to his original base."

However, it appears to me that the use of the singular to "touch base" necessarily excludes the ordinary situation where a runner is required to touch all bases as he passes them, in addition to the situation where a runner is required to go back around the basepath in reverse order so as to "retouch all the bases."

I suggest that the phrase under examination is merely another way to express the rule which requires a runner to "tag up" after a fly ball is caught.

"7.08   Any runner is out when . . . (d) he fails to retouch his base after

a fair foul ball is legally caught before he, or his base, is tagged by a fielder. He shall not be called out for failure to retouch his base after the first following pitch, or any play or attempted play. This is an appeal play."

When a runner "tags up" after a fly ball is caught, he needs only to touch a single base—that which he was legally entitled to occupy before the play began. When I touch base with an associate, I need only to make contact with a single individual.

I conclude that the phrase "to touch base" is more analogous with the latter rule. The typical usage carried the connotation of "returning" or "getting back to," as in "Jack, by now you've heard what happened on the Smith project. I wanted to touch base with you before I proceed with Plan B."

T. Alan Wyle
New York, New York

The column on cuckoldry described the unfortunate Actaeon as "cheatin'," implying that this provided motive for Artemis (Diana) to turn him into a stag, in which form he was torn to pieces by his own pack. This seems improbable inasmuch as Artemis had vowed to preserve her chastity, giving her little standing to resent any putative love affairs of Actaeon.

The story, as described by Robert Graves (The Greek Myths, Volume 1, pages 84–85) has Actaeon happening upon the naked Artemis, who was bathing. To ensure that Actaeon would be unable to brag to his friends that he had seen her in the altogether, she changed him into a stag.

I know of no received explanation for the cuckold's horns.

Richard H. Howrath
Reston, Virginia

One step beyond the hapless "cuckold" there is the contemptible "wittoe," whom the OED defines as "a man who is aware of and complaisant about the infidelity of his wife, a contented cuckold."

Harvey Fried
New York, New York

TRANSPARENCY, TOTALLY

Openness was just not good enough. *Scrutability* didn't measure up because that word is better known by its turnaround, *inscrutability*, and to use it seems laboriously *couth*, even *ept* and *kempt*.

Proponents of greater accessibility of information—ready to go to the very brink of revelation—needed a new term for organized, agreed-upon, mutual veil-dropping. ("Salome tactics" was too sexily insiderish.)

In diplomacy and foreign correspondence, cookie pushers and pencil pushers alike vied for some term of universal acceptance that would counter the cold-war secrecy prevalent in the late 60s and the back-channeling of Henry Kissinger in the early 70s. What was another noun for openness, perhaps a little longer and less familiar, to convey a meaning opposite to the dangerous secrecy and possibly corrupt opacity?

Frankness had a problem: In diplolingo, the adjective *frank* does not mean "candid," as it does in dictionaries, but has a code meaning in talks of "these guys were really hollering at each other," the opposite of *fruitful.*

What other word means "letting in the sunshine" or "pervious to light"? *Diaphaneity,* the noun form of *diaphanous,* is unfamiliar, and *pellucidity* could be confused with Pell grants. Coinages to define a concept are not easy to come by.

Visibility might have had a chance, but the airline industry had a lock on it. *Verifiability* made a hard run for the money. Ronald Reagan's adoption of what may have been a Russian adage—"Trust but verify"—gave *verifiability* a specific place in arms-reduction talks, but it never made the crossover to general vogue usage.

The science of linguistics—especially its category of phonology, the study of sound changes—offered a clue. Loosey-goosey linguists, unlike hard-line physicists, accept the notion that there are mysterious contexts in which a rule just does not work; they call this "the opacity of a rule." Now here comes our answer to the other side of darkness and concealment: In a 1971 linguistic survey, Paul Kiparsky—then of MIT, now of Stanford, where he laps the field on Sanskrit grammar—wrote, "Let us refer to the converse of opacity as *transparency.*" And the worlds of diplomacy (especially arms control) and trade (back when global was still international) said: Yeah, let us.

Transparency (rooted in the Latin *parere,* "to appear, to become visible") apparently swept through several fields: "The term was a convergence of, or developed concomitantly from, the two worlds of economics and arms control," says Vince Garnett at *The Foreign Service Journal.* The former ambassador James E. Goodby, representing us at the 1983 Stockholm Conference for Disarmament in Europe, recalls the word getting hot then: "The Russians didn't like the word at all, so I stuck to *openness.*"

Before that, in the spring of 1975, the columnist C. L. Sulzberger wrote in *The New York Times* about "spooks in an open society" and quoted the Swedish professor Stevan Dedijer as hailing "the *transparency* of social intelligence," where "the U.S.A. has an incomparable lead not only in relation to the Communist countries but in relation to the most open of the democracies."

Now the word is defined in *Brewer's Politics* as "the catchword for the openness of the operations of the European Community to the public gaze." In administrative law, *transparency* applies to rules with a well-defined and universally accepted meaning. In business, an NGO (for "nongovernmental organization") created to blow whistles at bribery calls itself "*Transparency* International." And in the merged worlds of economics and diplomacy, Tom Friedman of *The New York Times* wrote in 1997 about "the regulatory agencies, banking controls, *transparency*, bureaucratic professionalism, and civil society needed" to keep emerging nations stable.

When Standard & Poor's, the credit rating agency (like Moody's, its name ends with a possessive), reported on Asian risk, the *Business Times* of Malaysia reported that "the rating agency said the issue of *transparency* remains a challenge." That was a double: The paper coupled the vogue word *transparency* with the even more voguish word *issue.*

We have dealt with the *issue* issue in a scholarly diatribe (on page 169); now, however, we must come to grips with the Adverb That Ate the Language last year. When the casino tycoon Donald Trump wanted to help defeat Governor Christine Todd Whitman of New Jersey in her reelection bid, he announced, "I was *totally* a good friend to her, and she showed *totally* no loyalty."

Two weeks ago, when the White House aide Lanny J. Davis announced he was quitting the job of scandal spinmeister (either the crisis is over or the roof is about to fall in), we recalled his pronouncement: "The ads that both the Democrats and Republicans aired were *totally* legal. It is *totally* legal for the President and Bob Dole to sit and write the ad and to use soft money for that purpose."

Clarity and fundamentalism are out, and comprehensiveness is in. Only yesterday, the adverb *clearly* (akin to the noun *transparency*) held sway as the sentence adverb of choice, meaning "as any fool can plainly see." Then, elbowing clarity aside, *basically* took over, meaning "ignore all that folderol and let's get down to fundamentals."

But basics were not enough. An adverb was needed to encompass everything, top to bottom, seen and unseen. Enter *totally*, in its most overwhelming sense, as in "I *totally* totaled the car."

Here are a few variations for today's *totalists*. *Entirely* has a connotation equally sweeping but not as harsh; *fully* is not as emphatic; *perfectly* is somewhat defensive; *thoroughly* has a no-nonsense quality, but goes to depth rather than width; *wholly* is useful in print, but its homonym *holy* makes it confusing in oratory.

Keep your eye on *utterly*.

TROPE-A-DOPE

"Comfortable in his skin" was identified by Melinda Henneberger of *The New York Times* as "the favorite phrase of admirers of . . . former senator Bill Bradley." It appeared in a Howard Fineman article in *Newsweek* in July: "He came off as a relaxed public man *comfortable in his own skin*," and Eleanor Clift used it a month later on Fox TV: "The fact that he's more *comfortable in his own skin* is what makes him appealing."

The phrase's use in American politics was first remarked by Michael Kinsley in 1988, then writing in *The New Republic* about Democratic candidate Michael Dukakis: "Ironically it is the uptight, humorless Dukakis who seems most *comfortable in his own skin*, to cite the official standard of campaign-trail media psychologists."

It is also translated as *comfortable inside his skin* and is from the French *être bien dans sa peau*. The meaning of the Gallic trope is "at peace with oneself," or in current political terminology, "the balanced, centered state of being that comes when the person is not in conflict with the persona." (To be inside someone else's skin, which never quite fits, is presumably uncomfortable.)

Ms. Henneberger's recent use was to contrast the general acceptance of Mr. Bradley's skin-insidership with the news media brouhaha over the Gore campaign's retention, purportedly for image guidance, of Naomi Wolf. She is the author who once noted that she wrote in "the first-person sexual," a singular locution. Because her employment was concealed, her guidance that Vice President Gore act more like an *alpha male*—mentioned only in passing, she says—was seized on by pundits eager to ridicule any potential manipulation of images.

Alpha male, I am informed by Edward Lucaire of New York, is a coinage of Rudolph Schenkel, who studied dominance hierarchies among captive wolves (no kin to the Gore consultant) at the zoo in Basel, Switzerland, in the 1930s. It is the term now used for "top dog," employed by ethologists studying the micturation and mating habits of predatory canids. Among wolves, it seems that only the *alpha males* breed. We are now off on a tangent.

Back to work. Of Ms. Wolf, Ms. Henneberger wrote, "Her last book, *Promiscuities*, is about girls sexually coming of age and prescribes heavy petting as an alternative to early intercourse."

What a pleasure it was to see *heavy petting* back in use. That's old slang describing the sort of intimate caressing and fondling defined accurately but clinically in the *OED* as "noncoital sexual activity."

Its origin was "to treat as a pet"—that is, to stroke lovingly. Between humans, *to pet* came to mean "to fondle," or in slang, "to cop a feel," one step past *neck*, "to engage in prolonged kissing." In 1960 came the first cited use of the adjective-noun combination: Mark Caine, in *The S Man: A Grammar of Success*, wrote of "what is called *heavy petting*, in which frank exploration of each other's bodies is permitted." (I think it was used in the 50s, synonymous with a baseball allusion, "I hit a triple but not a home run.")

Euphemism is occasionally desirable. The generalized, even modest, *heavy petting* strikes me as more suitable in what used to be called polite company than today's overly specific *mutual masturbation* or *oral sex*, which may or may not be involved in medium-weight petting. If slang must be eschewed, another possibility is *outercourse*.

Back to the trope-a-dope of current politics. The knock being put on Senator John McCain as he creeps up on Governor George W. Bush in the polls is that he conceals a hot temper. "Most Americans do not expect their presidents to be Caspar Milquetoasts," the pollster Whit Ayres said, referring to the wimpish cartoon character created by Harold Tucker Webster in 1924, but "they also don't want him *flying off the handle* at inopportune times."

To fly off the handle was first recorded in 1843 by the Canadian Thomas Haliburton, author of a series of satires on a too-shrewd Yankee named

Sam Slick. "You never see such a crotchical old critter as he is," he quoted a character in a novel. "He *flies right off the handle* for nothing." The trope, or figure of speech, is that of the head of an ax becoming detached from its handle during a hard swing.

George W. Bush has been attacked for his lack of academic achievement in college. "According to the Yale document," wrote Jane Mayer and Alexandra Robbins in *The New Yorker,* citing school records, "Bush was a C student. (This, of course, was in a preinflationary time, the waning era of the *gentleman's C.*)" Bush, in self-deprecation, earlier used the phrase, saying, "That's the difference between a Phi Beta Kappa and a *gentleman's C.*"

Dictionaries are no help in tracking down that phrase. The earliest use I can find is in a 1959 *Journal of Negro Education* about bright students "poorly motivated, content to be a *'gentleman's C.'*" The quotation marks indicate earlier usage. In 1973, Richard Merelman wrote in the University of Texas's *Journal of Politics*, "Although such ascriptive practices as the *gentleman's C* are now dying out, the antiquated image of education they reflect—a view that education should legitimize a social aristocracy by providing it with marks of status—remains embedded in the schools."

This department will try to stay on top of the Americanisms cascading out of political campaigns. That's how word mavens stay *comfortable in their own skins.*

In Hebrew there is an expression, hu yatza me'oro, *literally: "He got out of his skin," meaning that someone either made an extraordinary effort to do something or burst out with something.*

Ambassador Zalman Shoval
Embassy of Israel
Washington, D.C.

I am writing in regard to your interest in finding the origin of gentleman's C. *Look to the venerable halls of Oxford and Cambridge universities for the answer to this question, where there has been a centuries-old tradition of granting a* gentleman's third *to members of social (as opposed to academic) distinction. A third is traditionally the lowest passable mark one can have at Oxford or Cambridge on the final examination and still take a degree. (I've heard Prince Charles got a* gentleman's third *at Cambridge, for example.)*

Since a third *is roughly equivalent to an Ivy League's* C, *it is not difficult to surmise that the phrase could have been picked up by a Rhodes scholar earlier this century and applied to similar practices at Yale. George W. Bush, after considering his academic performance in light of his pedigree, might certainly be considered as a* gentleman's C *candidate.*

Frank H. Thurmond
Anatolia College
Thessalonika, Greece

TRUNK SHOW

A hot phrase in retailing is *trunk show.* It is to the selling of clothes and jewelry what the tailgate party is to eating out in the parking lot at sports events.

"Emanuel Ungaro Parallele Spring 1998 *Trunk Show*" announces the Saks Fifth Avenue ad, "with informal modeling from noon to 4." That sentence triggered three questions: Does *parallele* mean that Mr. Ungaro is beside himself? (No—that's his ready-to-wear division.) What's "informal modeling"? (It's not an all-out fashion show, with runways and music and a bridal gown at the end—just a model or two hanging around the contents of the trunk.) And though even the most unfashionable language mavens know what a trunk is (originally a wooden chest, presumably first made from a tree trunk), what is a *trunk show?*

"*Trunk Shows* Hit the Road and Spread the Fashion News" was a headline in *The New York Times* in 1971. The article, by Joan Cook, reported that American designers were taking to the road with representative collections of classic clothes, countering the well-publicized European collections of cutting-edge fashions: "In some instances, the designer is on hand for an added smattering of glamour."

Bernadine Morris, a former fashion writer for the *Times,* recalls *trunk shows* starting before World War II: "Manufacturers would pack up a hundred things in trunks and take them to, say, Macy's in Colorado. The buyer was happy to have the clothes come direct to her, and sometimes invited a few clients to come and take a look. Then it got a little more formal and more public." With the rise of American designers in the 50s, the showing of "designer fashion" took off, and the *trunk show* was the vehicle for personal appearances by the new celebrities.

The attraction for the local store buyer, and for the ultimate purchaser, was an advance look at the designer's line. "I've never been able to do *trunk shows*," Hillary Rodham Clinton told *Vogue* in 1993, "because I can't think that far ahead."

The advance look available to a select group of high-end customers (*high-end*, associated with *top of the line*, is a euphemism for "rich") is today being extended to a wider clientele. With the ads, in come the crowds—and you can forget the original trunks.

"The word *trunk* is really out of date," the designer Bill Blass, who has been doing these shows for forty years, tells me. "These days the whole collection is packed in three or four really thick canvas garment bags."

Does this mean that the trunk—used by the Parisian dress-packer Louis Vuitton in 1837—is passé now that the era of the *trunk show* is upon us? "I still see some representatives with packing cases," Blass recalls, "coffinlike things laid flat with the clothes strapped in. They are a bit cumbersome, and I imagine the clothes get wrinkled."

TWILIGHT ZONE

At the Senate hearings into campaign finance scandals, Senator Arlen Specter examined a photo of the Democratic fund-raiser John Huang with President Clinton at a White House "coffee." The Senator apologized for being repetitious and—in a clear, easily heard voice—asked the witness, Karl Jackson, president of the Thai Business Council, to "tell us again precisely what Mr. Huang said that you heard where the President was closer to Mr. Huang than you were."

The witness's reply: "I'm sorry, Senator, I zoned out on you."

Whence the verb *zone out?* According to Tony Thorne's 1990 *Dictionary of Contemporary Slang*, it means "to lose consciousness or concentration," sometimes as a result of alcohol. The British lexicographer notes that it originated in a drug context, perhaps influenced by "spaced out" and possibly by the mythical "Twilight Zone," as in the name of the old television series.

"The earliest form of this expression is *zoned out*," reports Jesse Sheidlower, then senior editor of Random House Reference, "in the sense 'intoxicated by drugs or liquor; high.' This is first found in the late 1960s but is not representative of the period; it doesn't appear in any of the usual collections of hippie terms like *freak out*, *tripping*, etc. The actual verb *to zone out*, 'to become high; (hence) to become inattentive or dazed,' arrives by the early 1980s."

I think it was also influenced by *zonked out*, which is a close synonym. The letter *z*, recalling the buzzing sound of snoring, is a natural evocator of punchiness.

Zoned is a worthy successor to *zonked*, and now has an innocent sense of "preoccupied; mind elsewhere." Slanguists everywhere are indebted to Senator Specter for eliciting such a delicious citation in public hearings, to which much of the public was *zoned out*.

UP THE DOWN LADDER

WHO ARE THE JONESES, anyway, and why are we still trying to keep up with them?

They started out as a snooty family standing apart from the crowd in England. In *Memoirs of a Station Master*, E. J. Simmons wrote in 1879 about the social interplay at his public meeting place, the railway station: "The Jones's, who don't associate with the Robinson's, meet there." By 1913, the cartoonist Arthur R. Momand, who used the pseudonym "Pop," titled his *New York Globe* comic strip "Keeping Up with the *Joneses*." ("Pop" got the spelling right: it's *Joneses*, plural, not *Jones's*, possessive.)

Ever since, it's been a scramble keeping up with the puttings-down of the upwardly mobile. In 1924, the founder of social psychology as a behavioral science, Floyd Allport, wrote that "an inconsequential genealogy" might cause an ambitious young man to be labeled "a *social climber.*" That professor at Syracuse University's Maxwell School thereby coined a derogation that was popularized two years later in the novel *Mantrap*, by Sinclair Lewis: "You sniveling little *social climber!*" (Eager to claw my way up life's ladder, I audited a course by Professor Allport at Syracuse in 1950; he thought I was uppity, and now I know why.)

About the time Allport coined *social climber*, P. A. Sorokin was titling his 1927 work *Social Mobility*. In our more meritocratic times, social climbing is not seen as such an offense against good taste; it is better to be *nouveau riche* than not *riche* at all.

Upward mobility has become a positive value. *Status* is now worthily achieved, not born to, and while a *status seeker* juggling *status symbols* is considered a little tacky, the terms are not quite as pejorative as *social climber*, sniveling or otherwise. (That is usually pronounced STAT-us, as in *statistics*, by the hifalutin, and STATE-us by the hoi polloi. It comes from the Latin *stare*, "to stand"; in law, your status is your standing.)

The happy achievability of status, sometimes called the American

Dream, was hammered home in the theme song of *The Jeffersons*, a television sitcom that lasted an incredible ten years: "Well, we're movin' on up!/To the East Side/To a dee-luxe apartment in the sky./Movin' on up!/To the East Side/We've finally got a piece of the pie!"

VENERABLE

AT THOSE HEARINGS examining campaign finance scandals, a title was introduced not often heard in Congress. Three Buddhist nuns, explaining under immunity from prosecution how they altered and destroyed incriminating checks and documents, were respectfully addressed by their title *Venerable*.

What a nice word. Rooted in the Latin *venerari*, "to worship," and even more deeply in *venus*, "love," *venerable* is a title that is a degree more reverent than Reverend. In the Anglican Church, it is used for an archdeacon; in the Catholic Church, it is a title for a dead person who may be beatified on the way to sainthood; and in Buddhism, it is used by nuns, roughly equivalent to the title Sister.

As an adjective, *venerable* means "worthy of respect because of age and dignity." Its most famous use is titular, however; the Venerable Bede was a Benedictine monk and scholar who lived in seventh-century England. He was sainted in 1899 and is venerated by historians today because the widely read theologian was the first to scrupulously cite his sources.

WANDERING WORDS

"WHEN I USE A WORD," said Humpty-Dumpty, ". . . it means just what I choose it to mean—neither more nor less."

That is the voice of the hard-edged prescriptivist, in the quotation most often cited by those of us in the usage dodge to all of you semantic drifters who let meanings go fuzzy.

And yet years later, Lewis Carroll, author of the book in which the Mother Goose character Humpty-Dumpty makes that linguistic assertion, wrote, "You know, words mean more than we mean to express when we use them."

That takes the opposite view; descriptivists, like most lexicographers, hold that words have a range of meanings that change with the times, and can carry messages different from what the speakers choose them to mean.

I found that apparent conflict in Carroll's thinking about language in a recent article by Robert K. Merton, the great Columbia sociologist and the proud father of the 1997 winner of the Nobel Prize in economics.

"Here is Humpty-Dumpty speaking for the would-be exactitude of scientific *de*notation," writes Merton, "intent on abolishing overtones and undertones with all their interpreted ambiguities. And there is his reflective creator speaking, many years later, of the shades of meaning to be found in humanistic *con*notation, with its often more evident variety of meanings we need not wittingly mean."

Barnacles attach themselves to words, as crustaceans to ships' hulls, freighting a term with meaning beyond the ship itself. Merton found a resonation of Carroll's ambiguity in the works of Henry Adams: "No one means all he says, and yet very few say all they mean," wrote the historian Adams, "for words are slippery and thought is viscous."

Pity about the choice of the last word in that quotation; Adams meant "adhesive, sticky," still the dictionary definition, but most people now associate *viscous* with *viscosity*, having to do with the flow of oil in a cold engine. Besides, *viscous* looks like *vicious*. Better to have written "words are slippery and thought is sticky."

Why *sticky* and not *tacky*, which also means "adhesive"? Because *tacky* has been barnacled by usage with another sense as "low-class, unstylish, icky." Not a word that means what I choose it to mean.

> *Robert Merton is, I believe, also the originator of the concept (and the phrase) of the "self-fulfilling prophecy."*
>
> Frank Mankiewicz, Vice Chairman
> Hill & Knowlton
> Washington, D.C.

WAR WORDS

Every sailor enforcing a blockade knows the term of art for the warlike act of stopping a ship suspected of carrying contraband: *board and search*. However, in cutting off the supply of oil to Serbia, NATO's crack nomenclature specialists devised a more blockade-runner-friendly term so as not to offend vessels being frisked. The new, sugarcoated pill of war: *search and visit*.

As Naval Reserve Officer Seth Cropsey pointed out in *The Washington Times*: Board and search "is an invasive maneuver in which an armed naval vessel trains its weapons on the merchant ship and radios for it to stop and allow sailors to board to search. The sailors make their way by small craft . . . armed and loaded. It is not a relaxing situation." But Cropsey notes that "*search and visit* sounds like what most of us do when we are on vacation in an unfamiliar place."

Every war develops its own set of terms. The leader of the enemy requires consistent derogation. In the Persian Gulf War, Saddam Hussein of Iraq was a *bloodthirsty dictator* and *the butcher of Baghdad*, similar to the *genocidal madman* often applied to Adolf Hitler. Although many critics of Slobodan Milosevic of Serbia called him a war criminal, that term was unavailable to anyone in officialdom, because it prejudged a potential prosecution and also might make it awkward to negotiate with the one so called.

The castigation of choice is *thug*. In 1991, the *Boston Herald* was first to refer to "Slobodan Milosevic, the Stalinist *thug* who rules Serbia." Three years later, Anthony Lewis in *The New York Times* castigated "aggression by a *thug*, Slobodan Milosevic." Governor George W. Bush of Texas joined many other presidential candidates in using the phrase "a *thug* like Milosevic." In the Dow Jones database, the name of the Serb leader and the word *thug* appear near each other 343 times.

Thug may be the earliest word of terrorism, perhaps predating *assassin*, a member of the hashish-smoking terror group that struck at the Crusaders.

The Hindi *thag* is the root, meaning "deceiver," from the Sanskrit *sthaga*, "thief." The *Thugs* were an organization of murderers and thieves in India who specialized in strangling travelers. The purpose of strangulation was to preserve the victim's blood, symbolically offered as a sacrifice to Kali, often called the Hindu goddess of destruction and pictured as a three-eyed deity smeared with blood and sporting a necklace of severed heads. Many Hindus consider this grisly portrayal offensive.

The *Thugs*, its membership said to number ten thousand at its peak, practiced their predatory system of *Thuggee* for at least six centuries, killing more than a half-million people, making them history's longest-lasting terror group. In 1833, the British governor-general of India launched a campaign that captured thirty-two hundred of the murderous cult's members, hanged several hundred, and effectively ended the terror.

The historian Thomas Carlyle in 1839 was the first to extend the term beyond India by decrying "the Glasgow *Thugs*," and he also coined *thuggery*. The adjective *thuggish* was not minted until 1953, by William Burroughs in his novel *Junkie*. The *Thug Life* was a best-selling 1994 album by the rap group of the same name, whose young star, 2Pac, was gunned down in a gang killing two years later. So much for the word *thug*; what about the word *core?*

We've heard it a thousand times to define an international force that would ensure the safety of the Kosovar homeless when they return. At first, that was a "NATO force"; then it fell back slightly to "a NATO-led force," and then, as the Russians started to broker a deal between the warring parties, it became "an international force with NATO at its *core*."

The center of a piece of fruit containing seeds is the *core*; by association with the French *coeur*, it has come to mean "the heart of the matter," and the noun can be used as a modifier, as in *core values*. Because it also has a connection to the French *corps*, "body," Pentagon officials can paraphrase Gen. Douglas MacArthur's farewell to West Point by saying, "My last conscious thoughts of NATO in the occupying force will be of the *core*, the *core* and the *core*."

What is the term of art for the altercation between NATO and Serbia involving warplanes, surface-to-air missiles, prisoners of war, propaganda, population removal, blockades and promises of prosecution of war criminals? Not war. That nasty term has legal overtones, including declarations, rights and obligations of belligerents and neutrals, and the like.

Some use has been made of *international armed conflict*, as in "the Korean conflict," which was the official United States designation of the Korean War. (For a time, President Harry Truman referred to it as a *police action*.)

To emphasize the circumscribed nature of the *conflict* with Serbia, rather than call it a limited war, which has a connotation of quagmires, the choice of NATO word warriors has been *campaign*. This has a general meaning of "a series of military battles during a phase of a war," and in the case of the current semi-rubblization process, a specific meaning of the sustained NATO *bombing campaign*. However, in light of the coming political campaign, notably what critics have called President Clinton's "permanent *campaign*," this word lost favor in Washington to the neutral *military operation*.

Asked what it was we were fighting, Defense Secretary William Cohen hedged: "We're certainly engaged in *hostilities;* we're engaged in *combat*. Whether that measures up to a classic definition of *war*, I'm not qualified to say."

There is an understandable problem when you speak of the derogatory epithets used to demonize enemy leaders, such as "Saddam Hussein . . . was a bloodthirsty dictator *and* the butcher of Baghdad, *similar to the* genocidal madman *often applied to Adolf Hitler." I doubt very much if the term "genocidal madman" was applied to Adolf Hitler before his death in April 1945, since the term "genocide" had not yet been invented.*

It is my personal recollection that the concept of genocide in international law was created shortly after Hitler's death by Dr. Rafael Lemkin in the United States as a displaced person. In the early 1950s, Dr. Lemkin persuaded the United Nations to draft and the Security Council to adopt a convention on genocide.

John Foster Leich
Cornwall Bridge, Connecticut

WASHING OUR DISHES

"She was a straight shooter—and she had great *dish*," the book agent Lucianne Goldberg told *Time* magazine about her friend Linda Tripp, who accepted Ms. Goldberg's advice to tape-record conversations with Monica S. Lewinsky. To *The New Yorker*'s Jane Mayer, the literary agent explained: "I did it because it's . . . fascinating! I love *dish!* I live for *dish!*"

A language column's responsibility is to interpret, without taking sides or making moral judgments, the words churned up in the coverage of a story that has gripped the nation by its belt. What, then, does the noun *dish* signify?

Certainly not its standard English meaning, "a slightly concave plate on which to serve food." From that sense came its colloquial verb usage, to *dish it out*, meaning not just "to serve" but also "to administer punishment." Also from that sense of a plateful of food—this time delicious—comes the old slang usage "she's some *dish*," a lip-smacking compliment, as well as the adjective *dishy*, chiefly British, meaning "attractive," first spotted in the *Sunday Telegraph* in 1961: "He encountered the *dishy* St. Tropezienne on his holiday."

Nor does the current term, as used by the *dish*-loving Lucy, find its origin in the British slang verb *to dish*, meaning "destroy," first noted by the great lexicographer Francis Grose in his 1788 *Dictionary of the Vulgar Tongue:* "He is completely dished up; he is totally ruined." When the conservative Tories stole the legislative clothes of the liberal Whigs by passing the radical reform bill of 1867, the prime minister, Lord Derby, delightedly chortled, "Don't you see we have *dished* the Whigs?"

Focus on the American slang noun, first cited by J. E. Lighter in the *Random House Historical Dictionary of American Slang*, from Martin P. Levine's 1979 book, *Gay Men:* "Calculated camp, packed so that people will think she's bringing them the real '*dish*' from the inside." Lighter attributes this synonym for *skinny* to homosexual lingo, meaning "gossip; spiteful or malicious comments," rooted in a verb citation in Cory and LeRoy's 1963 *The Homosexual and Society:* "To gossip . . . often used when such gossip involves the person's sexual activities and amative interests."

My own speculation is that the current slang noun is rooted in the alliterative slang phrase *to dish the dirt*, as used by P. G. Wodehouse in 1964: "He thinks you fall short in the way of *dishing the dirt*." That uses dirt as "gossip" the way Ernest Hemingway did in *The Sun Also Rises* in 1926: "'Do you know any *dirt?*' I asked. 'No.' 'None of your exalted connections getting divorces?'"

Thus, when Ms. Goldberg exults, "I love *dish!*" she expresses her delight in dishing the dirt, which may have a political effect in *dishing* an American Whig.

> *Variety for many years in its daily edition has had a regular column entitled "Dish," and in 1937 Lorenz Hart wrote "Won't dish the dirt/with the rest of the girls" for "The Lady Is a Tramp" from Babes in Arms.*
>
> Edmund R. Rosenkrantz
> New York, New York

WATER, WATER EVERYWHERE

"As I travel around the country," said Senator Bill Frist of Tennessee, "people ask me, 'What's in the water in Tennessee these days, with so many presidential contenders?'" These include Vice President Al Gore for the Democrats and Senator Fred Thompson and the former Tennessee governor Lamar Alexander for the Republicans.

That led to the metaphor of the month from the former Senate majority leader Howard Baker, a Tennessean who now lobbies in Washington: "If Al Gore runs for president," Baker said, "and Lamar Alexander and Fred Thompson run for president, we'll pump so much money out of Tennessee that the surface will subside and the Mississippi River will run in and flood us all."

WE/US

In her annual address to her subjects, Queen Elizabeth II updated the "out of the mouths of babes" idea with this observation: "The young can sometimes be wiser than us."

T. R. Reid, London bureau chief of *The Washington Post*, commented: "*Than us?* I wondered: Is this proper English? So I dug out the *Oxford Guide to English Usage* and found that Her Majesty was wrong. No one was more dismayed than I."

Here we go again in the great battle between the Concerned Conjunctionites and the Proper Preppies. The crucial question: Is *than* a conjunction that must be followed by a pronoun in the nominative case (*I, we, they*) or is *than* a preposition that must take a pronoun in the objective case (*me, us, them*)?

Mr. Reid and his conjunctionite buddies do not have only the Oxford usagists behind their stiff-upper-lip stand. Erik Wensberg, reviser of Wilson Follett's *Modern American Usage*, says, "In the Queen's construction, *than us* is at best colloquial and at worst simply wrong." Then he adds: "But as she rightly sensed, *than we* is annoyingly starchy. The answer? *Than we are.* It maintains strict grammar and achieves better rhythm as well."

That's a cop-out; in this scrap, you gotta choose up sides (he averred colloquially). The *New York Times* stylebook is conjunctionite, demanding that *we* follow *than*, no matter what most New Yorkers say. Jack Kilpatrick, "The Writer's Art" columnist who is more prescriptive than me (whoops!), says: "I think the Queen was wrong in her use of *wiser than us.* It should have taken the nominative. *Us* sounds awkward, doesn't it?"

Not to me. I am a Proper Preppie. To my ear, keenly attuned to the actions and passions of my time, it's *wiser than we* that sounds stuffy, stilted and strained, not to mention cribbed, cabin'd and confined. And speaking of Shakespeare, how about "a man no mightier *than thyself or me*," said by Cassius about Julius Caesar? Or what of John Milton's use, in *Paradise Lost*, of "*than whom*, Satan except, none higher sat"? *Whom* is objective, ain't it?

There are those who believe that the combined judgment of the firm of Shakespeare, Milton & Safire cannot stand up to the *diktat* of the legion of Conjunctionites. I will grant that famed writers make mistakes; even Homer noodled. But we who dare to treat *than* as a preposition have our authoritative defenders. "We regularly hear *than I* and *than me*," writes Kenneth G. Wilson in *The Columbia Guide to Standard American English.* "Some commentators think that the conjunction is currently more frequent than the preposition, but both are unquestionably standard."

"I would allow *wiser than us* because it is perfectly normal English usage," says Robert Burchfield, retired editor of the *Oxford English Dictionary* and most recent reviser of *Fowler's Modern English Usage*, from his home in Oxfordshire. "In British English we use both standard forms. The Queen was right," he says, adding loyally, "She always is."

Henry Fowler himself noted in an earlier edition: "The prepositional use of *than* is now so common colloquially (He is older *than me*) that the

bare subjective pronoun in such a position strikes the reader as pedantic."
(By *subjective* he uses a synonym for *nominative*, the case required by the
conjunctive. That's what Saint Henry thinks is pedantic and to be avoided.)

Now let's review the bidding. On formal occasions, like an address
from the throne, most authorities would advise royal speechwriters to
stiffen the sinews, stretch the nostrils wide and treat *than* as a conjunction, followed by *I, we* or *they*. But even as they once more fling their bodies unto this breach, the Conjunctionites seem uncomfortable because
they can feel the tectonic plates of language shifting under them. That's
why they all say, "But the prepositional way is O.K. in colloquial speech,"
in a plaintive, real-life-is-passing-us-by tone.

By choosing the proper prepositional in a formal address, the Queen
decided the time was ripe to eschew pedantry even at the risk of being
criticized as grammatically incorrect. Because royalty is trying to escape
rigidity and adopt a common touch, she preferred on this formal occasion
to adopt the informal usage of commoners, which is sometimes called
common usage.

Those who are hip will hooray. All hail the prepositional *than!* Long
Live the Royal *Us!*

*Thanks for your column about Queen Elizabeth and "younger than us."
The response in Britain has been surprisingly divided. The* Daily Telegraph *agreed strongly with me, as did Gavin Esler and his panel of Sunday pundits on the BBC. The presenter on ITV news and many angry
callers to Talk Radio agreed with you.*

*Many Britons wrote me. Some agreed with me; some cited horrible
examples of bad grammar they had heard in the United States; several
used your argument exactly—that the Queen was combating stuffiness by
talking the way her subjects do.*

Tony Reid
The Washington Post
London, England

*In supporting the relaxed grammatical construction "than us" you demon-
strate that you are not "holier than thee."*

Henry C. Clifford
Wainscott, New York

WEAPONS OF MASS DESTRUCTION

"*Weapons of mass destruction* has become the stock phrase in describing Saddam Hussein's threat," Jack Gescheidt of San Francisco writes. "Is this some sort of shorthand for 'chemical and biological agents'? Does it include 'delivery systems' like missiles or exclude weapons everyone else has, like conventional bombs? And where does this infectious phrase come from?"

Most arms-control buffs think it's probably a Russian term: *oruzhiye massovovo porazheniya*, a phrase much used during the cold war that translates roughly as *weapons of mass destruction*. The Russian phrase originally referred to any heavy attack from the air, but during that era English speakers narrowed the meaning to what we called "nuclear, biological and chemical" weapons. The initials NBC made some electronic journalists unhappy. (Just as today, WMD is disliked by female doctors.) This led to *CBR weapons*, the initials standing for "chemical, bacteriological and radiological."

Thanks to some hard digging by James Goodby at the Brookings Institution, however, we may have the origin of the phrase now abbreviated as WMD. At a meeting of President Truman, British prime minister Clement Attlee and Canadian prime minister Mackenzie King on November 15, 1945, three months after the atomic bomb wiped out Hiroshima, the leaders recommended in a communiqué that an international commission be set up to make proposals for "eliminating from national armaments atomic weapons and all other major weapons adaptable to mass destruction."

Who drafted the Attlee-Truman-King declaration? Vannevar Bush, the MIT engineer who led much of the American scientific effort in World War II, claimed coinage in *Pieces of the Action*, his 1970 memoir.

Bush described an argument he had once had with a general in the office of the Joint Chiefs of Staff about the possibility of bacteriological warfare. "He smacked the table and said to me, 'Don't you realize that the Attlee declaration contains the words "and other *methods of mass destruction*"?' 'Yes,' I said, 'I knew they were in there; in fact, I put them in.' He did not believe me, naturally, but it happened to be true." Bush had suggested the language and, as he recalled, Britain's Sir John Anderson had promptly agreed. "We both thought that while we were attempting to bring reason to bear on one terrible weapon, we might as well include another that could be equally terrible, and which might have indeed become so if the atomic bomb had not taken the center of the stage."

That declaration formed the basis of the Baruch Plan for atomic arms control, presented at the United Nations in 1946, in which the elder statesman (in a speech probably written by Herbert Bayard Swope) spoke of "other *weapons adaptable to mass destruction.*" Then and now, the phrase included nuclear bombs but was directed mainly at germ and poison-gas warfare.

The Department of Defense's Dictionary of Military and Associated Terms (we lexies call it the Dictionary of Destruction) defines the term as "weapons that are capable of a high order of destruction and/or of being used in such a manner as to destroy large numbers of people." The DOD definition does not include the means of transporting or propelling the weapon, such as a missile or a suitcase, "where such means is a separable and divisible part of the weapon."

I've been interested in the lingo of bio-war ever since 1970 when President Nixon told me, one of his speechwriters, to draft a renunciation of United States use of biological weapons and to announce the destruction of our stockpile. Shouldn't we keep a few, I asked, in case we needed to retaliate someday? "We'll never use the damn germs," he replied, "so what good is biological warfare as a deterrent? If somebody uses germs on us, we'll nuke 'em."

It occurred to me, in drafting the renunciation, that we might have a pollution problem in mass-destroying our germs, so I called the bio-war man at the Pentagon. "No problem," he said in an offhand way that still gives me a chill, "we'll just stop feeding them."

While serving in the U.S. Army Medical service in Japan in 1945, I was sent to school on the island of Eta Jima. It had been the Japanese equivalent of Annapolis during World War II. The school was called Chemical, Biologic and Radiological Warfare.

Among other things we were instructed that the radiological measuring device was not a "Geiger counter," because it wasn't counting "Geiger." Rather it was a Geiger-Müller meter.

John Eliot Spofford
Boston, Massachusetts

WELCOME BACK, SARAH

"I was such an ugly baby when I was born," Henny Youngman used to joke, "that the doctor slapped my mother."

However beautiful the baby may be, the decision about its name is usually the mother's, according to Edward Callary, editor of *Names: A Journal of Onomastics*. Mothers of sons tend to stick with traditional names: *Michael* is still highly popular and cross-racial, along with the standbys *John* and *Matthew;* lately there has been a good run on *Nicholas, Jacob* and *Samuel*. Although no national survey is authoritative, it seems that *Christopher, Austin, Joshua, Zachary* and *Andrew* are holding their own, with *Brandon, Cody, Christian* and *Dylan* moving up in the kindergartens, but *Mark* and *Luke* are already in their 30s.

Macho names are fading fast: Fewer boys are named *Rock, Lance* or *Pierce*. (Whatever—now one word—happened to *William*, Looie? Way down the list with *Richard* and *Robert*, and it's goombye Charlie to the once-hot *Jason*.)

Girls' names, like their clothes, are much more subject to the swings of fashion. Surging past *Michelle, Jennifer* and *Jessica*, according to a list posted by Michael Shackleford of Maryland, the new Top Five includes *Emily, Kaitlyn, Brianna, Ashley* and—atop the list—*Sarah*.

It's nice to see *Sarah*, with its biblical overtones, rising to new popularity. I was blessed with two *Sarahs* in my life—my aunt and godmother, Sarah Siegmeister, and my longtime secretary, Sara Cutting—and spelled with or without the final *h*, the sibilant name comes lovingly off the lips, along with its diminutive *Sally*. With *Sarah* atop the Top Forty, can *Rachel, Rebecca* and *Ruth* be far behind? (*Ruth*, with its touch of sadness, is quite far behind, and *Hagar*, as Abraham's jealous *Sarah* made certain, is out of it.)

Mothers seem to be searching for the uncommon in daughterclature. *Kaitlyn* is very big these days, an updating of the ever-popular *Catherine*. *Brianna* is the feminine form of the Irish *Brian*.

Women in today's maternity wards whose names are *Loren, Karen, Linda, Lisa, Hillary, Michelle* and *Kimberly*—and whose mothers are *Barbara, Mary, Jane, Helen, Dorothy* and *Betty*—name their daughters *Megan, Alyssa, Hannah, Brittany, Haley* and *Jasmine*. (*Maria* seems to be falling from grace, as *Grace* did long ago. Not a trace of *Tracy*.)

Androgynous names abound: *Ashley* used to be a boy's name, as fans of

Gone with the Wind remember. (*Ashley* Wilkes was played by Leslie Howard; now even *Leslie* is a girl's name.) Taylor, Cameron and Madison can be borne by male or female. This means it is harder for prospective employers to tell a job applicant's sex when reading a resume, a possible reason for the choices.

As names make news, news makes names: A generation ago, *Jacqueline* was hot, as *Diana* is today. Controversy can make or break a name; it is too soon to tell if *Paula* will be many babies' *Monica*.

In hilarity heaven, Saint Henny will catch the groaner on *monicker*. Rootless etymologists think it is probably from the Shelta language of itinerants in Ireland; *monicker* began there as *munnik*, derived from the Gaelic *ainm*, in turn taken from the Greek *no-men*, meaning "name." From that stem sprout *noun*, the name of a thing; *nomenclature*, a system of names leading to *nomenklatura*, the names of the old Soviet elite; *anonymous*, no name at all; and *nomination*, the naming of a candidate. Contrary to Shakespeare, plenty is in a name.

I was shocked, shocked, to peruse your column at breakfast this morning and discover two howlers in a row. I cannot believe you would have perpetrated these errors. Has "On Language" become pseudepigraphic?

First: To say the Gaelic ainm *is taken from the Greek* nomen *is equivalent to saying that I am the child of my aunt Bill: wrong on two counts. The Greek word in question is* onyma, *which is cognate to the Latin* nomen, *true enough. To use the word* cognate *implies a family-tree model, which is still the most commonly accepted image that we have for the relations of the Indo-European languages: It ain't perfect, but it runs. In that model, Latin and Greek would be "cousins," that is, more or less of the same generation sprung from a common ancestor one or more generations back. Gaelic would be the "nephew" (am I supposed to say "niece"?) of the Greek or Latin word, but the direct descendant of neither. Its progenitor, the Old Irish word for "name" (whatever it is), would be the offspring of the same unattested ancestor.*

Second: Defame *and* diffame (diffamare) *are formed from two distinct prefixes, which have been confused in individual cases since ancient times. The former shows* de *as a negative, as in "debunk," deriving from the Latin prepositional meaning of separation. The latter is the prefix seen in "disperse," etc., winding up in the wonderful* diss, *which must come from "disrespect." Dis- is also now often negative, to my disgust, because of confusion with the Greek dys- (as in "dysfunctional," a macaronic horror), but earlier meant "in different directions" (the final s happily assimilates to a following consonant). But even the Romans said* dearmare *for "disarm." As Uncle Miltie used to say, "Whattayagonnado?"*

Reverend Nathan R. Vail
Department of Theology
Fordham University
Riverdale, New York

No-men *is* Latin! *Not* Greek. *The Greek is* onoma *(and obviously no source of* nomen) *whence "onomatopoeia." But you knew that.*

Reverend Thomas M. Catania
Glendale, New York

You're the Atop

ATOP THE LIST of popular names of girls, I wrote recently, were Sarah, Emily, Kaitlyn, Brianna and Ashley.

"The choices of African-American mothers are ignored," writes Sol Steinmetz, part-time onomastician in New Rochelle, New York, "despite the fact that in the past thirty years the most unconventional, counter-establishment baby names have been coined by black moms."

He got hold of a student enrollment list of a typical New York inner-city high school and examined the names of two thousand girls. Not a single Sarah. But plenty of teenagers named *Aisha, Malaika, Bashanya, Rashida, Shawanda* and *Keshanta.*

Finalists in frequency were *Latisha, Tamika, Shamika* and *Tawana,* and (envelope, please) the winner is . . . *Latoya!*

We must remember that these names were the preferences of black mothers of babies born fifteen years ago; no more recent surveys come to hand. However, notes Steinmetz, "it shows the 'Africanization' trend in baby-naming among African Americans is gaining momentum and bears watching by expectant mothers."

What strikes me is the prevalence of names that end in *a*. It recalls the time that Henry Kissinger was introduced at an Italian-American dinner and noted, "I think I'm the only person here whose name ends in a consonant."

Another letter triggered by that column came from William Zinsser, author of *On Writing Well* (now in its sixth edition—more than nine hundred thousand copies sold).

"Your sentence citing girls' names that are '*atop* the list' of popularity gives me an excuse to raise a question that regularly puzzles me," writes Zinsser, with nary a mistake in his letter, and believe me I checked. "I see *atop* all over *The New York Times* every day, in every section. Teams are *atop* the league, songs are *atop* the charts, hats *atop* the head.

"Yet I've never heard anybody say *atop*. I've always thought it a tenet of writing well that we should never say anything in writing that we wouldn't comfortably say in conversation, since our style is (or should be) who we are. You're not an *atop* person, and nobody else is an *atop* person. So how did it creep into daily journalism?"

Note the subtle allusion to George Louis Leclerc de Buffon's *Le style c'est l'homme même*, "The style is the man himself." (Language mavens send each other signals like this.) He then seeks a pattern: "Is there any other word in common use in print that never gets spoken? What would you call such a freak?"

The first part is easy: *decry*. Headline writers who don't have space for *complain about* or *disparage*, and feel that *whine* is loaded, usually settle on the short and never spoken *decry*.

On the second part—a name for a word common in writing but not in speaking—why should I break my head? (I can hear George Shearing singing now: "You're *atop*, you're the tower of Babel.")

Have you heard about the father at the bris twenty years from now who says, "We're naming the baby Shlomo, after his grandfather Scott?"

Ronald W. Meister
New York, New York

Max Frankel has used atop *in the second sentence of a column of his, "It is a struggle for your attention* atop *many of their best articles." If the* Times's *language expert and its former executive director both use* atop *automatically within two weeks of each other, that's my idea of endemic.*

William Zinsser
New York, New York

You wrote that you searched in vain for a mistake in Zinsser's letter to you. In the second part of the aforementioned quote from Zinsser, he writes ". . . since our style is (or should be) who we are." "Since" is used in a nontemporal fashion, "because" would be the more appropriate word choice. It is a bit picky, but it is an excellent example of a commonly accepted verbal usage that is technically incorrect and seems to be misused more and more frequently in the written language in recent years. Perhaps the fact that this misuse is common in the spoken language would justify Zinsser's misuse according to his tenet? I, for one, would prefer to protect correct word usage. As many of my students could affirm, I never let it slide when grading papers, so I think you are safe in calling Zinsser on the misuse.

Preston A. Britner, Assistant Professor of Family Studies
University of Connecticut
Storrs, Connecticut

WHAT AM I?

At a chic Washington cocktail party, Elizabeth Drew, author of *Whatever It Takes: The Real Struggle for Political Power in America*, accepted an hors d'oeuvre of chopped liver smeared on a cracker and asked: "Chopped liver is delicious. Why do people derogate it so? As in the expression, '*What am I, chopped liver?*'"

The earliest use of this phrase in its derogatory sense—that is, "something trivial; something to be scoffed at"—in the *Random House Historical Dictionary of American Slang* is by Jimmy Durante on his 1954 CBS-TV show: "Now that ain't *chopped liver.*"

In a 1980 monologue about the Reagan-Carter presidential debate, Johnny Carson noted Ronald Reagan's statement that if all the unemployed were lined up, they would stretch from New York to Los Angeles. "He came up with another one today," said Carson. "If everyone on welfare were *chopped liver,* you could spread them on a line of Ritz crackers from here to Bulgaria." A decade later, the actor-producer Michael Douglas applied the phrase to himself, complaining about his secondary role in a movie: "That hurt me in the industry as an actor, and it ticked me off. I thought, What was I—*chopped liver or something?*"

This show-biz usage contributed to the treatment of the ethnic culinary delicacy (in Yiddish, *gehakte leber*) as an object of disdain. It may have also been influenced by its sense in underworld lingo as "a beaten and scarred person," or by the urbanization of the once-rural expression "That ain't hay." Sol Steinmetz speculates: "*Chopped liver* is merely an appetizer or side dish, not as important as chicken soup or gefilte fish. Hence it was often used among Jewish comedians in the Borscht Belt as a humorous metaphor for something or someone insignificant."

Nobody who tastes properly made *chopped liver* can use it as a derogation. I turned to my *Times* colleague Marian Burros, author of *The New Elegant but Easy Cookbook*, for the recipe: "Sauté one finely chopped medium onion in two tablespoons hot chicken fat until lightly golden and very soft. Add 1 pound chicken liver and sauté until cooked through; process in food processor with one small raw onion and one hard-cooked egg. Season with salt and pepper and mix with enough chicken fat to make it moist and spreadable."

Then you can say, "I feel just *as terrific as chopped liver!*"

The enough already expression, while certainly introduced into American English by Yiddish speakers, is totally part of idiomatic German. The expressions Komm schon *(come already) or* hör schon auf *(stop already) or* schon genug *(enough already) are standard idiomatic German.*

Another point: You talk about an "inch-high, 102-point, block letter headline." There are 72 points to the inch, not 102.

Gerardo Joffe
San Francisco, California

With all due respect to the recipe you quoted for chopped liver, I am certain you must realize there is a reason why it is called "chopped liver" and not "blended or pureed liver."

The texture one gets from chopping the ingredients, instead of placing them in a blender or food processor, is what, in my opinion, makes the dish. The blended dish would be a form of pâté.

To the ingredients one could optionally add finely chopped "grieden," which for the uninitiated in middle European Jewish cooking are the chicken "cracklings," i.e., crisp fried chicken skin, and are a boon to cholesterol lovers.

Hanno D. Mott
New York, New York

Chopped liver *is simply funny. Jimmy Durante, Johnny Carson and the Borscht Belt comedians knew that intuitively. Plausibly, it's the* chopped *adjective implying that the speaker is a poor, beaten-up schlemiel. Also, almost anything Jewish is funny in a way—especially when out of the mouths of goyim such as Durante and Carson. In the Borscht Belt, it was probably funny because of its down-home familiarity to the audiences, in the same way that Jews make fun of kreplach. If Jimmy Durante had said, "What am I, kreplach?" it might have caught on.*

Robert L. Wolke
Pittsburgh, Pennsylvania

Enough already with the chopped liver! *When we read Marian Burros's recipe, we schried, "That ain't chopped liver!" Elegant and easy though it may be, leber lovers worth their chicken fat never eschew the chopped liver for the processor. The resulting texture is not chopped (as in chopped liver), but more like liver pâté, smooth rather than lying in that luscious limbo between pasty and chunky.* Genug shoyn! *First you render the shmalz . . .*

Carol Hochberg Holker and Ralph Holker
Islamorada, Florida

WHERE'S THE POETRY?

Have you noticed the paucity of poetry in American public life, especially in headlines? The Poetic Allusion Watch (PAW), once an annual event in this space, has been shut out for lack of examples. The last good entry submitted is from Donald Marks of New York, citing a headline in the science section of *The New York Times* over a story about snakes in Venezuela: "Splendor in the Mud: Unraveling the Lives of Anacondas."

The allusion is to Wordsworth's "Intimations of Immortality," written between 1802 and 1807: "Though nothing can bring back the hour/Of splendor in the grass, of glory in the flower."

And a couple of years ago, my colleague Anthony Lewis headlined a diatribe at "radical Republicans" who would leave social programs unfinanced as "Bare Ruined Choirs." That comes from Shakespeare's Sonnet 73 about the late autumn of life when the leafless boughs of trees become "bare ruined choirs where late the sweet birds sang."

To stimulate an alertness to allusion, MAW was founded: the Musical Allusion Watch, to detect veiled references to lyrics of popular tunes. Deborah Stapleton of Mountain View, California, noted a *Wall Street Journal* headline over a story about English environmentalists trying to preserve traditional hedgerows: "If There's a Bustle in Your Hedgerow, Don't Be Alarmed." This is a line from the 1971 Led Zeppelin song "Stairway to Heaven." Ms. Stapleton suggests: "The headline writer must have been bursting with baby-boomer pride. When handed a story about guarding hedgerows, he or she found a perfect opportunity to communicate to the Wall Street establishment through lines sung in youth, often in an altered state of mind. 'Too weird,' as we might have said back then."

With both PAW and MAW in a depression this year, what hope can we find for the return of a sweet-seasoned shower of civilized discourse? In an unexpected place: Resonances of our great traditions of lyric language can be heard in the political impeachment process.

At a historic moment in the House of Representatives, Henry Hyde, white-haired chairman of the Judiciary Committee, rose to rebut a charge that he was going to allow the investigation to roll on for years.

"Let me suggest to you," he told his colleagues, "who think this is going to go on, like Tennyson's brook, just on and on."

PAW members forget what he said after that because we were turning from the passions of the moment to Alfred Lord Tennyson's 1855 "The Brook." It begins, "I come from haunts of coot and hern,/I make a sudden sally,/And sparkle out among the fern,/To bicker down a valley." The poem's last stanza: "And out again I curve and flow/To join the brimming river;/For men may come and men may go,/But I go on for ever."

Chairman Hyde, by the way, has been referred to as a "Solomonic Solon." This is an amalgam of two eponyms: Solomon was an ancient Hebrew king noted for both his infant-splitting judicial gimmick and the world-weary wisdom of Ecclesiastes, while Solon was a humane Athenian lawgiver who reformed the harsh code of Draco.

Not all poetic-sounding phrases that resonate are allusions to poetry or musical lyrics, of course; some are rooted in dialectical metaphor. "In other days in the capital," intones a *New York Times* editorial, "the President could summon . . . wise and disinterested elders who, as the saying goes, had heard the owl and seen the elephant."

Although the authorship of newspaper editorials is always shrouded in institutional secrecy, a demonstrable need to know enabled me to get the lowdown from a member of the editorial board of the suthrin persuasion: "Just heard *heard the owl and seen the elephant* down South as a reference to people seasoned to wisdom by wide experience."

Deeper digging unearths an 1835 use by the southwestern humorist Augustus Baldwin Longstreet: "That's sufficient, as Tom Haynes said when he *saw the elephant*." And a 1936 dictionary of cowboy lingo reported, "To have many and varied experiences was to *'hear the owl hoot.'*"

In her celebrated 1970s book, I Heard the Owl Call My Name, *Margaret Craven wrote of the belief of the Kwakiutl Indians of Canada that an owl calls a person's name before that person dies.*

In the context you were quoting, I take "heard the owl and seen the ele-
phant" as meaning a person is n .,,ot a youngster, has been around and
knows the ropes, indeed, may even have lived enough years to be ready to
die.

Jeanette F. Huber
Scilly, Kinsale
County Cork, Ireland

Reference was made to the idiomatic expression "seen the elephant and
heard the owl." It restored a long-stored memory of my early readings of
O. Henry, recognized as one of the masters of short stories with his facility
for capturing speech patterns of quirky characters. In one of his stories,
"The Passing of Black Eagle," we encounter the following: "He talks all
spraddled out," said Cactus, "bout the rookuses he's been in. He claims to
have saw the elephant and hearn the owl." In another story, "The Mar-
quis and Miss Sally," the droll character Phonograph says, "I've viewed
the elephant with the Mayor of Fort Worth and I've listened to the owl
with the gen'ral passenger agent of the Katy. . . ."
Apparently, this is a colorful idiomatic depiction of a worldly-wise char-
acter, one who has "seen the elephant and hearn the owl." O. Henry may
not be the earliest reference to this expression, of course, but it is my earli-
est and long-lasting recollection.

Harry Shabanowitz
Horseheads, New York

WITH A EURO IN HER POUCH . . .

No matter what the bankers tell you at the Frankfurt headquarters of
the European Monetary Union, the *euro* is already in circulation.

Aboriginal Australians have long been familiar with the Westralian
rock kangaroo, which they call the *uroo, waroo* or *yuro*. English-speaking
residents of that continent spell it *euro:* "Wallaby, *euro* and dingo tracks,"
wrote I. L. Idriess in a 1933 novel, "showed how popular this cool rock-
hole was."

Those creatures, with their powerful hindquarters and front-loaded
method of carrying offspring in pouches, will have to share their name
with the European supercurrency in a few years. Residents of eleven
countries will soon be disdaining francs, marks, guilders, escudos and

pesetas, instead insisting their common currency is as "sound as a *euro.*"

The Germans wanted to call it the *euromark.* The mark was the name of a German, English and Scottish weight traceable to the year 886; in 1946, the deutsche mark replaced the reichsmark and became the symbol of German financial stability. But the French preferred the *ecu,* acronym for the European Currency Unit (and an old silver French coin, similar to the English *crown*).

Germans thought *ecu* sounded too much like *Kuh,* German for "cow," likely to lead to such wordplay as "cash cow" and "curdling the currency." Bonn countered with the *franken*—a Germanization of the French *franc*—but that struck many as too close to Mary Shelley's Dr. Frankenstein, not to mention his monster. The *monnet* had its moment, honoring Jean Monnet, the European unionist, but that suggestion sounded too much like the English *money,* and the Brits were not even embracing the new currency.

"The Germans insist on *euro,*" wrote Nathaniel C. Nash of *The New York Times* from Brussels in November 1995, a name their finance minister, Theo Waigel, "floated in September when the finance ministers last met."

And so the coinage was coined.

MISTEAK SANDWICH

"Ouch!" That is the full text of a note sent to me by William F. Buckley of the *National Review* attached to a clipping of a political column of mine that began, "'Conduct unbecoming an officer and a gentleman' is one of those phrases that sounds as if it comes out of Kipling." The ouchifying word was the verb *sounds.*

This is the second time he has caught me in that mistake. Only twelve years ago I wrote about "one of those little episodes in the relations between nations that illustrates the nature of alliances," and in came that little blue note from Buckley expressing dismay with his customary one-word excoriation. The offending verb in that case: *illustrates,* with an *s.*

One critic does not make a winter. I waited for the other shoe to drop, and in the next mail came a missive from Alistair Cooke, whose gentle BBC eye has not lost its sharpness. On the back of the envelope a battle cry from some forgotten war: "Remember the Ellipse!" And, like an anti-blurb, "Absolutely indefensible—Fowler."

I get two categories of mail, linguistic and political, reflecting my Jekyll-Hyde existence as political pundit and language maven. About the political correspondence: Surely, I am the only *Times* columnist whose angry mail is neatly typed and whose supportive mail is often scrawled in crayon. I resist the temptation to reply to the more caustic critics with the classic, "Some crackpot has been using your name in writing to me, and I thought you would want this brought to your attention."

The language mail, however, is the lifeblood, mother's milk and any other bodily-fluid metaphor you like of this column. The Lexicographic Irregulars—from Olbom (On Language's Board of Octogenarian Mentors) to the English teachers compelled to begin with the word *anent*—are my sources of inspiration and information. (What is an *ent?*) The mail clerk dragging his sack of "Man the ramparts!" pleas and "Uofallpeople" corrections is welcomed after he has made his way through the bomb-disposal unit.

Kissing the rod brandished by the author of *Buckley: The Right Word*, edited by Sam Vaughan, I can ease Bill's pain and mine: In the sentence beginning "'Conduct unbecoming an officer and a gentleman' is one of those phrases *that* . . . ," what is the antecedent of the relative pronoun *that?* Is it *one?* If *one* were the antecedent, then *that* would be followed by a singular verb, *sounds*, with an *s*.

But *one* is not the antecedent. (I think I'll memorize this.) To see what the antecedent is, turn the sentence around: "Of those phrases *that* . . . , 'conduct unbecoming an officer and a gentleman' is one." *Phrases* is the antecedent; it's plural, demanding the plural verb *sound*. (Use the singular verb when *one* is the only one, as in, "That is the only one of the phrases that sounds right.")

Come at it another way. In a sentence beginning "*One* of the language mavens who plants 'mistakes' in columns to draw interesting mail is . . . ," what is the subject of the relative clause? Is it *One?* No; it's *who*, referring to the language mavens, plural, and the relative clause that follows should have the plural verb *plant* (unless it's "the only one of the language mavens who plants . . .").

Therefore, in my lead sentence, "one of those phrases that sounds" should have read "one of those phrases that *sound*."

That takes care of the damnably rather-be-right Buckley. But here is where I get blindsided by Alistair (Remember the Ellipse!) Cooke.

The *Ellipse*, to most of us, is the place behind the White House. That sense, from the Greek for "falling short," is not a criticism of President Clinton's stewardship but has to do with the shape of the lawn—falling short of a perfect circle, squeezed down into a sort of egg shape, a closed curve formed by sectioning a cone.

That is not the meaning of *ellipse* Cooke has in mind. He is using the clipped form of *ellipsis*, "the omission of words that the context makes unnecessary," another falling short of completeness and perfection. (His shortening reflects a clip by the grammarian Henry Fowler that is not yet in most dictionaries, but language mavens often push lexicographic envelopes.) Scrupulous writers use three dots to indicate an *ellipsis* in a quotation when pithiness is desired but some stuffed shirt goes on and on. We don't bother with the three dots in everyday language when the meaning is clearly understood: When *if it is possible* becomes *if possible*, not even a pedantic copy editor kicks about the missing dot-dot-dot.

Now to Cooke's beef. Using brackets, we can put back into my sentence the words I left out, in undotted *ellipsis*, because they are understood. "'Conduct unbecoming an officer and a gentleman' is one of those phrases that sounds as [it would sound] if it comes out of Kipling."

The end of that sentence is cockeyed. Earlier, I agreed to fix the *sounds* to *sound*, but Cooke is belting and flaying me for a different mistake, one masked by my *ellipsis*. As the addition of the words *it would sound* (formerly in *ellipsis*) to my sentence clearly indicates, the use of the present indicative, *comes*, is flat wrong; because I am in the conditional, stating a possibility, it should be in the subjunctive, *came*. To use the present indicative *comes* in this case would be as bad as using *is* instead of the correctly subjunctive *were*—which is, as Fowler decreed in *The King's English*, "absolutely indefensible."

Cooke reparses the whole thing for me:

"'Conduct unbecoming an officer and a gentleman' is one of those phrases that sound as [they would sound] if they came out of Kipling."

We need not become "hot and bothered," to use a phrase Rudyard Kipling coined in 1923, about failing to discern the proper antecedent or failing to use the subjunctive with the conditional, but we can coolly remain on guard.

As Rudyard used to tell young Alistair and Bill: If you can keep all this in your head when all others about you are falling into error, then you're a man, my son, or a woman, my daughter, as the case may be.

The reference to your supportive mail being often scrawled in crayon makes clear to me that you are aware of the punch line to the effect that the writer goes on to apologize for having employed such a writing instrument and explains such by adding that "they won't let me have anything sharp where I am."

John T. Elfvin
Buffalo, New York

Diagrammed, the sentence looks like this:

Conduct unbecoming an officer and a gentleman, is one
of phrases   that sounds
those

The subject is: Conduct unbecoming an officer and a gentleman.
The verb is: is.
The predicate nominative is: one.
The prepositional phrase modifying one *is:* of those phrases.
The dependent clause that modifies that predicate nominative (one) *is:* that sounds . . .
Ultimately, both the prepositional phrase of those phrases *and the dependent clause* that sounds . . . *have one and only one purpose in life and that is to modify the predicate nominative* one.
The sucker play is to assume that the dependent clause that sounds *modifies* of those phrases, *but it doesn't. In this sentence,* of those phrases *is strictly a modifier and not a part of the core meaning or structure. But* one *is. We're talking about* one. *We're not talking about* of those phrases. *Therefore, because* one *is singular, the verb in the dependent clause takes a singular* sounds.

Rod Carlson
Coral Gables, Florida

NYAH, NYAH—GOTCHA!

This space has been hijacked by the Gotcha! Gang, a growing legion of readers who take preternatural delight in exposing the grammatical errors of the resident columnist. Their motto: "No Haven for the Maven." (Excuse me; *its* motto.)

From N. Lewis of Croydon, New Hampshire: "You write, 'A column in this space titled "The Asian Connection" had just appeared, followed the next day by a front-page article about John Huang's fund-raising in *The Wall Street Journal.*'

"John Huang was doubtless a very active fellow, but I doubt he was engaged in 'fund-raising in *The Wall Street Journal.*'"

Max Culpa for Mayor. Huang was surely not chasing the editor Robert Bartley down that newspaper's corridors seeking contributions to the Clinton campaign. A prepositional phrase like *in The Wall Street Journal* is a modifier and should cozy up intimately to the noun it modifies, lest another, closer noun be mistaken for the term being modified. In this case, the noun phrase being modified was *a front-page article*, but I put so many words in between that it is possible to think that *fund-raising* was the modified term. The philologist Richard Lederer had a good example of this abuse of prepositional-phrase position: "Lincoln wrote the Gettysburg Address while traveling from Washington to Gettysburg on the back of an envelope."

From Ed Cashin of Hastings-on-Hudson, New York: "You say, 'He offers the other *two branches* of government the choice,' but you mean '*the two other branches.*' Otherwise, we would have four branches of government."

You know, he has a point. I never thought of that before. *Other* is called a "postdeterminer" because it usually comes after words that are determiners, like numerals or other quantifiers that make a noun phrase specific. Thus, when I wrote *the other two branches*, it could be thought to stand against these two branches—totaling, as my eagle-eyed critic observes, four branches. But if I had written *the two other branches*, there could be no doubt that only three branches exist.

Some would call this pedantry, but I stand corrected, and in turn correct David Schippers, majority counsel of the House Judiciary Committee, for his castigation of the President's disdain for "the integrity of the other two coequal branches." Cashin is hereby appointed recording secretary of the Nitpickers' League, a highly sophisticated subgroup of the Gotcha! Gang whose membership is in constant turmoil about writing its name Nitpicker's League.

In reviewing Bryan A. Garner's *Dictionary of Modern American Usage*, I misquoted him by writing that "that *historic* differentiation" between *enormity* ("outrageousness") and *enormousness* ("hugeness") should be upheld. Garner correctly wrote *historical*. Robert Burchfield's *New Fowler's Modern English Usage* quotes a forgetful maven on that: "Any past event is *historical*, but only the most memorable ones are *historic*."

Now to the alleged mistake that drew the most mail. In a line about the pronunciation of *status*, I wrote, "That is usually pronounced STAT-us, as in *statistics*, by the highfalutin, and STATE-us by *the hoi polloi*."

From Jim Tart of Dallas: "My daughter Katie tells me that her eighth-grade teacher would have smacked her in the head with her grammar book had she said '*the hoi polloi*.' Katie says *hoi polloi* means 'the masses' and therefore should never be proceeded by *the*. Live by the sword and die by the sword."

Thank you, Mr. Tart. (And when Katie comes by with her spelling book opened to *precede*, watch your head.) Curiously, this seeming redundancy in regard to a foreign phrase apparently infuriates Greek scholars. "Wrong!" shouts Stephen Esrati of Shaker Heights, Ohio. "*Hoi* means 'the.'" No doubt about that. Wrote Ronald Serafine of Butler, Pennsylvania: "One does not say '*the* hoi polloi' for the same reason that one does not say '*with* au jus.' How plead you?"

Innocent with an explanation, Your Honor. Take that French phrase first: When you order roast beef *au jus*, pronounced oh-ZHOO, you are using the French for "in its juice" (literally, "with juice"). Your waitress is in error if she treats that phrase as a noun and asks, "You want the *au jus* on the side?" Correct her, and you will soon have a *chemise au jus*. In the same way, if you correct an inviter who writes, "Please RSVP," you won't get asked again to *Répondez s'il vous plaît* (literally, "Respond, if you please").

Those are two language redundancies not yet given absolution by all-forgiving usage. When we speak of "the *hoi polloi*," however, we are firmly grounded in an error that common usage over centuries has erased. Certainly, the *hoi polloi* translates formally and redundantly as "the the masses," causing speakers of Greek and members of the Squad Squad to look at you with disdain. But the English idiom is *the hoi polloi*. Sometime next century, we will write that as *hoipolloi* to reflect its Anglicization.

Robert Burchfield, in the third edition of *Fowler's*, calls the hidebound resistance to *the* in front of the Greek phrase "an attempt to force Greek grammar on the receiving language." He writes: "Dryden and Byron wrote "Οἴ πολλοί' and who is to quarrel with them? And who is prepared to 'correct' W. S. Gilbert's lines from *Iolanthe*, '"Twould fill with joy, And madness stark / 'Οἴ πολλοί (a Greek remark)'?"

Though willing to go along with the usage roundheels on permitting that redundancy, I hang tough on semantics: The meaning of *the hoi polloi* should remain "the masses," or in less-Marxist-sounding terms, "ordinary folk." When the writer Pete Hamill told the interviewer Charlie Rose, "Sinatra threw a party for Agnew in Palm Springs with all *the hoi polloi* in attendance," Francis Dyer of New York objected, noting that the phrase had not taken on a new meaning of "important people, upper classes or 'swells.'"

That upside-down usage occurs often. The confusion comes from the similarity of the noun *hoi polloi* and the adjective *hoity-toity*, a rhyming compound from the English dialect term *hoit*, "to play the fool," which has come to mean "foolishly snooty." (What a pleasure it is to get back to correcting other people's mistakes.)

You were criticized for using other two *instead of* two other, *claiming that the first implies that you started with a pair and then referred to another. This cavil is surely nonsense.*

You might say to a vacationer, "What do you do the other 364 days of the year?" (Though socially gauche, it's grammatically unimpeachable.) That question doesn't imply that there are 728 days in a year and that you've just witnessed the first 364 of them. I can't imagine any native speaker of English saying, "What do you do the 364 other days of the year?"

This merely shows that your usage was idiomatic. It would have been possible, of course, to say two other *in your column. My statistical sampling in Westlaw suggests that the two phrasings—the* two other *and the* other two—*run neck and neck. There are about 130,000 occurrences of each in recent news stories.*

The would-be gotcha is reminiscent of the old debate about two first *versus* first two. *You don't hear much about this anymore. Here's what a little-known usage guide, Robert Palfrey Utter's* Every-Day Words and Their Uses, *said back in 1916:*

The expression *first two* is sometimes condemned as illogical, on the ground that only one can be first or last. *Two first* or *first and second* may be used instead, but the objection to *first two* where the meaning is clear is pedantic. The pedants, by the way, are always careful to point out that one may correctly speak of the *first two* when the serried is a series of twos.

Despite the couple of entries in A Dictionary of Modern American Usage *citing Safirean solecisms, please be assured that I'm ready to jump to your defense when you've been wrongly accused.*

Bryan A. Garner
author of A Dictionary of American Usage
Dallas, Texas

WHAT'S PAST MUST NOT BE PRELUDE

It is time to get right with the old millennium. In the course of the last thousand years, and especially in 1999, I have made a few mistakes that I want to get off my conscience so I can start with a clean slate.

In a jeremiad denouncing "shoppertainment" in factory-outlet malls, I wrote: "Standing here in the epicenter of pre-Christmasism, laden with shopping bags of merchandise that proves my worth both as a provider and conspicuous consumer, a nagging thought intrudes: Is this the way I want to spend my leisure time?"

As Robert Peyser of Brookline, Massachusetts, writes, "Might you not agree that the participial phrase beginning with the words 'Standing here' ought to modify 'I'?" I might. That was a double dangling participle—hard to do—and it would be wrong to let it slop over to 2000. I should have written: ". . . consumer, I was struck by the thought. . . ."

In a factual lapse, I misinformed readers that Al Capone "died in jail—'nutty as a fruitcake,' as a gangland visitor reported." A mob of his Chicago followers pointed out that their hero, Scarface Al, died of cardiac arrest in 1947 at his Palm Island, Florida, home after being released from jail (but—as reported accurately here—nutty as a fruitcake).

"The fifty American states are not sovereign," I wrote in a column that sought to explicate the exquisite difference between *state* and *nation*, "no matter what they say in Texas and Hawaii (the only states that were once sovereign nations)."

An indignant troop of Ethan Allen's Green Mountain Boys came after me on that one. (*Vermont* means "green mountain.") From 1777 to 1791 the settlers of the New Hampshire Grants, as Vermont was first known, refused to consider themselves part of neighboring New York and functioned as an independent nation, issuing their own money and telling the thirteen states forming a union to take a hike. Finally the feisty Vermonters paid greedy New York $30,000 to drop its claim, which paved the way for it to become the fourteenth state. Senator James Jeffords, on behalf of his incensed constituents, was especially worked up about my error, and I hope this does not start a secession movement.

The Gotcha! Gang follows me from these pages to television appearances. I was heard to say *congratulate* and *accreditate* as if those words had no *t* but only a *d*. Leslie Hill-Levitt Latham of West Redding, Connecticut, wondered if this frequent mispronunciation would lead to a change in spelling to *congradulate* and *accredidate*.

Hats off to *congratulations*—the word is impossible to pronounce correctly. When a *d* or a *t* comes between two vowels, what linguists call "flapping" takes place, and we hear the sound of *d/t* or *t/d*, an amalgam of the two. Worse, as Ellen Kaisse, professor of linguistics at the University of Washington (Seattle), notes, "The *y* sound before the *u* makes the consonant *t/d* sound more like *ch/j*, and people pronounce this word in about three ways: *congradyulate, congrachulate* or *congrajulate*."

What's a kudos-giver to do? I will adopt slang's shortened noun form, *congrats*, but will still struggle along with the word I pronounce *congradulate* as a verb. However, I will not adopt that spelling, preferring to stick with the *t* for old times' sake. (As for the mispronounced and misspelled verb *accredidate*, I'll strike it from my mental set; the verb is "to accredit.")

And as for those lifting a glass at the big hooh-hah next week: a festive, neatly snipped-off, easily pronounceable and correctly spellable *congrats* to one and all.

A quick, pedantic note concerning your referring to the t/d *sound as a "flap." Flap is a feature of phonetic articulation in which the tip of the tongue rapidly hits the alveolar ridge or back of the upper teeth; it is manifested in one of the British pronunciations of the sound* r *as [d]d (and sometimes transcribed as veddy). But it might just as well refer to the American pronunciation of the* t *in butter—that is, not* budder *but butter without the aspiration normally accorded the intervocalic* t *in many dialects of British English.*

The substitution of a sound closer to d *for* t *in intervocalis position is called neutralization. Rather than go into a long(er) explanation, let me quote from my definition from the first edition of* The Random House Unabridged Dictionary:

"Neutralization . . . 3. Ling. The loss of a distinctive feature of one of a pair of phonemes that are otherwise differentiated on the basis of that feature, as the loss of a voice as a distinctive feature between the -t- and -d- of latter *and* ladder.*"*

In English, there are four distinctive features of phonemes: voiced/unvoiced, place of articulation, nasality/non-nasality and stop/continuant. Thus, to labor the point, /t/ (written between slanted lines when a phoneme, between square brackets when a phonetic element) is an unvoiced, non-nasal (or oral) apico-alveolar stop. (Apico-alveolar just means that it is articulated with the tip [apex] of the tongue against the gum ridge behind the upper teeth [alveolar ridge]). The only phonemic distinction between /t/ and /d/ is that the latter is a voiced, non-nasal, apico-alveolar stop. (Note that there might be other, phonetic distinctions between the two, like length or articulation; but those are not considered phonemic.)

Laurence Urdang
Old Lyme, Connecticut

ACKNOWLEDGMENTS

I stand on the shoulders of giants. (Nobody stands on the shoulders of midgets; that would be cruel.)

My gratitude flows freely to Fred Cassidy, the late editor in chief of the *Dictionary of Regional English;* his successor at *DARE,* Joan Houston Hall; Fred Mish, Joanne Despres and Jim Lowe of Merriam-Webster; Jesse Sheidlower and Erin McKean of Oxford North America; Joe Pickett of American Heritage; Mike Agnes of Webster's *New World,* and Antonette diPaolo Healey of *The Dictionary of Old English.*

OLBONOME, the "On Language" Board of Nonagenarian Mentors: Jacques Barzun and Alistair Cooke. Allen Walker Read died in 2002. Sol Steinmetz doesn't meet the age requirement, but I include him anyway. That's a wise trio.

Others I call on for lexicographic help include Fred Shapiro of the Yale Law Library; Gerald Cohen of the University of Missouri—Rolla; Ron Butters of the University of Georgia; Anne Soukhanov, editor at large of *Encarta Dictionary;* linguist and reference publishing consultant Wendalyn Nichols, formerly of Random House; Allan Metcalf of the American Dialect Society (and the many e-mailing members of the erudite group); Victoria Neufeldt of the Dictionary Society of North America; Connie Eble of the University of North Carolina; Bryan Garner, author of *A Dictionary of Modern American Usage;* Anatoly Liberman of the University of Minnesota; Paul Dickson, Christine Ammer, John Algeo and David Crystal of the University of North Wales; William Kretzschmar of the *Linguistic Atlas* project; Wayne Glowka of *American Speech;* Robert Burchfield, former editor of the *OED;* Constance Hale, Frank Abate and Laurence Urdang, founder of *Verbatim;* and Charles Harrington Elster, the pronunciation maven.

My copy editors at *The New York Times Magazine* are Rob Hoerburger, Abbott "Kit" Combes, Jeff Klein, Jaimie Epstein and Bill Ferguson.

The final filterers at Simon & Schuster include the legendary Gypsy da Silva, Rose Ann Ferrick and Jim Stoller.

In addition to Kathleen E. Miller's and Jeffrey McQuain's language aid, those helping me at the *Times* Washington bureau include my assistant, Ann Elise Wort, who keeps her eye out for current words, and Todd Webb, who keeps up with the snail mail and e-mail. The bureau's chief librarian, Barclay Walsh, and the librarians Marjorie Goldsborough and Monica Borkowski are always helpful. The saviors of my political column who keep the Nitpicker's League at bay are Steve Pickering, Linda Cohn and Sue Kirby.

The final thankees are the Lexicographic Irregulars, an army that includes the shock troops of the Squad Squad and the Gotcha! Gang. Man the ramparts! (No, that's sexist.)

INDEX OF NAMES

INDEX OF TERMS